D0945157

WARS OF POSITION

WARS OF POSITION

The Cultural Politics of Left and Right

TIMOTHY BRENNAN

COLUMBIA UNIVERSITY PRESS NEW YORK

Columbia University Press
Publishers Since 1893
New York   Chichester, West Sussex

Copyright © 2006 Columbia University Press

Library of Congress Cataloging-in-Publication Data
Brennan, Timothy
Wars of position : the cultural politics of left and right / Timothy Brennan.
p. cm.
Includes bibliographical references and index.
ISBN 0-231-13730-3 (cloth : alk. paper) — ISBN 0-231-51045-4 (electronic)
1.   Political culture—United States.   2.   Humanities—Political aspects—United
States.   3.   Conservatism—United States.   4.   Right and left (Political science)   5.
United States—Politics and government—1974–1977.   6.   United States—Politics and
government—1977–1981.   I.   Title.
JA75.7.B74 2006
306.2'0973'09047—dc22
2005049683

c 10 9 8 7 6 5 4 3 2 1

In Memory of Edward Said

CONTENTS

PREFACE

IN WRITING THIS BOOK, I found myself returning again and again to the same five-year period in American cultural life: 1975–1980, the period between the end of the Vietnam War and the beginning of the presidency of Ronald Reagan. It was during this time that a certain social democratic vision of the political past was banished from public discussion and a forceful shift from belief to being took hold in politics. Set against the backdrop of the religious fundamentalism now raging across the globe, this book—for all its emphasis on belief—has less to do with traditional religious faith than with a civic religion I call the "middle way."

We are still living under the common sense of this short span of years that might be thought of simply as the "turn." Its credos were first launched and are today reinforced in a process of interpretive violence. Many of the chapters in this book explore the details of that willfulness and place them in the context of alternative histories. In my view, the transitional moment of 1975–1980 is best characterized as the fusing of right and left positions still evident today, above all, in viewing the state as an arena of innate corruption to which no claims for redress can or should be made.

The many faces of conservatism explored in these chapters emerged, I would argue, from divergent sources acting in concert: the deadening effects of middle-class immigration and entry into the university of intellectuals who either were, or were related to, formerly colonized peoples, and who therefore automatically registered as the oppressed when this was often far from the case; the popularization of right-wing philosophies from interwar Europe in which a fundamental confusion reigned between conservative and radical rejections of capitalism; and, finally, a hyper-professionalism that put the humanities in competition with a postliterate media and entertainment sector in a climate of privatization, including the privatization of the university. The forces that brought about this convergence are predictably larger than the ideas themselves—so large, in fact, that they remain unnoticed, which is why they were mostly passed over even in self-critical accounts of academic life produced in the 1980s and 1990s. These forces were brought into an articulate array in a moment of reassessment and political fatigue that has provided the model for the following decades.

Throughout this book, I take the view that cultural scholars in universities were instrumental in shaping public sentiment and that their influence was for the most part mixed, at times even disastrous. The thinking that prevailed in the late 1970s and early 1980s, at any rate, bodied forth two doctrines that have since become so dominant they are hardly noticed any longer, and these I trace in the two sections of this book. First, in the section titled "Belief and Its Discontents," I explore how political belonging was ejected from the idea of identity. And second, in the section titled "The Anarchist Sublime," I examine the consequences of fleeing, as so many left intellectuals did in those years, any politics seeking to enter or make claims on the state. These two gestures are perhaps the only unambiguous political legacies of what was then beginning to be called "theory."

How exactly did this intellectual culture of the "post-turn" come to be, why, and with what consequences? Why is it typically cast in terms of "identity politics" when the real source of the underlying shift is more consequential and more historically resonant as an explicitly Heideggerian gesture—namely, the dissimulation of belief as *being* and the vaunting of a politics beyond belief, where "belief" is understood as the taking of positions or the setting of programmatic goals? This is the ideological outlook, we have to remember, that was popularly adduced in the media and in Washington think tanks in the 1980s and 1990s as American dissidence itself—a peremptory substitution of part for whole that has its own interesting history. As the civic Left was nudged off camera, deans, talk-show hosts, and think tanks were dubbing "Marxist" anything outside an uncritical embrace of the American free market. The genius of the defensive bulwarks of the neoliberal shift was revealed when the term "Marxism" was affixed even to a poststructuralist theory that wanted in fact to dismantle it, as though opinion makers had found a way instinctively to create a buffer between the establishment and its dangerous other by inventing a proxy. Consequently, the real social democratic alternative became an enemy so beyond the pale that it could not even enter the debate.

This politics of being has stood for a clear set of propositions, of course, although they are rarely presented as such. They instead assume the guise of inexorable forms of inheritance, although this assumption is not limited to university professors and their students. Too disconnected and amorphous to be called a group or tendency, perhaps, the culture of the post-turn is surprisingly unified across large and varied constituencies. I am not referring, then, only to the academic humanities but to urban avant-garde theater circles, alternative publishing, and middlebrow journalism. Within these circles, everyone has been reading and reciting the same shared canon of venerated texts (primarily Foucault and Derrida at first, but now, in an exchange of forms, Gilles Deleuze, Hannah Arendt, and Antonio Negri). This culture of belief was conceived during the turn and consolidated following the fall of the Berlin wall in 1989, by then already displaying the same self-protective instinct of all hegemonies, acting with a peremptory and impatient finality whenever challenged.

The grounds for this turn are varied. One might at first detect a peculiar shrewdness in this gesture toward being, which can be viewed as a clever response to the fact that American politics does not permit any dissent that challenges the pieties of the center (typically captured in prevailing media jargon as "centrism") and because in dissent there are no protections for marginalized political beliefs, only for races, genders, and ethnicities (as forms of being). The Hollywood blacklists of the 1940s and 1950s, the purging of the universities in the 1960s, the firing of journalists in the 1980s, and the refusal to publish or give airtime to dissidents of a certain stripe (as strongly evident today as in any moment of the American past, including the McCarthy era) all testify to the lack of a publicly accepted discourse of protection for unpopular or dangerous viewpoints operating outside the shelter of identity. Consequently, to cast oneself as holding a positionless position beyond belief, in solidarity with outlawed races and ethnicities (popularly dubbed "cultures" in the usual journalistic euphemism), obviates one of the principle obstacles to entering the mainstream on behalf of progressive causes.

However, the problem is that belief, too, although arguably chosen rather than merely inherited, confers on its holders a *culture*; therefore, if it does not have the protections given other identities there is no coherent reason to continue denying belief itself that privilege, particularly when those beliefs are responsible for generating the positions that "theory" has appropriated without acknowledgment and that society must rely on when civility and basic democratic rights are most threatened. I am, among other things, suggesting a perfectly inverted (and so arguably allied) view that belief systems as political outlooks are to some extent cultural and inherited. But even more pertinently, prejudice toward left belief cultures tends to be overlaid upon more well-known imaginative geographies that were first developed in eighteenth- and nineteenth-century colonial discourses. They were perfected in the political showdown between left and right traditions during the interwar era (from which most of today's intellectual leads derive). An example might clarify what I mean: An article appeared in the *New York Times* in February 2005 titled "Europe's Muslims May Be Headed Where the Marxists Went Before." Its purpose was to warn Europe's Muslims to end their "ideology of contestation" if they wanted to avoid Marxism's fate of irrelevance. This history of consonance between attacks on belief and attacks on culture is rarely explored in any depth, however. The slippage from anti-red to anti-Muslim sentiments takes place to most observers, left and right, as though it were a wholly natural substitution.

But there is also another sense of the term "culture of belief" that would take us to a discussion of those particular beliefs that were suppressed after the turn—suppressed, one should add, with the active participation of theorists of rupture and apostles of difference. I want to argue that once the political positions of this post-turn culture are clearly spelled out—that is, once they are translated back from the rhetoric of being to the mostly unstated positions underlying them—their participation in censoring an earlier and still viable Left is disturbingly plain.

What I try to document in extended individual cases is the way a post-turn discourse works—the way, in short, that targeted identities have been enlisted to crush social democratic belief cultures, conveniently placing the avant-garde of theory in a position of public respectability that harmonized with its desire for social status and official regard. I show that this was done by way of tortured logic, misread archives, factual omissions, and peremptory waves of the hand. While there may not be full-fledged conspiracies at work, not everything that has happened to establish the present regime of truth has been on the up-and-up. It would also be wrong to treat this intellectual repression, although it is very real and ongoing, as simply the result of bad scholarship or petulance.

From 1980 onward, but especially after 1989, the major theoretical alternatives within the humanities to religious fundamentalism at large have themselves been religious to the degree that they were driven by an ethical, non-interventionist politics based on a shared canon of sacred texts. I am not being merely metaphorical here, nor do I think I am exaggerating. An oracular mode of knowledge has taken hold, one that does not just avoid discussion and debate but actually targets it. Far from contenting itself with the neglect typically suffered by initiates possessing austere truths, this oracular theory has sought a place in the American mainstream and was readily granted that status for reasons that it, somewhat surprisingly, neglected to interrogate. It opposes right-wing extremism, while sharing, without appearing to, the American credo of the middle way, which it now expresses in terms retooled to avoid overfamiliarity: "difference," "hybridity," "pluralism," "the new Constitution," the "multitude," "new social movements," and so on.

Paralleling its far right counterparts, this oracular thinking finds its enemy in government. For, if a single idea resounds in cultural theory today it is the liberation attached to statelessness. Dishonest, corrupt, paralyzed, rife with a sinister compulsion to survey, spy, moralize, and suppress, the "State"—as a monolithic ghost rather than a variable political form—plays in theoretical circles of the humanities the role of original sin. "As little state as possible," wrote Nietzsche, the *fons et origo* of radical theory over the last three decades. But in practice, authority for this view is drawn from much homelier and less philosophical sources, ones in which the deep political ambiguity of absolute American individualism plays itself out. Mixed in with a critique of government repression is a confusion of left and right positions. Should one be for or against consumer pleasures, national sovereignty, tribal loyalties, or ambiguous non-places whose jurisdiction is in flux or indefinable? These are the contradictions plaguing humanities intellectuals today, one reason why they are so ill-equipped to respond to the political and religious extremism at the center of public life.

There is a more serious problem. The success of the humanities in playing a highly visible role in the *Kulturkampf* raging within ever-widening circles of American society has had lasting effects. The practice of abjuring all claims upon the state on the grounds that it is a site of political contagion can be said, paradoxically, to have helped pave the way for extremism itself. At the risk of overstating the case, I would argue that the humanities have played a large and influential part in the descending spiral of political options after 1980. I try in this book to tell the various aspects of this story in a new way, to make the present accountable to the past, not with the idea of turning back the clock, but to prove that the traditions excluded during the turn are still central to our ways of thinking and acting, which are also, of course, ways of being.

ACKNOWLEDGMENTS

THE IDEAS OF THIS BOOK TOOK SHAPE, appropriately enough, in debate. For the hours spent trading ideas on both sides of the Atlantic over the last six years, I want especially to thank Neil Lazarus, Neil Smith, A. Sivanandan, Benita Parry, Silvia Lopez, Klaus Milich, and Chris Chiappari, all of whose comments were formative and plentiful. Let me also thank for their insights Tamara Sivanandan, Manju Parikh, Michal Kobialka, Tim Heitman, Madhuchhanda Mitra, Peter Hitchcock, Jonathan Scott, Gary Thomas, Richard Leppert, Doug Armato, and Crystal Bartolovich. Some of those with whom I corresponded helped me more than they know—Khachig Tölölyan, Emmanuele Saccarelli, Gopal Balakrishnan, Neil Larsen, W. J. T. Mitchell, and Mieke Bal. My gratitude goes also to my colleagues at Humboldt University in Berlin, where the meeting of East and West was painfully obvious (Günter Lenz, Reinhardt Isensee, Renata Hof, Renata Ulbrich, Grit Kümmele), and the Society of Fellows in the Humanities at Cornell University, where the important matter of how ideas travel, and how influences are made, was hammered out with Dominick LaCapra, Susan Buck-Morss, Emily Apter, and Cesare Casarino. For moral support, thanks to Joan Dayan, Barbara Harlow, and Rick and Kathy Asher.

I am grateful to those who gave me the opportunity of presenting these ideas in public lectures: Tobin Siebers, Gaurav Desai, Graham Huggan, Berndt Ostendorf, Martina Ghosh-Schellhorn, Betty Joseph, Jeffrey Cox, Priya Jha, Ken Calhoon, Gregory Jay, Madhava Prasad, Emily Apter, Gautam Kundu,

Sukanta Chaudhuri, Anjan Ghosh, Ali Behdad, Ania Loomba, S. Shankar, Dan Brewer, and Mariam Said. As part of these presentations, and thereafter in ongoing exchanges, I benefited from the following communities: Tom Mertes, Perry Anderson, and Robert Brenner at the Center for Social Theory and Comparative History, UCLA; Bill Boelhower, Annalisa Oboe, and Anna Scacchi in the American Studies center at the University of Padua; Stefano Selenu, Silvia Albertazzi, and Mariella Lorusso at the University of Bologna; Neil Smith, Christian Parenti, David Harvey, Cindi Katz, and Gillian Hart at the Center for Place, Culture, and Politics at the CUNY Grad Center; Peter Hulme, Suvir Kaul, Jed Esty, and Ania Loomba at the "Postcolonial Studies and Beyond" conference at the University of Illinois; C. T. Indira, R. Radhakrishnan, Rajamanickam Azhagarasan, and S. Shankar at the University of Madras; and, over a three-year period, Will Coleman, Imre Szeman, Stephen Slemon, Diana Brydon, Gauri Viswanathan, Arif Dirlik, and Janet Abu-Lughod at the Globalization and Autonomy Project at the University of Toronto and McMaster University in Hamilton, Ontario. Earlier versions of some essays were published by the following journals and presses: *Critical Inquiry, Public Culture, South Atlantic Quarterly, Cultural Critique, Diaspora,* G. K. Hall, and Cambridge University Press. These essays have all been revised for this book.

A few special notes of thanks. Neil Lazarus was a gifted and invaluable friend and interlocutor. Zohreh Sullivan's encouragement and aid made much of the work actually possible. There is no way to gauge the help given me by Keya Ganguly, whose thinking influenced me at every stage. By rights, this book could easily be dedicated to her brilliance and tenacity, which is more than I can match. And, finally, to Edward, for his example.

WARS OF POSITION

CULTURES OF BELIEF

AT A RECENT PUBLIC LECTURE I ATTENDED, the speaker was asked to explain her use of the term "structure of feeling." She jumped into the answer with energy, happy to have the question, and set about saying how much she had learned from this novel idea in Patricia White's book on Hollywood cinema.[1] Some of us thought she was just being subtle, but soon it became clear that she did not know the phrase had been coined by the Welsh literary critic and socialist Raymond Williams; instead she thought she had clinched the point and established the term's provenance. This sort of mistake seems innocent enough—the result of little more than a generational shift of interest or, more charitably, a side effect of intertexuality (since that term involves no notion of intellectual debt). I would like to argue, though, that it not be seen this way. Higher stakes are involved here than simply failing to give a single author his due; nor does this happen because a few individuals are inadequately prepared or have failed to calculate the stress on theories as they travel from one context to another. Rather, this sort of elision is part of a process larger than individual actors—a pervasive rewriting of the past.

Similarly, more than loose fact checking would be needed to explain why the blurb of a current press catalogue refers to a translation of Henri Lefebvre's *The Urban Revolution* (originally published in 1970) in the following way: "*The Urban Revolution*," it reads, "marked Henri Lefebvre's first sustained critique of urban society, a work in which he pioneered the use of semiotic, structuralist

2 INTRODUCTION: CULTURES OF BELIEF

and poststructuralist methodologies in analyzing the development of the urban environment."[2] The author of this extract seems unaware that Lefebvre's intellectual resources came not from Ferdinand de Saussure or Claude Lévi-Strauss but from the French Liberation, and were tempered in debates over tactics and strategies within the French Communist Party. This example suggests something of the appropriative thrust of literary and cultural theory in the restrictive (and, I would argue, more precise) sense of that word that I give it here: that is, the Nietzschean and Lacanian trajectory of the American humanities between 1980 and 1995.[3] Lefebvre's inspirations and styles of thinking were what the schools of thought flagged by the blurb sought to displace or, indeed, take over; but his work has outlived these schools and was already in the 1960s adapted by them in much the same spirit as the speaker's use of Williams.[4]

We find in such examples a vivid illustration of what Sebastiano Timpanaro memorably described in 1970 as the "sophisticated charlatanry" of a certain kind of theory, which set into motion a mode of structured ambivalence, wavering between "scientism" and the "feeble rhetoric and false pathos characteristic of a particular French existentialist tradition."[5] My view in this book, however, will be that this panoply of apparently rich and diverse thinking was not at all ambivalent in regard to its goals. It combined a variety of means with a narrow repetition of ends.

I am not concerned here only with academic trends in theoretical criticism or with a body of ideas related to the displaced philosophy taught in literature departments. When I summon the word "theory," I am talking about a broad social phenomenon that is essentially mainstream as well as a substantial part of the kind of thinking that inspires Hollywood scriptwriters, advertising executives, and the composers of neo-punk bands. It is the ideology of the *turn* I am referring to: a system of ideas more patiently and systematically laid out in graduate seminars, perhaps, but widely practiced and believed in the culture at large, not least because of the successful dispersion of those ideas by academics. I want to point out one other example.

The Soviet philologist and genre theorist Mikhail Bakhtin—who enjoyed an extraordinary reputation in American literature departments throughout the 1980s—entered American graduate seminars as a kind of Solzhenitsyn figure. He appeared as a dissident champion of the *dialogic*, a term that was taken to be not an argument about the meeting of Eastern European languages and professional jargons on the genre of the novel (as Bakhtin intended) but an abstract democratic sublime where dialogue is considered a rejection of polemical confrontation.[6] Bakhtin typically enters the graduate seminar as an adjunct of the Russian formalists (the forerunners of structuralism and poststructuralism)—

again, not unlike the way that Lefebvre was made an ally of the intellectual camps he both preceded and subsumed. No careful intellectual lineage is exactly established, but in an atmospheric way Bakhtin and the Russian formalists are perceived as members of a common project. And yet Bakhtin, in his own mind, had fashioned his career with the intention of repudiating Russian formalism, whose attachments to a narrow poetic form he considered impoverished. In one sense, every bit as much a formalist as the formalists, Bakhtin—with the impudence of a young revolutionary enlivened by early Soviet energies—set out to one-up formalism's highbrow poetics by casting them in the drama of a new philology. He gave to the formalists' project the dimensions it could not imagine: a sweeping command of vernacular languages, population shifts, changing national territories, class-bound generic boundary lines, and explosive new forms of demotic creativity.

Bakhtin sought in philological inquiry the discursive traces of historical tastes, values, and linguistic intrusions. Even as the attention he paid to literary form was broadcast in American comparative literature departments as a kind of political allegory—the *multi*form, the anti-stratifying impulse, the centrifugal vs. the centripetal in politics, and so on—he himself had already clearly stated that language was not a thingly entity, not an opaque screen (in the modernist register of Russian formalism) but, as he bluntly put it in "Discourse on the Novel," a "specific point of view on the world."[7] Novelistic discourse itself was a concert of "ideologemes" (333). The politics of literature as Bakhtin understood it could be found in his observation that irony itself is a form of heteroglossia (324). Literary irony was thus not a mere figure mobilized by writerly style but a marker in the drama of ideas: part of that socially stratified clash of languages found embedded like an archaeological artifact in the linguistic layerings of the modern novel.

These neglected dimensions of Bakhtin's work emerge more clearly when one appreciates his efforts to give Eastern European criticism a model of literary theorizing more exactly linked to the region's national and ethnic divisions. In place of the Russian formalists' austere *poetics* (about which he was witheringly critical) he coined a more supple and expansive term—*prosaics*—to capture the messiness and unruliness of literary language as popular speech, the coinages and bowdlerisms of lower strata, and the ideological commitment to valorizing emergent modes of "vulgar" perception. While describing the jumble of class and profession that produced the voices of his dialogue, he did much more than transcend the typical caricature of socialist realism purveyed in contemporary American graduate programs. The entire sensibility of his project was, by today's standards, frankly socialist in outlook; and much of later literary theory was to be, paradoxically, based on it—belatedly or by way of a reaction, but unmistakably nonetheless.

"Theory," we are told, is over.[8] More than a decade ago, the American critic Paul Bové wrote a book titled *In the Wake of Theory*, and recent years have seen the publication of Terry Eagleton's *After Theory*, Michael Payne's edited collection, *Life After Theory*, and a special issue of the acclaimed journal *Critical Inquiry*, dedicated to the end of theory. It was Stanley Aronowitz who expressed this fashionable view in the *New York Times* a few years ago in the context of praising the work of the Italian theorist Antonio Negri. The *Times* briefly quoted him saying that Negri's writing had happily reinvigorated the project of theory after its long decline and after what Aronowitz saw as its replacement by more committed, local kinds of inquiry: the New Historicism, for example, in literary studies and the study of race, globalization, and the public sphere by graduate students too restless to be satisfied any longer by the textualities of the past that had dominated '68ist versions of thought in the post-WWII era.

This common view, I am going to argue, is misconceived. In fact, the announcement of theory's death can be seen as a preemptive gesture by theory's proponents, designed to pump new life into a failing project by giving it a different and more updated rubric (under the sign of "biopolitics," "local knowledge," "the cultural turn," and so on). Picking up where logocentrism and the discursive regime left off, similar constituencies with similar aesthetic sensibilities are now serviced by declaring themselves engaged in forms of thinking that go beyond theory itself. In other words, we have not seen the disappearance of theory, only its vulgarization—its transformation into a manualized list of ethical givens.[9] In practice, what people mean when they adduce "theory" is neither analytical engagement nor philosophical grounding but the setting in motion of poststructuralism's infinitely interchangeable metaphors of dispersal: decentered subjects, nomadism, ambivalence, the supplement, rhizomatic identity, and the constructed self—terms whose sheer quantity nervously intimates a lack of variation. Although these metaphors are not identical, they refer with a high degree of conformity to a manner of right-living, not, as they present themselves, to an epistemological shift.

If we are to understand academic fame, the power of tendencies, and the success or failure of certain books or fashions, what we would need is an objectification of middle-class value. Only paying attention to that question allows us to decipher the hierarchies of the journal mastheads, anthology selections, or academic book catalogues, whose names appear as highly regulated registers of a service performed to a quietly but fiercely shared set of middle-class assumptions. The policing of this ethic and camaraderie is vigilant and unforgiving.

The common sense of theory, understood in the above way, is what I try to analyze in this book in discussions that are very different from each other but that have at least two things in common: they all grew out of local conjunctures that involved highly public examples of the humanities entering the political mainstream, and they all shed light retrospectively on a key transitional moment in American public culture—what I have called above the "turn" (1975–1980).[10] I have chosen instances, moreover, in which theory was widely recognized by non-academic commentators as performing this role of ethical demarcation. The victory of theory in this sense, the way it has become the very air we breathe in the humanities and in art circles, did not just evolve in some intellectual version of natural selection. Its fortunes were linked to larger political developments that form its backdrop: the shift from a geopolitical arrangement based on three worlds to Francis Fukayama's end of history, as well as from the agreed-upon contours of the Cold War to a more permeating and resilient cold war, now directed (with all of its predecessor's weapons) against various stand-ins for communism: immigrants, exposé journalists, peasant nationalists, Iraqi villagers, Third World reformers, socialist academics, and even independent-minded European heads of state.

To those on the generational cusp—and coming of age in the Carter years, I count myself among them—the turn is probably more evident than it is to today's graduate students or (looking back) to those who marched in the demonstrations of Paris or Chicago '68.[11] In this respect, betweenness has its advantages, and I have written this book from the vantage point of being a part of a featureless generation that attended college in the 1970s. With a foot in two worlds and membership in neither, my generation is particularly aware, I think, of the frightening rapidity with which the pre-1980s past has been erased by ideological conservatives in the U.S. government and its media. But to state my more controversial position, that process dovetails with the work of academic theory. The point of contact between American theory and the American state, generally taken to be antagonists, resides in their shared identification with what I would argue is an American secular religion. And it is for that reason that I consider *belief* crucial during an era of filiative reassertion like our own that seems to render opinions, positions, and arguments secondary to modes of being.

THE POLITICS OF BELIEF

Edward Said's work provides a useful point of departure for this discussion, since he often drew a contrast between forms of belonging. On the one hand were group identities based on will, principle, and intellectual location and, on the other, those based on inheritance and circumstances of birth. Much of his writing was dedicated to giving the former the same dignity enjoyed by the latter, and he often spoke on behalf of communities defined by shared positions, ideas, and visions for the future—on beliefs, in short—refusing to accede to the conventional notion that durable communities can be formed only on the basis of shared bodies, unquestioned spiritual legacies, or the received wisdom that comes with ethnic customs or common places of origin.

Said, in fact, distanced himself from a politics of ontological belonging—above all, its damaging mainstream forms in the spurious concept of a "clash of civilizations" (against which he frequently railed) but also, and less noticeably, against the identity politics of current versions of cultural criticism; he tended to link such forms of belonging with a religious approach to knowledge in general, that is, the creation of like-thinking communities based on transcendental convictions. Such convictions, even if they are not themselves identities, are identitarian insofar as they act with all the intransigence of familial or tribal allegiances formed in holy veneration for a set of shared texts not subject to question. As he put it, even shared beliefs can be dangerous when they "more or less directly reproduce the skeleton of family authority supposedly left behind when the family was left behind."[12] With like mind, Pierre Bourdieu spoke of the way established orders produce "the naturalization of their own arbitrariness," what he called *doxa*, a form of faith.[13] If, to paraphrase W. E. B. Du Bois, the problem of the twenty-first century is the problem of the religious line, the secular response would be not only crucial but also deeply compromised if it shared features of religious thought itself: setting up holy texts, rendering debate impertinent, mobilizing group anger against reprobates, and (as Said once disparagingly put it) insisting on "solidarity before criticism."

If what I have said so far rings any bells, one would have to concede that of all parties subject to the charge of closing ranks, requiring loyalty oaths and adherence to a line, it is Marxism and Marxists, who have come in for the largest share of attack, particularly in the postwar United States. This book, I hasten to say, is not about Marxism nor even a defense of Marxism necessarily; rather it is about the edifice constructed against the bogey that looms in the name of Marxism. Actually, Marxists were not prominently on Said's mind when he developed his motifs against doxological thinking, although they too came in for some harsh criticism. But, oddly enough, what was on his mind was what has come to be understood as literary and cultural theory, a body of complexly varied positions and attitudes, to be sure, but unified around a vigorous self-presentation as Marxism's academic other (if by Marxism we agree to mean for the moment social democratic politics and left Hegelian critique).

This reversal of roles from villain to victim is arresting in Said's chronicle and demands more comment than might first appear necessary. Was Said calling theory doxological? And was his skepticism toward the project of theory the result of a training that was as misunderstood as Lefebvre's and Bakhtin's? If one cares to look closely, there is a pronounced if unexpected attraction to dialectics in Said's early formation, schooled as he was in the work of Georg Lukács and Lucien Goldmann, both of whose ideas he borrowed from and defended throughout the 1970s and 1980s. There were other points of contact with left Hegelianism as well: his admiration for anti-colonial independence intellectuals like C. L. R. James, Frantz Fanon, and Emile Habiby, all products of interwar Marxism. Even Said's apprenticeship in philology bore signs of these influences. He explored the philosophical tradition not only by way of the well-known case of Erich Auerbach, but through the writings of the interrupted philologist and Italian communist Antonio Gramsci.[14] In one of his last essays, his introduction to the fiftieth anniversary issue of *Mimesis*, he considered philology unthinkable without the philosophical traditions launched by Hegel.[15] Familiarity with these lineages, although not all Marxist, was enough to give him pause when faced by an intellectual environment in which all references to Hegelian "totality" were rendered simply as totalitarian in the academic culture he inhabited.

Despite all expectations, it might be fair to suggest that theory's intellectual modes as practiced in recent years have been static and impermeable. In graduate programs, the dense texts of the 1980s have now been internalized as rule-books for etiquette. Even without being told, first-year graduate students come to seminars equipped with a prefabricated vocabulary about difference, ambivalence, and the performative, all mobilized as though the multiple and the dispersed were qualities whose credentials on behalf of freedom no longer needed justification. On the contrary, the very mark of theoretical sophistication requires having made this slippage an integral part of one's thinking in advance. Even if they are predictable, these concepts should not at all be underestimated. Their force lies in their common currency and they have become a powerful prophylaxis against certain politically uncomfortable kinds of intellectual exchange.

The form theory takes in the university is thus very specific and illustrates its meaning in other contexts. It refers to a definite subdisciplinary formation—primarily Anglo-American—that emerged at the end of the 1970s out of a much larger and more protracted perspective in the human sciences. Although a number of thinkers seem united in believing that theory in this restricted academic sense can be said to have emerged from a "turn to language" brought about by the confluence of Nietzsche and the nonlinguistic structuralism based (often very inaccurately) on the work of Saussure, I do not hold this view.[16] A more inclusive definition is necessary. Taken in this categorical sense, theory must be seen—positively—as a critique of instrumental reason, a critique of an antiintellectual worship of capitalist efficiency, the tyranny of the practical and profitable, and the narrowing of the human sphere: a protest, in short, against the fate of philosophy, which had been prematurely condemned to death by a philistine general culture. Theory did not so much supplant philosophy (as Paul de Man had famously argued in *Against Theory*) as preserve it in the double sense of retaining while fossilizing. The critique of instrumental culture could not, however, be mounted within philosophy departments themselves because the logical completion of the very metaphysical positivism that, since Bacon and Locke set British philosophy down the very road of instrumental reason, had taken root there in the form of analytical philosophy.

As the inheritor of both the English intellectual tradition and the British empire, the United States made its own contributions, further deifying the experimental natural sciences and further disparaging the humanities as anything but an elite pastime. And so theory migrated into other wings of the humanities. Literature departments were the best candidates, since their disciplinary boundaries were traditionally in flux. It would be schematic but not incorrect to view the different branches of theory that emerged as mirroring bitter conflicts already well developed in interwar European thought. These were marked by an abrasive coexistence of two self-conscious tendencies locked in rivalry, both pitted against bourgeois mediocrity and its mind-numbing consumerism but to very different ends. On the one hand was a left Hegelian strain marked by a critique primarily of religious modes of thought, of spiritual and material alienation, and of capitalism as a world economic and legal system. Here was a strain that emphasized historical agency, the rootedness of social actors in a system of communal relations, and the need to bring speculative thought to bear on institutions and civic life. On the other hand could be found a later, and reactive, strain derived primarily from Nietzsche's work in the late nineteenth century and Heidegger's from the early twentieth. In its post-turn variant, this strain has viewed capitalism as an aleatory and chaotic system that is fundamentally ambiguous and therefore productive of both domination and liberation; its politics appear in the form of ethics, it stresses the dangers of totality and the mediation of all knowledge by language as well as the semantic independence of representation. This overlapping and antagonistic divide has, to put it mildly, created confusion, not least because this second strain stepped in to claim for itself sole possession of the term "theory" in England and the United States after the 1960s. And it has succeeded. For three decades, this has, practically speaking, been all that most people have meant by the term "theory."

Only in recent years have the modes of inquiry that originated in earlier Hegelian forms of critique been generally accepted under the rubric "theory" in ways that did not, at the same time, obscure their sources. In fact, many of the ideas ushered in have revamped the disciplines and set a vigorous new intellectual tone: studies of the Habermasian public sphere; theories, after Lefebvre, of space and place; studies, after Bourdieu, of taste and cultural capital, the materialist film theory of Miriam Hansen inspired by the Frankfurt School, the historically situated literary formalism of Roberto Schwarz; and so on. That the earlier monopoly is weakening and that the latter kinds of inquiries are beginning now to operate under the imprimatur of theory is precisely what is intended and targeted by the preemptive claim that "theory is over."

Theory, then, as I mean it, is an *American* and *British* translation of *French* refinements of conservative *German* philosophy. This geographical placement allows me to come to the core of my propositions. I do not want to be mistaken for addressing simply the weakness of various arguments in theory or its sloppy handling of its own histories, for this would only continue a long and honorable line of attack mounted by critics like Said himself, by Jürgen Habermas, Nancy Fraser, Terry Eagleton, Richard Wolin, Barbara Smith, Raymond Williams, William Pietz, Miriam Hansen, Neil Larsen, and others. I am saying that the ensemble of ethical positions known as theory—revolutionary in posture, openly hostile to the American state, and characterized as Marxist by the media—is a dissimulated form of an American religion of the middle way. It was called into being by the needs of a political restoration following the Vietnam era, and only in this dissimulated form could it perform its tasks in a larger intellectual division of labor. The individual chapters of this book attempt to substantiate this claim in greater detail.

The first aspect of my critique, then, would be that academic theory, hounded by the media and Washington think tanks in the 1990s, acted as a buffer or proxy for a social democratic enemy considered too dangerous to represent itself. It had to be represented. Trying to overcome their growing irrelevance to the corporate university, theorists understood that competing for the attention of mainstream audiences on terms acceptable to the market could be achieved without abandoning one's dissident self-image. But to do so, one had to fold self-interest into an urgent call for political renewal: making the one as a matter of convenience stand in for the other. A philosophy of concession was needed to repackage middle-class aspiration as an epistemological break, making the rush to the center appear a bold avant-garde leap.

Second, I am saying that theory has been much more than self-contradictory. As counterintuitive as it might seem, I take the position that it was a secret sharer with American liberalism, a position of officially tolerant intolerance from which deviation is not allowed. Theory formed a common front with mainstream liberalism in an effort to efface social democratic traditions in the public sphere and left Hegelian modes of thinking within forms of philosophical critique (replaying, in this way, a contest first codified in the interwar European milieus from which the ideas of theory are mostly drawn, and its precursors largely found). In other words, theory did not merely pave a new road, as it is tirelessly described as having done; it was censorious and dismissive in the process of doing so. At different levels of awareness, the practitioners of theory in the poststructuralist ascendant saw their task as burying dialectical thinking and the political energies—including the anti-colonial energies—that grew out of it. There was never a debate, never a contest among competing philosophical outlooks that theory "won," as it were. A highly one-sided interpretation of Saussure (to take contemporary theory's own version of its inaugural moment) was drummed into students' heads like a catechism. There he was refashioned as a sternly anti-historicist convert to synchronic analysis who had decoupled signifier from signified.

Saussurian ideas were conveyed at second hand through the numerous anthologies and overviews published during the 1980s, most failing to underscore the fact that he never actually wrote a book called *Course in General Linguistics*. No more than a handful of the most curious and independent students are familiar, for instance, with the work of Timpanaro, who masterfully pointed out that this move exemplified the vulgarization of a vulgarization. The literary structuralism from which theory derived was from the beginning a co-optation, riddled with errors, of poorly understood turn-of-the-century arguments within linguistics circles that were then cobbled together to create an intellectual style.[17] There was no debate that allowed these ideas to be placed in counterpoint to the prevailing orthodoxy; as a representative of materialist scholarship on language, Timpanaro was simply excommunicated and no students of structuralism made to contend with his devastating critique, which even today is not part of the received tradition—not even apocryphally.

Finally—and this is my third point—I want to argue that theory was premised on a shift from communal identities based on secular belief to ones based on being—a view that began as identity politics but that has lately effloresced into a Heideggerian resurgence centered on an ontological politics (one of many other examples of how interwar conflicts are replayed in contemporary theory). This shift is significant, for while opposed to religious fundamentalism, the peremptory dogmas of the middle way have contributed to the political extremism we are now witnessing by disabling those who might have fought it.[18] The terms of theory are, perversely, those of that inflexible mode of thought that acts as an unquestioned filiative bond ("before criticism"), as though the recoil from fanatical belief and the shift to the innocent victims of prejudice was a safeguard against fundamentalism. What I am proposing—and I mean this to be a perfectly contrasting parallel—is that communities of political belief are themselves forms of identity. They are not merely chosen as a matter of taste or arrived at by a process of reasoning but are inherited; more to the point, they possess their own proper *cultures*, which, like all cultures, are apparent in one's style or manner even before one utters an opinion.

But I have spoken of "the middle way" and need to elaborate what I mean. How can I justify calling the avant-gardist standpoints of theory a staid mean or middle? Indeed, what could be more unlike the revolutionary postures of Gilles Deleuze and Félix Guattari's schizo-analysis, Jean Baudrillard's desert of the real, or the sweeping philosophical broom of Jacques Derrida at war with the "metaphysics of presence" than the low-wattage business rhetoric of the Democratic Party or the homely language of rights in the philosophy of John Rawls? Is there not, after all, evidence that American liberalism reviles what it sees as the barbarous extremes of theory, either in its conservative variant, because it rejects theory's indifference to empirical evidence and moral fixity, or in the left variant, because it has no theory of organization or electoral politics and, more generally, debunks humanism?

Nevertheless, I want to suggest that theory subscribes to the middle way of American liberal dogma in essential respects, reinvigorating the clichés of neoliberalism by substituting the terminology of freedom, entrepreneurship, and individualism for the vocabulary of difference, hybridity, pluralism, or, in its latest avatar, the multitude (a term, incidentally, excoriated historically by Alexander Hamilton in debates with his contemporary, one Governor Clinton, who used the trope of the multitude in a way that Hamilton considered demagogic).[19] In the environment in which these terms take hold, alienated professionals play in the ambiguous registers of good conscience and conformity at the same time. The neoliberal doctrine defining freedom as freedom from the state was emboldened by theory Americanizing itself as leftist, further weakening the flagging social democratic elements of Democratic Party liberalism whose virtues it cherishes only in the form of the holy individual reborn as the subject of difference. On the one side, a celebrated micropolitics has blended, at times indistinguishably, with suburban self-help and go-it-alone schemes. On the other, an apocalyptic rhetoric of the new millennium has given us the likes of Paul Virilio and Gianni Vattimo, or self-styled "communists" like Negri and Guattari, whose politics more closely resemble the theater of anarchism than liberalism in its conventional guise. I position both sides within the politics of the middle way because they are underground, millenarian, and cloaked in the language of an *all* that can never be realized. Like Bakhtin's carnival, such currents represent no more than a venting of energies (although not the populist energies captured by Bakhtin but an anarcho-liberalism both religious and Nietzschean at the same time—a contradiction, one would think, that gave the believers pause). In the recent versions offered by Negri, this tendency is based on a refashioning of Spinoza on behalf of the "*multitudo fidelium*"—a Catholic vision of global solidarity grafted onto a socialist one in which the politics of state power has been replaced by a mystical communion of saints.

If, apart from everything else, theory conforms to a middle way, it is above all in regard to its hatred of a common enemy, what its confusing panoply of positions all share with the mainstream consensus and why the official consensus gives theory the privilege of being its scandalous antagonist in the media debates of the culture wars: that is, its war against left Hegelian thought.[20] Louis Hartz in his seminal book *The Liberal Tradition in America*, published in 1955, zeroed in on the tendency, as lively in the twenty-first as in the nineteenth century, of posing the salvational middle against two extremes—what Roland Barthes memorably called "neither-norism" in his collection of essays *Mythologies*. In Hartz's view, American liberalism confidently proclaimed that "hard doctrinaire mind[s]" are "not of the American type" and that "the concept of social upheaval [is] alien to the American mind."[21]

The inexorable double movement associated with the program of dialectics could be dissimulated as difference. Now without its left wing, the cultural Left disarmed intellectual opposition and helped produce not triumphant liberalism at all but the acute expression of the realignment of resources and the redrawing of forces that characterizes today's unequal fight between the wealthy and the poor. The forces of self-enrichment, rigged elections, and wars for oil— all operating under the unifying myth of a carefully packaged Christian belief— stepped in to capitalize on an abdication by a cultural Left that had abandoned debate over goals, programmatic statements of purpose, and solidarities based on common outlooks and tastes. The latter found it actually tasteless to wield power or even to seek it.

BEING AND DOING

I have said that theory was staged as a movement from communities of belief to communities of being. This would seem to exempt many of theory's most vaunted practitioners, many of whom propose to unlock the inherent Cartesian bias of such a move. Judith Butler, for instance, has famously emphasized the constructedness of subjectivity, the performativity of gender, and the cultural malleability of identity, seeking to decouple the body from essential notions of selfhood. Biology is precisely not destiny in her account. What, then, is the nature of my charge, since the facts on the ground of what Nancy Fraser once called "movements for recognition" far exceed recognition? Notwithstanding Butler's assertions, I would argue that her work still permits the notion, certainly adhered to by her followers, that the critic must be of a certain race, gender, or sexual articulation in order to comment authoritatively on political issues pertaining to the same.[22] Or, as Trinh Minh-ha, another celebrated critic at the moment, once complained: theory demands that one must be one to know one, a position later muffled in equivocations about "strategic essentialism" and the "axiomatics of the closet." A phrase such as "postcolonial intellectual," to take one example, did not in the 1980s and 1990s refer to a scholar who had declared an area of specialization, but to an American- or European-based academic born in a former colony, or related to those who had been.

The fact of the matter is that the hard ideological substratum of theory's enterprise has been identitarian from the start. Strange as it may seem, Nietzschean genealogy was itself a form of identity politics. It was not, of course, the German tribe that was Nietzsche's ideal per se, although he frequently made direct appeals to "we Germans" (or alternatively, "we Europeans") in his ongoing struggle to rouse his countrymen from their historical slumber. But even if he disavowed the tribal, Nietzsche based his philosophy on the intimations, if not the reality, of blood, inheritance, and pre-rational filiation. His intimate audience was the aristocratic few willing to pursue the joyful savagery of Darwinian "life." It should not be surprising then that, for his part, Foucault, as the profound Nietzschean he claimed to be, universalized the experiences of his own targeted identity in *Discipline and Punish*. Grand conclusions of general applicability about a historical shift in Europe from treating criminals with corporal punishment to making the body a "prison of the soul" were drawn from what, in the end, was a limited French case (a fact about his work's claims that is, disingenuously, I think, buried by him in a footnote in that work). The discourse of the rehabilitation of the sexually abnormal in nineteenth-century

French prison reforms gets translated by him into an overarching epistemology of modern penality—a new universalism against humanist universalism. As with other essentially religious arguments, the more extravagant the proposition in the world of everyday sense-making, the more transcendent (and therefore true) its propositions.

It turns out that there are more than a few exemplars of the theoretical middle way. As a Bulgarian émigré long established in France, Julia Kristeva is an ideal representative, in many ways, of the demonstrable lack of subtlety in theory when it comes to addressing the move from a culture of political belief to one of ontological virtue. With her we see again the pattern in which attacks on barbarian races are mingled with attacks on belief systems that are then, in effect, fused in the reader's mind. In studies from the early 1990s on cosmopolitanism and nationalism, Kristeva was already displaying an identification with French taste seen as a salvational mechanism inseparable from the democratic mind. This point has been made well by Dušan Bjelić in an essay titled "The Balkans: Europe's Cesspool." Bjelić explores the work of Kristeva in order to account for the way she diagnoses the political transformation of Eastern Europe after the fall of the Berlin wall by substantially accepting Samuel Huntington's thesis of a deep civilizational divide between West and East, where the former stands for the "civic" and the latter for the "tribal."[23] Mobilizing the powerful weapons of French taste, Kristeva decries the dangerous moral and physical hygiene of the unsublimated Eastern European, posing as they do a danger to the cosmopolitan purity of the Western ideal. Enlisting Heidegger's student Hannah Arendt as guide, Kristeva considers her embrace of French democracy to be insurance against dreaded racialist notions "of the *Volksgeist* stemming from a line of thinkers that include Herder and Hegel," which in Kristeva's view led to the disasters of World War II and then postwar communism (Bjelić, 8).

It is hard, however, to reconcile the disavowal of racialism with her actual words: "I lodge my body in the logical landscape of France, take shelter in the sleek, easy and smiling streets, rub shoulders with this odd people . . . possessed of an impenetrable intimacy. . . . An irritated, condescending, fascinated world . . . seems ready to follow them. To follow us."[24] For Bulgaria, however, Kristeva constructs an analysis of what she, not unlike Huntington, calls "the Orthodox psyche," which she reads not only as a psychoanalysis of religion but as a power discourse on "the Orthodox body" (her words). This Orthodox psyche is an incomplete self, she argues, and, as such, deviant and self-destructive. Like Heidegger and like the Arendt schooled by Heidegger, Kristeva builds her case on comparisons to the ancient Greek polis and to Greek philosophy seen yet again (as it was by Nietzsche) as the model of a glorious philosophical politics poised against the degraded modern nation-state, where, to quote Bjelić, "the aesthetics of the self and the politics of the public sphere merge in the art of living and are interdependent with the new and constructive use of repression and violence."

Discounting for a moment Kristeva's hauteur, her position might appear to be merely a local and inventive recombination of latent motifs in Arendt. It is, however, much more than that: one movement, rather, in a more systematic resurgence of Heideggerian thinking in cultural theory, a much more polished, high-octane version of theory's earlier fixations on identity as the quest for recognition. But there is little in the recent turn (which is really more of a *re*turn or recidivism) that has about it the air of equality, civic betterment, or affirmative action as would be found in the politics of identity practiced in the 1960s struggles for civil rights and equality. Rather, the imperative, as in Heidegger himself, is about transforming reification into an ecstatic "thingliness," turning revolt against conditions of capitalist alienation into a life artwork, turning thought itself into the aesthetic revelation of being. To that degree, it is about shunting the question of conflict away from discussion, debate, resolution, responsibility, agreement, or disagreement and toward the building of a sublime space in pockets that find themselves in, but not of, society.

In much of her work since 2000, Kristeva is invested in a reappraisal of Arendt, whom she admires for being "faithful to the teachings of Heidegger." Arendt elicited from the great philosopher's poetic thought, Kristeva argues, an otherworldly and non-utilitarian form of heroism, which was for Heidegger (and this is crucial) just the opposite of an escape from the everyday. On the contrary, Kristeva portrays the everyday as an entirely new virtue of the polis. In what has come to be a familiar, even epochal, gesture for a number of contemporary thinkers (see Agamben below), Kristeva seizes on Arendt's reinterpretation of Aristotle in *The Human Condition* (1958) in order to thrust political being into a new solitary and sensuous environment. Through Heidegger, Arendt crafts an entirely new way of being political—one that resembles the poetic refuge of literary modernism, uselessness, and grand *disposability*. The fullness of life is thereby made possible through an Aristotelian "praxis" defined as inactivity, as a purely aware existence—which is perhaps the clearest feature of the "freedom" that Kristeva emphasizes as her principal theme: "Part and parcel of the search for a new happiness—the equivalent of a new sacred—is the devaluing of *homo faber* in favor of *homo ludens*; this is something else May '68 called for."[25] Kristeva herself expresses perfectly what is most Heideggerian in this bold exegetical act: "that which we classify as an aesthetic activity is the true life of thought. Which is to say, thought vivified and incarnate in the desiring body, rather than just a set of calculating operations."[26] In this atmosphere thick with the urge for revelation, the coupling of the project of thought with religion is not so much challenged as reasserted in a profane philosophical register, one that manages to cast the liberatory past of the postwar youth movements in an alliance with the standard-issue jargon of interwar political reaction: "Infinite jouissance for each person at the intersection of happiness for all . . . is it anything else but the sacred?"[27]

Heidegger, who often presents himself as a lonely sage dwelling on the ancient Greeks and therefore above and outside the quotidian conflicts of his time, knew and even indirectly responded to Lukács's *History and Class Consciousness*, published four years before his own *Being and Time*, which alludes to Lukács at least three times in the text. Indeed, this connection has already been explored by Goldmann.[28] At the very least we would have to say that Heidegger's motives (as indeed those of his latter-day disciples) were specifically anti-Lukácsian. Heidegger's project is, among other things, a reactive attempt to arrest Lukács's explosive inquiry into reification and consciousness by turning it into a meditation on being, although it cannot be reduced merely to that, of course. But its stated goal—the end of metaphysics—could lead only, given the terms of his inquiry, into a tortured metaphysical language. At any rate, this certainly is a major dimension of the recent Heideggerian turn, which is the logical endpoint of theory's obliteration of the legacy of Jean-Paul Sartre, who, in the 1950s, appropriated and, as it were, defused Heidegger in *Being and Nothingness*. Not only the grounds of Heidegger's inquiry but his self-appointed role as historical foil to the Hegelian Left lies behind his current enlistment by the cultural Left of our own times. Heidegger gave theory, as Corey Robin memorably puts it, "a more intense, almost ecstatic mode of experience in the spheres of religion, culture and even the economy," all of which are conceived as "repositories of the mysterious and the ineffable, celebrating the intoxicating vitality of struggle while denouncing the bloodless norms of reason and rights."[29] In postcolonial theory this discourse now drives discussion of the "subaltern," a term popularized by Gramsci but taken more recently to be the sign of a structural blockage between the material limits imposed by history and the occult freedom of the lower depths. Within postcolonial quarters, the experience of existing outside and permanently estranged from public participation or intervention in politics is thus cast as the noble predicament of sly civility.

One could put these observations in a more forceful way: theory leans on the postcolonial, and is even parasitical of it, in the sense that an occult subalternity is conceived as theory's deepest and most irreducible value. The abject image of Third World marginality forms for the postcolonial theorist (and this is a variation on Kristeva) the projected moral center of metropolitan thought itself. The subaltern is portrayed as the one who teaches intellectuals about Nietzschean life. We see this for instance in Heidegger's tendency to position himself as a sort of village wise man wed to the avocations of thought without being, properly speaking, an "intellectual." Irresistible to this theoretical sensibility has been Heidegger's style of gnomic simplicity of expression based on an idealized and skeptical peasant as well as the imagery of soil, wood, stone, and forest. Subalternity, then, as one can imagine, becomes not an inequality to be expunged but a form of ontological resistance that must be preserved—but only in that form: in a perpetually splintered, ineffective, heroic, invisible, desperate plenitude.

THE COLD WAR AND LANGUAGE

The clearest recent embodiment of this gesture toward ontological resistance, and a perfect adjunct to Kristeva both in his habit of finding lessons in ancient Greece and in his reliance on Arendt, is Giorgio Agamben. One of several contemporary Italian theorists whose work collectively has received significant attention, Agamben exemplifies what I would argue is a mode of "new Italian thought" carrying on, in many ways, the sense of sophisticated ease and prophetic insight that had previously gone under the imprimatur of French thought. Although better known than others in the same constellation (with the exception of Negri), Agamben expresses a very similar, and in many ways identical, field of interests, circling around a perceived change in political *sovereignty*. On the one hand, the authority of the state is taken to be beyond law and beyond all limits or constraints; citizenship and civic life are held to be "naïve" notions (as Agamben puts it), and as a result sovereignty has become as brutal as it is total and permeating, reaching right into the very body of the citizen. As such, sovereignty achieves in the eyes of the new Italians a novel existential dimension. For this reason one must discount "every attempt to ground political communities in something like a 'belonging,' whether it be founded on popular, national, religious, or any other identity."[30] The response to total power must be a neatly inverted one: redefine sovereignty so that it means control over one's self, which by foiling the state's desire is an eminently political act.

In order to preserve bare life—mere existence—from the prying eyes of sovereign power, Agamben sets out to de-scale politics to a manageable dimension, a process Foucault had earlier called the "care of the self." Agamben bases the logic of this argument on the distinction in Aristotle between simple, bestial life—mere existence—and the "good life" experienced by humans in their proper capacity as political animals: which is to say, a capacity that involves discussing, debating issues of policy, arguing over principles, and laying out strategies. Citing Foucault with approval to the effect that "the species and the individual as a simple living body" have now become "what is at stake in a society's political strategies," Agamben follows Foucault also in contending that the "inclusion of bare life in the political realm constitutes the original, if concealed, nucleus of sovereign power."[31] Following in the footsteps of Arendt as well (in whom, as I have already suggested, the Aristotelian distinction centrally features), he borrows the notion that the "concentration camp and the great totalitarian states of the twentieth century" have made biopolitics all politics as such.

By now we are familiar with this pattern, first perfected by Arendt, of taking a term inflated by classical resonances (*homo laborans*, in one of Agamben's usages) and reinterpreting it in a process that gradually moves us along to the a priori goal. *Homo laborans*, perhaps unsurprisingly, is taken to mean not "making man" or "fabricating man" or "working man" but (in Agamben's upping of the ante) "biological life as such—the very center of the political scene of modernity." Most charitably, one could understand this semantic leap to be an enigmatic rehearsal of Marx's *Economic and Philosophical Manuscripts of 1844*. Agamben, so as not to belabor a point with which he assumes his audience will be already familiar, follows Marx in identifying the active transformation of nature by human beings as an essential feature of their anthropological being or, in Marx's words, their "species-being." However, in this context it is important to recall that Marx actually includes desire, instinct, and hunger, not merely labor, and most certainly not thought alone in his definition of species-being.

But there is no evidence that Agamben has these features of humanness in mind, nor is there a consistent attempt to read or interpret any of his precursors, whose language and leads he quietly borrows. Agamben conjures his fear of sovereignty for what one can readily grant are sound reasons. Our extreme times are indeed marked by the growth of fundamentalist responses to the market, which have created new and frightening forms of political repression as well as a whole host of biopolitical strategies of control, including the patenting of genes, subcutaneous tracking devices, and the scanning of the human iris for identification purposes. One can see the impulse to circle the wagons while protecting the last bastion of the person under an administered state. Why not, then, following Foucault and Agamben, consider the body the last outpost of sovereignty and the last monad that if kept free can prevent sovereignty from attaining the status of an absolute? The answer to this question is another question, which Agamben neither can nor wants to answer: which state?

Just as political liberalism summoned the fiction of the totalitarian state without differentiation, so recent forms of theory drawing on the odd triumvirate of Carl Schmitt, Heidegger, and Arendt conjure the state as a mode of being. The terror dome of the Paraguayan dictator Alfredo Stroessner is rendered equivalent to Roosevelt's New Deal or Hugo Chavez's Venezuela. Agamben's hasty remobilization of the theses of Theodor Adorno and Max Horkheimer on damaged life, the culture industry, and the authoritarian personality manages in this very act to announce itself as displacing rather than strengthening the left Hegelian tradition—not openly perhaps but in an unmistakable pattern of carefully chosen affiliations. But in the end Agamben is unable to question how sovereignty has ever exerted itself except over *zōe* (that is, bare life). What he cannot contest, and therefore does not ask, is how it is possible to rule at all if not to rule over bodies. Only by disciplining bodies can labor be extracted from workers and slaves, or sexual favors extracted from the traffic in women. His assumption that biopolitics is a new predicament within Western societies is both awkward and revealing, and leads logically to one of the book's more uncomfortable impasses: biopolitics is premised on an epochal shift in modernity, but this shift can only be seen on reflection as a narrower way of viewing a familiar system of coercion instituted by absolutist states and European empires. Granted, there are unique features to any historical event, and Nazi extermination policies were to that degree sui generis. But genocide, medical experimentation on captive populations, systematic population transfers, and the bizarre coding of human types in racial or ethnic hierarchies are all central features of European colonization *as a whole*, and they existed in an advanced, scientific state well before the mid-twentieth century. In other words, the predicament of human suffering is hardly a matter of a tear in the very fabric of history introduced by the Nazi death camps.

Agamben is caught in a bind prompted as much by his Nietzschean tutelage as by his clerical and Italian classical training, not to mention his utterly Europeanized perspective. He assumes that the primacy of *zōe* over *bios* is, after Auschwitz, peculiar to Western societies and that the novelty of biopolitics can be established "following the tenacious correspondence" that exists "between the modern and the archaic." But such a correspondence is based, just as it is in the style of argument employed (very differently) by Heidegger, on etymologies drawn from ancient Greece rather than from anything resembling current geopolitics. What historical or political purchase can an etymological argument in this context have? No one would think to base a theory of modernity on such local and elusive evidence were it not for Arendt's leads in such a venture, and their unquestioned acceptance as speaking to a universal condition (in the manner of the false universalisms of liberal philosophy in general). Herein lies the real elision, for the historical and political basis of *those* leads takes us not to ancient Greece or Rome but to the political motives of interwar phenomenology as well as to the contexts of its politically suspect and hysterical reception in the United States of the 1950s in which Arendt featured prominently as *the* left Cold War intellectual. About this conjuncture Agamben has nothing to say.

If theory conjures an abstract state as its enemy—outside space and time—mainstream political liberalism typically conjures the totalitarian state as the common territory of left and right extremes.[32] A key element of the Heideggerian turn, then, is to fuse *communismfascism* as a single complex: a force so elemental and obvious that no counterevidence need ever be marshaled. No reason, for instance, to explain the historical antipathy of communism to fascism (from the imprisonment of partisans to the decades of political theory singling out the other as its primary enemy) or, even more decisively, the integration of former Nazis into the United States and West Germany after World War II, a move that has no systematic counterpart in the Eastern bloc. To adduce her in this context again, Kristeva, for her part, permits herself to offer this amalgam with a formula—"statism in all its varieties"—while at the same time leaving Heidegger's very real fascism tastefully out of the discussion except in the form of a passing reference to an unfortunate biographical episode.[33] Thus, an even more pronounced aspect of this *doxa* is its silence about uncomfortable truths.

In another illustration, Jean-François Lyotard's book, *The Differend*, presents a cogent illustration of how the *doxa* opposed to secular belief cultures works today in that realm of theory deriving from nonlinguistic structuralism in Timpanaro's sense. Again drawing on the late writings of Heidegger, and in a somewhat more unorthodox manner, on Wittgenstein, Lyotard conceptualizes the *differend* as any conflict of "phrase regimens" that cannot by definition be resolved simply because no rule of judgment is applicable to both. He argues that phrase regimens, out of which public speech is largely composed, do not exist as a litigation, as that which can be debated (as in a court of law) but in impassive "genres of discourse" bumping up against one another in ostensible dialogue fated to collapse into frustrating cross-purposes. From these premises, announced (as one would expect) with oracular majesty at the very opening of his book, Lyotard builds his case, venturing the idea that in this impasse lies great potential: "the free examination of phrases leads to a critical dissociation of their regimes." In other words, the unintended language games that Wittgenstein found in common language and that destined traditional philosophy to well-meaning banter for the want of stable referents are here raised to a desired principle, since to do so, says Lyotard, is to "lay the ground for the thought of dispersion (diaspora writes Kant)."

Here once more we find those infinitely interchangeable metaphors of dispersal I referred to at the beginning. They come to occupy a status that is simultaneously cognitive (mental "dispersion" is taken to mean "freedom" in Lyotard's terms) and philosophical (inasmuch as they recall the eminence of no less than Kant); they are also vaguely historical, if the term "diaspora" can be uttered at all today without bringing along with it an association of minority or persecuted populations in full flight from intolerable conditions. This juggling of metaphors, whose force emanates from juxtaposition rather than argument, is precisely the purpose of Lyotard's aphoristic phrasing. The entire progression of his thought is disingenuously evasive, but more to the point, it is by now a formula. This is how theory works at present: allusive of the immediately political and worldly present, suggestive of a fair contest of ideas "in litigation," but eager to introduce a literary template that plays the role of leaving, as all literature does, an unfilled space into which the reader can pour a certain confidence that we are in the presence of deep thought.

To flinch at Lyotard's semantic anarchism, as so many journalists and conservative academics did in the face of his exotic pronunciamentos of the 1980s and 1990s, is to overlook an even more revealing subtext found throughout his work as well as that of his theoretical contemporaries. Since his major point in *The Differend* is that there are no "unanimously approved protocols" for establishing the "reality of the object of an idea," he attempts in the book to move us by inches to the notion that any thought under the category of the "whole," which is at the same time considered an "object of cognition," is *totalitarian*. It is difficult to capture the stubborn allegorical flavor of his notions, which present themselves as having been written (as Lyotard puts it after Barthes) in "a zero degree style"—homely, unadorned, affectless. And yet the seeming substantiality of his propositions rests on a few referents scattered here and there and designed to ground the book in a specific conjuncture and clarify its affiliations. There are, for example, abrupt outbursts on Stalin, or flashes of an argument on Hitler lasting only a few lines, and so on, in a book in which there are no chapters properly speaking, only entries as if in a notebook. One has little trouble appreciating Lyotard's meaning in passages like the following: "If establishing the reality of a phrase's referent according to the protocol of cognition is extended to any given phrase, then this requirement is totalitarian in principle."

Given Lyotard's mix-and-match operations, it is easier to see in him than in others a more general tendency under the regime of theory: the inextricable destiny of semantic indeterminacy and freedom, of auratic declarations poised against the always indistinguishable communismfascism endangering the middle way. If Agamben, Vattimo, Lyotard, and late Foucault leave us with an image of the social as either hollow shell or oppressive weight, we have with Kristeva and Lyotard much more than theorists drawing on ambiguous intellectual sources. Their positions do not merely resemble, de facto, those of their right-wing antagonists; indeed they are indistinguishable from them. Kristeva relies on a poetic essentialism with a checkered past, recycling Western European prejudices about its Eastern fringe in ways that are worlds apart from her reputation in theory circles as a champion of insurgent freedom and an explosive, even revolutionary, mode of thought. Lyotard, for his part, presents himself quite unironically as an enthusiastic defender of the triumph of U.S. capitalism in the Cold War, a view unguardedly expressed in one of his "postmodern fables" (as he liked to call them) following the fall of the Berlin wall.[34] There are other dramatis personae in the tableau of theory, whose views, long taken to be part of the cultural Left, are in some variants at least openly and not just ludically identical to those expressed within American and European neoliberalism.

The middle way of theory is popularly posed in graduate seminars today as the stuff of heroic subterranean discourse with its own innovative pantheon. Part of the story, as it is narrated, has to do with a mythology surrounding the historic lectures on Hegel delivered by Alexandre Kojève after the war. From there, the story takes us to the long overdue rehauling of the dialectic by a select and youthful legion of intellectual explorers and revolutionaries like Deleuze, Michel de Certeau, Foucault, and others, who did nothing less (according to this story) than invent a new logic and language to make future conservative restorations impossible. This was purportedly a new epistemology and a decisive shift to a wondrously unpredictable but certainly preferable politics of new left possibility. The story is about an obscure and carefully crafted set of talismanic ideas that require a lifetime to penetrate and admire, much like the phrasings of *Finnegans Wake*. Finally, as the narrative has it, after a series of apparent logical and political impasses during the period of old left dominance, the ghost of the holy State had been laid to rest, its arguments cut off at their very Hegelian source so that the organic circularity of a passionate, progressive idealism could now be confidently exploded into the much more inviting prospect of a shower of glittering fragments.

The narrative would seem less novel to those who had read British conservatives like L. T. Hobhouse, who in his *Metaphysical Theory of the State* in 1918 laid out the lineaments of this same anti-Hegelian argument. He railed against the "false and wicked doctrine" of the "god-state" that according to him was responsible for the outbreak of World War I, whose carnage was fresh on his mind. Herbert Marcuse quotes Hobhouse in 1941 in *Reason and Revolution* to show the persistence of the attempts in Anglo-American thought, already evident in the 1940s, to eradicate the virus of left Hegelianism—a pattern slavishly repeated today. For our purposes, it is vital to recall that Hegel's critique of religion entailed the observation that "religion is principally commended and resorted to in times of public distress, disturbance, and oppression; it is taught to furnish consolation against wrong and the hope of compensation in the case of loss."[35] The dangers of religion are that it diverts humans from their search for freedom, paying them "fictitious damages for real wrongs." In fact, as Marcuse rightly points out, Hegel comes to champion the rights of reason and self-consciousness, concluding that "it is not strength, but weakness which has in our times made religion a polemical kind of piety."[36] In this spirit, we could see the current turn to religion as the defensive response of everyday people across the globe to the fact that capitalism, now triumphant, was coming to clobber them. In an updated left Hegelian sense, religion would be—as a sort of anthropological factor—fear inarticulate, or to put this another way, terror in the face of capitalism expressed in the distorted language of devotion.

Absolute civil freedom demands a cruel historical accounting, and history, according to Hegel, is "the slaughter-bench at which the happiness of peoples, the wisdom of States, and the virtue of individuals have been victimized."[37] The resulting sacrifice of individual and general happiness is that notorious "cunning of reason" excoriated by the anti-Hegelian critics as though it were a prescription rather than a lament. And what is crucially lost in this moralism is that neglected feature of Hegel's analysis for our global, multicultural age. For, despite his stern defense of the rights of the bourgeois subject and his self-conscious identification with its interests, Hegel recognized that civil society under the rule of investors and merchants "increasingly makes the social organism a blind chaos of selfish interests and necessitates the establishment of a powerful institution to control the confusion." Marcuse is quite right to conclude that "by means of its own dialectic the civil society is driven beyond its own limits as a definite and self-complete society." In other words, "it must seek to open new markets to absorb the products of an increasing over-production, and must pursue a policy of economic expansion and systematic colonization."[38] The "police" in Hegel's thought, in other words, are his bid for curbing the excesses of the market. To embrace the principle of force as a means of resisting the colonial rampages of capitalist economic expansion is, in the received parameters of theory, to risk being branded a "Leninist" (or some other name designed to end all discussion), whereas it is a wholly reasonable response to actual conditions as well as one the Left would presumably have to adopt if it wished to continue existing.

A skewed version of intellectual history presides over this received narrative, effectively silencing certain strands of scholarship. To illustrate this point, think only of four paradigmatic texts from the last gasp before the turn: Oskar Negt and Alexander Kluge's *Public Sphere and Experience* (1993 [1972]), Jacques Attali's *Noise* (1977), Pierre Bourdieu's *Outline of a Theory of Practice* (1977), and Stuart Hall et al.'s *Policing the Crisis* (1978). These books demonstrate the vibrancy of the ideas of the pre-1970s upon which they were all based, and how even at the dawn of the great shift there were fresh and vigorous replenishments of earlier moments. They did not, in other words, come to an end because they had run out of steam. On the contrary, these studies still have a kind of subterranean fame today, a shadow existence, even though they are not a firm part of the canon of graduate seminars.

The logic of '68 ensured a rethinking of older forms of organization and styles of reading. How could it have been otherwise? But it seems odd, in retrospect, that the definitive experimentalist political text of the generation of '68 turned out to be not Negt and Kluge's expansion of Habermas's youthful work on the "public sphere" but Deleuze and Guattari's *Capitalism and Schizophrenia*. The former sought a bridging rhetoric, combining some serious homework with novel and energetic institutional analyses of the media, labor, and the changes worked upon the latter in the forging of new constituencies. It appeared to be the natural antecedent to a future radical social and cultural theory. How is it, then, that the left-wing of the humanities was drawn instead to the hypertrophic, self-consciously prophetic work of schizoanalysis and its post-Freudian rampage against the bourgeois liberation of mere subjectivity?

What is lamentable is that this tendentious narrative has gained institutional clout. Theory may well have opened up a space for more freedom of inquiry across disciplines—only one reason why humanities institutes offered a stage to welcome subdisciplinary formations like cultural studies and postcolonial studies in the decades following its institutionalization during the late 1970s and early 1980s. Nevertheless, the emphasis of both on human agency, historical change, and subaltern artistic practices is an uncomfortable fit with "theory" where the acting subject was always a ruse and where physical beings gave way to being itself, and history as a mobile army of metaphors marched to the beat of a thundering ressentiment. What was perceived at the time as a natural alliance was in fact a conflicted, self-contradictory process carried out with a fair

degree of coercion. Quasi-commercial academic publishing houses like Routledge in the 1980s and early 1990s, and more recently Duke University Press, created a theory-product that was effectively disseminated, anthologized, and refined within the humanities and codified by the special initiatives of humanities
institutes. Only by way of an energetic organization and a concerted process of
apportioning resources according to a prevailing political position could postcolonial study's critique of imperialism or cultural studies' confounding of class
prejudices in the popular arts be made to seem a natural ally of the free play of
signification, genealogy, and the subject effect. When the inconsistency was
pointed out, labels like "vulgar Marxism," "unreconstructed leftism," and "left
conservatism" succeeded in bringing debate to a standstill. No side, however, has
a monopoly on oversimplification, and whatever vulgar Marxism survives has
been more than matched by a vulgar poststructuralist common sense. As a result, political differences have been misrecognized as disparate levels of theoretical complexity, with theory designated the winner in advance.

What makes this attitude all the more paradoxical is that left Hegelianism
represents not only a more self-critical and agential politics but a majority of
the last century's most creative scholarship. The very belief culture consigned
to history's cobwebs has reappeared again and again in traduced forms, seen
graphically in the reemergence over the last decade of Marxists like Walter Benjamin, Adorno, Ernst Bloch, C. L. R. James, Gramsci, and Lefebvre, as "poststructuralists" *avant la lettre*. The left Hegelian tradition is constantly present
as a resource in whatever turns are invoked by theory to greet the shifting of
events. There it always seems to stand—muted, disguised, unwanted, unavoidable—in whatever statement of the new presents itself.

The ethical undercurrent of the politics of being stipulates that any larger
ambition than the self risks an imposition on others, a transgression on alterity itself. In this modality, belief is rendered irrelevant. One simply cannot understand the triumph of the American Right in recent decades without appreciating the paralysis this line of reasoning produced even in idealistic students
and critics, repelled by America's commercial wastelands and hostile to the national claims of empire. An entire generation has been taken out of politics.

THE MIDDLE WAY

In an aesthetic rather than political register, theory articulates dissidence and
compliance simultaneously. At least one reason why this precarious balance
can be maintained is found in the prevailing conditions of the postwar United

States in which a fissure has opened up between the site of contestation embodied by the law and unwritten directives governing acceptable dissent. We
have all grown accustomed, for example, to the assumption that the U.S. Constitution protects citizens against discrimination on the basis of "race, color,
and creed." In fact, unlike the UN's Universal Declaration of Human Rights,
there are no explicit protections for freedom of conscience in the U.S. Constitution apart from article 1, which protects against "prohibiting the free exercise
of religion." This has resulted in a series of negative pressures on North American intellectual life. While free speech in the abstract is protected by law, the
safeguards never specify the *content* of acceptable speech, leaving all with the
(false) impression that no restrictions are tolerated. Such abstraction does not
render free speech meaningless, but it hides its partial character. Freedom of
expression is, in this respect, fatally abstract and for that reason severely restricted without being meaningless.

One clear institutional exercise of free expression has been the policy of affirmative action, which attempts to allow doing to take place freely, to not be
foreclosed by a certain perception of being. On the other hand, affirmative action relies on a shift from identity-as-position to identity-as-location. So, many
still stubbornly assume, for example, that American-based scholars whose family background is Lebanese, Nigerian, or Mexican are born specialists on
Lebanon, Nigeria, or Mexico. Entire careers, not just the speakers' lists of conferences or magazine roundtables, operate with a brittle confidence in this
questionable homology between knowledge and being, analytical depth and
surname. A cellular epistemology has for several decades covered the thinking
and (more important) the policymaking of academic reformers and liberal
politicians as well as that of public commentators and mainstream news organizations, thereby opening itself up to a reactionary attack that has won favor
with sectors of the public.

In spite of the crucial points of dissonance between the media and academic progressives on matters ranging from the value of cultural studies to the
role of research in undergraduate humanities education, there is no disagreement about the subtle equation between black scholars and black thinking, if
one can use such a term. I use it here, at any rate, with intentional irony to refer
to that nervous overcompensation by well-intended administrators who still
actually believe in what they pretend not to: namely, the radical and essential
differences among people on the grounds of race, gender, and ethnicity. In this
liberal sentiment there circulates an amalgam of similarly harmful but widespread assumptions by the very people at the cutting edge, supposedly, of curricular reform, affirmative action, and postcolonial sympathy. Such assump-

tions include the centrality of the English language in a world where only a global minority speaks it, about the vibrancy and longevity of foreign popular cultures provided they are already subsumed into the U.S. media and are therefore translatable, or about the seductions of the European literary canon—a position that must ignore the competitive aesthetic brilliance of, say, Caribbean music when placed alongside European literature or, indeed, Urdu literature when juxtaposed with its European counterparts. In both media and academic venues, the defense of culturally dissonant thinking is given permission to *be* only in the imaginary form of the nonwhite, the woman, or the diasporic scholar. Very much like the Californian tourist in Mali, the liberal critic cannot wait to return home to a more secure and inviting environment. Beliefs breed ways of being, and the intolerance toward some has less to do with scholarly refutations than with a palpable unease in the presence of lifestyles and worldviews that demand of the stranger a painful, and often impossible, cultural conversion.

Outside the relative social fairness and moral conscience of the university, the key sites of opinion forming and decision making—Congress, the Washington talk shows, and somewhat less so, influential news feature and interview programs such as *CNN Reports* or *The O'Reilly Factor*—are so overwhelmingly white (or so predictably tokenized) that equations between affirmative action and alternative values seem almost axiomatic. Nonetheless, a set of arguments against gender and racial oppression is firmly in place, even though those arguments have not achieved anything like racial or gender equality. There is a good deal of evidence, in fact, that the unofficial is becoming the official, that trends in business and government are actually moving from de facto segregation to an open declaration that minority exclusion is justified.[39] This represents a shift in policy that mirrors the rise in anti-immigrant violence, the number of police brutality cases, recourse to the death penalty, and extraordinary campaigns by white supremacist organizations best exemplified, perhaps, by the wave of arson against Southern black churches in the late 1990s, or the post-9/11 government campaign against Arab men under the rubric of terrorism, or the utter silence regarding the fate of Palestinians at the hands of Israeli troops and settlers. Such campaigns and policy changes are not being enacted, however, without resistance, for the crucial reason that a firm rhetoric of racial and gender inclusions still remains a part of U.S. civic life. People still widely agree that genocide and racism are bad things, however seldom they are roused to protest them.

There is, however, no counterpart to this consensus in the realm of belief—no language combating discrimination against the cultures that belief generates. Even in the pallid disputes between white senators from South Carolina and white senators from Massachusetts, in which a culture of postindustrial welfare liberalism vies with Dixie recidivism, issues of belief bear on the above developments with painful clarity (just as they are swept from conversation in a flurry of euphemistic codes for "race" such as "teenage pregnancy" or the "drug problem"). Again, constitutionally, belief has a much less clear legal status in discrimination suits than does gender or race and when raised at all is almost always considered to be a matter of religious freedom.

Following the government crackdowns on dissent by the Justice Department under John Ashcroft, a new awareness of censorship against progressive thinking arose, particularly in the wake of highly publicized outrages to freedom of speech: high school students suspended for speaking out against the invasion of Iraq; the refusal of CBS to broadcast a paid editorial advertisement during the Super Bowl by MoveOn.com; the prosecution and conviction of defense lawyer Lynn Stewart; the Disney corporation's initial refusal to distribute Michael Moore's documentary *Fahrenheit 9/11*; or the demand to fire the Native American author and activist Ward Churchill from the faculty of the University of Colorado. The discourse of freedom of conscience has, moreover, enjoyed occasional prominence even before the assault on civil liberties under the pretext of heightened security concerns. Typically these have taken the form of perennial protests against the attack on arts funding or the banning of books in public schools or the tracking of the choices of library users. But throughout the American postwar period and until the grossly authoritarian policies of the George W. Bush administration, the campaign for freedom of conscience was usually limited to issues such as school prayer, Catholics or Jews denied membership in country clubs, the rights of corporations to be considered individuals when regulating advertising, or the tax-free status of radio preachers. Forms of conscience not restricted to religious belief rarely received adequate attention.

One might argue that there are at least two exceptions to this claim about the limits of the U.S. religious focus: the Federal Communications Commission's (FCC) Fairness Doctrine, which requires television and radio stations to provide contrasting points of view; and asylum law, which stipulates the right to asylum of those with a "well-founded fear of persecution because of their race, religion, nationality, political opinions, or membership in a social group."[40] But it still seems significant that the first of these regulations was overturned by the circuit court of appeals in 1987 and was never applied vigorously or with wide range. And the second relates not to domestic rights but to international ones, thereby displacing the concept of discrimination based on opinions from our presumably central democratic polity to other parts of the world—which can then be judged from this center as though they were the only places where ill treatment of unapproved political opinions actually occurs.[41] In 2004, however, federal hate crime legislation was amended by the U.S. Congress in a Senate vote of 65 to 33, adding to the definition of federal hate crimes those committed because of the victim's "sexual orientation, gender or disability." In its entirety, the law now applies in addition to these new features to race, color, religion and national origin but not to secular conscience. Even had the law been in effect earlier, it would have failed to protect the doctors and intellectuals of the Communist Workers League who were murdered in the early 1980s in South Carolina by the Ku Klux Klan with the aid of the local police, or the high school students who have recently been stoned or threatened with death by their classmates for refusing to say the Pledge of Allegiance.

According to the Scholars at Risk Network (an international agency dedicated to defending academics censored, jailed, or endangered for their ideas), the foreclosure of unpopular views, or those deemed to be dangerous, is not the work only of state powers. In a recent essay for the Social Science Research Council, Robert Quinn observes that in some places the repressive agent is

> only one branch or wing of a government, like the military, the secret police, a ruling political party or sub-national authority. At other times it may be a non-government agent, including militants and paramilitaries. Indeed, in some places scholars have come under attack from both the left, in the form of left-wing armed guerrilla movements, and the right, in the form of armed paramilitary death squads. These also include religious authorities, criminal organizations or even otherwise-legal commercial enterprises.[42]

Despite its welcome efforts to document repression, this particular protest above is without nuance. Quinn still thinks primarily in terms of direct and brutal interventions rather than sub-rosa exclusions or the invisibility imposed on others by those who control vast networks of information and influence. He draws no direct connections between the advanced state of technology and information dispersal of certain wealthy countries and the absolute (and therefore unnoticed) power they possess to destroy competing opinions. More tellingly, he underplays the severity of censorship in the United States compared to other offenders, who receive most of his attention, and he never discusses the role played by the United States in instigating the censorship practiced elsewhere. There may be well-honed indigenous forces in, say, Nigeria, Egypt, or

Myanmar, dedicated to strangling unwelcome criticism, but the United States has long been a major actor in setting up systems of suppression abroad, employing technicians and advisors to help devise programs of surveillance, conterinsurgency, and even torture, as well as passively dispersing its narrow worldview via the export of ready-to-go commercial media networks. We are slowly drawn into thinking of suppression in terms of jailings, physical threats, and assassinations. By contrast, U.S. and European blacklists, destroyed reputations, conspiracies of silence, "privashing," and slander campaigns may not seem as severe, but they cause great misery and are equally effective in quashing dissidence.[43]

What is at stake in the concept of a culture of belief becomes clearer in everyday acts of ideological wordplay. For a generation, the Berlin wall signified communist perfidy. Today Israel's wall built across the entire expanse of Palestinian territory violates signed treaties, land-ownership laws, and common decency while effectively consuming part of Palestine's shrinking landmass. But if it is not even acknowledged to be a "wall," and is referred to officially only as a "barrier" or "fence," this is perhaps because of the disturbing historical parallels as well as the transformation of victims into victimizers that many U.S. opinion makers would prefer to ignore. "Torture and repression in Cuba!" scream the headlines. Quite right, although not in Havana or Matanzas—rather in Guantánamo, where the U.S. military keeps prisoners without trial or hope. In both cases, the ideological is quietly translated into a matter of religious or ethnic integrity.[44]

While legal protections against discrimination based on belief are carefully excluded from the statutes, there is a persistent rhetorical undertone in discussions of public policy that such biases do not obtain. In other words, what is done on purpose is then justified as serving the higher purpose of freedom. The ensuing false consciousness has tended to monopolize the issue of prejudice itself with damaging results. Views borrowed from nineteenth-century European social theories of human nature as well as from an underlying cultural conviction of responsibility for sin, both lead to the conclusion that inequality may be objectionable for those who cannot help what they are but permissible for those who choose their being. But why should what one chooses freely be any less protected than the ineradicable conditions of birth? Even granting the questionable criterion that active choice exposes one fairly to the play of power's whims, is it really true that choosing one's membership in a belief culture is free in the sense of being autonomous? The Amish child, the Hasidic youth, the teenage Klan member, the red diaper baby inherit, as much as choose, their ideological positioning.

As a diligent form of legal protection against gender and racial bias (class is typically not included, since the system depends on it), affirmative action has always been relatively weak and decentralized. Neither federal law nor executive order, it was and is a rather a loose collection of local or institutional policies carried out in the spirit of a sense of right that had been chiseled out of the commons through an arduous process of political mobilizations in the 1960s and early 1970s. "Multiculturalism" came into its own at just the time that affirmative action was suffering its first serious defeats. One has to wonder, in fact, whether the success of the one was not linked to the failure of the other—the principle of equal access now restricted to distinct classes of bodily selves that are politely referred to in a language that finesses that fact ("culture"). The slippage from the one to the other parallels the turn in the sense that the dignity given by multiculturalism to unapproved or minority identities is presented as though it were independent of the ideologies that historically accompanied their ascent to recognition—ideologies that were not always socialist (many of them were not) but were usually characterized as "red" by mainstream commentators.

So it is ironic that academic theory after the late 1970s has stressed identity while at the same time avoiding identities of position. Those belonging to constituent cultures of belief have largely been positioned by critics of binarism in terms of intractable binaries. Theory itself, to that degree, echoes the U.S. religion of state reflected in the legal and social attitudes outlined above: a solidly liberal dogma about the importance of taking the middle road against the extremism of two sides. The Cold War intellectual purges of the 1940s and 1950s seem in this light to have been only one pronounced phase in a much longer and more deeply entrenched stifling of deviance from the religion of liberalism. The entrance of the far Right into the mainstream in the 1980s has not so much changed the calculus of liberal extremism as altered its modes of expression.

At some point, one also has to speak much less impatiently and more openly about Marxism, refusing to assume that the term has a secure definition. What I am insisting on is not a partisanship towards a particular figure or a movement, but a refusal on *scholarly* grounds to acquiesce to the violent prohibition of speaking about "Marxism" as anything but partisanship—a view that is intellectually empty and easy to refute: precisely anti-scholarly and tyrannical. It constitutes an *environment* of inquiry exemplified, among other places, in the instructions for applications to the National Endowment for the Humanities (NEH). There a Q & A page is offered to guide applicants: "Can I get an NEH grant to support a particular cause? No, NEH does not fund projects that are directed at persuading an audience to a particular political, philosophical, religious, or ideological point of view." This injunction is astonishing. Does the NEH imagine that people spend years writing a book just to showcase their assiduousness? Why else would one write a book if not to persuade someone of their interpretations, their values, their outlook on the world?

I am proposing a discussion of the term "Marxism" not as a political affiliation but as a kind of mental blockage.[45] Were the word suddenly to become nonsensical it would probably help in trying to penetrate the meanings it now obscures. For the cant surrounding Marxism makes it almost impossible to avoid symmetrically inverted dangers. One mentions the word and is taken automatically to be either a partisan or a tendentious debunker. This is why we often find people trying on the word in a histrionic display of bravery as though it were a badge of honor. How Marxism came to connote a hostile or peripheral constituency, a closed party structure, or set of formalized, unquestioning dogmas is not as easy to explain as it might appear. Suffering this fate is less difficult to understand when one is talking about American high school civics classes or the media's Realpolitik, where such caricatures have always been a more or less clumsy tool for defending the virtues of consumer societies. But it is curious to learn how this same caricature has come to occupy the common sense of authors, artists, and professors.

To the American media, "Marxism" is precisely that post-turn set of theories poised against Marxism, so that American dissidence is generally equated with those cultural issues that have been the principal means by which the American Right has short-circuited left options and cajoled the unemployed and the abandoned to vote enthusiastically for the politicians dedicated to destroying their livelihoods. What arises, then, is a monstrous doublethink: within theory social democratic Marxism's historical role in defending gay rights, helping to launch modern feminism, disabling racist campaigns, and inspiring anti-colonial movements is furiously denied by the post-turn cultural Left; outside theory in the public sphere, Marxism is nevertheless readily equated with cultural theory itself, whose shortsighted focus on political ontology at the expense of productive relations helps account for its institutional rewards and its notoriety. Marxism as the transformation of the economy and the abolition of class relations in this way does not even have to be confronted.

The coercive demands of moderation have helped cripple progressive opposition movements and set the stage for the very right-wing assault that now threatens moderation itself. If in the 1950s, liberal sentiments were voiced by those whose illiberal designs were a matter of public record, in the last two decades the pretense has been dropped by those in power whose extremism takes the form of public bragging. At the same time, a politics of identity, although carped at by the far Right or newspaper columnists, flourishes in the arts, journalism, and the academy, becoming in its own way hegemonic—as an ethical stand, at least, if not as a civic fact. As one might expect, this state of affairs did not simply evolve but was forged through political will.

It will be hard for many to accept that academic theory could have such an effect on society at large. But I am not arguing that it acted alone, only that its themes and motives were part of a larger division of labor with media, government, and think-tank intellectuals. All of them have felt their way to a hostility to left Hegelian traditions for reasons both unconscious and deliberate. Hovering behind the subjective conviction of left barbarity was a vague historical recollection of what happens to those reprobates who step over the line. In civil war and social crisis, communists are treated more harshly than criminals— even, as a rule, less than human. It would be foolish to claim that the extermination of dissidents is comparable to the chilling of academic dissent in the United States or Europe, but the former resonates with the latter.

Consider those who have actually experience extreme state violence and censorship. During the dictatorship in Argentina in the 1970s, for example, the author and essayist Beatriz Sarlo recalls that she and her contemporaries concluded that Marxism was undergoing a profound and invigorating change. Her narrative provides a glimpse of how the uprooting of a political past was perceived in parts of the world that, given the rightward pressures of a new governmental order (in Argentina's case, a military coup) appeared attractive for contradictory reasons. She gives testimony to the openness Latin American intellectuals felt towards the left Hegelian traditions before the coup:

> Like good Argentines, we were always looking at what was happening in other places in the world. And we heard echoes of this especially from friends who were living in exile in Mexico. All over the world, the sacred texts of Marxism were beginning to be reconsidered. We were enormously influenced by what had happened in European Marxist parties, especially in Italy. They were beginning to cease being communist parties in the classical sense. . . . We were very interested in this process because we had always followed what happened with the Italian Communist Party very closely because it was Gramsci's party and because it had always been the most open of the parties, the most culturally open. It also published important magazines. At the same time, we were following the reconstruction of the socialist party in Spain. We asked people to send us books and magazines—we continued to read things like *New Left Review* and *Topos* that were sent to a post office box. And we had our books. . . . This

was all to defend our identity. Our identity was this tradition. I wasn't
going to start dedicating my time to study 15th century Japanese art. My
identity was formed though the history of Argentina, Argentine culture,
Argentine literature, and Marxism.[46]

These comments, however, introduce another sort of account—how in the
mid-1970s (the coup took place in 1976) they were suddenly disallowed from
studying those texts, and they along with an avant-gardist underground buried
themselves in distant historical subjects and discovered psychoanalysis. Argentine literary critic Santiago Kovadloff, for example, points out that while books
with a Marxist orientation were expressly prohibited in these later years, it was
not just Marxist books that were suspect. Equally impugned were sociological
studies, works of political philosophy, historico-economic monographs on the
development of Western civilization, ecclesiastical studies of social injustice or
totalitarianism, political works with any party orientation, anything that studied colonialism, imperialism, or the subaltern classes, and anything about Latin
America.[47]

Nothing like this degree of repression was true of university circles in the
United States during the 1980s and 1990s, of course. But it is hard to imagine
that the confluence of themes is coincidental. More to the point, the relatively
minor miseries of canceled book tours, denial of tenure, or professional non-
personhood are possible because there exists a more general prejudice. In the
history of pogroms, genocidal campaigns against captive populations, and
massacres, it is safe to say that the victims colored "red" have rarely if ever been
accorded the respect of being thought a targeted people as such—a community
slaughtered for its very forms of being and belonging. In civil war, or in the
consolidation of power following failed revolutions, it is typically the leftists
who are the first to perish in the prisons and torture chambers. The Kuo-
mintang in Taiwan murdered 45,000 communist sympathizers in the 1950s and
arrested 90,000 more;[48] in Indonesia in 1965, as many as a million suspected
leftists were summarily executed.[49] In the late summer of 1999, a trove of documents in Paraguay was unearthed that revealed how the United States organized state crimes against leftists in Brazil, Argentina, Chile, Paraguay, Uruguay,
and other Latin American countries. Political dissidents were literally exterminated, by program, for decades. When the revelations surfaced, the official
American response was dismissive: "It's ancient history."[50] And so it is. The execution of communards in Paris in 1871; the shooting of strikers in Ludlow,
Colorado, in 1917; the mass killing of leftists after the fall of the Munich republic in 1919; and the SS death squads in a number of Central and Eastern Euro-

pean cities after 1933 are all instructive in that they reveal the prevailing political unconscious—not only in the Third World but in the centers of Western civilization.

In this partial recounting of cases of state terror against a specific population, we see confirmation of the thesis that we are dealing not only with the paranoid overreactions of governmental authority against insurrectionaries but also with a culture of belief—that is, with a population capable of being rendered alien, outlandish, subhuman, or disposable *as a group*, as a human type. Some restless critics might object at this point that as grotesque as this treatment of subversives was, it was premised on the victims' anti-democratic and therefore inherently dangerous worldview, not simply their existence. In principle at least, this view has merit, for transgressions can indeed be laid at the door of the Left. But belief can be stamped out so inhumanly only when belief itself is conceived as a cultural taint rather than a misbegotten choice. More pertinently, there is little effort to analyze what precisely these beliefs are, where exactly they are anti-democratic, or in what precise ways they are dangerous to the majority. In this approach typically, all beliefs are rendered formally equivalent, where formalism is summoned to establish a principle that relieves one from exploring the content of particular, contingent, or conjunctural beliefs.

It follows that in the middle way, all political contents are formally equal. Polemical confrontation, the jailing of opponents, and killing are condemned on the same moral scale regardless of how many benefited, what policies were being defended, or whether the killing and the jailing were defensive or peremptory. In the face of brutal facts, the critic often resorts to the view that the weight of social inertia will always be disproportionately felt: the socialist is by definition guilty. Having resorted to extremes, he or she must expect payment in kind. But the existent is already the mean, so to avoid extremes can only lead, as we have seen, to a paradoxical praxis of inactivity. Marxism and left Hegelian currents of thought (however disavowed or camouflaged they have routinely become) participate in this process in a weirdly misrecognized role. The crimes committed in the name of communism are real, but they have also generally been admitted, even officially acknowledged by the inheritors of the very regimes that committed them. Still, these crimes are certainly no match for the atrocities launched by liberal capitalism, which, far from being officially acknowledged, are completely disavowed or excused. Even more, communism and social democracy, by helping to launch the early women's movement, by helping to destroy the legal edifice of racial discrimination, by playing a key role in the struggle for the eight-hour workday, and by helping to establish the common sense of social entitlements, have theorized historically, and brought into practice, many of the same rights and social advances cherished by the exponents of democracy. They have often forced such demands at great risk into the discussion, making central and obvious what once seemed utopian. Even if one were to justify the outlawing of marginal political parties or movements one would have to explore actual contents rather than merely formal claims about the supposedly already-known illiberalism of their beliefs. Current theories of diaspora paint memorable pictures of Somali communities in Italy, Turks in Germany, or Dominicans in New York, but have nothing to say about Italians in Italy, Germans in Germany, or New Yorkers in New York who are effectively in exile because of their political beliefs. There is no exile so profound as being a dissident in one's own country. The social function of the left radical is that of a sacrificial lamb and lightning rod—the one who cleans up society's messes and for that favor is all the more banished and despised.

The fatal consequences of these post-sixties trends are still vividly evident. Hegel continues to thrive, by abdication, in the right Hegelianism of the makers and marketers of globalization's myths: in the afflatus of Francis Fukuyama, Samuel Huntington, Thomas Friedman, and, to a more limited degree, George Soros. In them, the centrality of Hegelian thought regarding the mastery of power stands revealed, as does the meaning of the anti-Hegelian turns of theory. Accordingly, Hegel is left to be taken over by those who understand the relationship between the state, management, and the creation of culture as policy. Meanwhile the humanist critic busily pursues a virtuous inaction.

Humanities intellectuals believe they speak freely, even subversively, while speaking a language that has been carefully created for them; or rather, one that they have helped create, but that is refined in media and government channels only to return to them in an alienated form. This dilemma is partly the result of a suppression of precursors (an unlearning of the past) that separates the cultural Left from the theories that would make them aware of these patterns. One can see the problem in a number of arenas, but let us take the way that a popular topic like globalization is routinely advertised on the Internet. Most academics are familiar with these advertisements for graduate student conferences, the launching of a new Internet journal, or similar events. What follows is the actual wording of one such conference posting:

"Flight Time": The present transformation of time and space is simultaneously opening up new potentials and engendering new hazards. Our decreased reliance on geographic, social and theoretical boundaries means increased movement of global capital, peoples and ideas. This conference is interested in the multiple implications of the concept of flight, and how flight, as an inevitable feature of contemporary life, transforms our very experience of time.

One can see from this passage how the generative concepts of globalization flow between constituencies in the professional formation of opinions and tastes. I mean the word "flow" here to signify more than what is usually meant by influence. It suggests a market-generated excitement for concepts where the borrowing of ideas is concealed in order to enact an individualized rediscovery of a dominant cliché.

Here, as in so many other places, we see the conceit repeated that boundaries of all sorts have broken down, the nation-state is at its end, post-Fordism has triumphed. None of these points requires any proof; indeed, proof would be difficult to find, since legally and politically it is more the case that boundaries have intensified. As most governments fully grasp, many nation-states react to the invasions of the global market by establishing a new resilience. For every disarticulated country operating without government—Somalia and Afghanistan, for instance—there are a dozen that have boldly reasserted their sovereignty. Likewise, Fordist modes of production and uncapitalized small-holder agriculture continue to account for the majority of the world's goods and services. But one is still constrained to read in the conference description above the equivalence posited among the movement of capital, people, and ideas—as if the forces that moved them were not only of equal valance but equally indeterminate. Notice too how the gist of globalization is expressed in the language of potential as well as hazards, benefits as well as drawbacks, and yet both of these are seen as part of a dynamic, irrepressible process and, therefore, on their own grounds inviting to students eager to valorize dynamism, complexity, multiplicity. Anyone who might seek to arrest this transformation of "our very concept of time" would surely be cast aside as reactionary or stale. The title "Flight Time" is similarly ambiguous, as though uncertain of what it felt about its own designation: is it a flight from time or the time to flee? And for that matter, flee what? Is "flight" meant to evoke guest-worker labor as well as intellectual diasporas and tourist travel, or only some of these? If so, what comes under its mantle, what remains inside? Is it too crude to ask for such clarity before the flight has taken off? Is there a hierarchy among these different valuations of (a) flight and (b) time? Who decides the value? It is not only that these points remain opaque, but their vagueness is precisely what makes them attractive.

This example suggests how theory addresses the public sphere in a self-consciously political register. In the 1980s and 1990s, theory saw itself as standing for a neomodernism poised against neotraditionalism. This traditionalism had an explicitly religious component in the form of the New Christian Right, of course, but also, and no less religiously, in the academic humanities. The famous case of Leo Strauss has attracted significant commentary in this regard. Strauss's readings of Plato and Aristotle trained a generation of University of Chicago undergraduates to remain vigilant on behalf of elite moral certainty and Euro-American supremacy. Strauss stood for a religious form of belief, if one understands by that a frank embrace of metaphysics, divine decree, and the utility of organized religion to the obedience demanded by authority. What one notices immediately is that neotraditionalism in both its religious and its mediated, Straussian forms stands for confrontation rather than negotiation. Theory attempted to immunize itself against the contagion of extremism by counterposing to it the equivocal and the multiple—the tags of aesthetic, and therefore modernist, belief. Against neotraditionalism, theory found its answer in irony. In a polarized age, it declared that polarization be abolished. This aleatory uncertainty, it turned out—not unlike the American pluralism it mirrors—simply ended the debate by foreclosing it.

PART 1

BELIEF AND ITS DISCONTENTS

CHAPTER 1

THE BARBARIC LEFT

THE ODDITY OF THE TERMS "EAST" AND "WEST" is that they allude both to the Cold War and to an imperial divide of race and civilizational conquest. If translation is a familiar problem of East/West in this latter sense, it is also embedded in the ideological divide of communism and capitalism. To say, for example, that "East is East and West is West" is to allude to the inability of certain human types to communicate with one another—a view that has a long history in the work of Rudyard Kipling, E. M. Forster, and other novelists of empire. There, the impediments to mutually shared meanings seem naturally bound to the bordered ghettoes of the colonial arena, whose languages remain obscure in part because colonial authors were so long (wrongly) supposed to have achieved very little in literature.

By contrast, communication is not generally thought to be the main problem in the "East/West conflict," a phrase belonging to a war considered ideological alone—one conditioned by prejudice and hardened by tendentious will. That particular conflict is even now, after the fall of the Berlin wall, cast in the confident mood of Alfred Hitchcock's *Torn Curtain*, where disagreements are not dignified with the recognition of a collision of values. Rather they are seen only as a kind of orneriness on the part of the East, which sticks to a dogma it purportedly never believed. The standoff of the Cold War is never seen in the West as being civilizational, in other words, only ideological—a mere struggle over programmatic spoils. What translation studies needs to recognize is that, just as much as the colonial encounter, the clash of systems involved differences in aesthetic taste and social value, intellectual excitement and moral intention, not only the more regulatory contests of administration, hierarchy, or sovereignty over land.

An imaginative geography, in other words, governs not only the cultural differences related to national or ethnic divisions (the "East/West" as Kipling understood it) but also the world political contests of the Cold War, as perhaps Nikita Krushchev or, later, Ronald Reagan rendered them. Soviet or Euro-American cultures of position are today overlaid upon more well-known and imaginative geographies that were first developed in eighteenth- and nineteenth-century colonial discourses, and they extend to affiliative networks that were neither Soviet nor Euro-American. As a consequence, the political is not seen as having a cultural life with its own affective and varied practices or styles.

I am interested in how this meeting of the colonial and the ideological affects translation. If etymologies bear the stamp of historical meaning in terms dulled by repetitive use, "East/West" might be seen as a linguistic tick that assigns hemispheres to social types, but ambiguously and while doing double duty. World socialism in the mid-1960s, when it was at its apogee, counted as its members primarily nonwhite peoples in agrarian settings in the eastern and southern zones of the earth—a fulfillment, one might say, of its promise from the very start in the writings of Marx and Engels from 1848. So it is not surprising that embedded in the term "East/West" is sedimentary evidence of a longstanding tendency in the West to associate the racial with the socialist other.

The temporal and the spatial are also brought together in this merging. The backward- and the forward-looking are here curiously entangled. At the center of two overlapping debates on the Cold War and the so-called periphery lie problems of historical time: the "future in the present," as the Trinidadian Trotskyist and novelist C. L. R. James put it. Throughout the Cold War, in other words, it was unclear to many whether socialism in places like Tanzania, Kerala, or Vietnam was merely a throwback fueled by peasant resentments or (by contrast) the snapshot of a future in which "natives" now represented something like the cultural and social avant-garde—the classic Maoist theory of encirclement, in which the wretched of the earth would surround and eventually vanquish the metropolis in the act of bringing it kicking and screaming into a collectivist future. Today, interventionary forms of Marxism flourish most among intellectuals outside the U.S. and European spheres. Innovations within Marxism are today being made primarily by non-Western intellectuals, or those who take their leads from them.

That the supposed triumph of the global market has made revolutionary encirclement seem unthinkable is also a matter of translation, for how else could one travel from the site of a political innovation to the wasteland of a defeated promise except by passing through a dimension inaccessible to those outside a given culture or belief? To have access to this dimension really means going through a conversion. I use this word "conversion" with a certain sense of risk. My reference is not to religion but to the fact that there is no real semantic contact that arguments can produce between the two lifeworlds of communism and capitalism. Typically, there are no grounds even for persuasion. The two worlds of belief are so utterly different one can only enter them by way of indoctrination or revelation, even though this alterity is usually denied in practice or reserved for more properly civilizational disputes. To make this claim for translation may seem to place me in a lineage of criticism in which the impossibility of translation is foregrounded—a view emphatic and extreme in the work of Martin Heidegger, enthusiastically seconded in the Heideggerian traditions of deconstruction (especially in Paul De Man), and significantly mitigated by Walter Benjamin without being completely denied by him.[1] My own point below is less about the degree to which equivalences are incommensurable in language than about the failure to accord uniqueness to a political culture that is not precisely linguistic, or for that matter, racial or geographic. Behind the doctrine of incommunicability is also, and primarily, the ghost of belief. But more on that later.

If to those conditioned by the North American press, my reference to conversion may conjure up the religious fundamentalisms of places like Algeria, India, or Palestine, it is only another obstacle to meaning—one that translations between ideological positions often entail. All three countries, forced by financial pressures to abandon or curtail successful secular reform movements, found the only available safeguards for sovereignty in religious mobilization. Large barriers divide cultures of political belief. The term "conversion" may seem too grand for my purposes, but it serves to counter the monopoly over belief by the members of those religions that draw hard lines between inside and outside the fold, or see conversion as a hardening of positions—a voluntary or forcible joining of what will then separate. At least the religious undertone helps us see the passage from one secular belief to another as involving a complete rethinking, and as such it pays respect to the differences breached. The assumption that belief cultures, even transnational ones like socialism that were at one point adopted by a majority of the world's peoples, can be easily dismissed is widely maintained in journalism and scholarship that continues to be highly regarded in the West.

What I mean by conversion might be clarified by using an analogy from translation itself. Translating German into English is an act of conversion in the sense that mastering any language reorients one's world and makes perfectly obvious any number of things that remain impenetrable to non-German speakers. While it is widely conceded that one must study a language in order to translate it, or while it is readily seen that unless one is, say, Chinese or has lived and worked in China one does not know enough to grasp the cultural codes of a Chinese translation into English, the same assumptions are not made about the invisible foreignness of the ideological, which is compounded by the world-historical manner in which geographic zones are apportioned to it, or the transparency of imperial conflict placed upon it.

The height of decolonization was also the height of the Cold War. The coupling of "North/South" tended to blend into the East/West while expressing a properly colonial confrontation: a Western ideal of structural and organic difference. This previous common sense is what now allows many to take stock of the collapse of the Soviet (or "Eastern") bloc by noting that various nationalisms have taken over for socialism as the enemies of U.S. Realpolitik—one way of looking, certainly, at the bombing of Yugoslavia in the early 1990s, whose unruly Slavic actors (from the mainstream U.S. point of view) stand in quite readily for the Soviets in ways that go beyond their defiance of the U.S. government or their supposedly criminal actions. They are *like* the Soviets, they look like them to U.S. eyes, they speak a language "like" Russian, they have the same religion, they are not quite European in the same way as are our NATO allies, they are from the same peripheral region to the east of the Europe that counts. This conflation of race and belief in the mainstream finds its way into the cultural studies seminar rooms as well. There the Cold War plays itself out in what Harald Kittel has called a *Schattenkultur* (shadow culture) both upmarket and downmarket. While cultural studies theorists want to get beyond a supposedly outmoded nationalism, they create an inviting terrain for State Department intellectuals who find nationalism an obstacle to Euro-American sovereignty. The post-Soviet mainstream analysis in the United States is frankly recidivist, returning to models taken from eighteenth- or nineteenth-century theories of climatic determination like those found in David Hume or Joseph Arthur Gobineau and to the language of medieval crusades against the infidel. The fundamental agreement of these analysts on a question as decisive as nationalism therefore deserves a closer look and a different kind of explanation than it is usually given.[2]

But perhaps I am reading too much into the phrase "East/West conflict." It can only sound banal to many today given the apparent obsolescence of the

Cold War or the widespread belief that theories of Orientalism have taken us beyond older pairings like that of the Orient and the Occident by showing their interpenetration and mutual portraitures.[3] But have these dichotomies really broken down? Certainly the ability of smaller states to maintain their political sovereignty has decreased with the passing of the Soviet Union (which is, incidentally, another way the Cold War bears on the postcolonial). For whatever one thinks of the former Soviet Union, there is no question that it prevented such annexationist and neocolonial adventures as took place in Iraq, Bosnia, and Afghanistan after 1989. But there are other dichotomies as well, for when there were still three worlds, many of the newly independent states of the colonial periphery were said to perform their proper roles in big-power rivalries. In this story, the West had its comprador elites and military-torture regimes throughout the Third World; the Soviet East, for its part, had a committed left intelligentsia and its own military regimes, often with skin-deep populist bent. It was commonly assumed that the Cold War expressed itself in tropical climates as well, often involving the intrigues of personnel on foreign assignment fighting an absentee struggle on someone else's land: what John Le Carré evocatively dubbed "Delhi Rules" in *Tinker, Tailor, Soldier, Spy*. Popular fiction is replete with instances of this ideologeme: from Graham Greene's *Our Man in Havana* to André Malraux's *La Condition humaine*, with their savoring of a parodoxical Third World and an equally paradoxical socialism brought together in such a way that cultural foreignness (Latin American and Chinese, in these cases) temporarily melts away in the presence of a familiar political barrier that is difficult if not impossible to cross.

To borrow a phrase, we might say that the political dichotomy of the East/West conflict has typically been exported for the purpose of re-importing it—although now it comes as "foreign correspondence." Here I am talking about how the familiar translation problems of correspondence to truth, or faithfulness to the original, have often lent themselves in practice to reporting from the strange *afar* a story that traced a familiar *here*. What was most culturally elusive—in Edward Fitzgerald's *Rubaiyat*, say, or Ezra Pound's Li Po—was for that very reason open to a projection of self onto an other now seen, in reflection, as a more profound self. In that sense, acts of translation often heroize themselves by claiming an alienation or a foreignness that never strays far from home. But the North/South divide seen as shadowland of the Cold War (as I have been saying)—this idea that posits that the bombings, assassinations, and noncompliance of colonized peoples were only the East/West conflict by proxy and without a meaning of their own—plays a smaller part in the story I am focusing on here. The point is not about communists and capitalists in peasant dress so much as communist or capitalist perceived of as barbarian, alien, or wog. This sort of East/West divide reverberates in two different directions. The political other of the Cold War has always been racialized. This largely unacknowledged fact affects postcolonial translation, both in the utilitarian sort of way that books from Latin America, Thailand, or Senegal are received in the West and in the very different sense in which vintage colonial prejudices spill over into and play major supporting roles in the racially ignorant annals of the state department, the Cold Warriors, and for that matter, Le Carré's novels.

An ideological politics underlying translation—at least in the sense I am suggesting—has for the most part been ignored by postcolonial studies. What it finds in the figures of creative hybridization or the postcolonial subject is a deferral modulated by an East/West logic buried under theorizations of race and diasporic culture. And yet, one reaches a sense of that intermeshing of alien languages not by conflating them but by bringing their peculiar inflections up to the surface. One grasps the North/South *in* the East/West only by acknowledging the different language each speaks—the disparity between their respective networks of mythology, star making, and jargon. Such differences do not in the end obliterate a common premise or similar social function.

Even though my emphasis thus far has been on a conflation of the two meanings of the term "East/West" concealing their underlying cultures of belief, there is also a rhetorical screen that often separates both senses while creating the appearance of an exaggerated discreteness that overstates the case, obscuring their similar logic. This discreteness—or segregation of meaning—exerts itself to relieve the critic from an exhausted or overfamiliar dichotomy. In other words, the discourse of East/West (or North/South) as it pertained to colonial foreignness, racial typologizing, or resource extraction required its own specialized tropes. Ultimately, it played to a different audience than did the hysterical techno-fear and the grim, ideological contest of loyalty and betrayal of the European quarrel known as the Cold War between two species that were the same "race." Both were a matter of otherness, of radical difference and suspicion, but each marshaled a different vocabulary, a different list of specialists and a different audience attuned to particular inflections of the incommensurable. It is only by making these inflections aware of one another again that my opening statements acquire the right meaning. Translation is a problem of belief.[4]

By looking at the colonial and the Cold War via translation, I am eager not to arrest the inquiry in a technical argument about linguistic equivalences or approximations, or as further proof of the ontology of language, or of the asymptotic frustrations of approaching, but never finding, the right words in passing from one to another idiom—or as Jean-François Lyotard puts it, from the "language of departure" to the "language of arrival."[5] Lyotard's "*differend*"—"phrases obeying different regimens that are untranslatable into one another"—is a perfect place to look for the kinds of confluences I have been tracing here. At once an extreme restatement of the tradition of untranslatability stemming from the linguistic turn generally, Lyotard's position is also an unusually frank statement of politico-ideological affiliation. His "*differend*" owes a great deal to a Cold War framework, implicit in his own biographical account of having abandoned his early participation in the radical "Socialism or Barbarism" group in France while retaining its bitter rejection of official communism. With the "*differend*" the whole process of legal disputation, of recruitment to a cause, of responsible persuasion is thrown into doubt. From a fear of disciplinary regimes he finds his way to a far more extreme, even hysterical, position: the impossibility of civic sense-making.

To say, as I want to here, that translation is a problem of the East/West of North/South is to say that the distances created by unrealized conversions of a nonreligious sort in the battles of a continuing Cold War are distances that provide a valuable (and as far as I can tell, slighted) resource for understanding the translation difficulties surrounding non-Western, peripheral, or racially othered meanings in metropolitan contexts. My invocation of the term "conversion" above may seem to place me securely in Lyotard's camp. Actually, I am implying that the binaries he wishes to arrest are concealed forms of debate. Far from being precluded by discourse, they are continually reproduced where they seem least likely to be. Crossing over into others' "phrase regimens" (which Lyotard discounts) is always implied by the interestedness of knowledge. Untranslatability is not a linguistic or epistemological "finding" but an active element of political belief in the resistance to an ongoing process of decolonization.

Two Stories and a Pattern

We might look at cases where the ideological meets the geographical imagination on equal footing. In graduate school, I once translated Tomás Borge's "El arte como herejía" (Art as Heresy) for a small literary magazine. Taken from a Sandinista volume titled *Hacia una política cultural* (*Towards a Political Culture*), the essay struck me as a useful challenge to reigning notions of literary value and as a call to a difficult but useful debate over the shifting, multiply positioned character of resonant, nonsynchronous ideas such as beauty and wit.[6]

I did not have the conceptual armature at the time to recognize fully what I was attempting to overcome. Years after becoming a professor, I came to appreciate the help offered me by a key theorist of Cold War aesthetics. Ernst Bloch, against all expectations, shed light on the colonial issues menacing the Borge translation as a whole. His famous concept of *Ungleichzeitigkeit* (temporal incommensurability) originally referred to peoples living alongside one another in a different time that was the same time.[7] Analyzing in 1932 the rise of fascism in Germany and seeking to account for the powerlessness he felt explaining his own views to fellow Germans who did not (as he put it) "exist in the same Now" (97), he sought in a critique of fashion-conscious youth, of the fissures between peasant and city dweller, and of the mutual silences between frustrated petit bourgeois shopkeepers and cosmopolitan bon vivants, a way to explain to himself and others why the Left had failed in Germany.

Although he never dwells in his work on non-Western cultures, Bloch was driven by the logic of his observations to a theory that derived from colonial contexts and was arguably inspired by them. Essential to his point was an argument drawn from interwar colonial debates as he inherited them in the 1920s and 1930s, and which dealt with the familiar correspondence between temporal designations such as the primitive, the backward, and the developing, on the one hand, and on the other, locational references to places farther East and South, where time was said to be standing still or at least moving very slowly.[8] And yet Bloch's powerful concept is not only a description of temporal dissimilarity (*ungleich*), but a mode of incomprehension. The inability to gauge what time one is in, or one's audience is in, can lead (as it did in post-Weimar Germany) to collapse. The Nazi outburst seemed odd and even incoherent to those on the Left who felt they had become mainstream, and who thought they had been communicating to the public at large. In Germany's case, the older, unmodern, supposedly superseded time belonged to the fearful outliers, the simmering, inarticulate mass that fell for the new führer. But in Borge's essay, the concept of temporal incommensurability reverses its polarities. The heroic modernism of Borge's essay—which many readers will at first imagine stale—can be seen as the very thing that Latin American "underdevelopment" has managed to rescue from the advances of the metropolitan cutting edge. The culture that is privileged in Borge's essay is more advanced for being more "behind." From a certain point of view—that of the Third World subject in revolutionary time—its virtue is greater the more vigorously it resists a lumbering postmodernity. The implications of such a reversal of value open up for review the supposed obsolescence of socialism after the fall of the Berlin wall as well, which again places the topic of backwardness usually associated with colonial theory in a friendly relationship to its hidden, ideological twin.

Taken as an aesthetic artifact, a case could be made for Borge's remarkably restrained performance in "Art as Heresy." For traditionally educated, North American literary critics, the essay might appear blunt without being bitter, colloquial but also high literary, even proud. It resembled Baudelaire's famous meditation on the dandy with its passages on youth revolt and sensual luxuriance, although the Borge essay is in the end very alien to Baudelaire. Because he had helped found the Sandinista Front for National Liberation and had spent much of his youth dodging police or avoiding capture in the political underground, his bohemia was not so much of the garret as of the jail, involving both sedition and aesthetic experimentalism at the same time, although not as the same thing.[9] Needless to say, it was difficult to render the essay in a language other than Nicaraguan Spanish for reasons that had little to do with language per se. The essay demanded not merely a medium but a nimbus of associations: the informality of Managua conversation, the laid-back literariness of the self-taught. It appealed to the sensibility of those who were formerly in prison, or the tortured, or those whose belief in martyrdom was unmediated by religion or legend. "In the world of capital," Borge had written, "the sun never shines. The colors of that world are not that of the sky, but of satin, the colors of a jeweled ring. The world of capital knows nothing of the fragrance of flowers. The smell of deodorant takes its place."[10] The translation came off to my editors as a reckless bout of swearing, and it was never published, being, as it were, both out of time and out of place.

To work properly within the postcolonial field means to go literally or figuratively east. I did so briefly in 1997–1998 while teaching in an American Studies department at Humboldt University in the former East Germany. Before being renamed by the German Democratic Republic (GDR) authorities, Humboldt was known as the University of Berlin when it housed the likes of Max Planck, Georg Simmel, Werner Heisenberg, Theodor Mommsen, G. W. F. Hegel, and (for a temporary but formative visit) the young W. E. B. Du Bois. The students were an uneven mixture from the former East and West. And in the spirit of the European Union, which is busy transforming the region into a Eurocapitalist megastate able to compete with the United States, many of those students were of diverse national origin—Greeks, Sicilians, Belgians, Americans of German parentage, and, on the other and Eastern side of the wall, Poles and Russians.[11] Speaking German with relative fluency, although with uneven levels of propriety or ease, all of them failed to live up to the image of *echt*-Germany, including those East Germans whose language had departed from the West's in more subtle ways, being more formal, sporting fewer cognates and neologisms, calling places and streets by post-1962 names rather than their pre-war names.

The same issues of cultural political translation found in the case of Borge had emerged in the context of German reunification. As Daniela Dahn has memorably put it, "Der Westen sieht rot, der Osten schwarz," which might be slightly modified to mean in our context that the West sees "red" (is angry, sees communism) *in* the blackness of the East.[12] The swarthy and the politically un-trustworthy coalesce in the mind of the West as a related fear. East of Europe is racially suspect Europe, even now in the period of a European Union that re-pulses Turkey's membership or that witnesses a war in the Balkans in which Western powers ally themselves with medieval converts to Islam in the name of fighting Serbian Orthodox Christians who are too Slavic to be anything but versions of the Russians of the Cold War. What the Berlin papers described as the German "*Kulturschock*" resulting from reunification has led to what Wolf Wagner has interestingly called "*die Grenzen des Kulturbegriffs*" (the borders be-tween cultural understanding)—a border that involved, much like Nicaragua vis-à-vis the United States in the 1980s, a politically charged speechlessness that was only intensified in the latter case by the fact that both East and West Ger-many spoke the same language but not the same "language."[13]

One commentator, Michael Weck, for example, has grasped the parallels between the brandings of ideological difference and multicultural notions of difference when he speaks of the West's "orientalizing" of the East Germans.[14] He observed that they had been constructed as the "*wild und ungezahmt*" (wild and undomesticated) in the very same breath that they were labeled "authori-tarian and autocratic"—as overly Prussian with *urdeutsch* habits that needed to give way to the Enlightenment principles of the free market. In a now notori-ous book, Hans-Joachim Maaz, an East German psychologist and psychother-apist adapting to the times, went so far as to call the East Germans "psycholog-ically defective, infected by a 'virus' of a pathological social deformation."[15] His much-discussed book (*Behind the Wall*) virtually consigned the East German populace to a perpetual anal stage of development, victims of what he calls the "deficiency syndrome" arising from the "damming up of the emotions" (83). The would-be countrymen of the newly incorporated East were transformed by the West in such writing into quasi-racial aliens—a transformation overlaid upon a traditional repugnance that Westerners in Europe have felt for those farther east. Newly politicized psychotherapy joins a suspicion toward Slavic hygiene sanctified by centuries of custom. Those farther east are subject to con-tagion; they are dirty, as are the barbaric ideas of the Russian East to which they had been subject.

The theories of Maaz are not unique. Drawing on her past as a Bulgarian-born French citizen, Julia Kristeva, to take one recent example, brings similar views to bear in *Crisis of the ~~European~~ Subject*.[16] Although she insists that she does not "ascribe to religion the power of a unique determinant of behavior" and dismisses "popular psychology," neither statement prevents her from offering more than sixty pages of clinical reflections on the Eastern European psyche.[17] The cultures of socialist belief are for her the logical extension of the mysticism and nihilism of the Orthodox Church, the dark fruits of a history of Ottoman occupation, and the perverse flowering of murky but compelling Orthodox founding fathers like Gregory of Nyssa and Maxim the Confessor writing at the edges of a decaying classical Hellenism. Her silence, except as invidious comparison, on the extensive Ottoman cultural enrichment of Eastern Europe is itself an astounding confirmation of the deeply conventional outlook that governs her observations. Her diagnosis? Eastern Europeans are, clinically speaking, masochists.

Her major contrast is between Orthodox spirituality (East) and libertarian progress (West).[18] She draws on Alexander Solzhenitsyn for proof that "religious pathos" (his term) has made the Eastern subject "indifferent to everything 'public,'" which is what has led to the post-Communist problems of corruption and extortion. In other words, it is not neoliberalism, not American and European ideologues seeking an investment advantage in the vulnerable legal structures of a now-occupied Eastern Europe that is to blame for corruption and extortion; it is not the financial and ideological pressures of the "Chicago School" economists, the Hoover Institute, or their European counterparts that unleashed the gangster capitalism to which she refers, but an aversion to the *public* already ingrained in the Orthodox Catholicism as a cultural norm. She goes so far as to contend that the autonomy and independence of the person enjoyed in the West as distinct from the "renunciation and retreat" in the East is a direct result of their different conceptions of the Trinity: in Orthodoxy the Holy Spirit works through the Son, rather than with the Son. Hell is a place to occupy, and even to revel in, because the vision of Orthodoxy is sensory rather than aesthetic or freedom-based.[19] She wishes, therefore, to cleanse herself of her Bulgarian past: "I hold onto a calmness punctuated with French words." She contrasts "French politeness" with "Byzantine unease." French sonority protects her from the "language of louts," which lacks "the piquant insolence of the surrealists." Bulgarian loanwords inspire only "pity" and give her "a migraine."[20] This is a critic, we have to keep in mind, championed by the cultural Left over the last two decades, which thinks of her as a dissident on behalf of radical freedom.

It is significant that in opposing the new nationalisms of Eastern Europe after 1989, she turns resolutely to the social symbolism of language and translation. Against the popular movements there to keep foreign investment out, she looks instead "to generate new beings of language and blood, rooted in no language or blood, diplomats of the dictionary, genetic negotiators, wandering Jews of Being who challenge authentic, and hence military, citizens of all kinds in favor of nomadic humanity that is no longer willing to sit quietly."[21] In one respect, this sentiment is startling. For apart from the odd and unexplained suturing of the nationalistic philosophy of Heideggerian Being (part of a historical lineage that was, of course, hostile to the cosmopolitanism she evidently favors) with the image of the wandering Jew—cosmopolitanism's historical emblem—there is also the matter of a separate contradiction regarding language itself. The belated societies of Eastern Europe, in her opinion, never got past the Middle Ages. When after 1989 they finally translated the masterworks of Western European literature (her list includes Shakespeare, Dostoevsky, Beckett, and, of course, Kristeva), the translators realized that "there are not enough words, and so they stuffed into this poor language of sensitive peasants and naïve thinkers a whole arsenal of tasteless and rootless loanwords. As syntax becomes more cumbersome without thought becoming more flexible, they thought it was a good idea to transfer this Esperanto for university-educated polyglots."[22] So much for cosmopolitanism!

Similarly, the West German distaste for the East German—or in everyday parlance, the Wessi distaste for the Ossi—replayed a familiar jargon of North/South colonial prejudice, an incomprehension in the face of rhythms of life and ethical disparities arising from two to three generations of politically divergent training. The cultures are distinct for all to see, even while existing among peoples who share contiguous territory, language, common history, and the physical characteristics typically given the name *race*.

In the early 1990s former GDR novelist Christa Wolf focused on the cleaning up by the West of what it considered the East's ideological extremists in an egregiously one-sided act of conquest and invasion. Agents of the new power, she reports, pored over the files left behind by the GDR state, "reduc[ing] people's personal histories to simple patterns of yes or no, black or white, guilty or innocent."[23] This cleansing of those with the wrong attitudes toward property and space was fertilized by a rich series of cultural barbs. In Wolf's words, Ossis had become "brothers and sisters from a family we don't know: ill-bred, plebeian, proletarian, and yet demanding" (296). The term of contempt for the Ossis among the West Berliners (which I witnessed often) was simply "prolie." To be proletarian, in this sense, was itself in many Western minds an unforgivable cultural barbarism associated with the ideological ill breeding of an entire national family, a former governmental entity now gone a-begging.

Life "*nach der Wende*" (after the turn of 1989) has apparently done little to erase the debates from before the fall of the Berlin wall. In *A Berlin Republic* (1995), Jürgen Habermas bluntly states that in Germany, "the petrified front lines . . . continue to reflect the political and intellectual trench warfare of the 1960s and 1970s."[24] One Ernst Nolte "projects onto the GDR all the horrors that long preceded its existence, and which are nevertheless supposed to justify, posthumously, its fascist opponents" (23). In a similar mood, Habermas goes on to allude to "the unholy alliance between the rancor of the old anti-Communist fighters and the injured subjectivity of the victims" as well as to the haunting disparity in the current discourse between "the West's slick magazine articles" and a GDR that is powerless to make its own case since it had not had "time to develop its own public sphere with its own infrastructure and discourses" (23). Habermas's collection of essays from this period bears a title allusive of racial and colonial difference in the context of a constitutional crisis brought on by intra-European and extramural immigration resulting from the breakup of the former Eastern bloc: *Die Einbeziehung des anderen* (*The Inclusion of the Other*).[25]

In Germany one hears the word "*spiessig*" come readily to the Wessi's lips. It means dull, culturally conservative, petit bourgeois, provincial, philistine, and it expresses very well the culture clash existing between East and West in the German context. The Wessi thinks of aesthetic modernism as the innovative extension of German classicism, which—this term posits—has passed the Ossi by, since in the GDR, modernism (although not modernity) had been considered unreliable and decadent, though only because of the Ossi's boorishness and laziness. Similarly, the Wessi complains bitterly of the Ossi's intolerable *Stolz* (pride, arrogance)—much too vacuous and imaginary to constitute an intelligible identity since it was rather an excuse for complacency or stagnation. *Kultur* as freedom, happiness, and knowledge—the common German inheritance of both East and West Germany—was here a term used to deny that the GDR had even been a place that one could lose. Many Wessis refuse to concede that the colonial occupation of the East by the West entailed loss or the recalibration of a way of life, evident in everything from filling out that strange thing known as an insurance form to dealing with the mystifications in the West about where the state begins and ends (an issue, needless to say, that was far less difficult to determine in Erich Honneker's GDR). Nor have critics in the West even begun to assess the significance of the shattered honeymoon with neoliberalism in Eastern Europe, keeping tactfully silent about mass demonstrations in Russia, the Ukraine, Slovakia, and elsewhere calling for a return to communism.

That translation is not only a linguistic or hermeneutic matter but also a cultural one is, of course, a commonplace today, and it is one, I would argue, that especially postcolonial theory has convincingly demonstrated.[26] The imbalance of historical learning means that citizens of Indonesia or the Caribbean know much more about Europe than Europeans ever know about Indonesia or the Caribbean.[27] Given the mental impasse produced by racialized difference outside national-cultural fealties, what people feel or know in Calcutta simply doesn't register in the metropolitan-commercial networks of distribution. There are peculiar forms of semiotic blockage in the colonial world that enhance what Edouard Glissant and others have called the "opacity" of culture.[28]

The idea of opacity can be understood in very different ways, however, and is exacerbated by the hidden Cold War referents that often underlie cross-cultural work. It might make sense to look briefly at a case where the political and the civilizational senses of "East/West" have both figured centrally in postcolonial translation theory. In *Primitive Passions*, Rey Chow, for example, considers the hostility of mainland Chinese critics to Hong Kong commercial film (one of her examples is Zhang Yimou's *Raise the Red Lantern*, 1991).[29] She casts translation into an East/West problematic while strategically and (to me) doubtfully moving the object of translation from language (Chinese/English) to genre. On the one hand stands film—leisure-directed, postliterate, globally disseminated, and aesthetically drawn to technology; on the other, anti-film, espoused by a conservative, Maoist/Confucian, primarily bookish culture of legal codes and regimentation in her rendering. She tries to move us away from thinking about translation as involving some posited national-cultural incommensurability between the Chinese and the North American. This, she argues, is an older problematic, superseded by the popular cultural exchanges of the media which has made all of us more or less equally modern, although this positing of a communication crisis is a view still put forth by the Chinese old guard as well as many well-intentioned, albeit orientalizing, Western critics.

Chow asserts that film signifies a globally ubiquitous modernity (she speaks in passing of "the more or less complete Europeanization of the world" [194]). For her, then, the incommensurabilities that might have required cultural translation on a massive scale have already ceased to exist. She does not feel she needs to promote so much as recognize "mobility, proximity, approximation" (183), and sees only a confusion of categories in those who hunt for "profound meaning" in a purportedly real foreignness. Above all, it is the postcolonial subjects, she implies, whose mobility is certified and who are able to see the elusive differences between a Europe and a China without confusion or nostalgia. Their mobility allows them to be faithful to a China without claim to source, origin, or intractable cultural difference, and that is already modern (imaginative, fluid), which the aesthetic of Hong Kong films amply demonstrates in her opinion.

Such presumptive mobility, however, has struck many others in colonial contexts as a good deal less welcome. Indeed, acts of translation do not always seek ways to communicate more accurately, but instead to mistranslate meaning subversively in order to ensure an incommunicability that can then, retrospectively, be posited as a linguistic or cultural law of separation. The theoretical representatives of this view, however, are politically divergent (and this confusion of positions troubles some of the argumentative moves Chow makes). In one form, the view is found in the various tendentious arguments surrounding the sheer *convenience* of incomprehension—for ardent Heideggerians, that Heidegger cannot be known outside of German, say; or for the U.S. military, that the Vietnamese had no word for "individual" and thereby betrayed a value system so unspeakably strange that hostility against it was warranted. By contrast, in colonial settings the view is also a defensive strategy, usually among linguistic minorities, as Edouard Glissant points out when he describes Martinican Creole as having "at its origin [a] kind of conspiracy to conceal meaning" by way of protecting a people from a forced assimilation made easier by the openness of its codes of value.[30]

One certainly understands the suspicion of claims to cultural authenticity that motivate Chow (it is postcolonial common sense). But her deconstructive circularity is too easily confused with dialectical reversal, for it positions the other as already Westernized, and thereby poses a much larger question about the status of deconstructive thinking within postcolonial theory generally, as well as the friendliness of that thinking, not so much toward European essence (in deconstructive terms, its logocentrism) but toward European programmatic interests.[31] The delicately performed circularity of Chow's argument subsides finally in a proposition that is much blunter and much less inclusive than one is led to expect. In effect, she is arguing that only "natives" transplanted to the West can know there are no natives, and this is what makes them natives, and what makes their nativism authentic. The danger in such postcolonial theory is that, while it refuses to claim epistemological authenticity for race or ethnicity, it allies itself with a Western political culture even as Western audiences grant its authority to do so because it is seen as being from a foreign place (and, in this case, as a refugee from communism). In that atmosphere, one is not sure that these methods successfully deconstruct the myth of origins or show them to be nostalgic so much as they efface the original; and once that happens, there is no outer tribunal to compare China against the West's translation of it.

An elaborate system of value coercively forecloses any serious discussion of an always foreign socialism as a culture of belief. The scorn visited upon kitsch in its social realist forms, for example (the heroic ultra-realist statues of lunch-pail-toting factory workers in bronze—like the one found on Karl Liebknecht Strasse in Berlin) is unloaded in contemporary theory without any sense of irony and with almost no dissent. According to accepted wisdom, the United States could not be freer of a socialist realist sensibility. But anyone who has traveled the country would immediately recognize the aesthetic as a common form of public working-class art under American capitalism, not only the former Soviet sphere. Could it be that this style codified and publicized under one regime was also present in the other, which did not, and could not, codify or publicize it? Could it be that it actually is a working-class aesthetic, just as the advocates of socialist realism had claimed all along? Vulgar and homiletic realism—what highly rewarded émigrés from the Soviet bloc have made careers out of sneering at as Stalinist kitsch—is vulgar to those from a fleshier, more delicate training. But rather than a ludicrous ideology forced onto a docile, retarded public, socialist realism turns out to be a rupture in taste between those whose hands are calloused and those who take their literary agents out to lunch at expensive restaurants.

The vilified aesthetic, called socialist realism, is not only the style of the Iwo Jima memorials, or the inevitable large bronze Indians (or African slaves) in the American parks and squares of those territories that once held slaves or exterminated Indians, but a vernacular form of epic, which is often a commercial epic. In Minnesota, for instance, one finds the *Determined Mariner* statue in the harbor of Duluth—more maudlin and steadfastly unmetaphoric than any poster of the Soviet 1930s. And along the way, spoking out from the Minneapolis hub, large whittled Paul Bunyans litter the roadsides on the highways north. They cannot be mistaken for the self-satirical humor of myth: they are the mirror gaze of the cabin-going weekend pioneers.

A FEW PROVISIONAL THESES

My translation of a Latin American essay into English presented what, by all accounts, was a perfectly traditional and familiar problem of translators in regard to language equivalencies. On the other hand, to pose these traditional questions in the social arena of a market-induced reception of non-Western work is to bring these various problematics into uneasy contact. Even if the technical issues of translation have an evident impact on the ability of metropolitan readerships to understand the original adequately, anyone who has attempted to present a foreign literature to a metropolitan public (and who at the same time *has* read it in the original) knows that questions of technique do not exhaust the matter. Expressive means are bent and shaped by issues that, if not outside language, are not containable within language either.[32] The conversions required by Cold War binaries intimates something of the ideological basis at work in non-Western literary reception as well, which has to do, among other things, with the distant reckonings of smaller peoples by overdeveloped intellectual communities.

An additional problem of translation affects understanding here: that of specific national histories, social settings, and disjunct customs in which language itself circulates differently, is owned differently, and is not, perhaps, as saturated with the digested information of the news or the elusive shorthands of advertising. Few have marked the similarity between these customarily postcolonial problematics and those articulated within literary criticism from the Soviet "East." They are similar in part because of the relatively less metropolitanized lives of Eastern Europe and Soviet Asia as compared to the West. In part also this is because of the popular sympathies of the socialist milieu from which even unofficial—even, at times, suppressed—Soviet critics benefited. Mikhail Bakhtin is one of these. He observed, for example, that the technique of novelistic hybridization "is not only (in fact not so much) the mixing of linguistic forms—the markers of two languages and styles—as it is the collision between differing points of view on the world that are embedded in these forms."[33] The closest counterpart to Bakhtin's theory of novelistic form would today be Pierre Bourdieu, for, like Bakhtin, he highlights the multiform, the anti-stratifying impulses, the centrifugal forces of the literary, not as somber, sovereign democratic ethos but as a parodic layering. In a real sense, Bakhtin sees the literary in terms of *play*, although not at all seeing language as deconstruction does, ludically. His comments on seriousness, on pathos, and on rhetoric paradoxically reveal his conviction that novelistic truth, and its role in authorial intentionality, is a matter of parody, of comic "play" (315, 323). The idea that conscious artistic structure accounts for only a fraction of what goes on parodically in the languages of the novel exemplifies, for Bakhtin, the process of *seeing oneself in others*, which is the serious and socially significant side of parodic form.

Bakhtin, in short, is talking about an intentional process of "bringing different languages in contact with one another." The many misperceptions of

Bakhtin's meaning are themselves informed by Cold War protocols of interpretation. As I pointed out in the introduction, Bakhtin was portrayed
throughout the 1980s as someone whose work was basically a long ethical argument for pluralistic modes of understanding and for democratic openness to
opposing points of view, operating (as though in a kind of allegorical cell) at
the level of subterfuge and double meaning where he launched an assault on
Stalinism under the clever rubrics of the "carnivalesque," "polyphony," and "the
dialogic" while living in internal exile. Once one dwells for a time in Bakhtin's
writing, and begins to reconstruct the debates in which his writing was forged,
this account of Bakhtin's influence begins to appear malicious nonsense.
Bakhtin was rather a philologist and Christian socialist suffering the indigni-
ties of all independent minds under Stalinism, but also hostile to the modernist
tendencies of Russian formalism—indeed, dedicated to exploding the literary
tendency of modernism from within by fashioning a literary formalism that
was, at the same time, sociological, anti-aesthetic, and plebeian. That he would
be taken as providing ammunition to the theoretical lineages of structuralism
is a profound irony, for he saw himself as its destroyer, although a destroyer
who conceded the insight of his opponents, appropriating them for different
ends.

Very much in concert with his Soviet milieu, Bakhtin's work situated itself
against an aestheticism then rising to prominence in the West, counterposing
to it a prosaics that would trace the genius of ordinary people's linguisitic
crudeness and polylingualism in the multinational contexts of his own country. This latter view, as is so often the case in the rearguard operations of those
espousing views outside the West's critical orthodoxies, has lately begun to
emerge just as Bakhtin's theoretical stock is falling. It arises, needless to say,
with all the testimonial evidence lacking in the first wave of Bakhtin scholarship in the United States. The new view of Bakhtin as critical Soviet subject and
anti-modernist is attested to by his friends and literary executors, Vadim Kozhi-
nov and Sergei Bocharov, who have done a good deal to help us see what
Bakhtin was really saying.[34]

The triumph of theories against essentialism and nostalgia make it difficult
to talk about cultural closure or uniqueness without appearing romantic. And
yet to many of us who study the Spanish-speaking Caribbean, for example (to
take only one case), it seems obvious that the social setting of its language gives
to its users a license to poetry or passion that audiences in North America cannot read without ironic distancing or embarrassment. Contrast this state of affairs with classic translation commentaries. George Steiner's *After Babel*, for example, confronts, from the vantage point of a withering urbanity a host of

translation difficulties that seem relatively minor when measured against the dilemma of rendering the simplest African or Arabic "prolie" fiction into a cogent, marketable English-language text.[35] Prolie fiction is not necessarily the brute, unmetaphorical narrative of harsh experience or autobiographical confession that we expect to find after reading dismissive or patronizing reviews in the West, but a fiction that often is immersed in an alternative value that constitutes an experimentalism—something of that alien view of place, property, or person referred to above by Christa Wolf. The same is found again in the writing of postwar Britain's most sensitive socialist, Raymond Williams, when he speaks of the Welsh industrial novel's translation of industrial life into novelistic form—the kind of work realized so memorably in the fiction of Pat Barker and Allan Sillitoe, among others.[36]

If translation theory takes us to issues of communicability, to the discussion of poetic-expressive means and the faithfulness of art to the original—or, as in Benjamin's rereading, to the revelations of language in the non-equivalencies of language manifest in the act of translation—surely there is a way to bracket these questions for another sort of inquiry. In a tentative way, I would like for the remainder of this essay to point to the kind of inquiry such a bracketing might yield, while returning at the end to the imaginative geography of the overlay "East/West." What is the current setting of translation in book-market terms? What are the uses of language, not as style or idiom or discourse but as national/political signifier or reservoir of historical memory? What kind of person is called forth to render it, on whose behalf, and at what sort of conjuncture? For whom does the translator write?

If one goes back to look at how the first accounts of European travelers, adventurers, and military men in the New World found a readership in the European sixteenth century, one finds that the Spanish, Portuguese, and Italian travelers were largely published by German publishing houses, often in German editions that were later retranslated into the other vernaculars following their dissemination. One could then say we are witnessing nothing particularly new in the properly colonial and imperial aspects of the translation process in book-market terms. But certainly the contemporary reality of vast literate populations in the G-7 nations with the money to purchase books is unprecedented. The power of fiction in translation to reach multitudes certainly gives some bite to the slogan of a "blurring of national belonging"—a slogan that has been rather too freely applied, and with a hint that this was the desired outcome, but which is for all that an accurate slogan when applied to literature and, more broadly, the image. It has, for example, become plausible to argue that among the most defining works of postwar U.S. fiction are works that were

written originally in other languages but that later carved out a space, in translation, in the U.S. literary canon. Certain books like *One Hundred Years of Solitude, The Book of Laughter and Forgetting, The Name of the Rose, If on a Winter's
Night a Traveler . . . , I Rigoberta Menchú* are "American" books to their North
American readers, and part of a national/political canon.

To say all this does not imply that readers are somehow confused about
these books' country of origin, or that they are perceived by readers as being
from the United States or as expressing some familiar or local American themes
or sensibilities. On the contrary, the reader is drawn to their foreignness, which
has become, through familiarity, a manageable foreignness. They are "American" books in their canonical role of providing a rite of passage to cosmopolitan literary maturity. Anyone who is an educated North American reader of
novels will be expected to know them and will be able to compare notes on the
same period of adolescence in which he or she came of artistic age while reading them. Moreover, these books are "American" by virtue of being the models
upon which the American novel is now based, a model primarily drawn from
Latin American and Eastern European fiction. Mass-market translation has allowed this process to occur not only among specialists but among middlebrow,
non-academic audiences in a sense quite different from the evaluative schemes
of the modernist canon of the turn of the century. And this foreignness occurs,
because it can occur, entirely in English.

What goes relatively unconsidered in translation theory are the networks of
conditioning and expectation within which translation operates. Today the immense financial resources of publishers offer a mind-boggling repertoire of
work written in languages other than English for monoglot English-speaking
audiences—a condition that finesses issues of faithfulness and poetic expression by presenting to an avid reading public a body of work that is known and
discussed entirely within English and that is often referred to in the translated
language of English even by literary professionals versed in a smattering of foreign tongues. And, of course, when one invokes "English" here it refers to much
more than a vernacular language. We are speaking about a North American
cultural industry that has built upon an earlier British educational industry in
a setting of empire whose current victorious dissemination is inseparable from
an America that "won" the Cold War.

Very much unlike the multilingual philological settings of high European
scholarship where many of the great theorists of translation operated (Heidegger, Benjamin, Steiner), contemporary North Americans are witness to a com-
mercially defined writing where it is possible for literature to be read and reviewed entirely in English while registering as foreign. The Leibnizian quest for

a universal language that found itself replayed in decades of undeserved fascination with Esperanto can now be said to have found its proper home in the
contemporary versions of those older, programmatic World English schemes
of I. A. Richards, C. K. Ogden, and H. G. Wells.[37] World English, in that sense,
is one of the central things the American empire "won" not (as Richards would
have it) by way of rational argument but by giving the world an argument it
could not refuse. Mainstream novelists in the United States and Europe nevertheless cop the gestures of a Third World literary scene, bringing it into view in
accessible ways.

It is crucial to note precisely what has been lost in translation. Through a
host of media interlocutors, this original impulse toward the Third World has
begun to decay, becoming in many cases a sort of politico-exotic, troping on
democracy in a setting of poverty, dictatorship, and revolution. Here one
comes to an unexpected impasse. Implicit in the acceptance of a construct conveyed as (but not actually called) "Third World literature" came a potentially
radical expansion of the degrees and types of aesthetic value appreciable in the
metropolitan centers, one whose politics was unashamed and central to its aesthetics. What actually happened en route to translating these values, however,
was different. The very emphasis on politics paradoxically disabled appreciation. Now that politics was out in the open, one could see *less* clearly the narrow range that politics was allowed to have at the aesthetic level. A formulaic
quality arose—what I am calling the politico-exotic—and another outlawed at
the very time that the salutary shock of a "political writing" about empire was
domesticated through popularity. It lost its ability to shock, and therefore to reorient value. A very unpredictable and asymmetrical set of conditions for literary reception has been the result.

Those conditions, among other things, link the exoticism of East and South
in the manner I have been describing. To return to Germany one last time,
Christa Wolf in *Parting from Phantoms: Selected Writings, 1990–1994*, takes us to
still another problem of language related to that immediately above—the problem (conversely) of the uncomfortable closeness of meaning, the inability to
hide what is one's cultural or national own from an invading enemy who knows
too many of one's codes to be fooled by tricksterism, allegory, or subterfuge—
the traditional ruses of the racial or ethnicized aliens under colonization (10).
The GDR was paradoxically more open to colonization, to cultural disarticulation, because of the relative transparency of its language to its invaders.

This important recognition, however, is still furiously dismissed. Andreas
Huyssen's arguments about the fall of the Berlin wall in *Twilight Memories* represent an extreme form of the anti-conversion thesis positing that cultures of

belief are not intricate views of the world but mere forms of mimicry: "East and West German intellectuals, who, after the collapse of the benefit of mutual exoticism, had found it immensely difficult to talk to each other, discovered common ground in a ritualistic, Third World theology and an anti-imperialism that mixes blatant and subtle anti-Americanism."[38] One must, I suppose, give Huyssen credit for obviating any special task of interpretation. His comments link East and West with a colonial brashness that is all but caricature: "The discourse of colonization and of a new Manchester capitalism overtaking the former GDR runs rampant among intellectuals when in fact the problem is that industrial capital does not colonize enough" (48). The unmentionable truth in the process Huyssen describes as industrial capital not "colonizing enough" is, of course, the financial arrangements that encourage investment in this globalized out-shipping of services, which depend on depressed wages, the absence of safety or pollution standards, and a heavily policed workforce. As always, these inhumanities tend to be more easily forced on people who are perceived as the "lesser folk and wild." Now it is the "prolies" rather than the cannibals who are brought into the light.

The book markets might be said, in this sense, to have placed Eastern Europe again resolutely at the center of an imperial problematic. There is, after all, a family resemblance in media commentary between non-Western literatures and the highly publicized literary writing from Eastern Europe in the wake of perestroika. In the mental space of the politico-exotic enjoyed by Third World writing in the metropolitan book markets, the literatures of Eastern Europe are similarly situated, spawning new publishers' series of high production quality and yielding predictions of literary renaissance. They arrive to their audiences in the same packaging: a world literature for an age of world music. To the North American reader in a bookstore weighing choices, Eastern Europe may not be fully Europe, but it is nevertheless much more like home than is Zimbabwe or Sri Lanka. At the same time, it can claim an attractive otherness for being a version of the colonies "at home." As a preparation for this linkage, bridges between the two regions had long been forged by journals like *Granta* in Britain and its counterpart, *Grand Street*, in the United States, which placed writing from India, Africa, and Eastern Europe under the same marquee, as it were. Mario Vargas Llosa alongside Milan Kundera, Ryszard Kapuscinski journeying through Africa.[39]

In the politico-exotic, there is a translation that precedes composition, one internalized by the author before the writing even begins.[40] Given the kinds of openings that exist, and the way that they are portrayed on the reviewers' pages, authors ranging from Brazil to South Asia tend to exist only as metonyms in an intertextual coterie that chooses them as much as they choose it. Placed in the company of other "hybrid subjects," they take their part in a collective lesson for North American readers of global pluralism. They are unable to enter the scene of letters as innovators in the way, for example, that a talented North American novelist without ethnic baggage might be packaged as the rude boy or girl of a new generation. Their movement is based on being rather than doing, and so it is not a movement so much as a retroactive categorization. At the same time, the oppressive persistence of the role the public critic implicitly asks them to fill—and rewards them for filling—conforms the novels they set out to write.

To subsume all translation under cultural translation is not my intention and may even be said to enervate language's privilege. For the more everyday matter of rendering Bengali or Tagalog or Patwah into readable English continues to vex the reception of non-Western literatures. My adducing the blood relationship between a Cold War cultural impasse and an imperial logic of distancing and dehumanization is not meant to circumvent the problem of translation as a problem of slippage in language's disparate modes of intention. This is, after all, what makes translation an intriguingly impossible task that nevertheless demands an attempt be made if for no other reason than to pay homage to language itself. But the less studied aspect of translation remains market inclusion and comparative cultural value: "a bazaar filled with all possible constitutions, where anyone can choose to perceive whichever variety they please," according to Jacques Rancière[41]—a process that has made of books in translation a proper domestic literature to a degree that it never had before.[42]

Failed conversions underlie experiences of incommensurate social value. It is worth recalling the opening of Benjamin's essay "The Storyteller," where he invokes the consequences of the historical rupture of World War I. The war had cast doubt among Europeans about the viability of their civilization and weakened European self-confidence to the point of making the first rumblings of decolonization possible. Although he does not emphasize that aspect of the problem, Benjamin does consider how the war had made people less and less able to express themselves: "With the [First] World War a process began to become apparent which has not halted since then. Was it not noticeable at the end of the war that men returned from the battlefield grown silent—not richer, but poorer in communicable experience?"[43] The ability to tell a tale properly had fallen into disrepute, he argues; experience itself had fallen in value, language had been stripped of its power, and it was no longer an adequate means of expressing what had already superseded it.

What has become politically inarticulate in our own time weighs us down and oppresses us because we too have experienced trauma. Important codes cannot be deciphered because whole lifetimes have been silenced by Western ideological colonizations after 1989. The story of the non-Western world, the meaning of the postcolonial, makes no sense without the socialist East and its elaborate networks of meaning, feeling, and valuing. It is time to translate that experience into a language that has so far only purported to understand the other.

CHAPTER 2

NATIVISM

ON DECEMBER 14, 1991, after two unexpected public appearances, Salman Rushdie emerged at Columbia University's School of Journalism to announce a strategy with two components: first, to pressure Western heads of state to help him win a reprieve from his death sentence, and second, to launch the paperback edition of *The Satanic Verses*. "*The Satanic Verses*," he declared, "must be freely available and easily affordable, if only because if it is not *read and studied*, then these years will have no meaning."[1]

This dramatic appeal to reading will prompt my own recourse to reading below. Obsessed in his essays with the Indian and British states, Rushdie wrote a novel that, by all accounts, had become a matter of state—and as such, created a condition that conspired against reading. What catapulted the novel into a matter of state, moreover, were charges that relied on the public presumption of inadequacy in two types of reading communities. The first was an ostensibly *mis*reading (or more often, *non*reading) community of naive Islamic faithful—the ones who had had the audacity, it was said, to burn the book without reading it, without even being capable of savoring the joys of an ironic literary knowledge. The second—in a much more localized and second-stage set of commentaries—a supposedly ill-informed community of critics from the metropole who sought to comment on the affair without personally knowing Islam or the Islamic world. The first had been exposed mercilessly by a powerful caste of reviewers in mainstream publications.[2] The second had been challenged by Muslim scholars and clerics in Europe and the Middle East who upbraided Western journalists in popular books and newspaper articles. At the same time both had been the target of a third type of criticism offered by scholars and professors, many of South Asian origin, writing in a climate of postcolonial theory in American and British universities.

The nativism of the first was held up for scorn under the aegis of a Western pluralism, whereas the *Western* nativism of the second had been rebuked by a postcoloniality immune, in its own eyes, to nativism. It is as an amendment to those views that I offer mine below. And I will insist that identitiarian obsessions (the being or not-being Muslim, Indian, Pakistani, dark, white) have here as elsewhere suffocatingly displaced a rhetoric more appropriate to the politics of position found in a figure like Rushdie, whose legacy to literature and to contemporary civic discourse is a peculiarly successful culture of belief marked both by the ideology of "migrancy" (which is well known) and a postwar British social democratic, parliamentary ethos (which is ignored).

What are the stakes of such a point? Over whom or what is this war of interpretations struggling? As a whole, the critical reception of Rushdie's work has been partial, although in uneven ways. A middlebrow, public-sphere commentary has jostled with an MLA-oriented expertise, with the former scandalously uninterested in the latter's knowledge and the latter eager for the former's notoriety but unable to gauge the ideological consequences of the former's prior setting of the Rushdian stage. Unaccustomed to entering debates over reading under the klieg lights, as it were, of a *literature of state*, professional literary critics often conflated distinct issues—on the one hand, the relevance of cultural criticism to foreign policy, and on the other, the Eurocentric gaffes of high-profile commentators whose notoriety (rather than their knowledge either of Rushdie's novels or of his precise cultural setting) had been their entry card into the debate.

One was dealing, then, with an unfamiliar set of interpretive problems. In Rushdie, the critic had to address a reputation so large—and so "now"—that the traditional luxury of working in separate critical spheres was not only in danger of confusing both but (as I have just suggested) was actually denied or finessed by the hermeneutic specialist seeking to break out of his or her academic confinement in a uniquely receptive commercial atmosphere. This was the case not despite but because the Rushdie affair demonstrated the impoverished view the public had of cultural criticism itself. Never before had a mass-market novel elicited official commentary from the likes of James Baker and Geoffrey Howe. And yet what the affair demanded, cultural criticism was best equipped to provide: for example, insights into problems of cultural transla-tion raised when fiction crosses borders; the way that book markets structure international tastes and create literary celebrities; the different status that the written word enjoys in different societies; the actual traditions of secular liter-ature within Islamic societies, as well as how that literature had previously en-gaged with the sacred writings of Islam; and importantly (perhaps most im-portantly), the problem of affiliation—the problem of how, in fact, to take Rushdie as a writer from India while being, in his own words, a writer also in and of England, a writer working on behalf of democracy but hostile to democ-racy's colonial interventions.

Rushdie first became an important author at a specific political conjunc-ture that needs to be repeated to be remembered. The affair and its aftermath are otherwise unintelligible. Despite the schematic nature of the account im-mediately below, I want to sketch that conjuncture at the risk of understate-ment or omission, since the more detailed and site-specific reading that I offer later depends on it. Rushdie, it should be recalled, first emerged as an author of renown in 1980, only two years after the government of Margaret Thatcher as-sumed power in a period of renewed U.S. imperial ascendancy that expressed itself in an emphatic riposte to a surge of anti-colonial insurrections marking the final moment of the immediate post-Vietnam era (Nicaragua, the Philip-pines, Iran, El Salvador). The gradual weakening of those anti-colonial move-ments and, in all but one of those cases, their defeat took place at the same time that his career was being launched—a career that grew and developed against a backdrop of neoliberal triumphalism. As the official public sphere rang with endorsements for ending the welfare state, the "second Cold War" (in Fred Hal-liday's phrase) was being carried out with a messianic vigilance, ending finally in the fall of the Soviet Union in 1989 as a result of that country's thoroughly unpredicted, and almost completely unapplauded, willingness to undergo re-forms. Today the transformation is popularly rendered as the result of Presi-dent Reagan's successful program of supply-side military spending.[3]

Meanwhile, a correlative movement of post-humanistic thought in the uni-versities and in the arts effectively disabled critical opposition to these devel-opments, announcing itself through a self-contradictory (but coldly efficient) claim that representation—in both its organizational and its semiotic senses—was a form of tyranny. Rushdie entered this prolonged liminal moment in a de-cidedly antinomian posture. His entire career, including the subjects and styles of his fiction, has been indelibly marked by a traditionalist defense of political and epistemological values against the public stream. A partisan of the Sandi-nistas, an ill-tempered enemy of Thatcher's new entrepreneurialism, and an unapologetic debunker of discursive theory, he set out to champion a brand of Left-Labor humanism bent on rehabilitating conscience in a frankly uncivil society.

Although the patterns of this transformation had been seen before (its history, in some ways, punctuates the entire postwar period), the important shift between 1980 and 1991 had been a grafting of traditional Cold War hostilities on to various nationalisms (Palestinian, Nicaraguan, Salvadoran, South African, Filipino), a meeting, as it were, of the enemies of the Anglo-American imperial self.[4] The decisive theoretical issues surrounding identity in the academy, as well as the prompting to an almost involuntary nativism of focus in the field of postcolonial studies, were both caught up in this shift and expressed it as a contradiction—that is, as a position hostile to an oddly universalized and abstract "nationalism" that failed to acknowledge its own congruency with official American policy toward insurgent movements of political independence, and as a position that drew energy from a renewed focus on alien ethnic and national specificities. The shift, moreover, produced a complex and self-defeating set of corollaries in which cultural critics, insufficiently attentive to the merging of diverse critical communities, found themselves.

The ethnic or national identities of postcolonial critics in the metropole simply *stood in for* entire regions of the authentic Third World even as the beneficiaries dismissed "authenticity" as a humanist fiction. Nationalism was furiously denounced in all quarters while the postcolonial critic was largely involved in promoting cultural nationalism—much like Franz Fanon's comprador bourgeoisie, whose primary critique of colonialism was to demand a larger cut of the action. Given the success of Iran and the decline of the Soviet sphere, nationalisms in Africa, Eastern Europe, and elsewhere turned their sympathy away from the classical anti-colonial model associated with the era of Bandung—the model later of the nonaligned nations, with broadly social democratic and critically "Western" sympathies found recently, for example, in Nicaraguan socialism and the Brazil of Luiz Inacio Lula da Silva. Disenfranchised from a coherent political alternative after the fall of the socialist sphere, these nationalisms increasingly took on the shape of religious, ethnic, or anti-Western movements. The political had become civilizational.

It is precisely in this shift that the interpretation of Rushdie gets complicated, and where the ambiguity and self-contradictoriness of the nativist readings reside. To resolve it, however, means to read much more than the famous affair or its proximate cause—*The Satanic Verses*—and so I will turn my attention below to aspects of Rushdie's career as a whole: exactly what is wanting in much of the helpful work prompted by his now global fame.

In spite of the aim of going beyond the affair, it is the affair, finally, that exacerbated the conflict within Rushdie's brand of social democratic and civil intervention, one that mobilized the *literary* on behalf of public decency and civil rights while situating itself securely within a framework of free debate that no nativism (including the West's) would allow him. The surprising unanimity of the public portrait of Rushdie as the displaced Indian of Muslim parentage, the renegade from color and country, is remarkable. Nor is it in broad outline inaccurate, except contextually, which has made that portrait tendentious. It extends, at any rate, from the *Times* of London, to the England-based mullahs of Bradford who first protested the book, as well as to a good deal of postcolonial criticism, although naturally the valence of that renegacy is utterly dissimilar in each case, particularly between the first two groups. The third (postcolonial criticism) takes a more complicated position that borrows from the others—a position in defense of authorial freedom, desirous of inclusion in a broadly accessible Western public sphere, but wearing the mantle of filiative authenticity. All, for their own reasons, quashed this other view—the one Rushdie tirelessly projected for himself, which had to do with an affiliation rather than a filiation: the venerable, new, proudly old-fashioned defender of the novel as a form, of the beneficent state, of tolerant public opinion, and of ethnic cross-dressing.[5]

Rushdie, as a whole, has been foreshortened by the affair. As Martin Amis memorably put it, he had "vanished into the front page." For those who had been following his career closely throughout the 1980s, *The Satanic Verses* appeared very different before the events of 1989 than it did afterward. To those of us who had the opportunity of reading *The Satanic Verses* in manuscript before its publication in England in 1988, the future was unpredictable and unknowable. Many of the expected gestures—the same humor, above all the same satirical targets—could be found there in what clearly amounted at the time to nothing more than the third installment of a trilogy he had begun in *Midnight's Children*, continued in *Shame*, and was now bringing to completion. There was nothing essentially new—no added virulence, no obvious change in tone, no special provocations. The savaging of Islam was dramatically evident in the earlier novels, particularly in *Shame* with its sustained parody of the Qur'an, which was compared there to the rantings of the Pakistani military. The difference was that the parody was not, as here, found in a book whose very title gave the jest away, and whose author had now attained a visibility *within* England that allowed the parody to be picked over by an avid international readership.

It was not, then, some newfound status as reprobate Muslim that caused the avalanche of protest and recrimination to fall; rather, it was a peculiar combination (one that a nativist reading explicitly denies): namely, the novel's

England-centeredness—which is not to say its Englishness in the now-transformed sense of that identity—along with, and in equal measure, the author's celebrity status. Religious apostasy may have been the proximate cause, but as in other sectoralist conflicts the real struggle was, as always, over rights, labor, and land. As perceived by the book's detractors, Rushdie's crime was the combined product of notoriety and an insider status that could effectively translate itself in Anglo-American surroundings, and do so in a context of palpable contempt for an immigrant community of believers in an era, as Syed Shahabuddin put it, of the "new Crusades." He had, in the view of Shahabuddin, "peddled his Islam wares in the West."

Following the fatwa, Muslim scholars seeking to explain what was outrageous in the book focused on his distance from the working-class Muslims and Hindus he typically wrote about—above all in England (and British Muslims were the first to burn the book publicly). What, for example, do we make of the fact that among them he was often referred to, with deliberate cruelty, as "Simon Rushton"? Postcolonial theory has at times alluded to the significance of these associations and the part they played in the ensuing controversy, but it has not emphasized them, for the view controverts the basic premise of cultural nationalism. After all, those who were arguably closest to Islamic knowledge and to the domestic complexities of religious politics in the Subcontinent saw Rushdie not as too Muslim to be understood by the culturally illiterate Western critic, but rather as too Western to recognize his own insiderism as a form of false advertising. They were exposing the luxury of a critique fully consonant with a British intellectual common sense, and challenging a highly rewarded author in an atmosphere of heightening rancor toward Muslim workers living in British exile, who were misunderstood, and who were now laughed at by someone considered to be (if not actually being) their own—only one example of the confusion of reading communities at work in the book's reception. He occupied both a different class position and an obviously different culture of secular-political (not only religious) belief.

But the post-fatwa Rushdie was a Rushdie robbed of his resources, even (as we will see below) by himself. He could only be seen through the veil of filiation. One has to struggle to remember how inappropriate such a delimiting was for a writer who in review after review had spoken on behalf of his own multiple identities and national fealties. And it looked past his elaboration, in essay after essay, of politics—of imperialism as a grand theme worthy of our century's greatest writers but as yet unexploited by them. He had always been drawn compulsively to those, as he wrote of Graham Greene, who have a "total addiction to everything about their time." As the affair opened a door between the uneventful reveries of literature and consequential public events, critics found themselves plucked into the light. While a generation of award-winning prose stylists scurried into the refuge of minimalist novels of gloomy contemplation, Rushdie bushwhacked his way into a different clearing. He helped recall for modern Britain what it had forgotten was there in Blake, Swift, and Orwell: big-theme Politics, the clash of states, the dramas of national heroism and betrayal, the perfidies and hypocrisies of a race-driven world system of empire, creating a festering sprawl of Babbitts, Bumbles, and Sebastian Flytes on the home front, living off the colossal spoils of colonial pillage. *Midnight's Children* exploded this literature of constipation, and threw open the doors to an entire generation of younger novelists for whom the British empire had been more tactile and obvious precisely because it was vanishing, and for whom the changing racial demographics of John Bull had led to popular commentaries of all sorts on immigration and religious fundamentalism.

Picking up on the mood, Tariq Ali had complained about the reception in London circles of Abdelrahman Munif's powerful five-volume novel, *Cities of Salt*: "The novel went unnoticed on the London literary scene. Naturally, the critics were preoccupied with slender, wistful accounts of middle-class life in New York. A short, light-weight, but clever book about a man warming his baby's feeding bottle was the rage at the time. Let me be blunt. Munif's work is worth much more than most of the junk being turned out by publishing houses."[6] And so it was with Rushdie, only that Rushdie drove home his point fully ten years before Ali, when few British authors with his connections thought in these terms, and he did so with the great exclamation point of a novel—a five-hundred-page mock epic that realigned English literature, making it more rife with possibilities, more uproarious, more carnivalesque, less European—but above all, more Political in the grand sense of that word. History in such literature resumed its status as time-honored burr in the flesh of the imagination, taking us back to the fictive musings over sweeping movements of social change.

Like his precise politics, the ideological aspect of his aesthetic achievement—formal stakes of his writing—has yet to be commented on adequately. They are lost in the battle of nativisms that jump, on the part of clueless British and American newspaper reviewers, to facile comparisons between Rushdie and Lawrence Sterne or Günter Grass and, on the part of defensive British and U.S.-based Indian academics, to claims that he has nothing whatsoever to do with Western authors but is interpretable exclusively through genres like the oral tale or languorous Urdu poetic forms like the *ghazal*.[7] These readings stamp a specious authority on an always very partial ethnic identification. They employ a threatening cultural specificity locked within an experiential "science" of the East in a mode of temporary amnesia toward both Rushdie's actual writing and his emphatic statements about what that writing contains.

Rushdie alludes, no doubt, to such genres and incorporates their formal aspects, and like every NRI (nonresident Indian), carries with him a special attachment to them, a fund of memories and a sensibility that is at once nostalgic and internalized. Rushdie's most fully realized and densely crafted novel, *Shame* (as I wrote many years ago), is a deliberate contestation at the level of form between the Qur'an that it parodies and the oral tale that it seeks to emulate, in which the plebeian and gender-inflected vitality of the latter is set against the scriptural certitude—the frozen orality—of the former. What has to be remembered, though, is that *Shame* is among Rushdie's most derivative novels in the sense that every aspect of its plot and situation is taken scene by scene from *One Hundred Years of Solitude*. It is only the most obvious moment where Rushdie's potent intervention into the book markets can be seen for what it gloriously is: a systematic reapplication of the lessons of the Latin boom to the Anglo-imperial world. The Americas were the source of the ideology of *mestizaje* that became hybridity in the hands of belated Anglo-Americanized exiles from the British colonies and that Rushdie captured in a new context as a "contemporary" phenomenon—the migrant sensibility—that had been the staple of a specifically American (above all, Latin American) discourse for two centuries. Neither Rushdie nor postcolonial criticism in general notices that it was in that particular school that Rushdie apprenticed—a point, by definition, friendly to the migrancy he elaborates. Nor is it appreciated that the political center stage then occupied by Latin America via the Nicaraguan revolution of 1979 and the contra wars of the early 1980s directly presented these aesthetic options to a Rushdie still struggling for a novelist's voice.

As a matter of form, however, or of the way that style is informed by signifiers of a distinctly national-cultural type, it has to be appreciated that there is no sustained attempt by Rushdie to work *within* the genres of Holy Book or oral legend except as a commentary upon them (for example, the role in *Shame* of the Qur'an and Bariamma's familial tales, respectively). He uses them metafictionally, in other words, and this use significantly alters their function in the context of a programmatic affiliation. In the case of *Shame*, for instance, the "oral tale" involves a point about women's domestic resistance to a male military elite. The flexing of the muscle of cultural capital that is seen in presentations of Rushdie as a mistranslated Muslim working in classical Oriental genres ignores the facts of his life. Let us recall a few important facts readily available from the public record.

A child of popular culture, Rushdie grew up surrounded by Bollywood and American comic books. In his own words, he was the joint product of *The Arabian Nights* and Enid Blyton. As part of what he described as a "very Anglophile and Anglocentric" youth, his father had hired a painter to decorate the walls of his nursery with animal characters from Disney films. He has stated that his most decisive single influence was *The Wizard of Oz*, the subject of his brief and brilliant study for the British Film Institute. Almost all of these early inspirations, moreover, appear again in *Haroun and the Sea of Stories*—Flash Gordon's rockets to the moon, *Alice in Wonderland*, the voyages of Sinbad, the heroic double lives of Clark Kent/Superman and Bruce Wayne/Batman, the riches of Ali Baba, and the colorful substitute home peopled with talking animals and forbidden cities of *The Wizard of Oz*. Many of the professional influences of his maturer years were also woven into that novel's fabric, with echoes of James Bond's *Dr. No*, the medievally tinged science fictions of Italo Calvino, the "bwana" adventure films of Steven Spielberg, and Satyajit Ray's spectacularly popular children's film about two bumbling bumpkins (*Goopy Gyne Bagha Byne*), whose names are given to the novel's two talking fish.

The secularized irreverence was in no way innocent of religious intent, on the other hand, even if Rushdie's romance with Sufism was insufficient to brand him, without many levels of irony, as a Muslim critiquing Islam from within. Having lived, like *The Satanic Verses*' Gibreel Farishta, "a childhood of blasphemy," he would as a child mimic the art of Arabic calligraphers by drawing the name of Allah so that it resembled the figure of a naked woman. Then came the years at Rugby, later King's College, Cambridge, where he took up his first serious study of Islamic civilization and, later still, discovered his romance with film—especially the films of Michelangelo Antonioni, Akiro Kurosawa, and Satyajit Ray—followed by his ventures into acting at the Oval and Kennington in the play *Viet Rock*, where, sporting long hair and a beard, he roamed London's counterculture, living his last college summer above a mod boutique on King's Road. Upon graduating in 1968, he declared, "I ceased to be a conservative under the influence of the Vietnam war and dope." During his short sojourn in Karachi, where he had planned to move after his parents' relocation there, he adapted Edward Albee's *The Zoo Story* for the country's government-operated television station. He ran afoul of the censors, however, for including the word "pork" in the script, and the magazine feature he then wrote on his first impressions of Pakistan was censored as well. In 1969 he returned to England in disgust and, apart from short visits abroad, never left again, until his recent move to New York.

His relationship to Islam in *The Satanic Verses* is impossible, then, to separate from a literary and civic project fed by the *soixante huitard* sympathies of a differently, but not uniquely, situated metropolitan. Of course, the Third Worldist passions of that ethos had for him a more immediate register than it did for the British who grew up beside him in England. He knew those passions personally, but what he knew was part of a reservoir of experiences with its own limitations. The novelistic India, Africa, and Asia of his upbringing—the ones immortalized in writing—were drawn from a world whose literary associations were stuck in a British "novel of empire"—the staid discourse of the Marylebone Cricket Club, gin toddies, barrack-room ballads, and stiff upper lips desperately out of character with the epic-fantastic that emerged in the international book markets following Vietnam in the intervening 1970s—the years of his novelistic apprenticeship.

The frustration of having a story that needed to be retold in an idiom appropriate to the time made *Midnight's Children* possible. And it led to a series of motifs of secularization operating at the level of form as much as theme—the elements that, once the field of the affair has been cleared, will bring us back to his writing. So one, even here, need not be sociological alone, but can return with pleasure to the issues of form. Recall what these formal characteristics have been. His narratives are constructed consciously as political cartoons, not (as is so often claimed) pastiche. Rushdie's fiction (as he suggests in *Midnight's Children*'s metafictional asides) is current-events collage, articles clipped from a newspaper. One wants to talk more about the seamless edge between his journalism and his novels, or rather, the journalism *of* his novels, their reliance on the logic of the headlines, and the subordination of character to the allegorical logic of news commentary.

We are dealing, that is to say, with a metafictional compendium that, unlike many of its contemporary counterparts, was resolutely non-postmodern. Many postcolonial critics, even widely read ones, continue to argue for his novels' postmodernity in what is surely a doxological gesture.[8] Rushdie's discovery of the world of the heart, of intimacy and conversation, is surprisingly evident and unapologetic in the 1990s. He found this intimacy first, after all, in the closing passages of *The Satanic Verses* in his portrayal of Chamcha's planting of a tree at his father's death—a fictional farewell to his real-life father, whose recent passing is memorialized there. Little has been said about this. One could easily argue that the significance of *The Moor's Last Sigh* is its attempt to extend that intimacy over the course of a novel via portraits of sexuality—in Rushdie's mind, for well or ill, a feminized strategy taken from the great women novelists of the English nineteenth century: "It's funny how books, the classics, order you to reread them when you are preparing for a novel. I've been rereading *Wuthering Heights*. Before that, *Jane Eyre* . . . these characters possessed by personal feeling." Having surprised himself by the power of the closing scene of *The Satanic Verses*, he set out to sustain it: "I've got to write about sex . . . there is very little sex in my novels, very little stuff at all about the deep emotions. . . . One of the things I have failed to do . . . is write about strong feeling, cathartic emotion, obsession."[9]

If it is form that needs addressing, it is the following that matters: his calculated use of loanwords (much richer and more natural than those of Kipling or Mulk Raj Anand), his angry wit (the most brilliant of his authorial gifts, and the secret of his stature), and his cinematic sense (cinema so often *in* his novels, but also *of* them in the fast-cutting, blurry close-ups and the melodrama). Apart from these is this premier fact of his placard prose, his two-dimensionality of character rescued from boredom by the multidimensionality of his political intelligence and frames of reference. It is an *intellectual* and satiric fiction whose aesthetic pleasures lie at the level of the phrase and of the idea rather than narrative development, an aspect that has led to many misunderstandings given the literary presuppositions of a public criticism still operating under the "end of ideology." Thus, *New York Times* reviewer Christopher Lehmann-Haupt's comment that Rushdie is "unreadable. . . . He couldn't write a sentence if his life depended on it."[10]

Out of the frying pan and into the fire. His postcolonial readership, under the aegis of nativism, has often caught him no better than Lehmann-Haupt did. In her reading of *Shame*, Sara Suleri cannot resist de Manian paradoxes, which remove all denotation from her field of vision and lead her to untenable positions—for instance, that *Shame* seeks comfort in a reflexive formalism, or that Rushdie "avoids melodrama." But Rushdie, of course, toys with genre; he is generically licentious, and melodrama (hoary villains, bald emotional appeals, sentimental plot devices) is part of his fiction's very fabric. Rushdie tries genres on, mixes them up, as if to express the multi-front novelistic war required to capture a place and a politics that are too painful to deal with in a single mode (as had been true of the novel's first draft). As for formalism, Rushdie's narrator in *Shame* is precisely anti-formalistic in the sense that the narrator here is Rushdie in a current-events and autobiographical mode. His strategy is a bit like Julio Cortázar's in *Hopscotch*—the author as critic of his own work, standing outside the fictive, forcing us back into an everyday history. The fairy tale self-destructs precisely because fictiveness is inappropriate to a contemporary dictatorship, and the political satire is so ill-humored and so literally based on news reports and police files that it fails as satire too. All of this is Rushdie's point, moreover, which is why his narrator is not a narrator at all but an author as confessor. "I can't do this," he keeps saying. "I hate these people and I have to say so openly," he continues, and "literature is such a small club, after all, against so large a beast." This is not the utilization of genre but a comment on genre: a joke, if you will, an intentionally superficial gesture calculated to display its own inadequacy. The formulaic quality of Suleri's points—their appeal to the clichés of literary modernism—did not harm their reception but rather, with the help of an unacknowledged assumption of authenticity, actually paved their way.

Rushdie set out to recover the Political in literature. Weak in plot, unable to realize character, he was strong in sardonic abuse and in the presentation of suppressed history. And this is what should be talked about—not the exaggerations that come from overreading, in which allusions become illusions, and wainscoting a foundation stone, as though Rushdie were the proper heir of Muhammad Iqbal in the land of the Angrezi *Dummkopfs*. The cultural politics of the Rushdie affair might at least consider the costs it demanded of his critique of empire, which screeched to a halt under the pressures of his own contradictory analysis of the forces poised against it. The affair was significant because it caught him, for a time, overtaken by events. Although his flight from the literary coteries of London to New York after the publication of *The Ground Beneath Her Feet* did not inaugurate his political turn to the right (à la Christopher Hitchens), transporting himself to the capital of the actual, not former, empire did exacerbate his tendencies toward prejudice and personalization that first revealed themselves in the affair. Already then, a decade earlier, he had begun to read Islam itself as a personal affront and to argue grandiosely that his own writerly situation was tantamount to the position of literary freedom at large. In time, the social democrat would become a social patriot, ardently defending the U.S. war in Afghanistan and, in concert with the George W. Bush White House, equating Islam with terrorism. Some close readers of Rushdie, myself included I must say, had seen warning signals earlier.

FIGHTING AND FORGETTING: THE AFFAIR'S FALLOUT

"These years," he writes in his Columbia speech. What, in fact, were the events that conspired to bring the traditionally Cold War and anti-Islamic discourses into a potent, and silencing, combination? As a prominent reviewer in high-

profile magazines on both sides of the Atlantic, Rushdie had had reason to assume that the publication of *The Satanic Verses* on September 26, 1988, would
be met with acute interest, if not open admiration. Indeed, the reception began
that way, although there were early danger signs. Even before September, the famous Delhi-based journalist and novelist Khushwant Singh—Viking/Pen-
guin's editorial consultant in India—advised against publication, warning that
the novel's blasphemous parodies of the Prophet Muhammad would cause
trouble. In an unfortunate interview for *India Today* on September 15, Rushdie
unwittingly alerted the Muslim community to the book's offensive contents by
declaring that his message was religious fanaticism. When the Government of
India banned the book on October 5, the measure only brought into realization
what had earlier been promised. For in the initial months after publication,
Viking had been deluged with calls and letters demanding the book's with-
drawal, along with a petition containing hundreds of thousands of names. The
first of many mass protests against the book took place in London on Decem-
ber 10, followed by demonstrations in every major British city with a sizable
Muslim population. As the book proceeded to be banned by all of the officially
Islamic countries, many other countries joined the ban, including Sri Lanka,
South Africa, Kenya, Thailand, Tanzania, Indonesia, Singapore, Venezuela, and
Poland.

Meanwhile, the demonstrations abroad had turned deadly. Ten were killed
protesting outside the U.S. embassy in Islamabad, five in Kashmir, thirteen in
Bombay, and hundreds more injured in Dhaka. As legal and public relations
maneuvers in both camps continued—with Rushdie writing an open letter of
complaint to Rajiv Gandhi and solicitors of the UK Action Committee on Islamic Affairs trying to quash the book by having England's antiquated blasphemy laws apply to Islam as well as Christianity—events took a turn that rendered both actions moot. On February 14, 1989, the Ayatollah Khomeini's fatwa
aired on Radio Teheran. Nor had these events died down immediately before
Rushdie's Columbia appearance. Thirty-seven had just died in a hotel in
Turkey in an apparent attempt to kill Aziz Nesin, the Turkish translator of *The
Satanic Verses*; in May 1992, Jamia Millia Islamia, a university in India, was
forced to shut its doors when its administrator, Mashirul Hasan, denounced
the ban on the novel; a few months later, Britain expelled three Iranians suspected of plotting to assassinate Rushdie, and Hotoshi Igarishi, the Japanese
translator, had just been stabbed to death.

What I am arguing is that the decisive issue of the affair—when one adopts,
as here, an approach to the career as a whole—is the interpretive impasse arising from Rushdie's insistence on publishing the paperback edition when its ap-

pearance amounted to death, deportation, and suppression on an international scale. A warmly social democratic public persona came in conflict with a liberal apotheosis of the literary in the context of a Western cosmopolitan triumphalism. And the insistence by certain critics on cultural particulars in a bid for authoritative reading stifled the issues to which his career had been geared: the role of the literary in the public sphere, and its capacity for liberalizing a climate of intolerance. For that reason, criticism needed to explore more fully than it did where the interpretive impasse arose, and how it played itself out in the public arena. That is what I would like to do here.

Rushdie's struggle to have others see *The Satanic Verses* as a matter of state won ground in May 1993 when British prime minister John Major agreed to meet with the author and be photographed. Rushdie had, one remembers, made the point of such a strategy clear in his Columbia declaration when he equated his own travail to that of "the Western hostages in Lebanon and the British businessmen imprisoned in Iran and Iraq." The enticements and threats that had finally freed the hostages should, he argued, now be used on his behalf.

As the location of the clearly desperate author and the Western heads of state began to coalesce over a site occupied by ambiguous U.S. embassy personnel in Lebanon and unnamed British businessmen, the mere symbolism of *The Satanic Verses* as secular irreverence began to assume the garments of state in a more brutish, more solemnly literal form. Mamoun Fandy's April 13, 1992, article for the *Christian Science Monitor* found reason to hope that "Egypt's burgeoning movement towards free thought and civilized debate might become a bulwark against fanaticism throughout the Arab world" on the very grounds that an Egyptian newspaper had printed Rushdie's Columbia speech. An article like this—and there were many—exemplifies some of the politics of Rushdian representation. Even tauter ligatures between book and event existed in the *Boston Globe*'s report of January 19, 1992, that high-placed government spokespersons feared that British Muslims, now two million strong, were becoming a "state within a state" over the heated controversy of *The Satanic Verses*. On July 25, Britain had expelled three Iranians suspected of wanting to assassinate the author.

In the great fear of Islam, it was unclear what exactly constituted "pressure" to free Rushdie—particularly pressure of the type that freed the American hostages in Lebanon. Was it deportation? There had been, one remembers, allegations at the time of transnational plots involving Iran in Lebanon, HAMAS in the Occupied Territories, and Egyptian revolutionaries in the first World Trade Center bombings. How can this representation of *The Satanic Verses* as a matter of state be set apart finally from the act of a Western power broker flexing muscle on behalf of a beleaguered, justifiably frightened author? This question had been raised in another way by Cynthia Ozick's odious essay in the *New Yorker* where Rushdie's emergence at a writer's conference in Paris occasioned a prolix meditation on the genetic sadism and boorishness of Islamic culture from an unrepentantly Zionist perspective.[11]

However bungled in some ways the parody of Muhammad in *The Satanic Verses* was, Rushdie's outlook had until then always been a world apart from that, but it was difficult to remember this, not least because Rushdie had begun to forget it himself. As much as *The Satanic Verses* had confused (in Agha Shahid Ali's words) "condemning fundamentalism with simply provoking it," it could only be after Rushdie's new strategy of state pressure that he would make the claim (as he did at Columbia) that the West finds "martyr-burning . . . improbable"—a claim made, it should be remembered, not long after the incendiary events in Waco, Texas, to take only one of many possible examples.[12] Nor would he have been likely to suggest that a "progressive, irreverent, sceptical, argumentative, playful and unafraid culture" can exist nowhere but in the lands of President Clinton and Prime Minister Major; nor would he have written of "mobs marching down distant boulevards baying for my blood" with its animal imagery ("baying") and its appeals to raw fear ("mob"). One had the right to reprimand Rushdie for using these resources so readily at hand and so abundantly supplied by an eager press and pro-Israeli political establishment, both of which were now dislodging him from his earlier views.

There are, in that sense, two kinds of points the decree and its aftermath should probably have raised, but generally did not. One of them occurs in a helpful and often overlooked essay by Ali Mazrui, where he concedes that the language among defenders of the fatwa who speak of "Rushdie's pornographic betrayal of ancestry" or his "treasonous" writing does not for the most part apply in the West to religious apostasy.[13] However, he points out that this very language and attitude are typically applied in the West to the religion of state—that solidly liberal dogma of the "middle way" packaged in a catechistic recitation of the benign intentions of American aid and American promise. On the matter of censorship, one might then well point to cases such as Britain's unapologetic silencing of IRA "terrorists" (or indeed, anyone even remotely connected to the IRA) or its suppression of Peter Wright's informative *Spycatcher*—examples that could easily have been expanded in the late 1980s to cases involving Muslims (as well as Arabs generally) in both the United States and Britain and which by the early 2000s had become the law of the land: ethnic profiling, persecution by the sound of one's name, summary deportations, torture, and assassination. One might counter that although censorship was originally at issue there, one was talking in Rushdie's case of something more than that: a decree of death. But here too, then as now, the Western religion of state has had its many fatwas, openly admitted and conducted with the same campaigning righteousness as that of the Iranian government—for example, the bombing runs in Libya to eliminate Muammar Qaddafi, the assassination attempts on Fidel Castro, the bombing and strafing of crowded Somali neighborhoods in order to murder Colonel Mohammed Farah Aidid, and later the drone plane assassinations in Yemen, the manhunt for Osama bin Laden, and the war on Sadaam Hussein's Iraq: only some of the better-known consequences of the Cold War shift to targeting oppressive "nationalisms" by issuing decrees of death.

Rushdie's second strategy—a *Satanic Verses* readily available to be "read and studied"—reproached the first, and did so for the simple fact that the neglected political center of the novel is a solidly social democratic demolition of Thatcherite Britain, its fatuous advertisements for a new middle class, its adventurist war in the Falklands, and its increasing police brutality and immigrant exclusionism. *This is the reading that the novel for the most part has simply not had.* The indelicacy of criticizing an author who has been condemned to death was justified if only because *The Satanic Verses* had almost from the start been a matter of state and was instrumental in mobilizing dubious forces on several sides of a multiple divide. Why was Rushdie unable to follow through on what should have been to him an obvious conclusion?

Fred Halliday in the *New Statesman and Society* gave voice to some of those "dubious forces" when he furiously regaled "the condescending rubbish produced . . . to justify attempts to silence Rushdie in the name of . . . 'understanding' the Third World"—a point repeated, in a similarly hysterical register, within postcolonial theory by a number of critics jumping on the media bandwagon.[14] Halliday's intemperance was palpable, and part of a familial intemperance shared in the affair by Christopher Hitchens, Faye Weldon, and others. To Halliday, critics of Rushdie (among them, Germaine Greer, John Berger, and Tariq Ali) were "a gaggle of windbags, fair-weather democrats and ignoramuses, unable to grasp the broader issues at stake, or besotted with some personal or parochial obsession of their own." They were "closet hooligans," "self-appointed censors," "back-seat heroes," "casual xenophobes."[15]

Surely writing this raw must perceive its target as seminal. Something particularly telling in the critique of Rushdie has set off this cascade of defensive peevishness. Could it have been, as Berger argued, that in *The Satanic Verses* there were "colonial prejudices"? that the battle for freedom of expression was not unalloyed by other, often countermanding, considerations, like the dignity and physical safety of "mobs on distant boulevards" who were dying in street demonstrations so long as the book's print run in India continued? So what freedom was served, exactly, by Rushdie's insisting that it continue to be printed in this atmosphere? Or what if the issue of human rights did not always point its accusing finger at the Islamic world? None of the reading communities, albeit for incommensurable reasons, were able to point out that the striking thing about Arabic fiction now available in the West was how consistently it failed to live up to the charges typically made against the culture of Arabic peoples: its mistreatment of women as the Third World horror of "traditional" societies, an assumption belied by what actually is found in the Arabic fiction of North Africa and the Middle East—extended studies of sexual politics whose point of entry is often the troubling image and reality of male sexual privilege, which is typically exposed and criticized with complexity and sensitivity.[16]

As a professor at the London School of Economics and an author of rightfully acclaimed books on Iran and Pakistan, Halliday did not try to fortify his position with reference to his own specialist knowledge. He must at least be thanked for that. This discretion, however, was not matched by other writers, especially within the academy, of whom some of the following comments were typical. One American-based Indian critic spoke of the "inside joke" of the number 420 in the novel, as well as the novel's generally "untranslated" and untranslatable colloquialisms, allusions, and sprinklings of choice Hindi epithets.[17] Another spoke of the "insider perspective of Rushdie's style," the "filmi slang," the "satire of Hobson Jobson."[18] Similar comments appeared widely in the journals where a territorial dispute over the valuable backlands of Rushdie's fiction had led to an exaggeration of difference in order to throw a specialist knowledge into bold relief. The point here, again, is not that these references to Islamic history or Indian popular culture are unimportant or universally accessible, only that a much more important darkness blankets this text than the ones created by missing allusions to the actor Amitabh Bachchan, the historical source of the Titlipur Ayesha, or the fact that the name Jahilia (a fictional place-name in the novel's dream sequences) means "ignorance." The number of insider references a reader needs to grasp The Satanic Verses is not large. More important, they are dwarfed by the novel's larger need to ground the reader in the look and sound of diasporic London.

The Rushdie kidnapped by the fatwa—the one who was also silenced and subverted, although this time by his protectors—was the Rushdie who had written The Satanic Verses as a novel devoted to lambasting a pretentious Western democracy of Paki-bashing policemen in the back of Black Marias, of imperialist longings for the exotic (what he is lampooning, for instance, in the

Rosa Diamond subplot of the novel set in Argentina—an allegory of the Falklands War), or the insipid commercial jingles of Thatcher's new shareholder
Britain of cheap commodities, garishly painted buses, and private ownership of
low-grade housing, all operating like a large happy face painted on the backdrop of the National Front. This novel exists in perfect symmetry with the
more publicized one whose space it shares—the one that attacked the anti-
democratic thrust of the religion of the mullahs. The failed parody of Islam is
importantly a twofold failure, it must be said, at once too obscure and too anx-
iously aware of its own ambivalence toward the very people he wanted to, but
could not, identify with.

The Rushdie of the early and mid-1980s is really the one lost in the uproar
and in need of recovery. In 1983 Rushdie had declared himself an enemy of
"nanny-Britain, straight-laced Victoria-reborn Britain, class-ridden know-
your-place Britain, thin-lipped jingoist Britain," which led him to say honorable things he could not, for tactical reasons, repeat when the affair broke out,
because he found himself relying on the British state for his bodily protection.[19] In the following passage from an essay of that time, he pretends to describe a fictional character whose name he borrows, characteristically, from a
Rod Stewart song:

> A Tory Prime Minister, Maggie May, gets elected on the basis of her
> promises to cut direct taxation and to get the country back to work
> ("Labour isn't working"). During the next four years she increases direct
> taxation and contrives to add almost two million people to the dole
> queues. And she throws in all sorts of extra goodies: a fifth of the coun-
> try's manufacturing industry lies in ruins, and (although she claims re-
> peatedly to have vanquished the monster Inflation) she presides over the
> largest increase in prices of any British Prime Minister. The country's
> housing programme grinds to a halt; schools and hospitals are closed; the
> Nationality Act robs Britons of their 900 year old right to citizenship by
> virtue of birth; . . . money is poured into the police force, and as a result
> notifiable crimes rise by 28%.[20]

The sustained fury of the passage, with its statistical overkill, leaves no doubt
about how deeply these images remained with him. They play an enormous
role in *The Satanic Verses* and, mutatis mutandis, provide the logic of his pre-
BJP (Bharatiya Janata Party) satire of Indian entrepreneurialism and Zionism
in *The Moor's Last Sigh*.[21]

More recently, the New York–transplanted Rushdie began his new sojourn abroad with the same credentials and same feisty spirit. One of his first interventions after arriving in America's cultural capital was a *New York Times* op-ed. He returns to familiar themes, but also comments on the relative badness of Hollywood films, the superiority of films produced elsewhere (China, Hong Kong, Iran, Britain) and so in the context of a threatened writers' and actors' strike, opens his piece with explicit support for unionization: "In the midst of this uncertainty [about the strike], the movie community awaits its annual festival of big business interests disguised as individual achievements." Later, after saying that Hollywood badly needs a wakeup call, he ends on a vigorous plebiscitary note: "When the world's finest filmmakers are coming after your audience, it may not be such a smart idea to shut your industry down."[22]

A crucial reading community not typically a part of the public clamor has missed this book, or turned it into its own chapters 2 and 6—the Jahilia episodes, where a specialist knowledge has a far greater field of play. If *The Satanic Verses* really had been "read and studied," what would one find? In terms of both narrative structure and sheer weight of pages, *The Satanic Verses* is principally about immigrant London; it is an "immigrant theodicy," secular in its bearings, flamboyantly syncretic rather than strictly Muslim, however one wishes to deem the Muslim treatments in it. Like most of Rushdie's novels, for example, this one casts his Muslim characters with intentional inappropriateness as Hindus experiencing (and reflecting upon) reincarnation, *the* central image of the novel. As such, it is important to ask what aims that portrayal of immigrant London sought to achieve, and on whose behalf it labored.

As an immigrant theodicy, *The Satanic Verses* sets forth a cast of characters continually exchanging their identities, merging with their others like the shifting sands of Jahilia, the immigrants' natural home. Exactly parallel to the coupling of Saleem and Shiva in *Midnight's Children*, or Iskander and Raza in *Shame*, Gibreel Farishta and Saladin Chamcha are the two that make one in Rushdie's world—the dialogue that, in a moment of fictional revelation, becomes the single mock Qur'anic "recital" of Rushdie alone as an internally divided author. To portray Rushdie, the author needed the dangerous, brilliant, famous, and unstable Gibreel as well as the unadventurous, proper, and toadying Chamcha—two aspects of the same self, a self that immigration as an almost spiritual state has made insecure, volatile, subject to revision, renewal, and self-redefinition. In the much-misunderstood dream structure of the novel, then, Ayesha the favored wife of Muhammad is also "Ayesha" the child prostitute, Ayesha as Allie Cone (Gibreel's lover), and Ayesha the fanatical Muslim girl who leads the people of Titlipur on a parody of Gandhi's march to the salt sea (another example of the Muslim *as* the Hindu in Rushdie's fiction).

One could repeat this process for most of the characters in the book. Farishta is Muhammad, the Archangel Gibreel, Shaitan, the real-life Hindi film star Amitabh Bachchan, and Azraeel, the exterminating angel. Played out this way to evoke the great dreamer Farishta's tortured mental life, there is, of course, also an implicit argument about the patterning of history, seen to be as repetitive as the designs on the border of a work of Islamic calligraphy—which is perhaps why the dreams of Farishta themselves are at once the ravings of a paranoid/schizophrenic, the calculated parodies of an immigrant trying to defend himself, memories of scenes from the sets of filmi "theologicals" that he had directed while in India, Brahma's dream of the universe, and a Qur'anic revelation. As in the allegorical levels of Dante (explicitly evoked in Rushdie's first novel, *Grimus*), all of these attributions coexist in the fake eternity of an ersatz Holy Book whose plausibility, under the rules of modernist literary form, is provided by the irreality of the mental life of its main character(s), suffering the tortured loss of identity and the descent into insanity.

The postcolonial critics who speak of "indeterminacy of meaning outside certain cultural contexts" are absolutely right, of course, provided one remembers that these indeterminacies are not always ethnic, linguistic, or national—in a word, civilizational.[23] They are also positional. In that sense, the point cannot be only the elaborate Islamic troping or the domestic Indian popular cultural allusions—both so organizationally central to the story Rushdie was striving to tell in his overt bid at a kind of crossover modernism of a nonindigenous type—but the often overlooked conditions of Rushdie's training. It was, after all, the result of a highly individual mixture of childhood memories, adolescent and early-adult accretions gained from his occasional visits home, and a deliberate (and belated) course of study carried out at Cambridge, in which the significance of Islam arrived to him (as it has for Indian and non-Indian students alike) via books. This is an important biographical detail: Rushdie's knowledge of Islam in *The Satanic Verses* was largely taken from his Cambridge essays.

To continue this sort of point, one might concede that it is not inaccurate to suggest that *The Satanic Verses* is a "love song" for an Islam that flourished in the Mughal period, although it is important not to overread this fact as dictating the overall structure of the novel.[24] The Islamic thematics of the novel are working less in the service of specific literary forms (the Urdu *ghazal*, the *dastan*, etc.) than a calculatedly irreverent reappropriation of Sufism, whose role in Rushdie's generically mixed narrative is free-floating and multidirectional, aimed at a variety of targets—among them the unquestioning devotees of the "Book" (in this novel, the Qur'an and the Bible), religious revivalism on the Subcontinent, and the very contemporary (that is, not originally Mughal) phenomenon of a politically insurgent Islamic clerisy, above all in Iran and Pakistan. To say that *The Satanic Verses* is not a novel so much as a misunderstood narrative convention drawn from the classical Muslim canon is to say too much, and to ignore the consistent (and appropriately superficial) employment by Rushdie throughout his fiction of disposable genres from a variety of traditions—although learning those traditions, and studying them independently of Rushdie's fiction is, of course, paramount in any informed interpretation.

This line of argument fudges an important fact. As anyone familiar with contemporary India knows, the romance with the Mughal period is a standard feature both at home and in the diaspora, and it is continually fed by the golden age of the Hindi cinema (particularly from the 1950s), whose frequent Mughal settings provide a ready-made repertoire of courtly splendor and aesthetic grandeur in the arts of painting, dance, song, and food. It is much more reasonable to believe that the filmic sources of Bollywood, rather than private attachments to Mughal form, were his inspirations. A certain edifice of firsthand experience is here coupled with a paralyzing challenge summoned by foreign language and broad specialist categories without regard to the contexts in which Rushdie actually used them. The proud nostalgia for the Mughal legacy in secular India also fuels Rushdie's writing, of course, even extravagantly so, but there is little mystery in it, nor does it require a native attachment, even if these shadings are missed in the (usually journalistic) readings of Rushdie as a sort of Günter Grass manqué.

Indeed, Rushdie carefully explains these references in his own essays—a characteristic act of self-interpretation that is, if not a guarantee of accessibility, at least a mild rejoinder to the kind of critic widely evident in postcolonial theory who insists upon the untranslatability of cultural dissonances while quoting Western scholars (Stanley Wolpert, H. A. R. Gibb, Laurel Steele, and others) as their own authorities. We have no more than assertions to tell us precisely why critics from India in the American and British academies are not, after all, Western; nor why critics who are not originally from South Asia must—by genetic fate apparently—"metropolitanize" their subject. Civilization displants position, and so it ceases to matter what individual critics actually know about Sufism, the Qur'an, the politics and personalities of postwar London, *mestizaje,* or the *Shahnameh*—the medieval Persian epic that provides one of the models for his early novel *Grimus.*

The point, I imagine, is whether more is at stake here than might at first appear—more than just an unworthy struggle over critical territory, the planting of one or another national (or personal) flag in authorial terrain in a gesture, as above, of cultural nationalism carried out as a critique of "nationalism" fully in concert with the vestiges of the European conquest and a resurgent American one. For the point—at least my point—is not to finesse locality, or diasporic experience, or the impasse of a missed cultural context, but precisely to underline what the nativist reading ostensibly stands for: namely, the importance of informing oneself about every aspect of a work's history, its literature, and its metaphoric import before offering theorizations about it. A surprising number of otherwise informed readings have simply not done so, and yet they have ventured forth with remarkable energy in the name of a civilizational contest heightened by the specific conjunctures I outlined at the beginning. They are the fruit of a period of renewed self-definition in an era of imperial resurgence fed by a diasporic professionalization. Filiation steps in as a substitute for a more civic and less parochial critique of empire sequestered and immobilized by a continuing Cold War criticism.

A familiar move in the nativist criticism of postcolonial studies revolves around the problem of purportedly false literary attributions. Several South Asian critics have jumped on the inevitable but shopworn subject of "magical realism" in accounts of Rushdie's fiction as though Rushdie had been misplaced once more within a literary heritage that superficially resembled his actual South Asian one.[25] It is, they imply, the kind of linkage that American or British critics rush to make, whatever the validity, since it fits in nicely with the familiar story of the Latin boom novelists and saves one from having to dig too deeply into the less accessible (to the outsider, perhaps even invisible) Eastern sources (not noticing, apparently, that the critic most associated with the linking of Rushdie to Gabriel García Márquez is Kum Kum Sangari, an Indian-based academic). The limitation of identitarian logics of these sorts—their imperviousness to textual detail—is dramatically illustrated by *Shame*'s systematic reapplication of García Márquez's plot and characters to the situation of Pakistan. Unless one believes that artistic form is unrelated to political outlook, one can see the problems this reapplication raised for Rushdie, since the condition of Latin America vis-à-vis the "nation" is so different from that of South Asia. The parodic distancing of the liberator/caudillo, Colonel Aureliano Buendía, becomes, for example, in Rushdie's Raza and Iskander, something much more desperate; what in García Márquez had been a sympathetic self-jesting in his portrayal of the foibles of village life becomes in Rushdie's account of the Baluchi separatist movement, the old canard about the "sheep-fucking" of mountain tribals. In his reviews and in his journalism, Rushdie dares not utter García Márquez's name (unlike the attention he gives to Vargas Llosa, Borges, and Jorge Amado, for example), for the reason that the parallels are revealingly close. The impropriety of transposing a specific Latin American experience to South Asia is Rushdie's, not that of the hapless Western critics targeted by the charge.

What the nativist line of argument does in essence is dance among the verbiage of contemporary Euro-theory to flesh out a familiar politics of ambivalence in order (contradictorily) to establish its indigenous South Asian valences; it casts itself in the garments of complexity and nuance, but ends by making precisely the same kind of point repeatedly. The painful necessity of this impossible attempt is to insist that Rushdie is not merely misunderstood by Western readers but, as one postcolonial critic puts it, that the very "Indianness" of Rushdie's "rethinking of Muslim public culture" places him "under the predictably hostile gaze of the West."[26] This kind of argument ups the ante considerably, shifting its claims to authenticity by wedding national-cultural identity to a specific politics. Seeking to carve a space of opposition, the argument avers that Rushdie did not merely attract the furor of Muslims for his apostasy but continued to be a feared and hated rebel against Western norms.

Actually, though, the ambivalent negotiation of cultural signifiers in Rushdie's writing—a formal option characteristic of a new international caste of intellectuals—points to a political outlook that in many ways (although not all) is comforting to emerging neocolonial arrangements emanating from within the liberal power centers of the West. Specifically, the argument obscures the decisive incommensurability of interest and outlook between the Muslim laborers of London and Rushdie himself. Rushdie has primarily concerned himself with building bridges between an English-speaking Asian middle- and upper-class readership, often in close contact with England and the United States through business and educational ties, and the enormous novel-buying public of Anglo America. The outrage among the immigrant Muslim communities would not have been so urgently felt had Rushdie been speaking only to the West. The nativist reader seems to think it requires a great leap of imagination for American critics to fathom that Rushdie is acutely interested in addressing an Indian readership, whereas it is the point of departure for the critique the nativist wishes to displace.

Nativism, it turns out, is not rectifying sources by drawing on background or contacts, but defending a political position of embattled privilege. One would never want to deny that Rushdie's enormously influential articulation of cultural translation has had the welcome effect of shaking colonialist criticism out of a two-dimensional victimology. The problem is that the very allure of his voluptuous complexities—fixed within the basically conservative figures of literature, the artistic conscience, the solitary iconoclast, and so on—has provided the means for a new caste of intellectual spokesperson working on behalf of the supposedly innate subversiveness of ethnic alterity to conceal its assimilating function. There is no such thing as "Third World literature." The phantasmagoric jumble of politics and parody that gave magical realism its multiple transnational manifestations is a mode of writing with unique appeal to metropolitan audiences, thereby submerging social realist, testimonial, *costumbrista*, and many other modes of literature found throughout the amalgam of flexible local cultures and peoples designated "Third World." Exile is a dead troping mechanism of modernism and the British novel of empire. But its ready-to-hand substitute, migrancy, does little to reinvigorate the original, although this is the goal of the nativist reading: a precise illustration of its assimilating function.

The critical focus of *The Satanic Verses* is thereby narrowed, and such a reading fails to appreciate, for example, the parallels in that novel to the Padma subplot of *Midnight's Children*. Again, those who have closely *read* his novels see in that subplot a key to what follows. It theorizes Rushdie-Saleem's anxiety about his own ambivalence toward the "people," a self-critique in which he casts himself as a protégé of the savvy, lower-class Padma who keeps interrupting him by saying he is too intellectual, too skeptical, too out of touch. The subplot parallels an aspect of *The Satanic Verses* but only in a cloaked way in the antagonism and friendship of Salman al-Farisi and Baal the satirist. If Rushdie had made a point about the adaptability of immigrants, and their tendency to try on identities in order to "turn insults into strengths," there is an aspect to the writing of these sections that are presented as strengths but that should in all justice be turned back into insults. It certainly was by many Muslim readers of the book.

Remember that Baal in the novel is a court hireling contracted by the Jahilian Grandee to satirize the village poor. His job is to practice on behalf of the state the "art of metrical slander." It is a key moment in the novel. When the novel arrives at his portrayal of the resistance of the black communities of Britain, we are introduced to their comically overweight leader, Uhura Simba (named after Tarzan's elephant?), and the fatuous deejay toaster Pinkwallah, the white black man—both vicious send-ups of British dub poetry and the sorts of popular resistance represented by Linton Kwesi Johnson, Darcus Howe, and other figures recognizable to postwar British, especially left, readers.[27] These portraits are combined with an almost unreadably condescending passage on the Afro-

British communities, an Orpheus and Eurydice parody in "Black speech," involving two lovers who work in the London Underground. One wonders why the first protests against the novel did not come from the Afro-British communities. It seems particularly depressing that one of the characters—Uriah Mosley—is given the same surname as Oswald Mosley, the 1930s leader of British fascism; a joke that, needless to say, falls flat.

From the perspective of the metropolis, there is a good deal of overlap, after all, between black people, working-class people, and the Islamic faithful. The village poor that the Jahilian Grandee first wants Baal to satirize are the water carrier Khalid, a Persian named Salman, and the black slave Bilal—the riffraff who become the Grandee's targets because they are early converts to Islam. The scene evokes a psychological truth, for Islam in the mind of many Western commentators is a religion of Semites of Arab extraction, Persians with dark eyebrows, laborers from the Punjab, and sub-Saharan blacks—the kind of people who, long before the Ayatollah posted his bounty, were demonstrating in Bradford, Detroit, and Karachi. What is Rushdie doing satirizing such people through his persona, Baal? Why is the historical Salman al-Farisi, Rushdie's namesake, the only original convert who flees, fearing the tyranny of the people defended by Islam (the former underdogs) once they have assumed power? Contrast this with his explicit statements about the novel in which he lays out clearly the position he thought he was taking toward Islam in the parody of the novel, one whose revisionist take on contemporary Islam was precisely to emphasize its originally progressive content as a looking back to a pre-Meccan (rather than pre-Islamic) culture codified in the word "nomad":

> Muhammad, an orphan himself at an early age, was in an excellent position to appreciate the way in which Meccan culture failed to care for the weak as dutifully as the nomads would have. . . . The people on whom Muhammad's word made the strongest impression were the poor, the people of the bazaar, the lower classes of Meccan society—precisely those people who know that they would have been better off under the old nomadic system. [Islam was in part] a subversive, radical movement.[28]

To say that Rushdie, in the actual performance of the novel, displayed distance from ordinary people is to make the point made glancingly by Berger when he referred rather unfairly to the novel's "arrogance"—a point that has either been savagely attacked, as Halliday has done, or (more commonly) overwhelmed by the antagonists of the other reading communities I mentioned—most of all the "naive" Muslim believers, the supposed *non*readers.

In the postcolonial academy, the two genres are often combined by dismissing the fundamentalist rabble's "failure of cultural imagination to countenance representation" at the same time that the inadequacies of non-insider readings of the book are underscored—an underscoring dramatized by Suleri in a presumptuous "open letter" to Rushdie at the close of one essay, replete with topical references to "the hill-station of Nathia Gali, which you may know."[29] She refers to a 1990 Pakistani film titled *International Guerrillas*, which others have commented upon as well—a film that stages the affair for the purpose of allowing its audience to witness Allah's righteous killing of Rushdie by movie's end. But the film's content exemplifies the weakness of her reading. For, having set up her argument to explore a formal paradox—namely, that the Pakistani faithful, seeking to censor *The Satanic Verses*, are here in effect publicizing it—she abdicates the opportunity of answering a more interesting and difficult question related to her theme of "representation." As depicted in the film poster, Rushdie wears a high-collared shirt, slicked-back hair, and sunglasses—potent images, indeed, of "Simon Rushton."

The issue, then, might be: what exactly in this representation suggests what the Pakistani (or more broadly Muslim) masses detest in Salman Rushdie? Aren't we missing the opportunity here of exploring meaning outside the stalemates of the conflict among religious hermeneuts, since this is a work, after all, of popular culture? It is this failure to imagine the desires and angers of ordinary people that links this brand of Rushdie criticism to Rushdie's own fiction, which has dealt with working-class life warmly and compassionately, but always in a comic register. His accompanying political motif—evident in his comment from *Shame* that the people, like Robespierre, "distrust fun"—has blended with these comic portraits in the most unfortunate way, and has much to do with the explosive anger that the affair produced. That reaction took by surprise only those critics who had overlooked his earlier condescensions, to the same degree that only those unaware of the blow to his social democratic sensibilities during the affair would be surprised by his warrior outbursts on behalf of U.S. imperialism in an op-ed article for the *Washington Post* in 2001 that describes the entire Iraqi village of Tikrit as a home of "homicidal criminals" and demands invasion because of Sadaam Hussein's "futile wars" and his "ruthless gang of cronies."[30]

On April 1, 1992, in the *Los Angeles Times*, Carlos Fuentes added finally another dimension to the acts of reading and misreading *The Satanic Verses*. He wrote that "Rushdie is the first victim of a religious atavism which filled the ideological void left by the end of the Cold War." Apart from the fact that the

Cold War is not over, this is a dodgy statement for other reasons and, one could argue, exactly the opposite of the case, since what is called "religious atavism" here did not arise suddenly after 1989 with the triumph of perestroika as though filling a void. It was instead, of course, the Western states that latched on to the neotraditionalism of Islamic movements as the major obstacle to globalization following the openings created by the fall of the Soviet Union—an obstacle, as well, to U.S. control of the oil fields and to Israeli geopolitical plans. Nevertheless, he forces us to ask clearly what *The Satanic Verses* has to do with the Cold War. That, I think, is a fertile question that could open up more interesting ways of reading *The Satanic Verses*. How has the criticism generated by what we could call "the *Granta* left" facilitated the climate of globalism? The record is mixed.

The Satanic Verses has to be applauded for diagnosing one of the key processes of this emergent globalism in Thatcherite Britain's rough displacing of traditional societies within domestic Britain and its creation of a new command economy whose true face can be seen in the disaster of the GATT accords. Nevertheless, much of Rushdie's writing, although pre-perestroika, had been proleptic. It was fully a part of perestroika's fervent hopes and frames of reference, as evidenced, for example, in his satire of the "magicians' ghetto" in *Midnight's Children*, aiming its humorous wrath at older but still viable forms of resistance in an India with (at the time) two states that were nominally communist—West Bengal and Kerala—and with strong trade ties to the Soviet Union. Given the current free-market open-door policy of the Indian government and what has since arisen in the form of the party of Hindu revivalism, the BJP, U.S. foreign policy toward India has decidedly warmed, not because of the decline of religious fundamentalism but because of its intensification at the expense of the Muslim communities of India. The politics and culture of the BJP are the great enemies of *The Moor's Last Sigh*, and forces of the Hindu right in Bombay attempted to suppress the novel in exactly the manner *The Satanic Verses* had been before.[31] In one of the best of his post-fatwa responses in 1990, Rushdie wrote:

> The point of view from which I have, all my life, attempted this process of literary renewal is the result not of the self-hating deracinated Uncle-Tomism of which some have accused me, but precisely of my determination to create a literary language and literary forms in which the experience of formerly colonized, still-disadvantaged peoples might find full expression.

This used to be true. The angry protests from within the community of nonliterary Islam forget that Rushdie had had little in common with those who indulged in scares over the civilizational threat of the "Islamic terrorist," even when the unhappy trajectory of debate over *The Satanic Verses* greatly strengthened the uncritical belief in Western freedom, which although real and appreciable, came predictably at the cost of a more global unfreedom to others.

Unhappily, this is no longer the case. In a climate of dangerous international tension and belligerent imperial designs, Rushdie has become a weather vane for the bellicose social democracy found in his adopted American home—progressive on domestic social issues but all caricature when staking out the enemy. Islam—*tout court*—in Rushdie's new view stands against "freedom of speech, a multi-party political system, universal adult suffrage, accountable government, Jews, homosexuals, women's rights, pluralism, secularism, short skirts, dancing, beardlessness, evolution theory, sex." According to Rushdie, one is no longer supposed to wonder whether the demonstrations in support of Osama bin Laden have anything to do with decades of U.S. occupation and humiliation. The universal answer to "chaos" is what he calls, in an embarrassing oxymoron, a U.S. peacekeeping force.[32] All of these positions have moved him very far from that of former British friends and allies like Harold Pinter and John Le Carré. If the evolution of Rushdie's public persona is more clearly understandable in the framework of professional pressures than diasporic insights (his need, that is, to find a space in the op-ed columns of the New York establishment, which considers itself at war), then it is also true that his adopted model for this reincarnation as immigrant cheerleader for the home team is more Christopher Hitchens than Gibreel Farishta. Finding his place in the latest right turn of the *Granta* Left, Rushdie is not abroad at all. Politically and professionally, he is at home. It is a matter of close reading to recognize that.

CHAPTER 3

HUMANISM,
PHILOLOGY, AND IMPERIALISM

THE HISTORY OF EDWARD SAID's *Orientalism* is already slipping away, the current legends are now firmly established, but some basic questions have still not been posed. With the book's twenty-fifth anniversary behind us, we might well ask: did *Orientalism*—as received opinion seems to be—launch a new scholarly field known as "postcolonial studies"? That the response has to be "no" is one that few are prepared to hear. Supporters and critics alike are unified around the understanding that *Orientalism* has created that field. What I argue below, then, has to be more than the reading of a book, since it involves a question with somewhat higher stakes and far-reaching associations than *Orientalism*'s meaning. One of these certainly (although it may seem at first glance digressive) is what the writing of Michel Foucault and other poststructuralists has to do with Edward Said.[1]

To answer these questions means to place *Orientalism* in its worldliness, by which I do not mean its global reach or supposedly transgressive crossing of borders—as the word "worldly" is often used—but rather its materiality, its self-positioning within institutions. This is the way, I would argue, that Said himself used it. What *Orientalism* came to symbolize militated against this positioning and prevented many of the important interests of new academic work on the history of colonialism from reaching a wider public. Many of those addressed by the book, after all, were general readers rather than academics. Others toiled in academic disciplines like history and anthropology where "postcolonial studies" came into being under other names, and without any claim to being a distinct subspecialty or field, as it did in English departments. My opening questions, which are intertwined, can be defended if for no other reason than that Said's *authority* has been from the outset both literary and academic. His entry into other spheres was launched in a series of complex arguments about the scope of humanism in literary criticism. My interest is to explore how that activity might be understood in a way that accords with Said's actual practice, which I take to be neither "idealist utopian" (as some Marxist theorists have called it) nor recuperable within familiar poststructuralist formulae.[2]

The first issue has to be the degree to which the success of *Orientalism* prepared the ground for postcolonial studies. It is important, first of all, to understand postcolonial studies not as a discrete subliterary field but a collection of attitudes and styles of inquiry arising in a variety of disciplines more or less simultaneously, including anthropology, geography, international studies, history, English, comparative literature, and music. At both ends of the spectrum of *Orientalism*'s reception this issue seems to have been settled long ago. Within specialized studies of language and literature as well as in the more catholic sort of criticism found in middlebrow journalism—and then again among the book's enemies in area studies and the media—there is agreement on one point at least: *this* book produced *that* field.

In my discussion of why I find this view untrue, I concede that Said himself was, at least publicly, a generous critic, quick to defend himself and others against assaults on various expressions of postcolonial studies. In the essay "East Isn't East," for example, he applauds some of the work going under its name as being "connected in its general approach to a universal set of concerns, all of them relating to emancipation" and maintains that one of its leading motifs has been "the consistent critique of Eurocentrism and patriarchy."[3] Although they find themselves inimical to postcolonialism in general, various left critics have also conceded as much. In other words, there is no desire on my part to establish that Said exhibited a simple hostility toward the predominant trends in research on the non-Western, even if his relationship to that research has been misrepresented in frustrating ways. Said's intellectual lineages have not received anything like the attention they should have, which has, among other things, led to misunderstandings among both the champions of postcoloniality and those materialist critics who consider postcoloniality an idealizing, neocolonial professionalism (Bryan Turner, Samir Amin, and others).

As a way of launching this discussion of lineages, I would like to begin with an unlikely premise. In spite of Said's public persona as a Palestinian spokesman, *Orientalism* is a profoundly American book. It could not have been written anywhere but the United States, and its legacy is fused, or confused, with an American national culture that is particularly impervious to what the book is saying. To call the book American is also, of course, to raise the issue of the authentically Third World dimension of the postcolonial intellectual as a way of probing the sensitive issue of metropolitan spokesmanship so caustically pursued in Aijaz Ahmad's *In Theory* as well as in other texts. But that is not my emphasis for the moment, although I will consider it briefly below. I am here underlining, by contrast, the special resistance in the United States to *Orientalism*'s moods and styles by pointing to the wedge that has been driven between the text and the public image, the lessons and the uses, of *Orientalism*.

The typical grouping of *Orientalism* with Said's poetical testimonies of Palestinian longing (*After the Last Sky*, 1986), or his interviews and conjunctural essays on Palestinian identity and Zionist politics, or the books that complete the trilogy of *Orientalism* (1978)—*The Question of Palestine* (1979) and *Covering Islam* (1981)—is primarily due to sensibilities that have arisen through postcolonial studies itself: the assumed identitarian allegiances underlying *Orientalism*'s subject matter.[4] But the problems with assigning *Orientalism* this position become most evident when examining the work that immediately followed the trilogy itself—*The World, the Text, and the Critic*. This volume reconciled the past with the present and forecast a line of argument that continued for more than two decades. Published in 1983, the volume was by no means a departure. It localized *Orientalism*'s themes, although now in the form of a collection of essays on problems of literary theory, the politics of the university, and the "treason" of intellectuals working in the United States.[5]

The World, the Text, and the Critic is tightly bound up with *Orientalism*, and has a special relationship to it. The collection brought together not only the outtakes of *Orientalism* (the chapters in the latter book on Islam and philology, on Louis Massignon, and on Raymond Schwab, for example, were clearly written for inclusion in the former) but also the essays "Reflections on American 'Left' Literary Criticism," "Secular Criticism," "Roads Taken and Not Taken in Contemporary Criticism," and "Traveling Theory"—all of them elaborating the mass psychology of a peculiar brand of American messianic beneficence and naiveté, the emphasis, after all, of *Orientalism*'s final chapter, "Orientalism Now." It seems significant that whereas "Traveling Theory" has been given its share of attention by the American critical community, "Secular Criticism" and "Reflections on American 'Left' Literary Criticism" have had less resonance here. Another essay from the volume, "Criticism Between Culture and System" (his original title, incidentally, for the volume as a whole), has been slighted to a degree that scandalously affects the interpretation of Said's work.

The Saidian persona, then, both as inheritance and as self-creation, has frequently been misinterpreted. His multilingual background was, after all, ambiguous. The entire first half of his career was characterized by a willing and untroubled assimilation; his childhood and early schooling in Lebanon, Palestine, and Egypt gave way to a gentlemanly privilege in Ivy League venues that was no less instrumental in constructing his identity (just as it was decisive in giving him tools to speak). Commentators on Said's work in the United States consequently miss his understanding of "home," which is far less literal than positional, less filiative than political. Exile for him was apart from everything else also about ideas and opinions, which is why he speaks approvingly at one point about the "executive value of exile," which some writers have been "able to turn into effective use" (WTC, 8). The personal accidents of life affect understanding, of course, but Said was particularly eager to insist that they do not constitute positions. Nor was the opposite the case. Ideological positionings are not immune from the repugnant inflexibilities of a solidarity reminiscent of those bonds formed by conditions of birth. In this vein, rejecting the systems, as he put it, of "Northrup Frye [and] Foucault," Said once observed that even affiliative (which is to say, ideological or positional) structures are dangerous when they "more or less directly reproduce the skeleton of family authority. . . . The curricular structures holding European literature departments make that perfectly obvious" (WTC, 23).

The entire matrix of meanings we associate with " 'home,' belonging, community," he further argued, is intimately bound up with the "assurance, confidence, the majority sense" necessary for the "power of the State" (WTC, 10–11). This is a very characteristic Saidian move. Home refers not only to a site of origin but also to the comfort of belonging among those of the same social outlooks and opinions in a sublime national-cultural conformity. What he meant to do here, among other things, was to reject deliberately the Third World authority accorded him as exilic Palestinian while conceding his privileged status in the America he criticized precisely as an insider, albeit from a special perspective. He also explored the compelling need in an era of sectarian resurgence and nationalist manias "to produce new and different ways of conceiving human relationships" (17). His point, however, was not what today is called transnationalism—given that he continued to believe in the necessity of national movements—but to flee sectoral categories altogether.[6]

> [The intellectual is a] wanderer, going from place to place for his material, but remaining a man essentially *between* homes. . . . Such notions as "exteriority" and "in-betweenness" . . . do not refer to a sort of fellow-

traveling critical eclecticism. Rather, they describe a transformation that has taken place in the working reality of the self-conscious writer.[7]

This shifting of the locational (being) to the positional (believing or knowing) is found throughout Said's work.

The American contexts of *Orientalism*'s composition arrest one immediately while rereading *The World, the Text, and the Critic*—a book that deals with much of the fallout that *Orientalism* produced, and the first that expanded upon, rather than simply filled out or continued, its concerns. Whatever else *Orientalism* might have said about the imaginative violence of European portrayals of Middle Eastern and North African cultures, its meanings arose by way of a sustained examination of individual philologists. What is being examined, among other things, in *The World, the Text, and the Critic* is the contradictory legacies of philology in the contemporary moment, one having to do with humanist sweep and public action, another having to do with the compilation of data and a withering technique marshaled on behalf of a critical order that Said portrays as all but Masonic.[8] In *The World, the Text, and the Critic*, many of the themes and much of the language (Schwab's "ingenuously obvious motif[s]" and his privileging of "historical moments, and large movements of ideas," are taken directly out of *Orientalism*. Only now they are placed alongside essays of surprising anger, which even at times rise to the level of wholesale dismissal of aspects of American literary theory. These essays stress, for example, the alarming religious turn in American criticism during the Reagan/Thatcher years, when (in Said's words) the "private and hermetic" took prominence "over the public and social," and where graduate students under the banner of the Left propounded "camouflaging jargons" while revealing a "haphazard anecdotal content enriched neither by much knowledge of what politics and political issues are all about nor by any very developed awareness that politics is something more than liking or disliking some intellectual orthodoxy" (*WTC*, 292, 26, 172). As someone who studied with Said in these years, I took his comments then, and do now, as a direct accusation against academic theory.

This can be put another and clearer way: *The World, the Text, and the Critic* examines the same social and political function of contemporary American criticism that *Orientalism* does in nineteenth-century Europe. The circuits of power that are traced in *Orientalism* between public and political figures like Disraeli and orientalists of formidable detailed, literary bent like Edward Lane are respectively captured in the relationship between the current-events media study *Covering Islam* and the more academic and literary *The World, the Text, and the Critic.* The complexities of the relationship involving government and fourth-estate intellectuals, on the one hand, and the academy, on the other, are now greater and more mediated—subjects that need to be treated over the expanse of entire books.

In *The World, the Text, and the Critic,* both the outtakes of *Orientalism* on philologists like Schwab and the more immediate commentaries on criticism at the present time have a common end. Despite the ways in which many admirers have interpreted him, when Said invokes the concept of secular criticism, for example, it is not primarily Middle East sectoral politics that he has in mind—not, at least primarily, Islamic or Jewish extremism. He is thinking about the emergence of an oppressive theoretical Americana—one so pervasive that it formed an epochal backdrop to a whole way of thinking, and as such went unrecognized. Those who nod toward Said while invoking the concept of secular criticism in response, say, to the Rushdean fatwa, are not wrong, but they have overlooked a vital element of the term's original usage. With some guardedness, it is in the essays of *The World, the Text, and the Critic* that he sets out to portray a mental landscape of imperial resurgence at the dawn of Reaganism as well as a situation in which critics were cramping the scope of intellectual life, a later example being the eventual reception of *Orientalism* in the spirit of a postcolonial nativism quite at odds with his purpose in writing it. Although few understood his words this way, his target in these essays was poststructuralist "science" seen as substitute religion with its own codes of enlistment, conversion, and mystification.[9] In this way he revisited *Orientalism's* analysis of that thoroughly European problematic, the sublation of religion and technics, a problematic continually shadowed by the triumph of reason implicit in Europe's tireless war on a conveniently ageless and resilient Islam.

By targeting poststructuralism, he did no more here than recall his own earlier arguments against the "science" of high humanism. He was frankly returning to the problem described in those passages of *Orientalism* that examined the fatal methodological borrowing by the philologist Ernest Renan from the naturalist Georges Cuvier. Those passages prepare one to understand many of his emphases in *The World, the Text, and the Critic.* As described in *Orientalism,* the result of Renan's affection for Cuvier had been what Renan tellingly, and damningly for Said, called "*la science exacte des choses de l'esprit* ("an exact science of all matters of the spirit [of cultural facts]")"[10] In ways that the American theoretical community was unprepared to fathom, Said was saying something rather subtle and unexpected: despite its assault on humanist mustiness with its arrogant Enlightenment grandeur, theory had assumed an uncomfortable resemblance to Renan. What Said in the collection repeatedly dubs the slavish attitude of American critics to their French sources had given way already (in his words) to a "secular priesthood" in the "era of scientific intelligence" (*WTC*, 173).

Here is the point at which I have to depart from Said's most compelling critical interlocutor of the 1980s and 1990s, Paul Bové, whose brilliant writing on the situation of theory and what he calls the "modern genealogists" specifically took up an older humanism in light of the American conservative turn.[11] With a good deal of supporting citation, he quite reasonably points to the characterization of theory in the 1980s as a "threat to civilization" by extremists in the National Association of Scholars and certain government spokespeople. Bové's objective is to show that theory's critical edge provided a redoubt for radicals during a suffocating neoliberal resurgence—one for which the belletrists and New Critics were the logical allies: "the cultural agents of Reaganism were and still are often the same as the 'anti-theory' agents within the universities and the media."[12] These views I would argue do not go far enough, as Bové himself suggests elsewhere.[13] In the early 1980s and thereafter, Said is arguing that theory is not the foil but the adjunct of American conservatism—its manifestation in a different realm, closer to home. This observation does not, of course, contradict the fact that many anti-theory stalwarts in the university were political conservatives, although I believe it much more accurate to say that the majority were on the liberal left—populists who disparaged theory for its infatuation with anything Continental and for its elitism (criticisms very different from Said's, or mine). Said goes on to declare that the state's desire to neutralize our "technical skill as critics and intellectuals" was succeeding by virtue of the critics' abdication of responsibility; that intellectuals in the 1980s were conducting cultural inquiry (as he puts it) without "genuine historical research" and without the goal of "understanding, analyzing, and contending with the management of power and authority within the culture" (*WTC*, 173).

In short, in and through the particular way theory was being practiced, American critics had begun to assume the status of state functionaries, although decidedly without portfolio. However much Said had cast Raymond Williams and Antonio Gramsci in a language of negotiation with a left humanism that hardly accords with either Williams's socialism or Gramsci's communism—taking terms like "territory" and "maneuver" to applaud the latter's suppleness and lack of dogma, for instance—Said nowhere violates their important emphases on specifically *state* power, an emphasis quite out of step with literary-theoretical trends then as now, which seek the "dissemination" of the state into a more manageable micropolitical realm. Despite the claim from the left that Said had simply appropriated socialist theorists for eclectic insertion in another mode of reading, it was rather the case that theorists like Gramsci and Williams (as well as anti-colonial intellectuals like C. L. R. James and Frantz Fanon) moved Said elsewhere, further toward the more deliberately materialist categories of *Culture and Imperialism*, which is inspired to emphasize imperialism's control of territory and conquest of land rather than its control over the locational spaces of discourse—*Orientalism*'s obvious focus.[14] Although not usually seen in this way, Said was borrowing from the political sensibilities of social democracy and the political legacies of the anti-colonial era.[15]

Today's graduate students cannot know—and others will not remember—how defining the early 1980s were for those with Said's sympathies. He was not alone in sensing a shift of depressing and far-reaching dimensions in which a newly emboldened far right wing began to permeate government and the popular sphere, and where a social democratic common sense was pushed to the margins as a lunatic fringe. This was the atmosphere in which Said happened to portray the development of theory in the United States, granting its achievements and its often honorable powers of conception but stressing also the fruit of its political instincts for a revolt that was, in his opinion, a submission. This is not the sort of dissent usually associated with Said's work, which is much more commonly thought to be about the stinging slights suffered by foreign professionals in the field of civilizational identity, or about larger, ultimately racial, constructs implicit in the term orientalism.

Enter postcolonial studies, which, on the face of it, had seemed to take up Said's critique in *Orientalism* for the purpose of realizing it in a comprehensive way and across an entire range of subjects and styles. In addition to its institutional forms, the significance of postcolonial studies could be found also in its interstitial effects. Apart from welcome changes in curricula and in hiring practices, the postcolonial moment gave writers and intellectuals who personally or by family lineage came from outside the United States or Europe a featured place on speakers lists and in opinion columns. It involved a new marketability for the arts of Africa, Latin America, and the Indian Subcontinent. There were important, and even progressive, achievements in academic and educational practice, which reached well outside the university. This is one of the arguments for rereading Said, the public intellectual, in this context, since the identitarian aspects of postcolonial studies, rather than the imperial-political ones, found a place not only in the graduate seminar room but in the program notes of local theater companies, church sermons, feature articles in *Rolling Stone*, and the VJ banter on MTV. The postcolonial and the multicultural would soon coalesce in what is now called the global, although its general process of outreach would allow both to keep their distinctive labels governing separate territories: foreign intellectuals on the one hand, U.S. ethnic minorities on the other.

Clearly, then, the prima facie case for seeing postcolonial studies as an extension rather than a departure from *Orientalism* is strong. But there are initial problems in doing so, and they are traditionally American. A colloquial version of postcolonial studies found in the newspapers was easily translated into ready-to-hand ideas about American pluralism. To that degree, the feeling of embattlement by foreign or minority professors and graduate students did not precisely fit the warm welcome given otherness in these years. Added to that were the very rules for inclusion that theory had, as it were, drawn up and made available. The racial and political as distinct from the phenomenological other were being spliced together as though they were the same thing, and in a manner that was simply unacceptable to Said—or acceptable only if one took account of the radical difference between coercion, imprisonment, and segregation, on the one hand, and perception of self and non-self, on the other.[16] The perceived unfitness of issues like imprisonment or military occupation for theory, in the sense that there was little of apparent interest in such brute contests to theorize, had been for Said a theoretical problem of de facto silence and evasion, although his ameliorative and broadly inclusive style of presentation often muffled this criticism. He returned to the critique repeatedly, at any rate. It was a problem, as I have been saying, that he deliberately took up in *The World, the Text, and the Critic*. The imperial subject annexed by the phenomenological other became in academic practice an alleviating substitute that violated a certain demand for frankness, for a contestatory witness, on behalf of which *Orientalism* had in its own way been struggling. Although Said could not have known this at the time, this slippage was part of what I have been exploring in this book as the Heideggerian turn. The full-blown rhetoric of warring forces is what Said attempts in *Culture and Imperialism*.[17]

There is no space here to dwell on the complicated trajectory of Said's career in general, or (especially) the contradictory role this book plays in his work. Suffice it to say that it is ironic that *Culture and Imperialism* has been taken by some to be his definitive statement on literature, for it does not measure up to other books in his oeuvre. Apart from rehearsing his early-career arguments less forcefully, the book never explores the extensive literature available on imperialism as a cultural and economic complex, and it even goes so far as to state (quite inaccurately) that no one before him had examined the relationship of culture to imperialism. Whereas elsewhere he adopts a language of non-closure as a form of resistance to system and to avoid pre-fabricated debates, his language in *Culture and Imperialism* sidesteps the difficult task of working through the real conflicts that had been papered over by more than a decade of obtuse and circumlocutory language. In a concessionary gesture very much at odds with his bracing tone in *The World, the Text, and the Critic*, he repeatedly indulges in the pious "two superpowers" language of the Cold War (an unconvincing stance, needless to say, during the first U.S. invasion of Iraq, when the book was written, and just after the official fall of communism). Not coincidentally, his assessments of theory take on a very different, almost uncritical, resonance, as if compelled to pay homage to the hegemony of the times, particularly evident in the decade of the 1990s (see *CI*, 57 especially).

But if these claims I am making are true, what of the forceful presence in Said's early work of Michel Foucault, which would imply a much less distanced view toward poststructuralist theory in the Said of the late 1970s and early 1980s? Not only in the university but in a variety of urban-underground or freelance intellectual enclaves, Foucault had been undeniably central to the formation of what I am calling the postcolonial tendency. Indeed, the French theorist attained this stature by way of a perceived Saidian Foucault, who seemed indisputably real following Said's panegyrics to him in *Beginnings*, as well as the critical common sense surrounding *Orientalism* itself, whose titular subject was, in Said's own rendering, a discursive construct—a "notion of discourse" (3). Said's densely detailed survey of vast institutional histories reminds one at once of the genealogical method of the Foucauldian/Nietzschean archive. Admittedly, it is easy to hear in the way *Orientalism* handles the words "power" and "history" an allusion to Foucault, an intellectual for whom Said had an understandably high regard both in *Beginnings* and in his testimony published in the journal *Raritan* following Foucault's death in 1984. In fact, most of the opponents and supporters of Edward Said have once again been united in the view that the concept orientalism in the book *Orientalism* played itself out as an epochal skirmish over Foucauldian power/knowledge.

But *Orientalism* is not Foucauldian, and the consequences of that fact are significant.[18] Many, of course, never took Said to be intellectually close to Foucault, and for them my argument will to that degree hardly come as news. Several friends and associates among scholars and activists from Asia and the Middle East, for example (such as Eqbal Ahmad), or those in the sizable wing of more traditionally humanist literary scholarship drawn to Said because of his sheer love of reading (such as Richard Poirier) show that the misapprehension I am referring to is not universal. Their Said was never Foucauldian. But one has to concede that the theoretical basis of postcolonial studies as practiced in the United States and in Britain—the one Said is said to have founded—is predominantly (although of course not exclusively) Foucauldian.[19] If the essays of Homi Bhabha clearly drew their orientation from Derrida and de Man, and if the work of Gayatri Chakravorty Spivak was an idiosyncratic mixture of Derrida and a textualized Marx—although this may only be a way of saying a Derridean Marx—the greatest influence, theoretically speaking, on the postcolonial tendency of the mid-1980s to the mid-1990s has been that of Foucault.

This was the case not only because (apart, perhaps, from *The Order of Things*), Foucault had the methodological feel of a more traditional sort of intellectual history and was therefore easier to adapt than Derrida or Lacan to fields like geography, history, and anthropology, but also because there were several early texts that applied Foucault convincingly to the postcolonial problematic, and did so across disciplinary boundaries in widely read studies. One thinks here, for example, of Michel de Certeau's *Heterologies* (1986), whose final chapters are dedicated to Foucault; or Gilles Deleuze and Félix Guattari's *Kafka: Towards a Minor Literature* (1985) where Foucault's guiding hand is testified to in key lengthy footnotes; or in James Clifford's influential crossover texts, *Writing Culture* (1984, coedited with George Marcus) and *The Predicament of Culture* (1987), the second of which contains the notable review of *Orientalism* as a failed Foucauldian imitation.[20] Nor does this begin to get at the rising influence of New Historicism, particularly via the work on the colonial encounters of early modernity by Stephen Greenblatt, whose famous confession on methodology pits Foucault against Marx, with Foucault the victor.[21] The influence of Lacan would be extensive also, but his influence took much longer to develop as it traveled through feminism and film studies, primarily, and found its expression in the postcolonial field by the early 1990s in work that brought the gaze and identity construction into union with a consubstantial racial other. However, the major source of Foucault's influence on postcolonial studies has been—and precisely for all the paradoxical reasons I have mentioned— Said's *Orientalism*, although an *Orientalism* that Said did not write.

The misunderstandings were not entirely negative, nor were the misreadings always unproductive. But objectively and programatically, Said's particular capacities for bridging the typically separate realms of the public and academic, the Eastern and Western, the belletristic and the sociological, made him a crucial ally for ushering in a mode of criticism with at least some welcome consequences. Without Said's prominence, his prolific writing, and (not least) his effective personal presence as a speaker, the process of breaking from an Anglocentric parochialism and moving toward more unsettling and linguistically diverse kinds of intellectual influence would not have proceeded as inexorably as it did. Obviously, what produced the theoretical turn, on the one hand, and the postcolonial moment, on the other (not to mention the conflation of the two) involved much larger and more complicated forces than those entailed by one man's career. Indeed, that is the underlying point of my argument. But given Said's combined authority as literary amateur *and* proponent of anti-colonial liberation in Palestine, the Foucauldian Said—however imaginary—did provide reasons for talented and resourceful younger scholars with a taste for the political to see a side of the French theorist that Said, somewhat tendentiously, sought to emphasize in his own early writing: one that popularized critiques of the West and placed literary critics themselves as credible arbiters of political value by virtue of the role of language in power.

Foucault, then, remains the obvious methodological link between *Orientalism* as a text and postcolonial studies as a field. Indeed, in a simple chronological sense, the relationship appears at first to be causal. Following the book's appearance in 1978, the texts that today make up the field began to appear, often citing Said as their inspiration.[22] Of course, studies of imperialism and culture were widely evident before Said's important intervention. The anni mirabiles of such work remain not the 1980s but the 1960s and early 1970s, where new ethnic and women's studies programs were built out of thin air and where much of the writing from the colonial world, writing on black liberation and imperialism, institutional critiques of cultural imperialism, media penetration, and "development," was either published for the first time, or first translated into English. The very luxury of having a tradition to improve upon or complain about in the 1980s was the work of the 1960s. It changed the debate in a much more abrupt and radical way than occurred in the academy of subsequent decades.

Within that perspective, it is easier to recall that several of the writers from these older traditions of cultural/imperial critique had been invoked by Said as early as *Beginnings* (a work of the mid-1970s, published in the year the Vietnam War officially ended) and, according to Said, they had been among his chief inspirations in the writing of *Orientalism*: Theodore Roszak, Noam Chomsky, Gabriel Kolko, Louis Kampf, Herbert Marcuse, William Appleman Williams, Bertrand Russell (see *Beginnings,* 374, 378). As oddly dissonant as this grouping seems, given our retrospective judgments about the kind of book *Orientalism* is, Said mentions these writers not once but several times in the final passages of *Beginnings,* particularly Chomsky, who arises again in the opening pages of *Orientalism* (11). In dealing with the problematic relationship of *Orientalism* to the outpouring of studies of imperialism and culture both before and after its publication, one has to recognize that the significance of the post-*Orientalism* 1980s is not the creation of a new field dedicated, for the first time, to the colonial problematic, but that a certain kind of imperial/ideological study—largely Foucauldian—became academically respectable. A constellation had gathered force, achieving critical mass by the late 1980s, its members bowing to *Orientalism* as their lead and commenting on the effective gloss on Foucault that the book seemed to provide.

This consensus, I am arguing, is deeply misconceived. Said had often enough commented publicly in the early 1980s that in writing *Orientalism* he had most in mind Raymond Williams—especially Williams's *The Country and the City*. But that sort of evidence would be unconvincing if it were not for the transitional quality, once again, of *The World, the Text, and the Critic*. Apart from offering a retrospective display of the full array of Said's interests and positions up to that point, it contained the transitional essay "Criticism Between Culture and System," which demythifies and demotes the work of Derrida and Foucault for an American audience while attempting to revise the penultimate chapter in *Beginnings*, titled "Abecedarium Culturae," an essay that is structurally identical to "Criticism Between Culture and System." Both are lengthy readings of the twin pillars of the Franco-American theoretical establishment. In the revisionist, or later, essay, he allowed skepticism and at times open rejection to replace his earlier qualified praise.

He returns to these two crucial thinkers for precisely the reasons outlined elsewhere in the volume and to which I have alluded above—namely, with the objective of stemming the drift of postcolonial theory as he saw it developing, or at the very least to clarify what he had tried to argue in *Orientalism* but that had not fully come across. This is not to say that there was no praise for Derrida and Foucault in *Beginnings*—nor, indeed, in *The World, the Text, and the Critic* itself—or that he did not thank them for their successful demonstration of the inadequacies of an unexamined humanist core knowledge, for their helpful attentiveness to linguistic details, or for their generous archival reach. And yet it is astounding that over and over again, from the overviews on postcolonial studies published in the *Sunday Times Magazine* and the *Chronicle of Higher Education* to more-scholarly analyses by Clifford and Dennis Porter, Said's counter-Foucauldian demur, his balanced conclusions based on a cautious, and finally emphatic, departure from the work of that French thinker have been passed over as though they could not really have meant what they said or as if they had not existed at all.[23] This, one could say, was a locus classicus of the hermeneutic violence I referred to in the preface. We indeed had the unintentional self-parody of Clifford's review of *Orientalism*, in which he shakes his head in disapproval at Said's failure to live up to his Foucauldian promise, citing those passages in which Said had inexplicably lapsed into humanist vagaries and materialist totalizations. What he (and from a very different point of view, Porter) cited as inconsistencies were the very items that the mood of the time dictated they would miss.

But this surely is an argument that Foucauldians will quickly seize upon as cutting both ways. The late millennial *episteme*, if we are to take the concept seriously, may only be said to have provided a setting of a linguistic will to truth from which Said vainly sought to extricate himself. The logic of intertextuality dictates in advance (according to this option) that a Foucauldian *Geist* haunts *Orientalism*'s every line according to a historical grammar—rendering heroic improvisation a self-deluding exercise. Said himself, I believe, would not try to deny the inescapability of such a riposte to the argument I am laying out here, so long as one unjustifiably accepted the terms of Foucault's own theories sui generis. If they happened not to, then it would not be the unyielding logic of the *episteme* but an ideological movement that was at issue, and as such a contestable one—a point Said without defensiveness, and with the full weight of the Vichian traditions behind him, had been developing since *Beginnings*.

In that book Said first announced his desire to make the early-eighteenth-century Italian humanist Giambattista Vico his point of departure, the person through whom he would reorient comparative literature and change the (to him) fatal directions of theory. Apart from being a not-so-subtle riposte to structuralism's death of the author and Foucault's emphasis on the determinations of discourse, the concept of "beginnings" as "will and intention" was—through Vico himself—a confident rejection of the entire Cartesian enterprise against which was emphasized history as making, understanding, and rewriting, and "novelty" as the emulation of the significant lives of worthy predecessors. Descartes was, to Vico (as to Said) the perfect twin embodiment of French philosophical idealism and a suspect scientistic methodology based on pure deductive reasoning that took little account of the messy stages of the development of peoples, their phases of culture, and the real-life pressures of political institutions. In other words, what Said means to say is that he identifies with Vico's struggle against the lonely ego of mathematical rationalism that leads, after so many twists and turns, to the Cartesianism (and now Spinozism) rampant in contemporary theory. In short, he is to Vico what "theory" is to Descartes, and Vico's "new science"—the science of history—was antipathetic to a notion of originality as rupture. It is interesting, in this respect, to see how vigorously Descartes' contemporary (and, with some important exceptions, his *semblable*) Spinoza, has lately been taken on as the principal theoretical resource for those involved in resuscitating the project of theory. One can only see it as proleptic that Said would have embraced the work of Vico, who appreciated Spinoza's radical undermining of official religious dogmas but who also recoiled from his syllogistic proofs equating God with the material world. In this respect, Vico argued that "neither the Epicureans who consider God to be exclusively material, nor the Stoics, who in this respect were the Spinozists of their day, and make God an infinite mind, subject to fate, in an infinite body were capable of properly conceiving, let alone upholding, law, institutions, and politics."[24] Vico, every bit as much a revolutionary as Spinoza, nevertheless disparaged the mechanistic purity of his ordered rational vision, complaining at one point that Spinoza "speaks of the commonwealth as if it were a society of traders."

Despite theory's claim to sophistication in regard to the utterance, Said had long argued that theory does "not seem to be interested as much as I would like in the sheer semantic thickness of a literary text," which is evident only by involving oneself in history, anthropology, political theory, and the conditioning forces of one's time and place.[25] He felt there was no reason to be overly impressed (as the default position then was) by Foucault's Nietzchean epistemological audacity of proposing that all evidence is simply a ruse, or that the will to truth is less the desire to discover truth than to present as truth what one simply wills to be true. Said's painstaking procedure had been to remind his 1980s audience that intellectual history had staked out diverse positions in regard to agency and evidence, even if the lineage he occupied had been lately assaulted by de Man and others as a hopelessly infantile or irrevocable past. For its part, the evidence in this argument of mine is of two types: what Said is on record as saying about his work and what the work internally shows.

The inconsistencies cited by Porter and Clifford were nothing of the kind. They were rather careful repudiations misunderstood by those who approached the work within a peculiar and dominant frame that I have been calling the turn. This is made clear in the last chapter of *Beginnings* on Vico. Again, the terrain was very different in the period between 1975 and 1983 than it is now. Foucault is for him still a marginal presence, ignored by the profession as a whole—a profession that is, for its part, locked in a sterile formalism: "Some notable omissions from the anthologies indicate this prevailing idealist and antimaterialistic bias. Michel Foucault is scarcely to be found, although more recently he has become a cult figure in his own right" (*WTC*, 148).[26] As a whole, his commentary forms the territory Said was staking out against theory—at least the religion of the self that many were beginning to put forth in the early 1980s under Foucault's name, marking what was perhaps a shift in Foucault's own later work from a primary focus on "power" to the "self" in, for example, the *History of Sexuality* (particularly volume 2).[27] A politics of the body is an entirely different thing from a disembodied power, and Said abreacted to the quietism and evasion of Foucault's supercilious self—the only response Foucault was able to devise against what he portrayed as an impervious and all-penetrating rule. Since Foucault's theory jettisoned any notion of meaningful political agency, he was little more in Said's book than a "scribe of power." These views—already pronounced, although unrecognized, in the immediate aftermath of *Orientalism*—became more and more emphatic in Said as the years went by, cropping up in informal conversation as well as in interviews and essays.[28] *The World, the Text, and the Critic*, one could say, was, among other things, Said's declaration that literary theorists had gotten *Orientalism* wrong.

Even the admiration for Foucault in *Beginnings* was a highly qualified one, and it took place in a decidedly different academic environment. In 1975, of course, the project was to open up the theoretical field, breaking out of an academic atmosphere in which Kenneth Burke and Northrup Frye represented the theoretical avant-garde. The burden of Said's argument was similar to that of Raymond Williams's at Cambridge—namely, to make a persuasive appeal to an Anglocentric professoriate by arguing that not all Continental philosophy was obtuse or irrelevant. The glowing, at times quite excessive, praise he showers on Foucault in *Beginnings* must be seen with these objectives in mind. His arguments here, at any rate, are attempts to recuperate a side of Foucault that he felt slipping away in his American reception.

By contrast, indeed, one is struck by Said's distance toward a theory of the discursive regime even here. Rhetorically, "Abecedarium Culturae" is much like a third-person chronicle as told by a foreign correspondent who seeks to translate a stranger's utterances for the bewildered villager. That is, it is an ideal representation of all that Foucault can be meant to mean to Said in his programmatic turn toward contemporary philology and historicism as outlined in the opening chapters of *Beginnings*. Said goes out of his way to note in parenthetical asides his nonmembership in the developing coterie of what would soon afterward be known as "poststructuralism" or simply "theory." Calling Foucault, Deleuze, and Derrida "structuralists" (itself a sign of the different times), Said writes: "The origin and the beginning are both hopelessly alien to, and absent from, the stream of discourse. (This is a structuralist position which, in the course of this book, I have implicitly been criticizing and modifying; here, however, I am presenting the position as they have argued it)."[29] The point here is not whether Said's distance from Foucault was always justified, but only that the distance is emphatically there, and to a highly formative degree. The point is not whether Foucault was always, in every case of disagreement, wrong, but only that the disagreement existed. In fact, Foucault's sensibilities toward prob-

lems of sexuality, for instance, or his frank ultra-leftism during the Maoist flirtation and the prison interviews, add dimensions to his work that escape Said's
range, although with debatable results.

In retrospect, then, it is apparent that the moments of strategic heroization
of Foucault in *Beginnings* take place with much throat clearing. Looking forward to the concerns of *Orientalism*, Said chose to compliment Foucault by
reconciling the apparent lapses in his offerings with their inspirational potential: "A frequent problem with the sociology of knowledge has been its reliance
upon a narrowly circumscribed Western, industrialized social paradigm; anything beyond that setting seems to resist the method. Foucault's criteria have a
tighter internal discipline and a wider general sweep than that" (310), although,
it is implied, they too partake of this "Western, industrialized social paradigm."
Timidly at first, Said backs his way into a series of accurate attributions of Foucault that will amount in *Orientalism* to accusations, although *Beginnings* does
not yet forcibly cast them that way. These have to do with those elements in
Foucault's work that amount to a "system"—a machinery of method—that
Said always opposed, and that became increasingly obvious in the Foucault of
the *Archeology of Knowledge*. "The paradox of Foucault is how he maintains
such severity, learning, and *system*—quite without dishonesty or trickiness—
with such wisdom and style. . . . And yet Foucault and the structuralists share
a gloomy theme in the idea of loss and, associated with it, man's unhappy historical insertion into a language game that he can barely understand. This has
led to a dominantly linguistic apprehension of reality" (*Beginnings*, 315).

In good Vichian mode, Said is eager to find countermanding—which is to
say, not merely "dominantly linguistic"—influences in this brilliant "structuralist." What he loves in this thinker at this point is a treatment of language
that exceeds its resemblance to a prison house. What he reads in Foucault is a
philosophy of language as "something with its own special history, geography,
and spirituality, as well as corporeality" (304)—a description that Foucauldians
might today find rather quaint if not suspect. The stress in *Beginnings* is on
Foucault's breadth and care for detail, the description of a scholar for whom
nothing scholarly is alien. The points are only fully understandable, though, if
we remember that he is writing for an older humanist audience unfamiliar with
theory. They often overreach in their search for common ground: "they are
structuralists—as, in a way, we all are—because they accept their existential fate
inside language, whose mode of being is pitilessly relational" (319).

Along with praise and acts of compromise, there arises in this chapter a
darker intimation of a point that becomes fully articulate in *The World, the
Text, and the Critic*. In *Beginnings*, he already writes that "all of Foucault's work

is an attempt to make the history and indeed the experience of knowledge something as specifically ordered as 'nature' has become for modern physics or chemistry" (313). These words, it should be clear to close readers of *Orientalism*, are not meant as praise. What Said in *Beginnings* goes on to call "linguicity"— an *order* that chooses syntax over semantics and beyond which it is impossible to think (327)—forces one, against their will, "to read language and reality together as if they were cleverly hidden in something like Swift's little languages, or in the puns of *Finnegans Wake*. The trouble with this fairly esoteric view of language," Said continues, "is, first of all, that rules insure the safety and the captivity of signification: in a sense, therefore, structuralism is conservatively safeguarding the assured certainty of its own activity" (339). "Assured certainty" was then, and is now, the intellectual mood Said ruthlessly rejected.

Beginnings concludes with a paean to Vico, whose *The New Science* Said frequently praised precisely because of the ironic ring of "Science" in its title. That is, the connotations for us of science are exactly what Vico problematized in his lumpy, expansive, accretive, and constantly shifting view of history as "willed human work" (*Orientalism*, 15)—a view that the major thesis of *Beginnings* attempts to emulate: "beginning [as] a consciously intentional, productive activity" (372). In the clearest and most unambiguous way, Said identifies Vico as his intellectual mentor, and it is in this final chapter that he seeks a rapprochement between Vico's philology and the "structuralists" who have occupied him over the previous eighty or so pages. It is an uneasy marriage, but one that Said attempts, establishing some important points of contact, but finally conceding that the incompatibilities are equally significant. What is crucial to grasp, however, is that Said's embrace of Vico the historian, philologist, lonely innovator, and great believer in the power to understand by emulating and by "re-writing" the already written, is unequivocal. His treatment of Foucault, by contrast, is hot and cold, often estranged, and at times actually suspicious:

> As with most of the structuralists, Foucault must presume a conceptual unity—variously called historical a priori, an epistemological field, an epistemological unity, or *episteme*—that anchors and informs linguistic usage at any given time in history; no structuralist to my knowledge has gone to such lengths as Foucault to ascertain and to articulate this "unconscious positivity." In *Les Mots et les choses* he writes that "in a culture, and at a given moment there is never more than one *episteme* that defines the conditions of possibility of all knowledge. One of the various chores this univocal assertion is made to perform is, as Steven Marcus has re-

marked, that it gives license to Foucault's literal faith in an era before the
modern dissociation of sensibility.   (*Beginnings*, 284)

Put plainly, the greatest praise Said is able to give Foucault, and this despite
what he describes as Foucault's "univocal assertions," is the French author's capacity to be a part of the "adversary epistemological current found in Vico, in
Marx and Engels, in Lukács, in Fanon, and also in the radical political writings
of Chomsky" (378). Although this generous view of Foucault's like-thinkers is
found in the Said of 1975, it would not be thereafter (no one would think this
constellation viable today). The adversarial lineage is, at any rate, Said's priority, and he begrudgingly allows Foucault to enter it in the closing pages.

The extravagance of the view, moreover, is perhaps plainest in the comparison to Chomsky, which would certainly strike most appreciative readers of
Foucault as highly odd if not actually embarrassing. It is, however, significant
to remember when one comes upon Said's expressions of debt in the introduction to *Orientalism* in which Gramsci, Williams, Foucault, and Chomsky are all
mentioned in the same breath (14), for it reveals that his citation of Foucault—
whom he has found it "useful here to employ" (3)—is part of a patented eclectic amalgam in which the concepts of discursive network, hegemony, the ho-
mologies of Lucien Goldmann, and cultural materialism all mix.[30] One
obviously has to look at the development of his relationship with Foucault in
separate works both before and after *Orientalism*'s publication and with a mind
to the contexts in which his appropriation of that thinker took place.

Despite the decidedly French bias of *Orientalism*'s framing and sympathies,
Said would soon afterward target Foucault's "flawed attitude to power," his "insufficiently developed attention to the problem of historical change" (*WTC*,
222), in that way echoing the charges that appear in the early pages of *Orientalism* where Said writes that "unlike Foucault . . . I do believe in the determining
imprint of individual writers upon the otherwise anonymous collective body of
texts constituting a discursive formation like Orientalism. . . . Foucault believes
that in general the individual text or author counts for very little; empirically, in
the case of Orientalism (and perhaps nowhere else) I find this not to be so" (23).
There is nothing in the book by way of praise for Foucault that begins to equal
the excitement Said has about contestations over issues of "hegemonic systems
like culture" and "politics in the form of imperialism" (14) that expresses itself
at one point in the claim that "one or two pages by Williams on 'the uses of Empire' in *The Long Revolution* tell us more about nineteenth-century cultural rich-
ness than many volumes of hermetic textual analyses" (14).

Quite apart from this commitment to interrogating power and interest as the shifting, contingent, and dynamic properties of historical actors, Said goes out of his way to distinguish the apparent genealogical method of *Orientalism* from that of Foucault: "Unlike Michel Foucault . . . the unity of the large ensemble of texts I analyze is due in part to the fact that they frequently refer to each other: Orientalism is after all a system for citing works and authors" (23). This embrace of a fairly standard notion of influence along with its implicit diagnosis of class symmetries and intellectual weight as being, after all, a factor of one's celebrity status—all of this is quite unambiguously distinct from the impervious textuality of Foucault's discursive network as it was brilliantly, and sensitively, described by Said in *Beginnings*.

An entirely new and deeper dimension of Said's distance from Foucault (and even his conditional hostility to him) would have to wait until the years immediately following the publication of *Orientalism*. In the essays of *The World, the Text, and the Critic*, Said finally pinpoints the challenge Foucault posed to precisely his own project: non-European histories and anti-colonial mentalities. That is, we find Said quite unexpectedly implying that the inheritances of theory may well be antagonistic in many respects to the project of decolonization and to the ability of Europeans to entertain alternative cultural values from other civilizations. Foucault underestimates, says Said, "such motive forces in history as profit, ambition, ideas, the sheer love of power, and he does not seem interested in the fact that history is not a homogeneous French-speaking territory but a complex interaction between uneven economies, societies, and ideologies" (*WTC*, 222). "Foucault," he continues, "seems unaware of the extent to which the ideas of discourse and discipline are assertively European" (222).

If, in the light of *Orientalism*, such a charge was not itself a decisive repudiation, Said's language becomes even more uncompromising later in "Traveling Theory": Foucault's theory of power, argues Said, has "captivated not only Foucault himself but many of his readers who wish to go beyond Left optimism and Right pessimism so as to justify political quietism with sophisticated intellectualism, at the same time wishing to appear realistic, in touch with the world of power and reality" (*WTC*, 245). The accusation is followed by an outright attempt to go over the author's head: "We must not let Foucault get away with confusing [Logos with words], nor with letting us forget that history does not get made without work, intention, resistance, effort, or conflict, and that none of these things is silently absorbable into micronetworks of power" (245). Quotations such as these could be multiplied, and they could also be supplemented by the comments Said often made in public speeches or in casual conversation.

But instead of adding more evidence, I would like now to bring my two themes together.

The interpretive conflicts I have been tracing between *Orientalism* and postcolonial studies, on the one hand, and *Orientalism* as an American book, on the other, are interrelated. Whereas *Orientalism*'s critics have frequently complained about its apparently self-contradictory embrace of a misrecognized *real* Orient set alongside a misrecognizing discursive orientalist construct, this complaint dissolves in the book's site-specific Americanness.[31] The ideas coalesce in the book's final chapter, which compares the scholarly machinery of nineteenth-century humanists and twentieth-century media intellectuals: both construct a reality in concert with policies and interests, of factions and parties and status groups, rather than by the natural properties of a rigid semiosis. The implied interplay of American media experts and their urbane academic counterparts is very roughly drawn, however, and left mostly implicit. Nor is this to say that the book is secretly, or allegorically, or only about the United States, for that surely would be an overstatement. The personal retooling that Said underwent in the early 1970s, and the rethinking of his own project as a result of crises created by the continued Israeli occupation of Palestine—all of this had profound effects on his scholarship and political orientations, and *Orientalism* would obviously not have been written without them.

But it is important to remind ourselves of the New York and California environment of the book's composition—the media and academic obsessions of this particular metropolitan center in which cultural and global capital mixed in a site-specific way. There are significant echoes in Said's project of much earlier progressive academics fighting against the stream of an oppressive science of culture under radically different conditions but a similar national-cultural dominant. As a student of Richard Blackmur and later a colleague of Lionel Trilling, as an intellectual whose formation took place in the Ivy League environs of Princeton, Harvard, and Columbia, Said could not have escaped the historical example—if not the substantive sympathies—of William James and John Dewey. The parallels, at any rate, between the pragmatists' lonely resistance to icons like Herbert Spencer and William Graham Sumner during the political reaction of the late nineteenth and early twentieth centuries, along with Said's distrust of poststructuralism in the New Gilded Age of the 1980s, are remarkable. There is nothing like an attempt on his part to resuscitate pragmatism, of course, and there is almost nothing to bind Said's project to that of Richard Rorty, for example. But the radical role that liberalism plays in moments of reaction does connect Said's project, in some respects, with that of the pragmatists as it concerned the humanities. Like Said's work, pragmatism thrived on the principle of antagonism to "'block-universe' philosophies . . . impervious to chance or choice," as Richard Hofstadter puts it.[32] The emphasis, particularly of James, was on active human effort and the innovations of unusual or outstanding individuals against sweeping complacency of hierarchy and system.

Orientalism is in most respects deeply unlike the postcolonial work that enlists its name for the reason that it mounts a criticism, proleptically, of the U.S. theoretical arenas in which postcoloniality grew up and through which that tendency expresses itself. The fact is that very few of the current younger generation of postcolonial critics have even read Orientalism; it certainly plays next to no role of importance in their calculations. The book's ability to be proleptic relied on its capacity to be retrospective—that is, deeply and didactically invested in a historicism that, in Said's view, was alone capable of attaining the multiple dimensions of the literary text as well as the mysterious and conflictual agencies of any text's author. What is more, the book has been antagonistic to most of the work found in postcolonial studies in the practical sense of its style of performance. In the very country that professes individualism as a national creed, in the land in which multiculturalism is an imperial shibboleth, postcolonial studies has understandably worn the clothing of identity in the often obtuse and willful psychoanalytic register of the "subject position."[33] Postcolonialism hypostasizes experience and then substitutes experience for one or the other variety of ethnographic representation. In the Saidian terms of Beginnings, this operation is filiative rather than affiliative, and in that sense, apart from its purported outreach and cultural sensitivities, postcolonial studies emphatically strengthens a culturally specific and suspect American obsession with ethnic identity as authority. Hence my allusion early on to Said's very different kind of authorization as a positional one.

Here I would like to repeat my opening claim that Said's literary training is bound up with his political positioning by turning, finally, to my own reading of Orientalism. Without appreciating his attempt to elaborate a politics by way of philology, it is hard to understand his public and politico-literary success. Orientalism's reception did indeed come about as the result of exploiting an identitarian contradiction in Euro-American consciousness, with its emphasis on name, race, immigration, color. Orientalism seems in this sense to be primarily a text by a postcolonial intellectual speaking back to empire, a crossover study whose importance lies in the license it issues to scholars from other parts of the non-European world. My refusal to see the book's importance as an identitarian one may seem to be a merely subjective convenience on my part.

But I would argue it cannot be written off as such.[34] In the United States, the dissident intellectual has had to choose between the powerless prophetic anarchism of beat poetry and '60s counterculture, the plaintive radical liberalism of C. Wright Mills, or the reputable, but slandered, traditions of American communism, made toothless by Cold War prejudices. Part of the significance of *Orientalism* was that it managed an American critique that fell into none of these categories while drawing on all of them (although the first least of all). Its intellectual importance was a matter of its positional freshness not only its geopolitical or racial location.

A good deal of postcolonial studies drew on *Orientalism* without being true to it, in other words. The book's theory traveled, and it did not travel well. Many found there warrant for the construction of the postcolonial intellectual as a necessarily racial or nationally inflected mind/body. Its message for them was that one can write about one's personal and foreign situation from within literary theory as practiced in the U.S. academy. Such a model allowed a certain kind of criticism, and critic, to be taken seriously, for to be serious one had to be theoretically adept, and Said's supposedly Foucauldian text was approved theory. In order to reprimand the imperial center for purveying an offensive colonial discourse rife with racist assumptions and provincial conceptions of value, a certain payment was exacted. Such a critic had to repel accusations of relying too much on a rough-and-ready civil rights discourse, virtuous but intellectually vacuous. In short, the postcolonial critic had to write within *theory*, which meant poststructuralist theory, given the years of its emergence. But not only that. After *Orientalism*—which exploded into public and professional territory far outside the pockets of academia where these concerns were paramount—the literary theorist as poststructuralist was authorized, paradoxically, to write about historical or textual matters with the assurance that such commentary was always ultimately about the self. It was understood that a hovering emphasis would be on an epistemological divide based on national/ethnic/psychic being.

Said's own training and his intellectual lineages suggest that these uses of *Orientalism* chafed against both his "intention and method" (as the subtitle of *Beginnings* put it). His method—as he pointed out in numerous essays—was always based on an intellectual generalism borrowed from many writers, but above all Vico—to whom he had been introduced among others by Auerbach. Said's attraction to both came at a time when comparative literature sought a rationale to escape its status as the humanities' disciplinary remainder. *Orientalism* might seem to have provided this rationale in the new non-Western emphasis that came with postcolonial theory, but actually the non-Western gesture had been an aspect of comparative literature from the start.[35] According to Fritz Strich, even Goethe did not consider world literature to be synonymous with European literature.[36] What is more, "in the decade after 1810," as Said pointed out, "[Goethe] became fascinated with Islam generally and with Persian poetry in particular."[37]

It is true that Auerbach's modernization of philology did not clearly retain this aspect of the Goethean emphasis, and Said was perturbed enough at one point to pronounce Auerbach "no longer tenable" on the grounds that Auerbach's precious Europe was better seen in terms of what E. P. Thompson had called "Natopolis"—countries long dominating peripheral regions where "new cultures, new societies and emerging visions of social, political and aesthetic order now lay claim to the humanist's attention."[38] He complained that during Auerbach's wartime exile in Turkey, "there was no discernible connection between [him] and Istanbul at all; his entire attitude while there seems to have been one of nostalgia for the West."[39] But this was less a concession than a pedagogical tease, for more than any modern critic, Auerbach exhibited the mastery of the history of rhetoric necessary to win adherents to a program of comparative literary expansion. In one of his last pieces of writing, Said described Auerbach's style in words he would have loved for others to use about his own: an "unruffled, at times even lofty and supremely calm, tone conveying a combination of quiet erudition allied with an overridingly patient and loving confidence in his mission as scholar and philologist." With obvious emulation, Said described Auerbach's lifework as comprising a "handful of deeply conceived and complex themes with which he wove his ample fabric," and Auerbach condemned the "failure of German literature to confront modern reality" as Said had American literature from his earliest days as a young professor.[40]

His links to Auerbach, then, went much deeper than adopting the latter's atmospheric humanism. Both saw the expansion of literary study into new canonical territories as being among the first, but least essential, imperatives of disciplinary transformation. The more important task was to grasp that literature was now extra-literary—that is, the field devised at a time when leisured reading performed the true, anthropological, function of value formation now achieved its ends via more disparate forms of knowledge.[41] Auerbach was invaluable above all for constructing a method that acted as a wedge against the "division of intellectual labor" that Said took to be a pernicious "cult of professional expertise" designed to force intellectuals to sell themselves "to the central authority of a society."[42] *Beginnings* was the first of Said's books to lay out a case for the conclusions he had drawn from his apprenticeship in modern philology. It was a case for what might be called intellectual generalism.

It is in this concept that so much of Said's formative thinking was invested, and it is a concept that derived in large part from a brand of literary Marxism (although this has not been widely acknowledged). As early as 1966, one finds him drawn, in his very first published piece, to the work of Goldmann, whose argument "stands in the center of a highly challenging and flowing pattern, a 'dialectic,' whose every detail sustains and is sustained by every other detail."[43] It is clear that many of his most insistent motifs—among them his repudiation of the phenomenologists' "lonely ego," the "rigorous intellectual effort" that forms the inner coherence of an author's work, the value of "historical consciousness," and so on, are all emergent precisely here. At this moment, in the presence of the dialectical tradition, which he then deliberately connected to *les sciences humaines* (the human sciences, that is, the humanities) of Wilhelm Dilthey, Vico, and Auerbach, he established his own continuity of thinking with Marxism (448, 447, 445, 444). What excited him about Goldmann's effort, among other things, was the theory it posited of the way "in which individual parts can be said to make up a whole greater than a mere sum of its parts"—a view, he argued, that led away from a monadic consciousness to a relational "group consciousness," which is not simply Hegelian but philological (444).

It is a point probably lost on those who already "know" Said to be the founder of postcolonial theory's politics of discursivity, but one needs to recall the exact way he put the matter of dialectics on the eve of *Orientalism*'s appearance almost a decade later in 1975:

> I have a great deal of sympathy for what [Marxist groups within the MLA] are trying to do, but I think it is a fundamental misjudgment of reality to base one's political work on an unsituated effort to show that Marxism is principally a reading technique. . . . What I am saying is that . . . to turn a literary or intellectual project immediately into a political one is to try to do something quite undialectical. But to accept the form of action prescribed in advance by one's professional status—which in the system of things is institutionalized marginality—is to restrict oneself politically and in advance.[44]

This, clearly, is a rejection not of Marxism's extremes but of its timidity in the American context. In that spirit, it is to Goldmann that he returned again almost a decade later in "Traveling Theory" in an effort to translate the meaning of dialectics, colloquially put, by way of analyzing what he called the "tamings" of reading over time as texts passed from one to another social circumstance: in that case, how the concepts of reification and totality passed from Lukács to

Goldmann to Williams and Foucault.[45] And again dialectics reasserts itself in his thinking in the mid-1970s, just as he was finishing *Orientalism*, in a review of Béla Királyfalvi's study of Lukács's *Aesthetik*, where he considered the Hungarian's logic to be "Hegelian in its dynamism, but more radical . . . in its thrust into totality."[46] Although Said's reliance upon these strains of thought cannot be doubted, he resisted being identified with them—strategically perhaps, but thereby leaving his thoughts to the interstitial comments of a long-term dialogue: "Marxism has . . . always struck me as more limiting than enabling in the current intellectual, cultural, political conjuncture" (that is, 1992).[47] The unexpected point is that there were always tight linkages in his mind between these influences drawn from the Left of European theory and the philological substratum of comparative literature, even though the latter in others' hands would be presented with a decidedly liberal flavor.

It is remarkable, for example, that no one has observed that Said's discovery of Vico may well have derived from Lukács's "Reification" essay in *History and Class Consciousness*, not only from Auerbach, as is generally supposed. The influence of Vico was at the very least enhanced by Lukács and may have given Said's reading the peculiar twist that struck contemporary critics (Hayden White, for instance) as "baffling." Even if it were not for the clear documentation of Said's fascination with Lukács (he offered seminars on Lukács in 1981), the "Reification" essay forcefully articulated the primary themes of Said's attacks on the system thinking of theory—a theme that permeates *Orientalism*. Here Lukács strikes a note found throughout Said's book:

> The ideal of knowledge represented by the purely distilled formal conception of the object of knowledge, the mathematical organization and the ideal of necessary natural laws all transform knowledge more and more into the systematic and conscious contemplation of those purely formal connections, those "laws" which function in—objective—reality *without the intervention of the subject.*[48]

This focus in Lukács is not merely made in passing; it is the principal idea of that famous essay, which looks for support to Vico himself, who stands in the essay (much as he does in Said) as an alternative to the antinomies of thought in the Western idealist tradition. This tradition, for both men, is never able to concretize the image of the thinker in his or her own social contexts, and so is unable to see why thought that violates the political interests of the theorist is, for that reason, literally unthinkable (hence, an "antinomy"). It is very difficult not to hear Said in the following passage from *History and Class Consciousness*:

The idea that we have made reality loses its more or less fictitious character: we have—in the prophetic words of Vico already cited—made our own history and if we are able to regard the whole of reality as history (i.e. as *our* history, for there is no other), we shall have raised ourselves in fact to the position from which reality can be understood as our "action."[49]

In a general sense, Said was acquiescing here to the more recognizably Sartrean claim that Marxism is a humanism, and that if one were to defend the humanist legacy in an age of religious thought, it was to Marxism that one must logically turn. Just before his death he again acknowledged, more clearly than before, that the work of Auerbach "arose from the themes and methods of German intellectual history and philology; it would be conceivable in no other tradition than in that of German romanticism and Hegel."[50]

In another respect, of course, the intellectual style of Lukács's Marxism did not capture well what Said intended by intellectual generalism. Said beckoned his circles to read widely, freely, without plan, and without prescribed divisions. And yet even here the goal was not that cost-free tolerance about which one so often and safely speaks in the American academy. Such a position on reading might be taken at first as a brand of textual politics; it claims for language no radical revision of existence. The Foucaldian gesture toward a micropolitics of dispersed power, playing without agents in the regimes of discourse is a wholly alien series of ideas to Said, here as elsewhere.

His idea in *Orientalism* is rather that the literary intellectual in the analysis of literary texts most matters by remaining, as it were, in literature, speaking to an aesthetic need that is also a social need. The model he lays out for others to follow is one about learning to speak in a way that attracts audiences by assuming the role the public grants them: namely, as readers, as purveyors of ideas of consequence, as speakers of words well chosen—in short, as critics. From Said's point of view, it is there that a literary intellectual develops a vocabulary and defines concepts capable of nudging thought itself into a gradual change of emphasis. Compounded over time by altering the questions asked or by giving a name to what has rarely been talked about before, the critic is able to find something new and valuable. There is for Said no master discourse, in other words, that rivets together the political and the literary in a single act: the enunciation in general (*pace* Foucault and Emile Benveniste). He stands, instead, for a differentiation of those modes of involvement and for speaking in two minds with a general interest that takes the registering of political opinion out of the mouth of specialists. He has always stood for a disciplined roving, a catholicity of reading and awareness, outside the stable languages of a field.[51]

Orientalism, in the end, served antagonistic purposes. But if it did not offer a Foucault ready for use—a Foucault seen as brilliantly consonant with a new, non-statist, more strictly epistemological assault on colonialism by virtue of his demolition of humanist universalism—then what was its real worth? This is a question that some of his Marxist critics, it would seem, were best poised to answer. But despite their important deflation of the sort of untouchable myth of Said—which stifled a needed debate (for example) on what later came to be called globalization in postcolonial theory, I do not think they were altogether accurate in assessing *Orientalism*. My own view is that the book mattered so much precisely *because* of the very culinary humanism that often rubbed the materialist critic the wrong way. The book allowed people who were uncomfortably aware of contemporary empire to talk about imperialism in an acceptably humanist language. Perhaps the least that can be conceded is that Said knew how to speak to his audience in a manner both unforgiving and concessionary, cutting off idealist escape routes in an impassioned language of justice and rights while holding out for a sheer savoring of the intellectual enterprise itself. *Orientalism* does not simply address the relationship of literary intellectuals to the state in a series of French, English, and German cases in the nineteenth century. The book goes much further than that. It models itself on philological humanism.

Orientalism was, among other things, an attempt to arrest—or at least redirect—the drift of Euro-theory in the American university. It did so, however, in a historicist project whose allegorical resonance for the present (an allegory found in Said's charges against Renan's "*science critique*") was admittedly lost on an audience that saw primarily race in large letters, or the Arab-Israeli conflict in costume, or an urbane Afrocentricity in Arab garb—an Occidentalism, as some of his critics put it. The linking of *Orientalism* with postcolonial studies by the advocates of the field or by journalists seeking to account for the field's origins is somewhat less caricatured than that of the conservative public intellectuals. But it is not of a qualitatively different type. Both miss Said's devotion to the apparatus of erudition in the best literary critics as well as his calculated admiration for humanist specializations, sweeping syntheses, multilingual generosity, sheer aesthetic indulgence, and of course, unapologetically totalizing appetites. It is somewhat surprising, actually, that critics consider *Orientalism* in some essential way Foucauldian. In spite of pointed Foucauldian allusions, both the method and the substance of the book are in the end opposed to the French thinker's practices and views, as Said had already made clear in *Beginnings*. Indeed, from 1967 on, Said was trying to lay the groundwork for a Vichian rather than a Cartesian intellectual tradition, and so was employing Foucault tactically for the very purpose of showing his shortcomings during an era in which he was the principal unit of theoretical currency.

Indeed, the book's success had much to do with bringing the humanities into a battleground that poststructuralism seemed in the 1980s to be abdicating—one involving the politics of government, of network news, of political parties, of media exposés, of liberation wars. It addressed the readers of newspapers, the enraged television audience of Washington talk shows, especially in the concluding chapters. It was, of course, also a book that invoked the Arab, but usually from the historical standpoint of regional power contests in both an ancient and a modern world system. Its conscience enfolded that population of Arabs and Muslims for whom racism was, and is, almost blasé—the ones against whom racism has been so caustic and so familiar that it appeared almost second nature to U.S. audiences. Here, again, is what makes *Orientalism* an American book in that Said was attempting to finger that murky unconscious of American racial typologizing in which the Arab had conveniently taken over for the Jew in the annals of American anti-Semitism. Said cast light upon the very group associated freely with a millennium of hostile rivalry to the West—not, of course, an American pastime alone any more than anti-Semitism against Arabs is unique to the United States. However, the stronghold of Zionism abroad was certainly in the United States, as were the most powerful allies of the people occupying Palestinian land. One forgets that *Orientalism*, whatever else, is written with palpable anger. This anger cannot be underestimated in accounting for its success, particularly outside the academy, and it is of course not at all what postcolonial studies has in mind when it invokes the book's formation of its field.

Said was trying in scholarship to express a commitment on behalf of a specific people and a named movement—a movement, we should remember, of which he was once a formal member, and for which he had worked as translator, delegate, and spokesman. But this fact alone did not make him unusual in the scholarly company of intellectuals like Albert Memmi, K. M. Pannikar, Gerard Chaliand, and Abdallah Laroui. What is surprising is that the book received the welcome it did in the academy. For he demolishes there a certain kind of disciplinary etiquette. This violation of what is often called collegiality is rarely so warmly rewarded.

Not that the book had no dissenters. It had been pointed out that either "Orientalism" as a concept is eternal and therefore ahistorical or it is an entity that requires a discrete definition that Said nowhere provides. It seems rather clear, though, that an epochal hostility toward the Arab world could extend from Aeschylus to Conor Cruise O'Brien without that position being historically undifferentiated. And it seems equally clear that Said is not resting on the point that European philologists or contemporary area studies experts got the Orient wrong, but rather that their Orient took no account of the Orientals' ordering of themselves. Said does not argue, for example, that there is no such thing as a real Orient, or that it has only a discursive life. It is rather that he does not pretend in this book to describe that brute reality to which he repeatedly refers, and to which he gives a priority of place. His is rather a point about the relative indifference of Western intellectuals to that reality, about the confident building and elaboration of ideas and images that rely on the ideas and images that have preceded them within the same constellation of value. It is about how intellectuals create a reality.

This is not how discursive networks function in Foucault, obviously, and Said's dedication to the concept of agency—at times most emphatic—is an additional rejoinder to any claim that *Orientalism* is intelligibly Foucauldian. The evidence necessary to prove this is not difficult to find in the text; the much greater task is to explain why the book has been taken otherwise, which can be done only by examining some of the special needs of American and Western European literary-critical intellectuals in the early 1980s—what Said along with others frequently referred to as the "Age of Reagan." The attempt to do just this, as I have been saying, can be found in *The World, the Text, and the Critic*. If we take up the issue of agency, we can see that the biographical methodology of *Orientalism*, for instance—the way it courses from Edward Lane, to Richard Burton, to Ernest Renan, to Raymond Schwab in lengthy, loving portraits of admirable lives—is a deliberate construct, put there to highlight the historical stakes involved in the careers of named intellectuals who have made something by force of will and by rhetorical skill. This emphatic insistence on the intellectual as historical agent, and on the direct influence of some thinkers on others by way of emulation rather than the impassive dissemination of textually embedded ideas is profoundly contrary to Foucault. The past is known by thinkers who, as Vico understood it, rewrite the past in their own idiom.

The problem, of course, is that most of the future proponents of the field of postcolonial studies needed a Said, and approached the book with an orientation he himself had not had, nor (more importantly) had attempted to impart to his readers. Anyone familiar with Said's training, or with his articles of the early and mid-1970s (on Auerbach, Vico, Joyce as a postcolonial author, Arabic fiction, late Lukács, and so on) knew that Said was too Vichian to have more than a qualified interest in the author of an odd theological confession such as Foucault's Preface of 1970: "*Sept propos sur la septieme ange*").[52]

Orientalism's targeting of the terminological and ideological tyranny of a Western humanist apparatus is not merely un-Foucauldian, of course (for example, it does not reach anti-humanist conclusions when it locates and attacks a peculiar brand of imperialist humanism). It is also—to take a much more tenuous legacy of Foucault—resistant to national or racial filiations. It is vital to recognize that for Said the ideological bludgeon of Orientalism is not a matter of some civilizational taint or genetic prejudice from which, say, the white race suffers, but a matter (as he would later put it in *Culture and Imperialism*) of "positional superiority." European knowledge production vis-à-vis the Orient took the form it did because it could. It controlled the land, the trade, the government registers, and the means of disseminating information. The process painfully described in *Orientalism* is this: no one could counter the European view, and this lamentable hegemony gradually gave way to the belief, backed up by a sensitive scholarship, that no one need question it. It is essential not to deny that Said is speaking about a propaganda system in the latter chapters, and about mass fantasy throughout (those issues that poststructuralism supposedly superseded), even as he emphasizes in the early and middle chapters neither the one nor the other—rather, a self-generating system of images and values that professional intellectuals in a specific social setting devise and propagate.

Orientalism, then, documents how the academic intellectual is involved in the formation and legitimation of state policy—a conclusion that does not lead, as in Foucault, to a Nietzschean escape from the state as internalized discipline (or "governmentality") but to the demands of orientation in an inevitable political contagion. It is no coincidence that *Orientalism* begins with a personal reminiscence of the civil war in Beirut, nor that the reception of the book flourished in the catastrophic invasion of Lebanon by Israeli forces in 1982, only a few years after the volume first appeared. Said's emulation of verbal mastery and textual power are, needless to say, not at all Chomskyan. But like Chomsky, Said is grounded in the appalled witness of applied terror, an embodied rather than a disembodied power. It is, once again, precisely here where Said leaves Foucault behind, and the *The World, the Text, and the Critic*, then, can be seen perhaps as bringing to completion Chomsky's famous debates with Foucault on Dutch television.

When one sees *Orientalism* in its proper time and place, it becomes clear that its central construct is not discourse but institution. Said's point is the inescapable fact of dominance in the act of amassing information on an area whose coherence is predicated on an internal, or domestically defined, set of attitudes. The outlook is itself inseparable from the pursuit of policies of expansion, forced inclusion, and appropriation—the themes he would take up even more explicitly in *Culture and Imperialism*. The Orientalist system of knowledge conceals preliminary assumptions of an unreflective sort by easing us into the sheer mass of intricate details and documentary "proof" placed in the service of the original concept. The finesse of scholarship is, as it were, made naked here; its very formidability and grandeur bears an inversely proportional relationship to the more basic questions that prejudice makes elusive: why is one an Oriental only in the West and never in the Orient itself? Why have the subjects never been given (as Said was to put it in a later essay) "permission to narrate"?

This pointed—one is tempted to say impish—invocation of the term "narrate" in an atmosphere of theoretical textualism points to an implicit critique of postcolonial studies before the fact. The tireless demonstration of *Orientalism*, after all, is of the mutually contributing work of academic disciplines acting in concert and with an astonishing unity of purpose. Said is setting up a homology not only among disciplinary enclaves but among historical periods, forcing the reader to entertain the view that the imperial absurdities of the high nineteenth century—relatively easy to ridicule in retrospect—live on in the supposedly enlightened technologies of the contemporary news media and in literary theory. To that extent as well, the book is contextually American, for it inserted into the British and French colonial enterprises described in the early chapters a contemporary U.S. imperial dynamic. What had in the French and British cases been sanctified by the lure of tradition and cleansed by their relative weakness (their pastness) in regard to the geopolitics of the present becomes, especially in the late chapters, dangerous and immediate. That final chapter is dedicated to the American media and its intellectuals.

Orientalism exploits a creative tension located in philology—a fundamental doubleness represented on the one hand by Schwab and on the other by Renan. These two figures form the poles of a continually repeated standoff in Said's work: on the one hand, the admirable power of textual nomination and deliverance found in the best of the generalist intellectuals; on the other, the typologies, the taxonomies, the cantankerous arrogance of humanist "science." The book for a variety of reasons—not all of them good and not all of them the result of Said's planning—became an enormous success. Without taking anything away from its execution or its versatility, one has to stress that it became so out of intellectual moods and transient conjunctures largely outside Said's control. As Clifford rightly suggested in his review of *Orientalism*, many other scholars had argued basically what Said had argued before him, and there were a number of earlier eloquent studies that, in retrospect, seemed to achieve the same clarity in regard to the function of imperial scholarship, the East/West civilizational divide, and the destructive power of the media mind. Had Said, for example, not written the book in the United States or had he not been Palestinian, or had he not written it at a particular juncture in U.S. imperial resurgence, or had he not been a Columbia professor—or, for our purposes here, had there not been a transitory need within the academy for a curricular and discursive shift to account for the collapse of anti-colonial liberation movements and the new demographics of American graduate schools—*Orientalism* would probably not have had the impact that it did. Seeing the book in that milieu is the only thing that allows us to understand why the book has been in key ways misread, or why it has been enlisted on behalf of a body of postcolonial scholarship with which it has had a quarrel all along.

It is true that Said admired individual studies in postcolonial theory. More often he uttered his distress at its evasive personalizing of issues, at the psychoanalytic linguicity that dominates the field he is said to have created. Taken outside of its history (or worse, left unread) *Orientalism* will appear to be the progenitor of the sterile self/other dichotomy that has paralyzed postcolonial studies in the hands of Said's epigones. To change an entire field by making it more Saidian is a rather tall order, but at least we can be clear about what the text did and did not have to do with it.

CHAPTER 4

GLOBALIZATION'S
UNLIKELY CHAMPIONS

Neither "globalization theory" nor "postcolonial studies" is a term that easily reveals its meaning. The areas of knowledge to which they refer are not what they seem, and a great deal of confusion surrounds their uses. Readers would be forgiven for thinking that the first denoted an emergent body of writing called forth by inexorable developments in technology and communications, as well as radical shifts in the world economy and in geopolitics, all of them presaging the rise of a truly global culture—the obliteration of state sovereignty in a world marked by fluidity and border crossing. In turn, these readers might suppose that the second term referred to an inaugural critique of Eurocentrism prompted by a new diasporic wave of intellectuals from the former colonies resident in metropolitan centers who—informed by postwar theories of language and representation—began in the late 1970s to cast older versions of "Western Man" in doubt in an act of writing back to empire.

Actually, neither is the case. One has to begin by distinguishing between the study of global issues or colonial pasts per se and the fairly recent creation of schools of thought that retrospectively appropriate the more general cases fleetingly echoed in their names. When invoked in European or North American universities in the last decade, globalization theory and postcolonial studies turn out to be very specialized discursive formations passing for older and more varied types of inquiry. This slippage between connotation and code is one of the first things to understand about the conjunction of the two terms.

There have been many earlier traditions of investigating, on the one hand, globalizing features of world history and human societies and, on the other, colonial practices and anti-colonial challenges in the cultural field. Indeed, these now separate foci were in earlier periods conjoined. The ancestors of both, as unified phenomena, include systemic analyses of colonization dating from the early years of the European conquest in the sixteenth century (Las Casas, Montaigne, Raleigh),[1] Enlightenment tracts protesting the ravages of imperial intervention in the eighteenth century (Graffigny, Voltaire, Raynal, Smith, Bentham),[2] studies in the nineteenth and early twentieth centuries of the origins and dynamics of capitalism as a global phenomenon (Marx and Engels, Marx, Melville, Hobson),[3] comprehensive economic critiques of the division of the globe at the apex of European colonization prior to World War I (Graham, Morris, Kautsky, Lenin),[4] new forms of global or broadly regional historiographies associated with the *Annales* school and other historical schools after World War II (McNeill, Hodgson, Braudel),[5] Marxist world historiography based on the initiatives of the anti-colonial movements (Kiernan, Stavrianos, Wolf),[6] dependency theory (Frank, Rodney, Santos),[7] and particularly—and very directly—world systems theory (Cromwell Cox, Wallerstein, Amin).[8] We will look at some of these efforts in more detail below.

In spite of reaching back several centuries, and despite being well developed, extensively documented, and self-conscious, these intellectual movements with their own canons of texts and scholarly pantheons are frequently discounted in contemporary globalization theory even as they are quietly accessed without acknowledgment. In a similar way, postcolonial studies—although in part resting on these foundations—draws on more immediate precursors, especially the anti-colonial intellectuals of the 1950s and 1960s whose work was anticipated by, and directly inherits, interwar Marxist networks of anti-imperialism (Nehru, Mao, Guevara, Fanon, Lumumba, Ho Chi Minh).[9] Motifs of cultural difference, epistemological othering, colonial subjectivity, and social contradiction—all common in later postcolonial studies—were inaugurated by that earlier generation of politically engaged intellectuals, who were often members of actual governments following formal independence. These "independence intellectuals," if one can call them that, were in turn the inheritors of a tradition forged by intellectuals from Africa, Asia, and Latin America who were resident in Europe between the world wars and who in the communist milieus of those years had begun to forge a rhetorical and theoretical apparatus for studying colonialism as a comprehensive phenomenon and, even more importantly, as a morally corrupt system of economic enrichment that could be defeated by organized counteractivity in which intellectuals from the colonies would play a prominent role.

The tendency of contemporary intellectual trends to supplant predecessors by erasing the history of their own making is not a chance occurrence, nor is it simply the work of uncharitable scholars. It is rather a characteristic feature of contemporary capitalist societies, which are at once *presentist*—that is, viewing each moment as the only reality while expunging the past in a gesture of calculated anti-historicism—and *modernist* in the technical sense of needing to judge every current discovery as an utterly new departure, an absolute rupture with all that went before. This intellectual reflex is, in fact, a central feature both of what globalization theory argues the world has become and of what that theory unwittingly demonstrates about itself.

Contemporary modernism celebrates what earlier modernists greeted with suspicion or disparagement (as in the work of those writers of the early twentieth century, like Franz Kafka, Marcel Proust, and William Butler Yeats, who despised mass culture and the decline of an aristocratic sensibility of the refined patron of the arts). Today, by contrast, mass culture is enshrined in terms of obscure and refined aesthetic pleasure with populist pretensions that form the bedrock ideology of the most wealthy and the most privileged. Both versions are "modernist" in that they cast the new as the never-before-seen: in the first case, as a heroically constructed, formal experimentalism that preserves the unsurpassed intelligence and insight of the chosen few of the past, serving as a bulwark against the vulgarity of the masses; in the second case, as a radical break with a history considered to be heading in an unpredictable direction, which is then valorized precisely for that reason. Although one speaks of *post*-modernism today, the "post" does not connote a time after, but rather a heightening. What is meant by the term is less the supersession of modernity than *ultra*modernity.[10] The modernist does not merely express a neutral belief in the "year zero" of the now, as though dispassionately describing a fundamental historical fissure that evidence had forced him or her to accept. Instead, modernism (including its postmodern variant) is normative. The "now" is the new, and the new is rapturously and exuberantly embraced. Without ever questioning the fundamental self-contradiction of the move, the modernist then vigorously urges on a future that *should* unfold (because it is good) while simultaneously arguing that it *must* unfold (because it is inevitable). This style of thinking informs both globalization theory and postcolonial studies, and is another of the major links between them. Let us now develop in more detail the arguments outlined above.

As a term, "globalization" is marked by a fundamental ambiguity. On the one hand, it holds out hope for the creation of new communities and unforeseen solidarities; on the other hand, it appears merely to euphemize corporatization and imperial expansion. At its base, in other words, lies a tension be-tween *process* and *policy*. Is globalization theory about describing a "process": that is, an amalgam of material shifts, spatial reorderings, anonymous devel-opments and movements, the inexorable concatenation of changes in com-munication, transportation, demographics, and the environment? Or does it describe a "policy" (and is it a part of that policy): that is, a mythmaking oper-ation whose purpose is to project a world order that a small group of national and/or financial interests ardently desires to be the future for the rest of us—a future that has happily not yet arrived? There is, as well, a normative dimension to this tension. Does globalization presage a new openness to the previously foreign and the out-of-reach, or is it rather (and paradoxically) just the oppo-site: a veiled way of alluding to the Americanization of foreignness in a world dominated by U.S. power following the fall of the Soviet Union?[11] As expected given our observations above, a similar ambiguity—structurally identical, in fact—marks postcolonial studies, as various critics have wondered aloud whether assaults on "imperial discourse" or the "epistemic violence" of colonial mentalities is the more sophisticated way of battling the Eurocentrism that their authors claim, or merely a rendering of earlier radical positions of dissent in a form more accommodating to power by a professional diaspora to the im-perial centers.[12] Questions such as these interrogate globalization, but are al-ready outside "globalization theory," which does not typically open itself up to this kind of self-questioning. In particular, globalization theory would consider raising the issue of the interestedness of academic knowledge to be imperti-nent, for reasons we will describe.[13]

Current globalization theory, in its restricted sense, cannot logically doubt itself in the manner I have suggested because it does not merely claim that eco-nomic or cultural integration is occurring on a global scale. The import of what is being said goes significantly beyond that. The intended point is rather that the world is being reconstituted *as a single social space*. One might interpret this to mean that the world is becoming more homogenized, that we are seeing the creation of a single, albeit hybridized world culture whose pace of life, tastes, and customs—conditioned by a similar regime of commodities consisting of cars, computers, and cellular phones—had increasingly fewer local variations. It could also be taken to mean that we are on the road to global political inte-gration. But it is worth recognizing that it does not necessarily stipulate either of these positions. To say "a single social space" still allows for complex and dy-namic internal variations across an interconnected system of localities and re-gions. The key component is that there be a governing logic or social tendency that brings all these localities and regions into a unity unknown before.

The idea is further posited that globalization has become its own explanation: that is, not only has space/time been "distanciated" as a result of analyzable causal forces (that is, distances are less relevant to one's particular experience given the instant availability of images, objects, and information from afar); what is being claimed is rather that social theory itself has undergone a spatio-temporal reformulation in which the earlier modes of analysis are no longer tenable. Class antagonisms, geopolitical rivalries, the entrenched defense of privileges, imperial designs, the blunt arguments of war and profit making—all of the earlier mechanisms of historical causation are, in globalization theory, implicitly downgraded into second-order explanations.

As these are cast as vestiges of a vanishing social logic, globalization theory looks rather to a "new" dynamic forged by the happy chaos of an infinitely mobile citizenry, a constantly self-defined subjectivity, a terrain of virtual space consisting of multifaceted niches of an always malleable and morphing freedom. As such (the argument goes) the mandate of reliable definitions crumbles away; the researcher, in order not to be left behind, sprints frantically after a reality vastly more innovative on its own than earlier utopias had been in the imagination. Social sense-making is no longer determined by students of history or the organizers of thought known as philosophers; in the view of the globalization theorist, their structures of understanding only impede their ability to recognize the future unfolding before their eyes, which is being created by investors, technologists, managers, and organizers not—thankfully not—working according to plan but swept along in a process that is anarchic and autopoietic.[14]

The paradigmatic tone and style of globalization theory is perhaps provided best by the sociologist Anthony Giddens, who gives a clear indication of the type of argument found in the field in our restrictive sense. For Giddens, people in ultramodernity live apocalyptically, experiencing levels of risk unknown before. As social institutions become more and more complex, they operate (and force us to operate) at increasing levels of abstraction, now built into the fabric of individual life. As a result, the subject is forced to *trust*, since abstract systems tend to "disembed" the subject from immediate experience, transforming intimacy from the previously anchored criteria of kinship and obligation to a "life politics" based on controlling one's own body. As deskilling renders most of us utterly dependent on expert systems whose functioning we simply have to trust, this biopolitical control becomes more important as a response to the "runaway world" of modernity and the unitary framework of experience, of which we are constantly reminded. Doubt as a pervasive feature of modern critical reason now permeates everyday life, becoming part of its existential dimension. Time and space are separable and controllable by way of the technologies of clock and map. Although aspects of this vision sound threatening at first, our initial impressions are deliberately confounded by Giddens's jubilant conclusions. For him, our ability in ultramodernity to outgrow providential reason produces an increasingly secular understanding of the nature of things, and so intrinsically leads to a safer and more rewarding existence.[15]

Such an explanation is obviously at odds with a systematic account of financial forces or the impure motives of privileged agencies. By taking these conflicting approaches into consideration, one comes to recognize that globalization is not waiting to be found, discrete and safe, in the world of living social communities. There are no facts to be rehearsed in order to determine either whether the term "globalization" is merited or whether (if so) this *thing* has not existed for many centuries without it being accompanied by the heraldic futuristic utterances that are now widely evident (utterances that often have the ring of a campaign). By themselves the facts, such as they are, are mute: for instance, the ownership patterns of transnational corporations (TNCs), the explosive rise in Internet traffic, the radical breakdown of treaties governing international law, the increasing recourse to offshore banking, the orchestrated planning imposed by the Bretton Woods institutions (International Monetary Fund, World Bank), or the flows of migrant labor in Southeast Asia.

To this extent, it is vital to grasp that debates over globalization are discursive. That is, they are debates over theory: over which explanatory mechanism makes the most sense given a body of (usually implicit) ethical and political objectives. The ensemble of theories of globalization invoked at the outset of this essay—centuries-old critiques of capitalism, Enlightenment protests against colonial excesses, conscious attempts over the past fifty years to write a fully world history, and the more recent exuberant "globalization theory" that characterizes both poststructuralism and neoliberalism (often in similar terms)—all of these taken together have yielded five basic positions that again and again arise in various guises in the now massive literature on globalization. Heuristically, it might be useful to spell them out at this point.

The first position argues that globalization—however much it is the unintended result of economic logics, technical discoveries, and population growth—finds its only real significance as a political promise. Here, finally, the great Enlightenment program of Immanuel Kant for a single world government under universal law is perhaps realizable.[16] Possibilities at last exist for either world citizenship under a single governmental entity (a new world state) or some flexible federalist structure allowing significant local autonomy. It is an exciting and welcome development, taking us beyond the petty factionalism, ethnic rivalries, and bloodletting of the past, associated with the ancient, pre-modern, and modern nationalist eras. Globalization, in this view, is welcome.[17]

By contrast, the second position argues that globalization is not so much a matter of formal political outcomes as the development of *trade* and of *finance*, in which the pure freedom of exchange revolutionizes human contact along with the potential for understanding, leisure, and cultural sampling. It is not political actors but the transnational corporations that are responsible for globalization, and therefore what is happening is happening deliberately *outside* political structures, and even in opposition to them.[18] There is no clear local, or national, beneficiary of globalization, since the transnationals are in-different to nations (they are, after all, technically owned by people from many countries) and hostile to them (they naturally desire the permeability of bor-ders). They supersede nations, which have therefore become obsolete. In this variant, globalization can be considered either welcome or unwelcome. A the-orist such as Jagdish Bhagwati, for instance—an economist at Columbia Uni-versity who celebrates capitalism—considers these developments the fruit of the marvelous rationality of market forces, while Félix Guattari and Toni Negri (post-Marxist intellectuals who describe themselves as "communists") share much the same view, considering the runaway market as unleashing powerful utopian energies.[19] By contrast, the billionaire financier George Soros deems the unrestricted mobility of finance to be a human catastrophe, since it renders developing nations acutely vulnerable to collapse when shaky market condi-tions prompt capital flight.[20]

The third position combines the emphasis on politics and trade while shift-ing the criterion to geopolitical motive. In this variant, globalization is the re-sult of developments in technology, transportation, and financial/corporate re-structuring working in concert with an underlying ideology that is basically American.[21] Thus globalization, although undoubtedly permeating the rest of the world and in some ways benefiting actors in several countries, is struc-turally American. It is the United States that primarily benefits, not only di-rectly as a specific nation-state but in the more ambitious sense that the United States is a mini-model of the future world—the world as it will appear when globalized. Were we to examine this recognizably American ideology as the dy-namic contemporary expression of capitalism (the argument goes), we would see how important it has been in facilitating technological developments in media, travel, fashion, and entertainment in a wild and intrepid search for nov-elty without any thought to consequences. But in a more localized sense, it is the American twist on capitalism that has made globalization seem desirable and has done so by making the following concepts widely believed in, either because they are thought inexorable or because they are thought attractive (the fusing of the two qualities, again, is paradigmatic): pragmatism, pluralism, individualism, and suspicion toward the "state." Here globalization can, again, be thought either good or bad, with Thomas Friedman offering perhaps the most outspoken and extreme views on behalf of an irrepressible American genius and beneficence and Paul Krugman, the economist and, like Friedman, op-ed columnist for the *New York Times*, tirelessly exposing the emptiness of neoliberal ideology and the rampant corruption and cronyism at the heart of American profit making.[22]

A fourth variant is less evolutionary than the third while retaining its focus on the United States. It explicitly ties globalization to the problematics of the colonizing West. Here, globalization is basically the form that imperialism takes in the late twentieth century.[23] It is a shibboleth whose emergence as a master term coincided exactly with the fall of the Soviet Union and the Eastern bloc—that period, in other words, in which the last credible adversaries to U.S. global hegemony were removed. Most of the features said to characterize globalization are American, and they are coercively imposed on others as a universal norm. Rather than the hybridity that is widely acclaimed as being on the rise, we are instead seeing the violent incorporation of global difference into a single national project that is importantly, even vitally, not perceived as such. Although the forms and styles of this imperialism are crucially different from those of the past, the intentions and effects are identical (conquest, occupation, and the stealing of resources continue, and enrich distinct national entities, but they are now performed not under the sign of "civilization" or "God" or "Britain" but in the name of "globalization" or simply the "new," which universalizes the interests of that distinct national entity). This analysis presents globalization as a largely fictive enterprise, either cynical or guilty of wishful thinking. Here, globalization is seen as a threat.

The fifth position is the most distinctive. It avers that globalization does not exist. Although it concedes that travel and communication are much easier and more accessible than previously, and although it readily agrees that this increased human contact has had profound effects on the way people see the world, nothing qualitatively has changed. The nation-state structure is still the international norm; ethnic, linguistic, and religious divisions have only intensified; most of the world's people are entirely localized, provincial, traditional, and cut off from others, living not only outside this supposedly new globalized world but outside modernity itself. Globalization is therefore not a description but a projection; or more properly, it is a projection that passes itself off as a description. Once again, this is a mixed view, with globalization being thought either good or bad. As the self-styled Metternich of the late twentieth century, for instance, Henry Kissinger is not particularly happy to observe that globalization is an overweening fiction.[24] With grim pragmatism, therefore, he counsels his readers to be wary of obstacles still remaining to American supremacy, wishing in fact that globalization were more real than it is. In both Immanuel Wallerstein and Janet Abu-Lughod, by contrast, globalization collapses as a concept not because so many scholars or commentators are guilty of wishful thinking but because they have failed to examine adequately the full range of relevant documents, or to compare the present to earlier periods.[25] An investigation of material relations makes it vain, in their opinion, to distinguish our own time from the high Renaissance (or even earlier); both eras are "global" in more or less the same ways, just as both equally fail to approximate the complete integration fancifully described in globalization theory.

These representative positions display more than different diagnoses or emphases; they are methodologically at odds as well. For instance, in his own primer on globalization, Anthony McGrew assumes that global society is uncontroversially real, seeking to introduce the topic only by discussing the conflicting explanations for this reality given by major voices in the field. He does not mention the fact, but his discussion reveals a paradox.[26] His own argument is representative of only one of two major methodologies—which can be found throughout globalization discourse—that emerge as perfect dialectical opposites. A seesawing between the multiple and the unitary is highlighted in both, but the two elements play very different roles in each. On the one hand, the proponents of the view of an already achieved "global village" (McGrew's position combines the second and third positions above) often tend to see a multiplicity, randomness, and disconnectedness at the heart of an overall, fortuitous unity portrayed as the result of a progressive telos. By contrast, some of the critics of globalization—both those skeptical of its desirability and those doubtful of its presence—see behind globalization an underlying, comprehensive set of motives and related processes working on behalf of limited and localized interests: a symmetrically inverted position. Theirs is a *total* explanation based on the repetition of patterns of power brokering from capitalism's past, whereas McGrew's represents a modernist enthusiasm, and is, as a matter of taste and principle, individual, separable, and "federal," if you will, at the same time that it resists the suggestion of being little more than a very familiar defense of the market in highly charged ethical terms.

The concept of totality employed by some critics of globalization theory is reminiscent of that theory, but again, inverts it. Totality does not merely stipulate a unity but suggests that any contingent or local problem is clearly seen only when viewed as being conditioned by its place in a total relationship of objects and events, all governed by a dominant logic. So, for example, the idea presented by a globalization enthusiast like McGrew that Immanuel Wallerstein, James Rosenau, and Robert Gilpin pose incompatible views on globalization because Wallerstein emphasized historical capitalism, Rosenau the shift from industrial to post-industrial order, and Gilpin the power and legitimacy of a hegemonic liberal state would, from the vantage point of totality, be a crude way of seeing the matter. A theory that conceives of society as a totality would tend not to separate the economic, the political, the social, and the aesthetic in this way. These modes of societal interaction all devolve from interests and material conditionings such that, say, the preferred goals of historical capitalism could be said to *demand* at a certain point precisely a "hegemonic liberal state" to oversee its concerns, managing the vast division of labor that involves moving basic industry to the Third World while drawing on the highly trained citizens of the wealthier countries to set up information- and service-based businesses (the "post-industrial" ones). Capitalism is the logic in each phase of this operation, and there are not three explanations, but one.

In all of its variants, globalization theory presumes a knowledge of the following key terms:

• *Modernity.* Apart from suggesting widely available technologies associated with "modern life" (televisions, cars, high-rises, computers), modernity more generally refers to a cast of mind, an attitude, and an approach to problems as much as to a period. Modernity begins with the Enlightenment and never ends (we are still in modernity). It centrally involves the idea of the "new," the break, the departure. Earlier, intellectuals (church clerics, for example) tended to base their arguments on Aristotle, Scripture, or the like. In modernity, legitimacy and authority are thought to be based no longer on principles derived from the past. Rather, the questioner (of law, of right, of religion, of truth) offers his/her own justification. Modernity means to create one's own normativity out of oneself.

• *The West.* A historical rather than a geographical construct, it means developed, industrialized, urbanized, capitalist, secular, and modern. Any society that shares these features is usually thought of as existing in the orbit of the "West." Derived originally from the division of the Roman Empire, and later by the division of the Christian churches in the eleventh century, it took on a new, ideological coloring in the era of the Crusades, when the Orient (which referred at first only to Islam) was then allowed to stand in for everything east of it as well (China, India, Persia, and so on). In the Cold War, a new binary opposition arose using the terms "East" and "West" with a slightly altered (but fundamentally similar) geopolitical significance.[27]

• *Space/Place.* The significance of the turn to space/place in globalization theory lies, first of all, in the overcoming of temporality. Time is supplanted by space in a worldview that (a) perceives the conflicts of history as being decisively decided in favor of one of the warring parties or (for exactly opposite reasons) (b) allergically recoils from the Hegelian notion of a progressive telos to history and is therefore drawn methodologically to a synchronic analysis, expressed in metaphors of spatiality (we identified these opposed, but complementary, features of globalization theory above in the terms "neoliberalism" and "poststructuralism"). In harmony with the assumption that globalization is an irrepressible unfolding, the logical issue is no longer what will happen, but when it will extend itself over a vast but finite territory. The optic logically shifts from tempo to scale, and from the chronometric to the cartographic. As a matter of theory, the dual expression "space/place" means to suggest that a struggle over value is embedded in the way one thinks about spatiality.[28] "Space" is more abstract and ubiquitous: it connotes capital, history, and activity, and gestures toward the meaninglessness of distance in a world of instantaneous communication and virtuality; "place" connotes, by contrast, the kernel or center of one's memory and experience—a dwelling, a familiar park or city street, one's family or community. An ambiguity of value is obviously contained in the pairing, since the former is both bloodless and forward-looking while the latter, although personally vital, is also static.

• *Cosmopolitanism.* Colloquially associated with broad fellow-feeling, world travel, openness to cultural otherness, and so on, cosmopolitanism discursively accompanies globalization as the political ethic of the humanities intellectual. It both describes and endorses (endorses *as* it describes) the creation of a singularity out of newness, a blending and merging of differences becoming one entity. Furthermore, it stipulates a theory of world government and world citizenship in which the term's cultural meaning is carried over to its political one. In that sense, it is distinct from internationalism, which sets out to establish a global network of respect and cooperation based on differences of polity as well as culture. Cosmopolitanism sprouts from an already existing culture of intellectuals and middle-class travelers, researchers, and businessmen. Internationalism, on the other hand—although based no less than cosmopolitanism on the facts of global interpenetration, the homogenization brought about by capitalist mass culture, and the cultural consequences of mass migration—is an ideology of the domestically restricted, the recently relocated, the exiled, and the temporarily weak.[29]

• *Neoliberalism*. This position became prominent in policymaking circles (and later in journalism and the academy) following the conservative electoral victories of Margaret Thatcher in Britain and Ronald Reagan in the United States. With the goal of dismantling the welfare state, neoliberalism argues that an unrestrained market logic, freed from governmental constraints, will cure social ills and lead to general prosperity. As Pierre Bourdieu explains, it "is not a discourse like others. Like psychiatric discourse in the asylum, as described by Erving Goffman, it is a 'strong discourse' which is so strong and so hard to fight because it has behind it all the powers of a world of power relations which it helps to make as it is, in particular by orienting the economic choices of those who dominate economic relations and so adding its own—specifically symbolic—force to those power relations."[30] It is a faith rather than an analysis, and it creates its own truth by imposing itself on the supposedly free agents of economic choice.

LINKS TO POSTCOLONIAL STUDIES

Globalization theory and postcolonial studies ambiguously evoke an ethical program while presenting themselves as iconoclastic departures from older modes of studying their fields of interest. A teleology of shared mores links them. On the one hand, postcolonial studies carries on the sensibilities formulated by anti-colonial intellectuals who, given the conjunctures of foreign policy, caught the attention of metropolitan writers and thinkers at specific times. The influence on European and North American thinkers came most strongly from resistance intellectuals from Latin America throughout the nineteenth century, China of the 1920s, India of the 1940s, Algeria of the 1950s, Vietnam of the 1960s, and Central America of the 1970s. Within the United States, many of the central motifs of postcolonial studies were formulated already in academia in the 1960s as a result of the anti–Vietnam War movement and the radicalizations that produced new black studies and women's studies departments. On the other hand, "postcolonial studies" is often taken to be something much more specific. It was less a well-defined disciplinary formation than a broad attitude toward expanding the field of inquiry to include histories and points of view from outside Europe and the United States. Postcolonial studies in this sense alluded to its early parentage, but thought of itself as being more directly influenced by poststructuralism; indeed, the growth of "theory" in the late 1970s and the rise of postcolonial studies in this more restricted sense were virtually contemporaneous.

In the broadest sense, postcolonial studies is an intellectual movement driven by a critique of Eurocentrism and patriarchy. In its general arc, the work involves collecting and disseminating information, formulating arguments, or explaining concepts with the end of achieving emancipation for minority, marginal, or formerly colonized peoples. However, it is also and at the same time involved in questioning value—that is, it seeks to reorient cultural values attendant upon learning to understand and aesthetically appreciate the cultural achievements of those outside the European sphere. It seeks to show how earlier scholars in the West have been narrowly obsessed, culturally limited, and tendentiously ignorant of many of the world's most consequential artistic and intellectual creations. Many trace the origins of the field to the publication of Edward Said's *Orientalism* in 1978, and the elaborations later provided (in a very different vein) by Gayatri Spivak, Homi Bhabha, and others. In practice, these later elaborations (unlike Said's) tended to merge colonial or non-Western themes with deconstruction, discourse analysis, and Lacanian psychoanalysis, whereas Said was more consciously drawing on an earlier philological and social democratic tradition of historians and activists.

There has been a good deal of argument about the term "postcolonial," since it suggests that colonies no longer exist (a suggestion that does not bear scrutiny). The term has, however, survived in part because it successfully euphemizes harsher terms like "imperialism" or "racism" in professionally respectable academic environments, but also because many of its practitioners believe the fight over the independence of sovereign states (which had once characterized the colonial struggle) was no longer the issue. In an age of globalization the issue was about Eurocentric assumptions rather than military occupations. Hence the *post*.

As a matter of intellectual precedent, however, one clearly sees the ties of globalization to the problems of imperial practices, and so can appreciate a rather different kind of bond between them as well. Some of the intellectual precursors that have been ignored or downplayed in scholarship of the 1980s and 1990s presciently fused the global and the imperial foci kept artificially separate by the two fields examined here. "World systems theory," for example, is often cited as the most obvious forerunner of globalization theory, and either Immanuel Wallerstein or Samir Amin is usually considered its most commanding presence if not its founder. Who came first is of less importance than that a left critique of development ideology arose in the 1950s and 1960s, creating the basis for much of what later became known as the theory of "globalization." Amin was formulating its basic tenets in his dissertation in 1957 (published in 1970 as *Accumulation á l'échelle mondiale* [*Accumulation on a World Scale*]). For his part, Marshall Hodgson was publicly using the term "world system" already in 1965, and that was a year *after* Oliver Cromwell Cox had completed the third volume of his neglected trilogy on the foundations of capitalism as a world system.[31] The central arguments of world systems theory are (a) that intricately organized systems of trade, cultural contact, and borrowing are extraordinarily old, even ancient, (b) that capital accumulation is the motor force for such contact, (c) that history must be founded on a rejection of Eurocentric assumptions or by the artificial separation of cultural and economic questions, and (d) that world systems have a center/periphery structure and alternate between a hegemony and rivalry marked by economic cycles of ascending and descending phases.

A related predecessor would be dependency theory, which is, again, inexplicably ignored by the purveyors of the new. If the colonial era's naively ethnocentric evolutionary argument of European superiority gave way after World War II to modernization theory, the latter nevertheless adapted many of the former's assumptions: for example, Europe is supposed to have entered history in a dominant posture by way of the "European miracle," its unique mastery of reason, freedom, and individualism. These cultural traits distinguish it among world civilizations.[32] Hence the rest of the world is on the way to modernizing itself, but it cannot do so without the diffusion of European traits. The dependency theorists, primarily based in Latin America and the Caribbean, arose to contest this narrative. They argued, by contrast, that the dominant countries deliberately underdeveloped the Third World and that First World wealth was derived not only from the theft of resources from the periphery but also from pressing home the artificial advantages won in an earlier period of conquest.[33]

Theories of globalization, then—as Justin Rosenberg points out—are not necessarily "globalization theory," just as studies of colonialism, anti-colonialism, and imperialism are not necessarily "postcolonial studies."[34] In the university at least, these two latter and late-arriving trends were driven by a set of ethical postulates popularized by poststructuralist theory: the striving for ambivalence as a matter of principle; the ardent belief that answering a question forecloses it; the elision of meaning in pursuit of epistemological doubt as a desired goal; and, most of all, the deployment of a variety of tropes such as "migrancy," "nomadism," "hybridity," and "decentering," which are marshaled in order to make the case that mobility and mixedness—not as contingent historical experiences but as modes of being—are states of virtue. What is implied is that these conditions are *ontologically* superior and that political life should be based today on approximating them. It is important not to confuse this ethical program with theories of globalization in general, since many critics believe such a program to be precisely an adjunct to the very corporate (and American) globalization being analyzed. To its predecessors, as well as to its critics, globalization theory shares with postcolonial studies a dubious relationship to the power it purportedly questions. In these circles, one would want to emphasize not ethics but the large-scale structural determinants of both fields of inquiry: namely, capitalism and the West. Those who are skeptical of globalization theory in its restrictive sense wish above all to expose the tyrannies of value lying behind the creation of the myth of the West—a myth continually reinvented in each subsequent era in order to outmaneuver the disrepute into which the older discrimination had fallen.[35] But if globalization is a continuation of colonialism, what exactly is colonialism?

Both colonialism and imperialism entail the subjugation of one people by another. Traditionally, neither term refers to individuals within one society subjugating others within that same society. What is meant, rather, is that people who live in one region of the world—not just living together, but acting as organized members of a recognizable political territory such as a nation-state—subjugate those of another part of the world. So the concept suggests not only the largeness of the operation, or the ethnic, racial, or cultural differences of the parties, but the global scale upon which it is carried out. When we say "subjugation," we mean forcible, often violent, control over others: the rendering of people "subjects," which is to say placing them in a situation where their freedom is contingent upon the will of the dominant group.

Colonialism and imperialism, unlike other forms of subjugation, are not based on rank or privilege alone—as, for instance, in the inequalities experienced by people of different social classes in eighteenth-century France. That is, the dominant group is not composed only of the rich and powerful, or the generals who did the conquering, or the businessmen who profited from the conquest. On the contrary, the key idea that motivates colonialism and imperialism is that *everyone* from the conquering country is civilizationally superior to the conquered people. One can feel that one belongs to the dominant group simply by virtue of one's race (the racial identity that is preponderant in the home territory), one's nationality (whether one is a citizen of the conquering country), or one's cultural identity. In this way, the poor, the subservient, or the discriminated against within a given country often support imperialism because in that relationship they are considered members of the superior group.

What prompts this form of subjugation? Historically, several different factors exist at times in combination: to acquire new territory for expansion or settlement, to acquire raw materials needed in production (ones that cannot be found in the home territory); to acquire labor by enlisting laborers who can be forced to work for free or for less money than in the home country; to set up businesses that could not exist in the home territory (because of the climate or the distances from essential commodities or because they would not be tolerated at home, given the cruelty of the operation, or the amount of pollution the business generates, or other legal or moral reasons). Other motives are less immediately linked to the extraction of wealth: to have a place for expelling unruly social elements (criminals, religious dissidents, unwanted racial populations, the diseased, or the insane); to have a place to flee persecution and so to become the persecutors in turn; or, simply, to create new markets. Here the point is not to *take* things from the colony or to make things in the colony less expensively, but to create a new culture that will be receptive to the things one makes in the home territory so they can be more readily sold there. This last point often entails the export of ideas and values: the setting up of new educational systems; the establishment of new local customs; the dissemination of books, dress, musical performances and other artistic and broadly cultural practices, as well as religious indoctrination, in order to transform the local population into a "familiar" one.

There were many ancient and modern empires—that is, attempts by a people to conquer the known world and bring it under a single jurisdiction: the Persians, Macedonians, Romans, Mongols, Mughals, Ottomans (Turks), and Spanish all had extensive empires. But when one uses the word "imperialist" today, it does not refer to these empires. It is rather a modern, and more specific, term for a system that grew out of European colonial expansion between the fifteenth and nineteenth centuries, and it involves a comprehensive interconnected economic system, as well as an accompanying cultural penetration and unification rather than simply a conquest, as in the ancient empires. Coined in the late nineteenth century by critics of empire who saw the global system as an organic outgrowth of capitalist expansion, the term "imperialism" in practice refers to the French, Dutch, Spanish, Portuguese, and especially British empires, but also to the U.S. empire, which after World War II inherited the system that these European countries created.[36]

The basic difference between colonialism and imperialism (for they vary greatly from case to case) is that imperialism is a later and more systematic organization of the foreign exploitation pioneered by colonialism. Another way of expressing this idea is this: imperialism makes the process begun by colo-

nialism more efficient and generalized, and often (although not always) reduces the need for a bald, direct confrontation of peoples from two different
cultures. In general, colonialism characterized the period before imperialism—
roughly the fifteenth to the nineteenth centuries (it is, in this sense, a chronological term). Although widespread and even concerted, it tended to be pragmatic, occasional, and unsystematic. Colonies, especially in their origins, were
often run by private ventures or holding companies rather than states. They
were carried out either for purposes of settlement or for economic exploitation; they were largely conducted in terms of a confrontation between the
"White"and the "Dark" races; they often involved direct military occupation,
and the setting up of alternative cultural institutions for the purpose of creating a native caste that shared the same culture as those in the home country.
Imperialism, by contrast, grows out of colonialism, both by extending its logic
and by responding more subtly to the demands for political independence
launched by the freedom movements in the colonies during the twentieth century. It tends to be comprehensive and systematic, ruled by a central authority
like a state or decisive financial or political institutions effectively controlled by
a state or an alliance of states. Imperialism can and does involve military invasion and/or occupation, but usually not for the purpose of settlement.

Under imperialism, conquest is often maintained from afar, by the threat of
military invasion or by means of economic coercion. In its classical sense, imperialism is above all a structured system of economic disparity that places certain countries of the world in a position of dependence on those states whose
economies are strongest and whose strength is artificially (and coercively)
maintained by unequal rates of exchange, punitive lending laws, and other financial and commercial means. One of imperialism's classic definitions, therefore, is simply "the export of capital."[37] Under imperialism, the cultural institutions in a foreign country that serve the imperial center are no longer run by
the imperial center itself (at least directly). A whole sector of "native" intellectuals and elites, inherited from the colonial era, identify with the imperial center and carry out its wishes either out of conviction or through payoffs, bribery,
personal networks of affiliation, and so on. The ideology of civilizational superiority incipient under colonialism becomes under imperialism a given, and is
used by the imperial center as a natural justification for all its actions. There is
no open enlistment, as under colonialism, of the rhetoric of a righteous cause,
or a confrontation of the enlightened versus the benighted. These categories are
rather fully internationalized, bureaucratized, and no longer controversial.

One can appreciate, then, why globalization theory so carefully dissociates
the process of globalization from *national* identifications, ethnocentric atti-

tudes, forcible inclusion, or the discourse of civilizational superiority, since unless it does so the continuities between its purportedly "new" and liberatory panorama and older exploitative arrangements would be obvious and uncomfortable. Taking globalization theory at its word, the classic features of colonialism seem not only alien to globalization but its very opposite, since the latter is relentlessly cast as popularly willed, anonymous, permeating, and unplanned. But can this assumption be confidently maintained? One notices, for instance, that colonialism always worked by playing cultural differences off one another in the name of acquiring material advantages. Differences, as such, were critical to a strategy of profit making that relied upon the *dissemination* of local values in the guise of global ones. If it is obvious that cultural differences were greeted negatively in earlier centuries whereas they now stand at the very core of the universal ethic of global pluralism, the stark contrast is perhaps a little too easy to misinterpret. Rather than being opposites, these positions are complementary. In each case, a carefully nurtured separability of locality, political knowledge, and cultural practice allows an educated caste with means to manipulate sectoralism, benefiting from the disparities that keep them in competition while calling forth a self-image as unifying force whose "inevitability" renders self-interest both invisible and benevolent.

What we are seeing today under the banner of globalization repeats a process, with some changes, that we saw more than two centuries ago with the emergence of national markets.[38] The significant development today is only the larger scale on which the process occurs, and the smaller number of beneficiaries. Much has been made in recent years of the necessity of nations to create an artificial sense of belonging—a distinct national culture via print media and invented traditions.[39] In globalization—often portrayed as the transcendence of nationalism—the same dynamic pertains: homogenization takes place as a concentration of power on the road to monopoly. Samir Amin's account of the rise of finance capital demonstrates from another angle this parallelism between globalization and national state formation. Via immense deficit spending, the United States dictates terms of structural readjustment to other countries, just as the Bretton Woods institutions (under U.S. tutelage) form the nucleus of a new global megastate.[40] Capitalism, he argues, has been falsely associated by many commentators with "development" and "the market," whereas it is actually hostile to both. It thrives, rather, in the zero-sum contest of mobile finance drifting around the globe in search of investment, victimized by its own victorious monopolization, hungering for new worlds to conquer.

The underlying logic linking globalization theory and postcolonial studies has, in at least one respect, a perverse cast. The mutual hostility of both to the nation form (particularly as nation-*state*) is projected as an irrepressible ultra-modernism. In turn, this ultramoderism in its contemporary variant is given an almost aesthetic accent in which mobility as an ontological condition is portrayed as the exciting play of an infinite self-fashioning. The cast is perverse because in accordance with such a logic one is forced to contemptuously revile, even while resonating with, a specific and conjunctural national-statist project (that of the United States), which in a vigorously broadcast system of images and slogans embraces the same hybridity, modernity, and mobility of globalization theory. Like that theory, it depicts the world as having moved *past* colonialism and imperialism.

It would be an enormous irony, of course, if this shared logic were purely and neatly self-contradictory. In fact, both discursive formations have helped generate, often in spite of themselves, a more complicated and internally riven set of theories. Even in their restrictive senses, both are institutional arenas where a welcome intellectual generalism has lately begun to flourish, pushing researchers into a rudimentary knowledge of sociology, economics, and social history. Particularly in the last few years, cultural theorists have moved past interrogations of methodology and epistemology (however important these gestures always were on their own terms, and however admirable when contrasted with the relative methodological complacency of the natural and social sciences). The globalization theorist him/herself has at last become part of the object of inquiry, placed in a field of interests and seen as functioning in a larger division of intellectual labor. In the shift in academic fashions, which has driven many postcolonial theorists to retool themselves as globalization theorists, this "economics" of the cultural intellectual may be the most consequential future field of action.

PART 2

THE ANARCHIST SUBLIME

CHAPTER 5

THE ORGANIZATIONAL IMAGINARY

IN THE CLINTON IMPEACHMENT SCANDAL, the organizational strategy of the New Christian Right (NCR) was to adopt one of feminism's only practical political proposals: the legal campaign against sexual harassment. Whether this act constituted a borrowing or a theft is not exactly clear. The rough parallels between the Right and the Left were not simply incidental but represented the sort of disturbance implicit in Clintonism itself with its conservative economic and foreign policies, on the one hand, and, on the other, its liberal policies on symbolic issues (among them the issue of gays in the military). Campaigners against sexual harassment have not been confined to the university, but they have tended to see the university as the thin edge of the wedge for testing culturalist political theory in general. Anti-harassment policy has been, above all, an experimental policy on college campuses, which in this case links feminist practice to culturalist theory.

If the plotting against Clinton by the NCR took its cue from one obvious predecessor (the only one close at hand in the cloistral surroundings of Washington), it sought to preserve it by canceling it in its original—for them, nightmarish—form. This predecessor was, of course, the Anita Hill–Clarence Thomas hearings, which dealt with a spectacular case of alleged harassment. Many congressional impeachment leaders considered themselves to be replaying and revising this drama, seeking a poetic justice that was almost biblical. Admittedly, these symbolic parallels may not have played a role for all of the major NCR actors, but the momentum of the impeachment effort certainly accelerated because of the overall climate in which harassment had become a plausible and pervasive charge. Here the cultural Left was closely involved, both directly and as a foil—the latter because the Right's adoption of left strategy, here as elsewhere, was an appropriation and a perversion. It fit into a pattern of reenacting while revising 1960s leftism by learning from its evil genius.

Playing the unwilling role of secret sharer with a radical Right that exaggerated the former's power and obsessively modeled itself on the former's glory, the cultural Left meanwhile had been busy abandoning the organizational focus that brought the Right to the verge of "revolution." That term—which is the Right's itself—suggested to everyone who closely followed the Clinton impeachment that we had all somehow rudely returned to a politics of *state.* Like the actions it described, the term drove home the stakes involved in a revolution that was surely cultural but that was also more than cultural. It did this by setting up a stark contrast with the moralizing spectatorship of the anti-statist politics that for more than two decades has defined the cultural Left.

As I have argued above, the theoretical foundations of the left academy have been generally anti-statist. In the decades in which theory has held sway, an antagonism to what is usually called simply the State (as though there were only one) has been absorbed precritically by graduate students and younger professors as a matter of routine in American universities. I have tried in the Introduction to explain how this came to be, and to point to the intellectual lineages that produced it, but it is important to reiterate that we are not speaking here only of the Americanization of a particular French Nietzschean tradition, even if anti-statism as such is clearly articulated there. This tradition dovetailed with a homegrown individualist anarchism that is as iconically American as cars and westward expansion. At any rate, because the confluences are both historically and nationally varied, I address them in more detail below. The parallels I am setting up between the cultural Left and the NCR, at any rate, although outrageous, are not without truth, and they have been noticed before.[1]

Why outrageous? For one thing, there can be little doubt that the likes of the NCR's spiritual and organizational founders—among them James Dobson and Gary Bauer—are attempting to destroy the cultural Left, not make an alliance with it.[2] Clearly, the NCR defines itself as culturalism's opposite, siding with moral absolutes, family values, a vicious anti-gay rhetoric, and bitter opposition to the culturalists' "chaos of relativism." Using a blanketing Cold War language, the NCR sees the academic theorist (very inaccurately) as Marxist or worse—something more cowardly, indulgent, and confusing than Marxism: a target that will not sit still, that hides rather than dies in the open like the noble stalwarts of the old Left conveniently did. The NCR is *anti*postmodern in the way that one speaks of antimatter, being the movement within American conservatives that historically emerged in the '70s as a cleanup operation on the 1960s.

But although it might seem unfair to say so, there are at least some senses in which the two are complementary opposites. Both draw their energies from the postmodern. The NCR and 1960s youth both built their first underground constituencies on AM radio, both distrust secular government, both attempt to legislate morality, and both exist in "a vigorous but marginalized subculture, strong in the faith" and bent on transforming society radically through "culture."[3] And the subculture of both is more imagined than real. Both are much more hegemonic than they like to believe. As Ronald E. Hopson and Donald R. Smith put it, an understanding of the NCR must consider the resonance of its own rhetoric with "hegemonic American culture in its exploitation of a postmodern cultural climate. . . . The postmodern cultural condition has not only provided more credible sites of opposition and self-identifying contrasts for religious conservatives, it also finds the core rhetoric of the Christian Right finally 'at home' in a larger debate from which it no longer may be marginalized as 'fringe.'"[4]

I am not arguing that the cultural Left can be branded as an accomplice to the NCR, or that superficial parallels are enough to allow one to say that the former is guilty simply for having made the latter angry. I am saying, though, that there are some important strains in the thinking of the cultural Left that are right wing (although not a rightism of the NCR type), and that some of these find expression in the Clinton affair. Because it lacked an adequate theory of organization—in fact, possessed a highly theorized hostility to organization—culturalism aided those it opposed. The relationship between these two constituencies, which others have commented on as well, is usually portrayed as a one-sided war by the NCR against the cultural laxness of the 1960s. However, I am saying more than this. There is a way in which the political legacy of the 1960s can be seen, in Angelo Quattrocchi's words, as "the beginning of the end."[5] After sketching out my general argument about organization, I want to offer an alternative genealogy of the 1960s that bears on the organizational crisis on the cultural Left revealed by the impeachment.

THE FRUITS OF ANTI-HARASSMENT LAW

When I write "organizational imaginary" and make it my title, I am referring to a collective subject. To partake in this imaginary entails an ethic of self-denial or deferral that flies in the face of poststructuralism's millennial ethics and, in general, its replacement of politics by ethics. Immediate intellectual pleasure is placed in the service of the real, and the real is consequently seen as a sublime, as though all merely imagined sublimes were to the real what a circle was to a square. Partaking of this imaginary means "finding a rational solution in human practice and in the comprehension of this practice."[6] To invoke organization is to do more than talk about a division between the abstract and the concrete, or between theory and practice, as we are typically used to hearing about it. Entailed by the division is rather a series of binary conflicts in which binarism itself is resituated centrally in logic and in action. Although the dispute over organization lies between advocates of identity and advocates of the programmatic group, and while one is never far in this arena from talking about the familiar clash between micropolitics and a politics of state, the discursive rift surrounding an organizational imaginary exceeds these particular contests and extends to a number of corollary problems.

For example, implicit in the defense of the collective subject is a view that is difficult to articulate within (and to) the cultural Left, as though there were no longer any vocabulary for doing so—namely, that in politics, *formal* similarities are ethically irrelevant. Not all violence is the same; not all coercion is unjustifiable. This proposition affects all of our analyses. Lying behind the organizational imaginary as I mean it is a view that culturalism sees itself disparaging, but that I think it just does not understand. To be political in a sense that is relevant to engaging with the NCR in the public arena is to grasp that strategies of control, leadership, policy, or direction can be condemned only conjuncturally, not as a matter of principle.

Formalism is the banal ethics of theory, as in Jacques Derrida's widely imitated sentiment that "we cannot formulate a single destructive proposition which has not already had to slip into the form, the logic, and the implied hypothesis of exactly what it is trying to refute"—as though the same form guaranteed the same position, stand, or outcome for actors and subjects.[7] What remains essential is the basically *political* understanding of activity, which is not ignorant of the matter of truth but not subsumable within it, either. For the political, the questions are always: for whom, how much, on whose behalf, to what end, and (especially, and as a warrant for the others) is there any other way? I am well aware that this sort of logic can be easily passed off as sophistry or left barbarity. Leszek Kolakowski, George Lichtheim, Jean-François Lyotard, and other conservative thinkers have made their careers doing so.

But what one most misses in the cultural Left—which of course would not see itself in light of an older type of Cold War intellectual like Lichtheim—is

the acknowledgment that being involved in politics means taking responsibility, assuming the conviction that running from power does not absolve one
from power's outcomes. How easy, after all, to renounce the state, as if societies
existed without states, or as though, in our absence, others would not run the
state. Fleeing power—and the Clinton impeachment showed this as well—is to
take responsibility for those who have assumed it in our absence. The collective
subject of politics is never all-inclusive. One fights on behalf of some, not all—
even at the expense of others. One's principles are always unevenly applied,
which is all the more reason to pick them carefully and argue them openly.

This sort of balanced, committed thinking is precisely what theory has effectively set out to disarticulate. And it is far from merely incidental that this
theoretical climate is, among other things, an anarchist one—in the different,
but related, traditions of Nietzsche, Bataille, Deleuze, and the Foucault who
wrote of "governmentality."[8] While this strain of thinking works at the level of
ethics and argumentation, it does not, of course, prevent an organizational
imaginary from being present in academic professional life. The contradictions, even absurdities, of the world of purity that is theory's *dégagement* are
never faced or evaded. From the running of English departments to annual
meetings of the editorial boards of scholarly journals, academic intellectuals
spend 50 percent of their time in the force fields of bureaucracy, counting votes,
preparing policies. Academic unions at some schools hold hearings, file briefs,
and petition the legislature; ad hoc organizations like Teachers for a Democratic Culture and the Union of Democratic Intellectuals used to print newsletters
and place op-ed pieces. But in general, the writing in cultural studies journals
is, purely speaking, anarchist in its politico/moral positioning. It is not an
interventionist anarchism à la recent anti-globalization activists like David
Groeber or John Sellers but an anarchism that follows the *echt* protocols of the
philosophy-as-art of Nietzsche and the psychoanalytic politics of pop Lacani-
anism, where one posits the body as a substitute regime for mere government.[9]
There one need not suffer guilt for exploiting others, since one's body ventures
nowhere, takes responsibility only for itself, and allows each subject to enjoy
that happy antinomy of a universal experience in a particular being. This is not
a move restricted to the theoretically well versed or the widely read. It has become a common sense and is bolstered by a convergence, on the one hand, of
a forbidding poststructuralist armature and, on the other, of a rather lazy
American individualism.

This anti-statist outlook has myriad corollaries. In some wings of globalization theory, it leads to denouncing defensive nationalist struggles abroad;
in postcolonial theory, it reduces liberation strategists like Amilcar Cabral,

Ahmed Sékou Touré, or Frantz Fanon to unethical demagogues while raising the postcolonial critic to an honorable observatory role; in domestic debates over the public sphere, it champions the micro-heroisms of critic, hacker, artist, and flaneur against the sullied arenas of politics as usual with its horse trading and its constituency politics. Above all, the stateless ones discover that in abdication a theory of virtue can be built, for it is not sufficient to denounce the state on the grounds of its meaninglessness or irrelevancy; rather, it must be denounced on the grounds of its inherently criminal nature.

One of the reasons the Clinton impeachment process became so dangerous early was that left intellectuals were confused by the fusion of left and right ideologies in cultural theory. Several years before the first hint of impeachment, James Carville was urgently arguing that the recently appointed special prosecutor, Kenneth Starr, was not really a judge. He was an interested witness by virtue of his financial ties to right-wing fund-raisers and his professional and personal relationship with figures suing the president. It hardly matters, in retrospect, if Carville was correct in later saying that the entire affair had been orchestrated by Newt Gingrich as a bid to consolidate executively what the NCR had already consolidated legislatively. The impeachment was an attempted coup. That is the first point. It was a plan with a prehistory and a long, cynical course. The only really startling aspect of the plan was how few were willing to concede its meanings as they unfolded in plain sight of day. The Republican revolution, announced jubilantly by Gingrich and others after the electoral successes of 1992, was here simply coming to pass. But no one would take the perpetrators at their word. Representative Barbara Lee (D-California), however, got close: "This process and this action are the real crimes against the American people and our democracy. This march to impeachment is an attempt to undo and overthrow a duly elected President . . . creating the appearance of a one-party autocracy."[10] She was joined by House Judiciary Committee members Maxine Waters, John Conyers, Barney Frank, and others who did not fall short of saying the process was an attack "on the rule of law."

The events, as they unfolded, did not so much prompt conspiracy theories as produce paranoid facts. The events actually demanded conspiracy theories, for only that kind of theory explained what was happening.[11] Buoyed by legislative successes and greater access to key players in government, the NCR plotted to depose Clinton as the only institutional obstacle to its agenda. It is true that a prima facie case against this reading can be found in Clinton's own program, which was a Republican one as it concerned military spending, labor rights, antitrust law, the "drug war," communications law, imperial policy abroad, and domestic civil rights. It was, predictably, in the cultural realm that the Right found displeasure. Clinton opposed outlawing abortion, bringing prayer to public schools, and further criminalizing homosexuality. With powerful allies among corporate revanchist secularists—their issue was not prayer but still deeper and more permanent tax cuts, something Clinton refused to fulfill—the NCR had a viable network of activist federal judges, Washington lawyers, and ambitious members of Congress eager to help them within the plausible bounds (of course) of the "rule of law." "Judge" Starr was their hand of God.

Unable to find impeachable acts in Whitewater, Starr mulled over the commonplace infamy of Clinton the philanderer—a ready-made issue, with a chorus of potential accusers. We cannot escape drawing lessons from the logic of Starr's choice about the unfortunate climate created by academic cultural theory, however. Blurring the boundaries—as here—between ethics and morals, he prepared and perfected an already existing discourse on sexual harassment, deeply a part of the national mood in the late 1990s. Juridically as well as discursively, distinctions between conduct in the workplace and conduct in life (the distinction between ethics and morals) were unclear in part because of the lessons drawn from earlier anti-harassment campaigns. Without it having to be that way, the puritan setting and the culturalist bases of those campaigns conspired to confuse issues of abuse of power, on the one hand, and squeamishness over various proscribed forms of genital play, on the other (extramarital sex, infidelity, fellatio, daddy-daughter role playing, and other interpretations of the Lewinsky/Clinton affair).

If the House would later, in its own mind, set out to rewrite the ending of the Anita Hill drama by providing it with a different moral, Starr set out to replay and revise the drama of feminism's sexual harassment campaigning. Using the enemy against itself, he cast sexual harassment in the role of a stage prop: a noose for the "abortion president," as the Right had begun calling him. The intentional irony of his plan lay in the hope of using women to draw women's support away from the womanizing Clinton, in much the way that the Right had mimicked the sit-ins of the civil rights movement by occupying the lawns of women's health clinics. Accuse him of philandering, entrap him into denial, impeach him for perjury. The utterly valid and important issue taken up by feminism, then, was purposefully twisted into a Dantean punishment for Clintonesque sinning.

Again, I am also suggesting that this was Starr's plan prior to Clinton's first testimony. There was a series of precedents that suggested a favorable outcome for Starr and his minions. People in positions of authority who could not be defeated in any other way had been successfully disgraced from power under the sexual harassment banner. It allowed itself to be used—and it was used—

as a form of *political* censorship and as a settling of scores in cases of professional jealousy. Given such precedents, Starr had reason to believe that whether the charges would legally stick or not, shame alone might drive the president from office (it did drive Speaker-elect Robert Livingston out not long afterward). Thus, the nauseating fake surprise on television talk shows that this president was "incapable of shame." Whatever the reputable intent, and however much harassment as such needed to be faced and fought, there was an organizational naiveté in the arguments defending college women by way of sexual harassment policies that were drawn up so broadly as to include consensual sex and all relationships of "unequal power."

Here we return to the problem of formalism. In thoughtful and lengthy feature essays throughout the 1990s, the premier non-academic magazine of academic issues, *Lingua Franca*, had examined the unromantic realities of sexual harassment policies on college campuses from a number of unexpected angles. Along with exploring cases that one would have expected—young male professors denied tenure for affairs with students—the magazine also ventured into more controversial territory by examining how irreversible were the formal charges of abuse when they involved a well-known psychoanalytic feminist (Jane Gallop).[12] Not at all the sort of anti-PC outrage against harassment policy found, for example, in David Mamet's play *Oleanna*, the magazine's position was perfectly clear about the need for protecting students—primarily women—from coercive sexual favors. And yet its overall editorial policy took the rare position of casting doubt on the extremes of the anti-harassment enterprise.

According to one piece, Adam Weisberger at Maine's Colby College, for example, was denied tenure not for illicit consorting, but for eliciting personal stories of students' families as part of their sociological coursework. Without ever having his case investigated by Colby's administration, and without ever having the chance to face his accusers, he was made a pariah, forced to move off campus, and eventually fired. Later seeking relief in a civil suit for "defamation, intentional infliction of emotional distress, invasion of privacy, and . . . breach of contract," he found little relief from the Equal Employment Opportunity Commission guidelines, which "stipulate numerous legal protections for sexual harassment complainants, but none for accused harassers."[13] One student in the affair sought to extend the meaning of sexual harassment to include any situation in which a student is made to feel intellectually or emotionally uncomfortable. In Weisberger's words, "'Uncomfortable' is a word I came to despise at Colby. It's the tyranny of absolute subjectivity, a way to censure another person without having to give any content." He had a point.

Contradictions between the apparently progressive and the juridically re-actionary lie embedded in the Clinton affair, forecast in miniature in Antioch College's sexual harassment code, which stipulates that in sexual encounters, a man must specifically request to touch each part of a woman's body before doing so (a procedure that, despite its excessive care, still finesses when "yes" actually means "yes.")[14] The point, however, is not to associate all sexual harassment policy with the goals of the special prosecutor. That would be disproportionate. Starr, for one thing, was a conspirator. As we now know, he ignored exculpatory evidence, repeatedly attempted to extort false testimony incriminating to the president, financially ruined and disgraced Clinton's friends, colluded with prosecutors in a separate civil case, and refused to charge, or even investigate, participants in the scandal who clearly broke the law (Linda Tripp). The point is rather the cultural Left's lack of an organizational imaginary. Sexual harassment policies in too many cases ignored the means/ends dilemma implicit in a situation where the rights of willing sexual partners are denied in the name of protecting adult women from their own free choices. An absolutist morality found comfort in an absolutist identity politics, not because they were the same but because the former knew how to mobilize the passions stirred up by the latter for explicit, and devastatingly effective, organizational ends.

None of this is to say that there is no validity to identity politics either. Without drawing any spurious equations, it cannot be coincidental that the great historical actors on behalf of reason for the Democratic Party Left on the Judiciary Committee, or later in the House, were primarily black and gay (Maxine Waters, Barbara Lee, John Conyers, Jr., Charles Rangel, Barney Frank). The leaders of the Right in the House and the Senate were boyz-n-the-(white)-hoods (Bob Barr, Trent Lott). But as a strategy across the culture, identity politics provoked without defending; it angered the satirists without offering any organizational relief or programmatic options. And while it fizzled, the NCR was busy with revolution—but not the revolution imagined by Quattrocchi in his memoir of the 1960s: "the ecstasy of history: the moment when social reality and social dream fuse (the act of love)." Love, indeed.

The apparent ecstasy of much of the NCR's path to revolution was mediated by a day-to-day drudgery of fund-raising luncheons, lobbying junkets, and well-packaged brochures. But it was no less revolution, for the impeachment process involved a deliberate revision of the Constitution by eliminating the separation of powers—a strategy that has become more and more obvious and crude under the presidency of George W. Bush. It sought to make future opposition to Republican *diktats* untenable by muscling forth a view—the ultimate end of American electoral policy—that the winner takes all. This volatile mixture of corporate hubris and missionary zeal sat nicely with the NCR's conviction that majorities rule from above in mimicry of God's harsh love. Discussion and debate are impertinent. The mission of every majority is to drive home numerical advantage by shortcutting future opportunities for dissent.

There was nothing new in Monica Lewinsky. She followed in the steps of Elizabeth Ray, consort of Ohio congressman Wayne Hays in 1976, later posing in *Playboy*, writing a tell-all titled *Washington Fringe Benefit*, and living out her life "as a punchline."[15] Donna Rice (and Gary Hart) came later. What was new was an organization to take advantage of the situation, and a cultural climate that allowed it.

RIGHT YOU ARE

The enduring value of the cultural Left—its true contribution—comes from clarifying the political arena that is culture itself. At least that is the argument many of the cultural studies journals make. But this view is simply wrong. Let us leave alone the career of the word "culture" from the early nineteenth century onward, where it was emphatically yoked to politics in the work of the Young Hegelians, and later the early poetic sociology of Georg Simmel, among others. A more immediate response to culturalist self-flattering might be to point out that the Right has known about the politics of culture for a long time. It represents their signal borrowing from the 1960s, expressing itself as an attack on welfare moms, the "culture of poverty," Ebonics, gay lifestyle, and in what it (positively) calls the Judeo-Christian value system of the traditional family unit and biblical principles in American life. Issues such as school prayer and abortion typically top the organization's agenda, and many of them are directed precisely at the arena of schooling and education in the guise of well-funded campaigns against "tenured radicals" and on behalf of "creation science" and "intelligent design."

Looked at organizationally, the key contribution of the cultural Left lies elsewhere, a contribution by negation. It decenters, dissipates, and atomizes in the name of plurality, heterogeneity, and the supplement. In this intuitive leap toward a new world fashioned as personal choice—as though the world would change one person at a time if only our guilty lust for power could be cast off—the Left ignored the mechanics of recruitment. How had the NCR coalesced into a fighting force in the 1980s and 1990s when only a decade or two earlier it had been reduced to suffering its alienation in private, listening to the angry lyrics of Merle Haggard songs? As it jettisoned the accumulated organizational wisdom of earlier generations, the Left fatally underestimated the necessity for any political movement to have what the NCR had lately learned to mobilize— namely, *myth*. The NCR has the myth of Christianity, to which owners of radio and television stations already adhere; the cultural Left has an emergency myth, but it is based on negations and evasions: the end of Enlightenment reason, critique of Western metaphysics, exchanging binarism for the logical running-and-dodging operation of deconstructive logic, in which it cannot call its own concepts "concepts" but must call them "anti-concepts." The cultural Left conspires against the very universalism that a political myth must have to recruit and expand. Instinctively, the cultural Left understands this and, in a bid for expansion, cops to a preexisting myth that it would publicly disavow, and that it camouflages and denies in itself: the myth of the creative, entrepreneurial, capitalist subject waging war in the shifting realms of consumption.

To grasp the necessity of myth to organization we have to rehearse briefly where the NCR came from and the role it plays in the self-styled centrism of the American state. To begin with, the extremist Right is already in the same universe as the Republican Party generally. The Right's positions are fundamentally those of all American business. It differs only in its style of extremity, in its hatred of secularity, and in a handful of cultural issues. It is possible to argue, in other words, that the advances of the NCR have little to do with organizational brilliance. Blaming the cultural Left might be at least partly misplaced if the Right's power is the result of a hegemony that existed when it first entered the scene, not that it constructed it from scratch or against great odds. One plausible reading of the NCR's rise is that people already in power simply came forth under the spell of an epochal mood to join what was always spiritually there. Strictly speaking, the Right had to win no one over; it did not have to persuade, cajole, or recruit. In its fundamentals, the material interests of hegemony were conceptually the same between the far Right and supposedly "moderate" wings of Republicanism. The NCR had only to become visible as actors, achieve enough discursive coherence to make sense in the pursuit of what the powerful by custom sought. The cable TV owners and radio moguls had only to learn its shtick.

In fact, in other senses as well, the NCR is not a marginal movement. White evangelical Protestants make up about 25 percent of all registered voters. Having found its start in Jerry Falwell's Moral Majority in the late 1970s, the NCR reemerged with more sophistication and better connections in the Christian Coalition of the 1980s, launched by cable television owner Pat Robertson and political strategist Ralph Reed. "A lot of groups have a great Washington presence and some have great grassroots," observed one member of Congress, "but few combine them both."[16] Waiting for the NCR to crumble under the weight of its own successes (and subsequent dilution into the theist American center) became a common pastime following the Republican takeover of Congress in 1994. It is unlikely to happen, however, since the NCR is primarily a political, not a religious, movement (religion is only its myth). In this case, a political program spawned a religious strategy, rather than a religious conviction prompting political involvement.[17] Ralph Reed has admitted as much about himself.

Once again we come back to the shadow dance of Left and Right. The NCR thrives on the imagery of being a persecuted minority defining, negatively, a social ideal. "The effect of such terms is to stigmatize just those persons who historically have been excluded from equal participation in normative culture and have long been considered cultural 'outsiders' and 'troublemakers.'"[18] It takes the place of the Left in the absence of the Left.

War on the '60s? No, War of the '60s

Let us entertain the following rough genealogy. In the 1960s youth woke up from its Cold War slumber, initiating protests that largely looked with horror and hope at events in various parts of the Third World—Vietnam, China, Algeria. This relationship to the Third World borrowed from the language of the pre- and postwar avant-gardes at the same time that it borrowed from the party solidarities of international communism, mixing (on the one hand) the likes of the neo-ethnographic fantasies of the conservative and despairing modernists of the College de Sociologie with (on the other) those geniuses of cultural theory who had committed themselves to organizational work—Antonio Gramsci, for example. The outcome of the struggle between these two very different traditions was determined in advance by the official intellectual climate in which revolt itself was occurring. Given the persistent reinvigoration of Cold War hostilities from above as well as the moribund rhetoric of the European Left's parliamentary strategies; and given the self-gratification among youth of a psychosexual and generational freedom as well as the middle-class identities of many of the protesters, a radical, utopian protest of grafitto and *dérive*, rather than electoral strategy or labor party, was inevitable.

Through many mediations, the generational break found expression in a renunciation of party for consensus and the spontaneous act (what, in a different era, the great nineteenth-century agitator Mikhail Bakunin called the "revolution of the deed"). In academic circles, the break with party Hegelianism found comfort, among other places, in philosophical sources that tended to yoke together anti-statist notions with Third Worldist evocations (the "other," the "subaltern"). The combined effect of this new trend—what came to be known as poststructuralism in theory and as postmodernism in the arts and architecture—was and is, politically speaking, anarchist. It did not merely reject modernity as an Enlightenment project, as one popular formulation has it.

Nevertheless, this movement toward the post entailed the conflation of Eurocentric with non-Eurocentric modernisms. Eurocentrists and elitists like Edmund Husserl or Nietzsche could be marshaled against Marx or Fanon in the name of supporting the Third World subject and his/her society. The paradox was that one was reducing complexity in the name of expanding it. Attacks on a dangerous universalism that critics located in Marxist or anti-colonial internationalism were predicated on what in the end was an absurd linkage between those modes of thought and eighteenth-century accounts of "Man" delivered in the now infamous contexts of the slave trade and the rise of scientific racism. What appears to be a conflict between the modern and the postmodern, or between reductive references to class and more inclusive or differential investments in the new social movements, is a structural ruse within a broader culture of capitalism itself, in which protest (with youth as the key player) is itself colonized by the fetish of philosophical idealisms, vintage European nihilisms, and the subtle uses of Third World imagery, referents, and styles to exoticize and dramatize Eurocentrism itself. This was not, of course, the exclusive legacy of the 1960s either organizationally or intellectually. But it was one that came into prominence in the newly corporatist Europe and United States of the 1980s and 1990s. All of this was highly successful, at any rate, because it took place not as an argument meeting others on the same terrain of the political, but as a "fucking with the categories"—as an attempt to outwit thought, and to destroy the very means of possibility of liberatory thinking in its older sense.

In place of critique, poststructuralism and postmodernism offer us a curious and morbid anatomy. They offer a prognosis but absent of rage or satire, focused on the future but evoking only an endless string of repetitions. They say, "we need not make" because "we already are"—and anyway, we have no choice. I am, therefore I resist. None of this takes away from their strong ethical component, of course, which on its own terms must be given its due. This ethical stance reminds us that not all politics takes place within parties; the repressed are not always to be understood in terms of poverty or economic exploitation; media saturation does, in fact, change the nature of awareness and action in ways that give new prominence to struggle in and through culture.

But postmodernism alludes to and mimics (without being) a critique of commodification. The proof of Habermas's dictum that modernity is an unfinished project lies in the modernism of postmodernism itself, in the sense that, like Baudelaire in his own time, postmodern theorists are driven by an anxiety about their own redundancy in the unchallenged supremacy of a market-generated popularity in culture. Everything that matters to the public at large seems to fall outside the critics' jurisdiction. They are motivated by the worry that they exist beyond the boundary of the public's frames of reference. But unlike Baudelaire, the postmodernist is unable to make resistance to the popular a highly valued form of aesthetic refinement; he or she must now appropriate the popular, call it their own, and fill it with a content that ensures the need for an interpretation that only professionals can provide. Social analysis is in this way aestheticized, and resistance is located in the activities of spectators within the networks of commercial culture.

For postmodernism, resistance already exists, and political work is an act of looking, discovering, uncovering, and interpreting the dramas of subversion that take place, as it were, automatically in everyday life. It has no theory of action. At its core, postmodernism is difficult to assimilate to a progressive politics since it is actually enabled by consumerism's ideological constants. It gives metaphorical support to the American illusion that we live classlessly when it speaks of the leveling of high and low art; it supports the worship of technology when talking about the liberatory potential of the video camera, public access television, Internet communities, and "subversive consumption"; it glorifies the important consumerist concept of novelty—implicit in its own claim to represent an epochal break—whose value lies precisely in being new: the new product. It stands in this way for a disposable tradition, an ideological planned obsolescence. Positing an epistemological break that is not there, it wants instead to *effect* a break. In short: it abandons as passé what it eagerly helped to destroy.

Postmodernism fixates on surface phenomena and allegorizes them. Thus, decentering, for example, alludes in celebratory language to the efforts of local neighborhoods or ethnic groups to speak for themselves at the same time that it unmistakably alludes (of course, without intending to) to corporate strategies of diversified management and niche marketing. Like the nightly news report that juxtaposes information about the Gulf War and police crackdowns with sporting events and fashion tips, everything that supposedly matters is delivered on the same level. Everything is simply the same, even as it operates under the rubric of difference.

Postmodernism purports to speak for youth and against outmoded rhetoric—a key category of the post-'68 variant. The principal claim to political relevance of postmodernism has therefore always been precisely this: it relates. But which youth? In this discourse, the Left has ceased to be spoken about as church groups, community organizations, trade unions, party activists, or campus ethnic groups. It is instead columnists and writers of books, New Ageists, ecomilitants, magazine editors, gay clubgoers, performance artists, and computer hackers—audiences that suggest class and racial biases usually denied by postmodernism's own careful rhetorical gestures of inclusion.

Its stance is basically theatrical. It dramatizes modernity's great philosophical banality: epistemological uncertainty. Enacting submission in the costume of revolt, it performs its politics *within* epistemology, where the critic already finds a home, and locates epistemology within the subject. Freud for them is therefore primarily a theorist of subjectivity rather than a clinical analyst of neurosis; Benjamin is primarily a theorist of shock or *Sehnsucht* (longing), rather than of the industrial-architectural-economic portal onto modernity, the Parisian Arcades. It is a stay-at-home sort of politics, a praxis of spectatorship.

As a politics, the post-'68 spin on the postmodernism debate adds to the earlier ontological description of a social state two normative strictures: (a) to organize on the basis of biological identities and (b) to be epistemologically modest by observing the limits of any claim to know or speak for others. But if it is a coalition politics, its enunciation remains incoherent. The organizational questions are suspended. The "how" of power goes by the wayside. Its obsessions therefore lie with the meaning of individual artifacts at the expense of the circuits and networks of distribution and control. Although clearly left in its motives, since it asserts the value of popular taste, accords agency and intelligence to supposedly passive consumers, and defends the rights of those involved in targeted lifestyles like homosexuality and youth countercultures, it fails to ask: How do cultural expressions or alternative forms of perception link constituencies or organize them into a politically potent force? And once linked, around what set of goals? It telescopes the process of Americanization and, by telescoping, urges it on, acting as its de facto advocate. Thus, the claim that the postmodern sensibility has been inherited rather than invented, that it is a cultural dominant, reasserts American centrality.

Shibboleth du Jour

The concept of an organizational imaginary is largely untheorized today, even in those Deleuzian and left-Lacanian circles where we would most expect to find it (Alain Badiou, Slavoj Žižek).[19] One looks for it in vain, for example, in the one book of cultural theory of the 1980s and 1990s that most greeted as the blueprint for a new activist politics. Ernesto Laclau and Chantal Mouffe's *Hegemony and Socialist Strategy*, however, is a book whose inexplicable fame for more than a decade concealed a tendentiousness that was quite planned and consciously carried out. Its distortions cannot be simply written off as confusion either. Laclau's organizational past in Latin America makes it unlikely that he did not realize that he and his coauthor consistently superimposed the Second International on the Third. "Marxism" as such in their book is equated with the policies and procedures of German social democracy of 1880–1914, and they ignore the innovations of the interwar communist era from which he and his contemporaries were quietly borrowing. This sleight of hand is fundamental to the structure of the book, and immediately apparent to readers aware of this political history. Not only does the book surreptitiously appropriate the very critique of the writers it then renders passé, it has the audacity to cast these stolen lessons in ensemble in the guise of its own novelty, which is then said to obliterate the intellectual milieu that enabled it. This is not to say, however, that the ideas are competently stolen. The authors' instrumental deployment of Gramsci, for example, reduces the Italian writer to an unrecognizably sentimental and drifting figure. Since, however, the failings of the book have already been detailed by others, it is only left to observe that in the broadest sense, the book is subject to a startling irony.[20] The Third International that the authors revile was among the first political tendencies to understand and to organize what today are called the "new social movements," which it did inadequately, perhaps, but no more so than other pioneering efforts.

Culturalist theory has eagerly defended itself against charges of political posing and organizational immaturity following a series of public reprimands—symbolized by Alan Sokal's famous spoof exposing the editors of the cultural studies journal *Social Text*, for having published essays the editors never in fact read. Lacanian-inspired feminism has especially mounted a defense since its claims to represent an insurrectionary politics of performance have been most pronounced. And, in fact, Judith Butler's essay "Merely Cultural" in *Social Text* signaled the start of the period we are still within. Theory pushed by the substitutional logic of the political self ratchets up its claims, invites external rebuke, and ends up reeling before the blows. But the blows no longer come from a traditionalist old guard alone; they include left critics like Barbara Ehrenreich, Thomas de Zengotita, JoAnn Wypijewski, Robert McChesney—writers and activists publishing in venues of integrity, irreproachable on intellectual grounds, who cannot be dismissed as being part of the machinery of bad faith set in motion by the conservative acolytes of the culture wars.[21] It is revealing that a Lacanian theorist like Butler, unfairly ridiculed by a conservative academic journal for being a bad writer, chose to defend herself in an op-ed column for the *New York Times* by building her case on the writing of Theodor Adorno and Herbert Marcuse.[22] And it conforms to the thesis I have been building here. These Frankfurt School theorists, after all, played almost no role in the work that established Butler's academic fame. It is ironic, too, that both Adorno and Marcuse had identified precisely the culturalist tendencies of American criticism that are arguably found in Butler's project as the impediment to thought and political responsibility. As Adorno uncompromisingly put it in an essay from 1955:

> The isolation of the mind from material production heightens [cultural criticism's] esteem but also makes it a scapegoat in the general consciousness for that which is perpetrated in practice. Enlightenment as such—not as an instrument of actual domination—is held responsible. Hence the irrationalism of cultural criticism.[23]

These sentiments sound a good deal like those Butler and others were dismissing as "left conservatism," right down to its charge that American cultural criticism of the 1950s had already learned to rely on what would become a poststructuralist standby of the 1990s: a rejection of the Enlightenment. Disregarding this specificity, Butler is forced to defer to its good sense. Theory suddenly protests that it was really about praxis all along, translating itself into the mimicry of a program as the judgmental readers of the *New York Times* look on.[24] Butler's acerbic jabs in *Social Text* against those critics who refused to grant that the revolt in theories of language was equivalent to the emancipation of the individual are a locus classicus of this move, and linked to the impeachment by way of her bid to transform "the ways in which sexuality is socially regulated" as a function of "political economy" (271).[25] The vitality of a critique of the social regulation of sexuality, brilliantly worked out in earlier decades by Alexandra Kollontai, Simone de Beauvoir, and then later (in the moment of theory) by critics like Audre Lorde, Rayna Reitner, and Butler herself, is here hypostasized. Would that oppression in the form of sexual regulation was worked out by Butler, in addition to her other effective means, also in terms of political economy; in fact, sexual regulation as such is its substitute. Adorno certainly would have denounced such a move. Apart, then, from the merits or demerits of her charge, it is this appropriative gesture and partial retelling of the past that has to be objected to.

These feints of culturalist theory—as well as its ill humor when crossed—are not limited to the Lacanian Left or to journals like *Social Text*. It is rather that keywords like the polyvocal or even the term *culture* itself are universally taken by left academics to show up and face down traditional forms of party organization or parliamentary coalitions. By way of circuits of influence that crisscross fields as diverse as Continental philosophy, aesthetic criticism, and radical sociology, this gnosis extends in many directions. Some of this logic even shows up, of all places, in the essays of American studies, Renaissance literary criticism, and theater history, forming part of an osmotic field of theory. To give an example both of the unchallenged ubiquity of this move and of its weaknesses, I turn to an essay by someone whose work I happen to admire, in order to develop the point that we are dealing with the aftershocks of a historical transition that laid waste a vibrant political culture. The essay has the advantage, as well, of weighing in on the intellectual inheritance of a generation that has preoccupied me throughout the writing of this book, for it looks back to the years of the transition now cast in a different light. In the essay in question, Eric Lott squares off against Richard Rorty and others while lampooning what he calls the "boomer liberals."[26]

Displaying the courage to name names at the cost of professional ease, Lott typifies many of the strengths of public political engagement in the academy. An analyst of race in American public life, he has written well on a variety of important issues. I want to look closely at this essay because it lies squarely in the anti-statist tradition I have been tracing here, although above all because it does not do so in any recognizably postmodern sense. Precisely because Lott's work cannot be confused with the excesses of verbal play or the gnomic utterances of the Heideggerian tradition in general—as, for example, in the neo-Schmittian oracles of post-2000 theory—it is important to deal with its organizational assumptions, and to notice the intellectual constellations he assembles, while heralding its by-now-familiar pantheon. At the same time—and this is another reason I turn to Lott—he adopts these pro forma positions in a curious blending. In place of the austere circumlocutions and aestheticist striving of theory in its overdrive mode, he displays the verbal sting represented by the best writing in the *Nation*, the *London Review of Books*, or *Harper's* (publications that have not generally had much time for the effete anarcho-sublime of academic theory). About the "boomer liberals," says Lott with a sneer, "these left-leaning suckers are in dire need of an anti-white, *anti-statist* critique" (24).

Clearly, coalition is one of the principal objectives of any attempt to organize a political force. Given academic jealousies, it would be easy to jump unthinkingly into a dispute in order to one-up the other side, as though one's own shrewdness were the only thing that mattered in the exchange of cultural capital that establishes academic reputations. But in the context of this essay particularly, it would be self-contradictory. The venom of Lott's own essay when dealing with the "boomers" implies a decision to treat his critical targets as outright enemies, perhaps following the common organizational tactic of removing the proximate first. It is a tactic, one could argue, that I have been using myself in this chapter. Admittedly, one begins a debate only after deciding whether one's opponents are on the same side or not. It is a fair question, and a necessary one, organizationally speaking. Lott apparently does not believe he and the boomers are. But I believe he and I are, so I want to conduct my intervention accordingly. The fight below, then, as I see it, is about not ends or intentions, but an imaginary that underlies current academic political thinking as one legacy of the 1960s that is not understood as such.

Among its myriad other differences, Lott's essay is more publicly focused than Butler's "merely cultural" even as it joins her in responding to culturalism's post-Sokal accusers, although now a different branch—the social democratic journalists (rather than left academics) who have attacked culturalism in light of the NCR's legislative successes. The cultural Left and the NCR are typically set against one another in these attacks, and positioned as foils. Hence, the unexpected parallels between Lott and the Butler of the essay here suggest a degree of merely cultural confusion over political stakes and philosophical genealogies within the cultural Left generally—and that is what I want to address.

The ripostes of Lott and Butler both start out with a similar inaccuracy: the opening gambit of both is to make a great deal of their critics' charge that identity politics is a failure primarily because it threatens left unity. This thesis allows both to point out, rather easily, that this purported unity is specious. According to Butler, the anti-culturalists speak of "a sense of a common history, a common set of values, a common language, and even an objective and universal mode of rationality," considered essential to political movement and romantically associated with a pastoral era before poststructuralism arrived with its purportedly "factionalizing, identitarian, and particularistic" cultural politics.[27] Butler is, of course, correct when she points out the coercive fallacy at the heart of these appeals to seeing national culture as a happy family. The problem lies not with her countercharge but with its application. The view that she successfully attacks is much more the stock-in-trade of establishment liberals like Arthur Schlesinger, Jr., or Harold Bloom than of her actual critics (with some exceptions)—the so-called left conservatives of the Modern Language Association and the academic journals whose positions closely resemble those of Adorno above (that left Hegelian, social democratic grouping I alluded to in the Introduction). More important, picking an easy target conceals the organizational weaknesses that she would prefer not to look at too closely and that she covers up in calculated terminology, as in her use of the term "political economy."

Similarly, Lott's boomer liberals—a group he implausibly cobbles together to include everyone from Richard Rorty to Todd Gitlin, Jim Sleeper, Greil Marcus, Paul Berman, Joe Klein, and Sean Wilentz, among others—are not primarily challenging culturalism's breaking of ranks, although that is an element in some of them. Their larger point is that culturalism is amateurish, un-serious, and self-indulgent—which are claims that Lott ignores. The focus of most of these writers is not the sectarianism of the cultural Left, in other words, but its bad faith. In their eyes, it is too hung up on racist imagery in popular film to articulate an analysis of the tax base; too vocal about the psychotraumas of otherness to be articulate about class violence in housing and education; too eager to speak about identity to scrutinize laws, policies, and unions. Lott may be on firm ground attacking the boomers, but on these points they rather than he are right.

Aside from the dubiousness of the list as a list (Joe Klein and Greil Marcus—not to mention Jim Sleeper and Richard Rorty—simply do not belong together in any meaningful sense that is not so abstract as to demand a much larger list still, indeed everyone), there certainly are lines of attack that can be made against the boomer liberals, just not the ones chosen. Blaming the boomers for being white boys only jumbles real differences and resorts to stock epithets that are easily transportable and, in spite of the appeal to poststructuralist difference, surprisingly nondifferentiating. To talk about liberal racism and white ideology is never irrelevant, but in this context it misses a more important point. The subtlety of these particular charges obscures the real reasons one should have animus toward the boomer crew: Rorty's nativist patriotism, for example; Berman's right-wing fascination with left-wing causes and celebrities; Gitlin's Zionism and his apologies for U.S. imperial intervention in Iraq, Latin America, and elsewhere. What ought to be challenged is the claim of some of these fellows to *any* Left. Rorty is a Cold War liberal, Berman an Orwellian spook. All of that story is sacrificed to a reduction, in which race plays the major ideological role. Rather than pinpointing an emergent fraction of conservative, primarily white leftists, anxious about irregular identities demanding their own forms of organization, Lott has instead assembled a broad sampling of divergent opinion united on only one point: the conviction that the cultural Left has no realizable politics. It is perhaps the only point that could unite them, because it is so pervasive, so urgent, and so obvious. In other words, he has helped to show the precariousness of his own position.

As always, Lott is effective in prying loose the hidden subtexts of racial bigotry (he has a field day reading between the lines of Rorty's unctuous prose). Memorably and mercilessly, he ridicules the simplifications and peevish dismissals of the journalist social democrats. But he never concedes the saliency of the boomers' basic charge about organizational naiveté, and his overall argument collapses as a result. Announcing itself as a holdout for the rights of African Americans, immigrants, women, and gays to shake up the false unity of a "color-blind" socialism, the essay only underscores the power of identitarian shibboleth. It implies that an earlier, organizational Left had no theory of subclass formations, never weighed in on the particular problems of race and gender, never participated in special forms of organizing along identitarian lines. Something is very wrong when someone of Lott's caliber repeats these legends, which are untenable and easily disprovable by considering the work, among others, of Karl Kautsky, Nancy Cunard, Langston Hughes, and C. L. R. James, as well as a number of other figures whose intellectual and political development took place within the traditions of socialism and the labor movement. Of course, the boomer liberals might very well disown a lineage as red as this one, but Lott is targeting an old white Left whose traditions extend back to these figures in a present largely derived from them.

The real issue is whether a post-1960s poststructuralist theory is guilty of disabling or trivializing protest during the Right's march to power. The authors skirt that issue, unfortunately, contenting themselves with taunting their critics (in Lott's case, a "white male cadre badly in need of a rationale," 27). Such language is gripping in its anger, and thrillingly ad hominem, but obscures the theoretical conflict inherent in identitarian logic. For example, there are obvious candidates for inclusion in the boomer liberal camp that Lott ignores because they are either not white or not male: Cornel West, Katha Pollitt, both of them eloquent exposers of culturalism's dead ends. Nor is the problem only one of exclusion. Making fun of Rorty for droning on about the virtues of Irving Howe even as Rorty busily ignores A. Philip Randolph (a good point there), Lott holds up for praise such "bona fide intellectuals" as Lani Guinier in order to demonstrate Rorty's narrow focus. But the invocation of Guinier in this context is odd. Whatever her considerable merits as a legal voting strategist, Guinier is a paradigm of Clinton liberalism, an uncritical fan of Janet Reno, her mentor, who is a politician that the Left and Right alike should have wanted in jail for her criminal handling of the events in Waco.

If attentive to history, one would suppose, Lott would find it hard to contest at least some of the boomers' barbs—for example, that labor at some point must be organized for the Left to thrive. But while Lott almost certainly agrees with this proposition in general, he instead rebukes the boomers' "fantasy" of a newly buttressed AFL-CIO, adding that the "white guys" might learn from "activist movements all over the country . . . what it's actually like to work in today's strikingly recomposed labor force" (31). True enough; there certainly are a number of "white guys" who deserve this lesson. But he is wrong to suppose that the AFL-CIO is not organizing blacks and women, or that the union movement is not theorizing the newly recomposed labor force, making it the center of its discussions. The condescension here is startling. Lott's positing of collective guilt, his circular reasoning (black liberals like Guinier cannot be boomers because boomers are by definition white)—both rest on a single problematic basis: an assertion that a middle-aged, 1960s-trained white Left is ignoring contemporary black activism because it feels left out.[28]

But there are two things wrong with this approach. It fails to concede the active relationship that culturalism itself has to the legacy of the 1960s and it never characterizes black activism. Is it really cut off from the white Left he wants to associate with the 1960s as a basically segregationist liberalism? That is, does he really suppose that the likes of Gitlin or Sleeper would oppose black activism in the form of a modern A. Phillip Randolph? Clearly they would not. Their demur has rather to do with the specious triumph of a multiculturalist inclusiveness that pays scant attention to cultures of belief.

Much of what riles Lott when he takes up Todd Gitlin, for example, has to do with the logic he himself employs—that of "removing the proximate first." On the surface it appears that the charge against culturalism by the boomer liberals is merely that of culturalism's abdication, as though its sin were indulging in a pretentious surface identification of minority status with desirable position. But lurking unmistakably in the likes of Gitlin or Pollitt is a different kind of charge entirely: that the cultural Left is perhaps on the other side of wrong. They implicitly ask: could it be that a certain kind of cultural leftism was an expression of a historical lineage of right nihilism and aristocratic "radicalism" of the sort represented by the *incroyables* of the French Revolution—a politics of style designed to save it, above all, from the vulgarity and passions of the populace? This culturalism may talk of popular movements, they imply, but it is basically a prop for the academy's lumpen intelligentsia.

I think there are traces of truth in that account, but that it goes too far. The theoretical legacies of 1960s France and the United States that inform culturalism have obviously been positive in many respects: challenging anti-intellectualism; undercutting America's "show me" commonplaces; adding weight to the critique of American technophilia, functionalism, and empiricist faith; and forcing a showdown on issues of race, gender, and sexuality in various media. On the downside, they have often endorsed the American self, dignified consumerism, neutralized the language of protest, contributed to Cold War rhetoric, and offered themselves up as a ripe target for the religious Right, which, unlike culturalism, never forgot about the state. More than anything, they lacked an organizational imaginary, and sought to destroy it in others.

CHAPTER 6

THE EMPIRE'S NEW CLOTHES

The Futurists: A group of small schoolboys who escaped from a Jesuit college, created a small ruckus in the nearby woods, and were brought back under the rod of the forest warden.
—ANTONIO GRAMSCI, 1929

OF ALL THE PROBLEMS WEIGHING ON CULTURAL THEORY, the most troubling (because most rife with self-reflection) is that of the intellectual at work. Why at the very moment of emphasizing, even exaggerating, the importance of the intellectual in political life has cultural theory had so little to say about its own social function?

In posing this question, I am not implying that the moment of theory has passed or that the energies of various theoretical movements in the post–World War II period have been totally sapped. The implications are more direct and contentious: namely, that theory has become a code word for relatively predictable positions in the humanities and related social sciences, most of which turn on the ideas of social transformation, historical agency, the disposition of selfhood (however understood), and the heterogeneity of cultures—all posed in the context of a critique of Enlightenment thought. But to the extent that such ideas have become routine in their very disruptiveness (or the other way around), our most vaunted theoretical figures today may well resemble the generation of futurists, whose pretensions to revolutionary and avant-garde originality Gramsci lampoons in the above epigraph.[1]

If the claims to intellectual oppositionality sound equally hollow these days, this may have as much to do with the general difficulty of distinguishing what counts as opposition or novelty as it does with an anarchist will to truth. At any rate, this is the position I will try to elaborate and justify by looking

closely at Michael Hardt and Antonio Negri's *Empire* and the related work of
Giorgio Agamben, for it seems to me that we have to traverse some distance before we can square the critical reception of these authors (which has been nothing short of dramatic) with the actual arguments, analyses, and proposals offered by them.[2]

One of those proposals is implicit in the very title of *Empire*. Emblazoned
across the cover is the first of many double meanings whose purpose is to enact
a kind of productive ambiguity. For *Empire*, it turns out, has almost nothing to
say about the actual peoples and histories the empires left behind.[3] There are,
of course, discussions of the "end of colonialism," of the effects of the Vietnam
War on the American government and European youth, on the disasters of the
nation for the anti-colonial movements; and there are several vignettes of postcolonial identity (on Toussaint L'Ouverture, for example) and references to
Marx's writing on India, as well as Sartre's essays on race. But the authors barely
nod in the direction of guest-worker systems, uncapitalized agriculture, and
the archipelago of *maquiladoras* at the heart of globalization's gulag. Apart
from a handful of passages where they are fleetingly adduced, the colonized of
today are given little place in the book's sprawling thesis about multitudes,
biopolitical control, and the creation of alternative values.

Empire's authors would argue that there is a good reason for this apparent
inability on their part to give a tactile sense of what is entailed by "trade" in
places like Colombia or Afghanistan—the brute hunger and brutality of the
operation—and their willingness to adopt a more prophetic tone about an
inviting future already contained in the present. On the terms they lay out, their
title is not meant to refer to imperialism, after all; so they cannot be criticized
for failing to summon the meanings appropriate to that term. "Empire," as the
authors make abundantly clear, refers to an acephalous regime of value operating from below, superseding national states and dissipating vulgar governmental agendas. They consciously coin this term to leave readers with an enabling
and inexorable expression of popular will, which it is the authors' desire not
only to thematize but to call into being. One of the first things to understand,
from the authors' point of view, is that this tear in the fabric of an older rhetoric of emancipation and resistance implied by the term imperialism is not just
a rending but an opening. And the authors may also be aware, at least subcon-
sciously, of other potential critiques of their neological ambitions.

It cannot be said that *Empire* is indifferent to the religious/ethnic missionary zeal of the classical and modern empires themselves. The book gives some
space to talking about such matters. The complaint would have to be further
qualified: that although the authors briefly turn to such concerns, they do so

only to allot them a place in the past. Their focus is never on imperialism as an infrastructural necessity (of either capitalism or some other social force). What preoccupies them, by contrast, is the historical ambivalence of imperialism's various *epistemes*, where European conquest is seen as having been a utopian project. To put this another, but no less problematic, way: the main interest of imperialism for Hardt and Negri lies in the new forms of identity it unleashed across the globe—a view that fits, mutatis mutandis, very comfortably with a mainstream perception that America's global influence has been largely positive. It would be difficult, even foolish, to separate *Empire*'s favorable coverage in the mainstream press from this aspect of its argument.[4] This bulky, and to the public certainly obscure, book—part a retelling of the history of European political science, part futurology, part popularization of the work of Gilles Deleuze—has been championed in the media for a simple reason: it argues that there is no such thing as U.S. imperialism and that contemporary capitalism offers the subject a new mode of being, one of infinite possibility. Mainstream news sources were understandably attracted by a book of radical theory that coincided so closely with their own official story.

One can account for the subtlety of *Empire*'s intentions, but to ignore the incompatibility of the book's governing themes with political events would be no more acceptable than an overly literal reading. As the United States ushers in a new government in Baghdad, criminalizes those who quibble with its military plans, and thumbs its nose at the Geneva Conventions, *Empire*'s thesis that imperialism has ended is likely to seem absurd. The authors seem not to understand the risks of defining new paradigms against the lurid backdrop of military invasion and repression. But if this contrast too is contained in their calculations, one might then conclude that since the deployment of ambiguity is a conscious strategy on their part, controverting the book's arguments alone would miss the point, for either the book's diagnosis is less foolish than it seems or theory itself suffers from a more self-defeating aspect than mere error. *Empire*, I am suggesting, is worth looking at in order to give this aspect a name.

At the heart of Hardt and Negri's project are four basic arguments: first, that the age of imperialism has given way, through globalization, to a new age of "Empire"; second, that a tradition of radical thought from Italy is uniquely situated to broker a wedding of Deleuzian theory with Marxist practice—the philosophical amalgam necessary for bringing Empire to recognition. Both propositions require, in turn, a third, an updated analysis of the new types and shifting parameters of postindustrial labor. It is here that one finds an attempt to portray a new "subjectivity of labor" manifest in the "multitude"—a social formation unprecedented in appearance and incalculable in importance, like

Gramsci's subaltern in that it avoids an overreliance on the analytic of class. Finally (and this is *Empire*'s most provocative gambit, and its only claim to originality), the revolution long sought by the Left need not be planned or hoped for. It has already taken place.

Readers captivated by such far-reaching, even foundational, assertions are, however, immediately confronted by a dilemma. Why, at a moment of American imperial adventure almost Roman in its excess, is the end of imperialism confidently announced? And why by intellectuals on the far Left for whom the older legacies of communism are not radical enough? The imperatives underlying these questions seem so contradictory, in fact, that one hunts for a dialectical mode capable of explaining how a deeply ambitious theoreticism—the full flower, in fact, of three decades of refined '68ist Continental philosophy—could come to sound, in *Empire*'s hands, so pragmatic, so cheery, and if one can put it this way, so American. The critic begins to see at this juncture that *Empire* signifies beyond itself; that it is meaningful not as the originator of something but as the unwitting record of an older something; that the reason to explore it has nothing to do with its faddish explosion onto the scene, but with its poignant embodiment of a deeply ambivalent left/right impulse derived from the theoretical legacies of the 1960s. I would argue that criticism desperately needs a vocabulary for describing how the very ability to distinguish between resistance and conformity has, in the U.S. context, become elusive. Moreover, that elusiveness defines the present climate of cultural theory itself.

VALUE AND SELF-VALORIZATION

Let me now turn to a closer examination of *Empire*'s conceptual apparatus. *Empire* is above all a return—a "recapture," as Gilles Deleuze and Félix Guattari have put it in a very different context.[5] If we take only its most prominent themes, *Empire* reprises the globalization debates of the last two decades in fairly straightforward ways.[6] In its pages, readers again find the history of Bretton Woods, the routine treatments of the Treaty of Westphalia, the obligatory references to the British East India Company, and the birth of the Internet, all described in superfluous detail because they have been treated in any number of previously published books. Its turn to biopolitics closely follows the arguments of Anthony Giddens's "life political agenda" in writings from more than a decade earlier.[7] Moreover, the authors' basic premise is part of the stock-in-trade of earlier cosmo-theory: namely, that the age of imperialism has passed.[8] The great powers of old, we are again told, ruled in the name of single nations, whereas today we find a supranational entity that coheres without coherence and rules without government (Hardt and Negri's term is "Empire," but others have given this basic concept other names: "the global ecumene" or, in a more critical variant, "McWorld").

In its practical demands, moreover, Negri's work (in *Empire* as elsewhere) is indistinguishable from that of an earlier time. In many ways that work squarely fits within the traditions of council communism of Europe of the 1930s and 1940s, which rejected programmatic political organization as dangerous and counterproductive and placed its stress on spontaneous eruptions and on a tactical orientation based on a rhetoric of "given possibilities." Like the council communists, Negri considers capitalism so ubiquitous and penetrating that it cannot be directly opposed. The council communists had similarly argued that workers must exist inside capitalism, finding their own "mass rhythm," basing their collectivity on "social average labour time" until they plan their own productivity.[9] While these ideas may seem familiar to readers of *Empire*, I am quoting them directly from the writing of interwar thinkers unmentioned in the book—Anton Pannekoek, Karl Korsch, and Otto Ruhle.[10] *Empire*'s ideas in ensemble, and even at times in their literal wording, are substantially the same. Many of *Empire*'s arguments, in other words, are seven decades old. At least some of the admiration for the book depends on the sad historical fact that the histories of the labor movement have become unfamiliar to audiences, and so these latter-day echoes of that past appear novel.

But to speak of *Empire* as a return is also a way of alluding to its emergence from a new Italian political tradition—its having grown out of a milieu provided by the autonomia movements of the Italian far Left of the 1970s, whose theorists have lately presented themselves publicly as a "front": the descendants of earlier street clashes now seasoned by the sophistications of Franco-German theory.[11] *Empire* is a new Italian text, in that sense, and must be seen within that constellation. It should be remembered that Hardt and Negri stress these national-cultural associations themselves—that is, they repeatedly draw our attention to the specifically Italian radicalism they espouse, the particular advantages of coming to politics in what Hardt and Paolo Virno call "laboratory Italy," and the public existence of the front that constitutes, in their terms, a new "Italian radical thought" as such.[12]

Like that earlier impossible unity "French theory," new Italian thought involves an orientation to a national past, an intellectual corpus, and—above all—an instinctive understanding of the strength in numbers that comes from a national-cultural identity. This is an important feature of the purported globalism that Hardt and Negri say they represent; as in so many other instances of globalization, the national-cultural retains its force and enables the very discourse that veils its continued existence. Italy's peripheral place in southern Europe, its notoriously weak and short-lived postwar governments, its hothouse radicalizations of the 1970s have all coalesced in an image now stamped on the reader's imagination in an act of self-making by a new irruption of theory. A new Italian theory reinvigorates its earlier French counterpart, taking over in the wake of lagging French energies and the fatigue of its intellectual stereotypes.[13]

But not all of *Empire* has to do with these restrictive or local inspirations. There is much to praise in Hardt and Negri's enterprise. Negri has long understood that politics today requires a common obsession to inspire, and that progress never happens through patient persuasion alone. Political myth, in this positive sense, also played a crucial role in their precursors—most elaborately in Georges Sorel's myth of the General Strike. Gramsci, one of Hardt and Negri's chief Italian forebears, famously compared Sorel's invention of this idea to the proto-Jacobin myth devised by Machiavelli, who had conceived, in Gramsci's words, an "imaginative and artistic" conception of the "collective will" in the image of the ideal condottiere, the "Prince."[14] Although opposing Sorel in the end for evading the problem of organization, Gramsci applauded him for being like Machiavelli, who had created a "concrete phantasy which acts on a dispersed and shattered people to arouse and organize its collective will."[15] Hardt and Negri, it must be said, understand this rhetorical aspect of politics and use it to great effect. Later in this discussion, I will take up the paradoxes of the treatment of Gramsci in their work; for now, let me turn to a reading of the economic theorizations of *Empire*, which are at the core of the authors' reconsideration of value and where, therefore, its arguments stand or fall.

The economic theory of *Empire* proves to be a minefield, which is, among other things, starkly illustrated by the difficulty that reviewers have had in summarizing it. Writing in the *London Review of Books*, Malcolm Bull tries his best: "Since Marx had shown that social relations were not, in fact, the seamless web of bourgeois mythology, but rather the battlefield of economic conflict, the class struggle could be waged more effectively if the working class disengaged from waged labour and sought autonomy for itself."[16] This primary postulate of the book—that which must be allowed for everything else to follow—can be more baldly put: liberation is achieved by declaring oneself "autonomous," by "disengaging" from labor. Autonomy is about proclaiming autonomy. Not only Bull but also other reviewers, like Gopal Balakrishnan and John Kraniauskas, have had trouble convincingly characterizing the substance of the argument because it is so obviously tautological.[17] It is an inauspicious beginning for a project that Bull, apparently without irony, dubs "the most successful work of political theory to come from the Left for a generation."[18]

If it is odd to propose an economic analysis of the condition of labor by re-cusing labor from the economy, what follows is far more formulaic than an apparently radical proposition might lead one to expect, for the portrait of economic change offered by Hardt and Negri bears a striking resemblance to the sort of analysis routinely offered by the *Economist* and the *Wall Street Journal*—namely, that capitalism has abruptly realigned its economic priorities in favor of the intellectual component in formerly manual work, a process to which the new Italians assign the term "immaterial labor." The language of management theory has for more than a decade bulged with a figural repertoire demoting sweat and muscle in favor of "skills," "insights," "ideas," and "speed." The trope of the end of the physicality of labor—a persistent fantasy of capitalism throughout its existence—is now little more than a cliché of the management genre. And yet, apart from the belatedness of discovering this largely fictional fact about the new economy, this is a scenario that *Empire's* authors do not merely lament. Rather like the columnists of the business press, they are encouraged by a systemic shift that makes them optimistic (in much the way that in the early 1990s the post-Fordist critics of "New Times" discussed the oppositional potential of consumption and the attendant subversiveness of the de-centering introduced by niche marketing).[19] While enlivening its terminologies by placing them in new philosophical registers, the authors' devotion to New Times credos is unwavering.[20]

Against the backdrop of a vast manual system of interlocking armed work farms in the clothing industry, the prison-labor system, massive new infrastructural projects (in the laying of fiber-optic cable, for example), and new Arctic drilling ventures, the world economy is for Hardt and Negri resolutely postindustrial. Even as Brussels vetoes U.S. corporate mergers, George W. Bush raises steel tariffs, and Chile indicts Henry Kissinger as a material witness in the trial of General Augusto Pinochet, the nation-state, we are told, has lost all sovereignty. In what can only be called a bracero economy of controlled "illegal" immigration and the reinstitution of slavery (in the Chinese tenement halls of the United States as well as in rural Sudan and Myanmar), we are told that knowledge rather than brute physicality is the constituent element of new labor. Consequently, the supersession of manual by mental or immaterial labor turns out to be a matter of faith rather than anything resembling an analysis of the record.

Hardt and Negri would no doubt respond to this charge by insisting that they were speaking only of a historical tendency in capitalist production rather than a predominant, already demonstrable, fact. This response would, however, be a temporization. Neologisms aside, their revelation that manufacture is being "informationalized" simply begs the question as to why such relations of domination cannot adequately be understood, say, in terms of combined and uneven development (as Neil Smith, for example, has argued).[21] It takes no specialist to recognize that manufacture is being informationalized. This is common knowledge. It is quite another thing, however, to pose this informatization as an exhilarating sign of the sophistications of capitalism as it frees up the biopolitical sphere while facilitating the refusal of work—and then to further portray it as an anagoge of high theory performing its grand conceptual tasks. This romantic view prevents readers from noticing how the aura of such thinking in practice mystifies the reality of globalization, which is a vast enterprise set up to encourage capital mobility while domesticating labor. The elasticity of motifs in *Empire* ("multitude," "biopolitics," "refusal," non-places) does not of course gainsay these realities; it merely binds them in metaphors of irrelevance.

A great leap of the imagination, therefore, is demanded in order to grapple with *Empire*'s diagnosis.[22] We enter a controlled environment of the "as if," a primarily subjunctive horizon. In the posited slippage from politics to ethics, the reader is made to pass through a realm of pleasure in which economics is beheld as an aesthetic artifact rather than a material calculus of scarcity and demand, utility and disutility. As a positive potentiality, its ethical utopia immortalizes precisely what is weakest in Marx's work while attacking Marx's strengths—his vivid descriptions of the logic of capital and the human toll it takes. If the Marx who wrote of "communism" as a utopian outcome is the least convincing Marx, it is the only one Hardt and Negri retain.

What unfolds in *Empire* more successfully than in Negri's earlier books is the development of a rhetoric of ambivalence designed to suture the worlds of Sorelian workerism (accented with references to a more explicitly Marxist revolutionary tradition) and '60s counterculturalism: the mapped territory, in other words, of Negri's divided origins. To this end, the book's slogan, "the refusal of work," for instance (taken originally from Mario Tronti), is crafted to evoke earlier and more familiar forms of labor resistance like the strike, the slowdown, or industrial sabotage, on the one hand, and on the other, an anti-authoritarian dropping out—a rejection of the workaday rhythms and disciplines of "voluntary servitude" (*Empire*, 204).[23] However, in Hardt and Negri's usage it means neither exactly. As Tronti, a lifetime member of the Communist Party of Italy (PCI), had developed the idea in his highly influential *Operai e capitale* (1966), the capitalist is the one, paradoxically, who provides labor while the worker provides capital, not the other way around.[24] The refusal of work, then, is for Tronti a revolutionary opting out of the perpetual cycle of the transformation of labor into surplus-value rather than a merely temporary stoppage of productive relations as takes place in a typical strike.[25] The original move by Tronti was a bold attempt to remind laborers of their power in the context of organizational struggle and to attack the very underlying logic of the relationship of commodity production in order to push organized labor beyond the mere search for a better deal. In the hands of new Italian thought as exemplified by Hardt and Negri, by contrast, refusal becomes a substitute for organization.

The seeds of this substitution do not lie in ideas alone; they have a historical basis. The new Italians are only one of several manifestations on the Left of a Europe-wide response to the era of sacrifice instituted by nominally left-wing governments of the 1970s. These governments abandoned resistance to long-term, double-digit unemployment, which became endemic; indeed, high unemployment levels were a precondition for entrance into the European Union.[26] In effect, younger Marxists, restless in the face of this structural impasse and cut off from their natural constituency, turned unemployment into a virtue. In a parallel move, the Krisis group in Germany, for example, has published a Manifesto Against Work, asserting that Marxism has been unable to transcend bourgeois modernization theory and that issues like exploitation and class rule were "derivative" because the deeper problem lay in a "commodity-fetishistic system" based on wage labor. As one of the members of Krisis puts it, "work is not an antagonistic counterpart to capital, but only its other pole within the taken-for-granted reference system of the commodity society."[27] Predictably enough, the Krisis group seeks not a liberated work but liberation from work, proposing a guaranteed "citizen's income."[28] *Empire* is easier to assess when one is familiar with the structural basis for a grand anarcho-philosophy bred by the betrayal, in its authors' eyes, of the European left intelligentsia.

Perhaps the wider context of other European experiments in speculative economics can help contextualize why or how the entire new Italian plan for political being, as distinct from acting, is contingent upon its economic theory. Readers of *Empire* may not be aware of the genesis of its underlying economic ideas or their development over the span of Negri's oeuvre in dialogue with his new Italian compatriots. For Negri, as for the other new Italians, escaping the regimentation of a job (not "selling out" in its '60s sense) undermines capitalism itself. As a result, politics can henceforth be based on forms of noninvolvement and insubordination rather than on alliances or agendas. Practice too can be a deliberate non-practice safeguarded by inaction from the taint of an unseemly power. Invoking mass insubordination as a principle—the refusal of work—*Empire* strives to escape the merely circular trade-offs and inversions of power politics and sees itself as delving into the very foundations of political motive: replacing the principle of material interest with that of "desire." Postulated as being more fundamental, desire is viewed as more radically enabling, more an absolute precondition of activity at the genetic level, so to speak. In the same bid to radicalize the political by internalizing it, *Empire* tries to replace the exercise of governmental power with that of "possibility." Here we find another calculated double meaning (a philosophical problem solved by a terminological splice); both "possibility" and "power" are simultaneously present in the Italian in the authors' choice of the word *potenza*.

As early as the 1990s, new Italian theorists such as Paolo Virno had transmuted this duality of politics and power into a purified "will to be against."[29] This will, as new Italian thinking presented it, was poised not only against the state but against the traditional parties and trade unions as well. "Immaterial labor," another transitional theme, at first seems to signal nothing more than a reference to the symbolic analysts of the information economy as they have been described by former Clinton labor secretary Robert Reich, Anthony Giddens, and others.[30] In their own account, Hardt and Negri do little to extend the term, and they are quite open about its having no special meaning. Just as it suggests in the work of Reich, for instance, it refers in *Empire* to labor that "produces an immaterial good, such as a service, a cultural product, knowledge, or communication" (290).

But immaterial labor has enormous ambitions within new Italian thought generally, and to review the course of its elaboration clarifies its role in Hardt and Negri's book. In Virno and Hardt's *Radical Thought in Italy*, for example, Maurizio Lazzarato claims that the term explodes the concept of labor by focusing on its cultural content, a form of labor that "defin[es] and fix[es] cultural and artistic standards, fashions, tastes, consumer norms, and, more strategically, public opinion."[31] Both in this text and in *Empire*, an older sense of countercultural street wisdom blends with a reverence for a much more traditional exegesis of texts from classical Marxism. Such nods to traditionalism, even orthodoxy, represent a highly significant maneuver in new Italian thinking, which feels compelled to claim a continuity and rigor it does not possess. Hardt and Negri, like other new Italian thinkers, live in a world of divided sentiments, morbidly obsessed with the rhetorical gestures of early Marxist parties and struggles (indeed, unable to slough off their inspirations) while driven by the antagonistic counterlogics of a theoretical climate that is allergic to battles of this older type. It is in this spirit that Lazzarato follows Virno and Negri in turning to Marx's *Grundrisse*.[32] Like them, he bases the theoretical panacea of immaterial labor on a short passage of that work—a passage to which the new

Italians continually return as though *Grundrisse*'s 904 pages were crystallized in this one section.[33] They even give a special name to the passage—the "Fragment on Machines"—as though Marx had done so himself. This pattern of citation and emphasis is already evident in Negri's *Marx Beyond Marx,* where he zeroes in on Marx's reference in that passage to the development within capitalism of mass intellectuality—a phrase the new Italians transform (with Marx's imprimatur, as it were) into what they call the "general intellect."

This peculiar juggling of sources allows all three to make crucial claims for their redefinition of politics, and it is important to understand how this relationship to the past works. Virno, for example, argues that Marx asserts that abstract knowledge becomes "precisely by virtue of its autonomy from production, nothing less than the principal productive force" (*RTI,* 22). And yet, were one to approach the *Grundrisse* outside this carefully prepared rhetorical frame, it would be very difficult to find anything in Marx that attested to such a hypostatization of thought. The passage of the *Grundrisse* to which Hardt and Negri refer is about the contradiction inherent in the creation of surplus free time by mechanization. Marx points out that this process poses a problem for capitalists who wish to turn free time into surplus labor. So when Marx alludes to the "general intellectual"—which in the original is a passing phrase rather than a major category—he makes clear that he is speaking of the role of industrial planning ("intellect") in increasing the ratio of fixed to variable capital (that is, the ratio of machines to human labor). In other words, there is no hint that Marx equates managerial planning with theoretical inquiry as such, much less that he projects a future in which immaterial values displace basic production as the motor of capitalist profit making. The *Grundrisse* sets out to describe how the clerical abstractions of gifted statesman educators and political economists (Marx's "theorists") would become more and more important as capitalism progressed, not—as Hardt and Negri argue (echoing Reich)—that knowledge would become the primary productive force.

For Hardt and Negri, the general intellect is both a threat and a promise (much as it is for Reich) in a sense similar to the way in which Empire is both a system of command from above and a potential structure of popular will. Capitalism may be tough, they imply, but it is good. Computerization, for instance, apart from being an enticing technological innovation, may have the negative appearance of helping management normalize the work of laborers— standardizing and disciplining their behaviors. And yet, at the same time, it represents the "liberation of living labor," for it relies on the "constellation of powerful singularities" (61). Hardt and Negri put the same idea in another way as well: capital creates an "open space" in which the subject can constitute "a new position of being" (61, 64). Instead of swallowing up subjectivity within production, making "the total person part of the process," capitalism creates "a polymorphous, self-employed, autonomous work . . . a kind of 'intellectual worker' who is him- or herself an entrepreneur" (*RTI*, 135). The vocabulary here flirts with its assumed opposite, a market-driven triumphalism implicit in the word entrepreneur. It is deeply, and intentionally, ambiguous whether this flirtation is a cleverly dialectical posture or an abject concession. In other words, one might at first take the word "entrepreneur" as an ironic reference to that excess produced by capitalism that is, for Hardt and Negri, a specific grounds for optimism: the contradiction left to exploit. The dialectical notion here would then be that capitalism produces a re-empowered subject who is better able to resist the regimentation forced on him/her in the name of productivity. On the other hand, one might see this gesture as not ironic in the least. It would then appear to be an enthusiastic admission that capitalism's emphasis on the supreme "I"—the sacrosanct individual—should be communism's emphasis as well. The part of Negri's work that forms the basis of *Empire*'s economic theory strongly suggests that the latter option is more strongly inflected. "My effort [is to] define ontological categories of subversive subjectivity against the dialectical categories of the relationship struggles-restructuration. . . . Inventive labor . . . reconstructs society itself, revolutionizing it through a process of subjectivization."[34] His effort, he continues, is to "invert praxis" in the frame of the current form of value, insisting (and making us see) that the political and the social are indistinguishable, and that the social is day-to-day life, just living. For its part, revolutionary consciousness is defined as "radically, ontologically autonomous" consciousness. A purer quietism could not be devised.

Accordingly, even if prescriptive management attempts to make us all predictable, albeit supple, subjects, and even if the system fails to "eliminate the antagonism between hierarchy and cooperation," the focus of new capitalism on personality creates the conditions for a "silent revolution." To put this another way, the "'raw material' of immaterial labor is subjectivity" (*RTI*, 142), and therefore capital's international tensions express themselves in a strengthening of the liberated individual in a happily chaotic network of other individuals forming Empire's multitude: "New figures of struggle and new subjectivities are produced in the conjuncture of events, in the universal nomadism, in the general mixture and miscegenation of individuals and populations, and in the technological metamorphoses of the imperial biopolitical machine" (61).[35] The most intense radicalism (that which pushes beyond mere needs to the irreducible cell of biological desire) finds its refuge and answer in capitalism itself, the sources of a revolution more radical than mere ressentiment.

The rhetorical accomplishments of this yoking together of Marxism, counterculturalism, and liberal business wisdom are remarkable. The terms of political economy mutate from structure to atmosphere, from employment to feeling, from workplace to environment. The fluidity of production appears not only as capitalism's new structural adaptability; it constitutes the potential destruction of hierarchy or, as *Empire* somewhat dodgily puts it, a "smoothing of the striation of modern social space" (329). The focus of politics must then logically be on "forms of life . . . modes of being and feeling that determine the common emotional situation" (*RTI*, 26). The book's restatements of post-Fordism and globalization theory are bound up with an all-too-familiar identity politics whose authority, in this case, is part of a larger Heideggerian amalgam within which the new Italian diagnosis historically developed.[36] The objective is to outradicalize radicalism.[37] If the orthodox Marxist position is that communism is implicitly contained within capitalism, *Empire*'s authors up the ante: capitalism's dynamic revolution, they suggest, has already provided us with an inchoate communism.

Unlike Foucault, therefore, who regarded governments as evolving from cloddy "discipline" to a more subtle and pernicious "control," Hardt and Negri echo that radical thinker of our times, *New York Times* op-ed columnist Thomas Friedman, in contending that people have lately increased their options for self-definition:

> Empire's rule has no limits. . . . [It] posits a regime that effectively encompasses the spatial totality . . . an order that effectively suspends history and thereby fixes the existing state of affairs for eternity . . . operates on all registers of the social order extending down to the depths of the social world. . . . Power cannot mediate among different social forces, it rather creates a new milieu of maximum plurality and uncontainable singularization. (*Empire*, xv, 25)

Hardt and Negri offer us a playful, dual-purpose portrait of uncertainty about who leads and who benefits. For them the march of the juggernaut—as ominous as it is anonymous—is at the same time the victory march of the disorganized followers and witnesses of the new anti-regime who blend imperceptibly (and conveniently) into the regime itself. At one with neoliberalism's fearful warnings of the seeping of the state into every crevice of society, the passage above conjures an irrepressible mass subject that conquers the state by virtue of capitalism's need for "maximum plurality"—a gathering of subjectivities (the multitude) who never actually meet or converse and who therefore can never be guilty of repressing their political foes or, for that matter, of exercising their political wills.

Central to *Empire*, then, is not just the notion that imperialism is passé, that nations are defunct, or that the United States has lost its hegemony. Indeed, these views—although demonstrably false—are held by significant wings of the mainstream social sciences and the business press, and are also hegemonic in globalization theory. What is new in *Empire* is its argument that working-class and student militancy from the 1960s and 1970s created globalization from below, and that capitalism co-opted its innovative forms of dissidence by mimicking them.[38] This astounding thesis is stated with insistent clarity (and, it should be said, in a revealingly theological tone): "The multitude called Empire into being" (43). How the unemployed, the de-skilled, the reified, the politically disenfranchised, and the mercilessly propagandized accomplished this or, more to the point, why they did so, is a problem *Empire* never pretends to work out. Only the blanket equation of "the state" with oppression could prompt the authors to confuse, as they routinely do, deregulation with emancipation, the center with the periphery, and the IMF (International Monetary Fund) with the GPAs (that is, those "Global Peoples Assemblies" that political scientists like Richard Falk and Andrew Strauss have been promoting as the only hope for a new international civil society).[39]

Consequently, despite an enormous apparatus of citation, *Empire* is simply unable to see the sharp historical differences between globalization and internationalism (the two are actually opposites), concluding that "the decline of the nation-state shows that proletarian internationalism won" (50).[40] Vigilant readers are forced to notice the enormous irony of all this. The very forces on which *Empire* draws and with which it identifies (council communism, post-Fordism, Deleuze and Guattari), all stand opposed to economism, positivism, and evolutionism—taken to be the untenably mechanistic legacies of Second International Marxism. But here are Hardt and Negri professing, in a particularly unguarded form, a mechanical/organic theory of inevitability.

The discordant modes of expression evident in the book's dual authorship, although necessary for the book's success, undermine an already challenged economic analysis. Negri's prolific output over three decades might lead to the expectation that *Empire* is a tour de force of economic and traditional Marxist theory, that his mastery of its older forms was on display, and that he had creatively, even epochally, refashioned it with the translative capacities of Hardt. For those who have followed Negri's career, however, *Empire* is clearly a recapitulation of arguments found in his earlier books, which had a much smaller readership. Hardt's contribution was to have found a contemporary theoretical language for those arguments.[41] So given the decades of apprenticeship, it is especially surprising to see a number of simple gaffes. One of the key rationalizations offered in *Empire*, for instance, is the conceptual monad of labor and labor power. Hardt and Negri have the habit of adducing labor power as an agent or subjectivity (as the worker him- or herself) (223). But this appears to be a misprision, because the term traditionally refers to the quantum of labor as commodity that the worker sells—that separable entity of physical force whose usefulness has the unique property of creating exchange value. This is roughly analogous to confusing value with price, or profit with surplus value, as many casual readers of political economy are wont to do. It is contextually clear that the authors are not redefining tradition, only sloppy in their use of it.

In his introduction to *Radical Thought in Italy*, similarly, Hardt writes that "in Marx's time revolutionary thought seemed to rely on three axes: German philosophy, English economics and French politics. In our time the axes have shifted so that, if we remain within the same Euro-American framework, revolutionary thinking might be said to draw on French philosophy, U.S. economics, and Italian politics" (1). Everything is confused in this passage. One notes its magisterial tone, and the friendly embrace of a common cause, as well as the strategy of placing new Italian radical thought at the center of current events. But of course the problem is that it was not revolutionary thought but Marx's personal intellectual development that combined these factors, and it was not primarily English economics but English economic theory that was crucial—a theory that has no real analogue in the United States, whose economy certainly dominates but whose most brilliant diagnosticians have been scholars (usually left or centrist) from a variety of national formations. Italian politics, of course, has nothing like the centrality that France's did, but—even more important— French utopian socialism, although decisive in Marx's formation, was in his opinion dilettantish and confused. And Marx, we may remember, ridiculed Proudhon and Saint-Simon, reserving his bitterest polemics for the "critical criticism" of the Young Hegelians in passages that look forward to today's critiques of cultural theory from the Left (in, for example, Terry Eagleton, Edward Said, Nancy Fraser, Alex Callinicos, and others). The simultaneous draining of energy from a past while inserting it into a convenient combination occurs throughout new Italian writing, and often with as little care for detail.

In addition to errors, one is also confronted by unsupple interpretations that can, at times, lead to embarrassing oversights. Take, for example, the following passage from *Empire*, based on Deleuze and Guattari's concept of "desiring production":

Whereas "outside measure" refers to the impossibility of power's calculating and ordering production at a global level, "beyond measure" refers
to the vitality of the productive context, the expression of labor as desire,
and its capacities to constitute the bio-political fabric of Empire from
below. Beyond measure refers to the new place in the non-place, the place
defined by the productive activity that is autonomous from any external
regime of measure. Beyond measure refers to a virtuality that invests the
entire bio-political fabric of imperial globalization. By the virtual we understand the set of powers to act (being, loving, transforming, creating)
that reside in the multitude.   (357)

But are not the available economic indicators (state budgets, the census,
marketing projections) formidably detailed "regimes of measure" designed
precisely to address the desires of those who believe themselves autonomous in
order better to exploit an illusory choice? Virtuality, similarly, can be understood in this passage only in a highly metaphoric way because corporate activity always unfolds in locatable (that is, non-virtual) countries, cities, or build-
ings.[42] As such, "non-places" are not really non-places at all, except in that
juridical sense so convenient to corporations in the act, say, of money launder-
ing, offshore brokering, or escaping the white-collar crime unit of the FBI.
Moreover, the "productive context" evoked by the authors can only be that very
desire they identify as the new reality of labor, whose power now resides in an
intransitive being, loving, and self-transforming, at the expense of a concerted,
disciplined anti-institutional agency. In the slippery syntactical constructions
of the above passage, labor is desire, and yet (for this is how ambivalence
works) the only labor that is desire is the authors' labor of desiring a new labor,
which they rhetorically produce.[43] This writing, which typifies *Empire*, has the
unintended effect of promoting the same legalistic and rhetorical legerdemain
of capitalism's apologists.
    However, the problem with the conceptual conflations has less to do per-
haps with syntactical matters than it does with the fact that *Empire* operates in
terms of an interstitial logic. It plays in the theoretical registers of plausible de-
niability. Favorable readers of the book are quick to observe, for example, that
it is not capital the authors are talking about but the *command* of capital, just
as the focus is not on imperialism but on a new "system of command" called
Empire that strives fruitlessly to discipline its mass creators while laying governments to waste, preparing the multitude for its rightful inheritance. Within
this conceptual no-man's-land (the non-place that is their new place), the au-

thors can never be reproached for leaving out history, or for liquidating opposition by assuming their opponent's forms, since the ready riposte can always be that the reader has merely misunderstood; the commitments of meaning are by nature ambiguous in their strategy of "indirection." Presumably relegated to the status of bogus proof-mongering, neither method nor supporting evidence need detain one over the subtleties of *Empire*, whose elaboration lies in the construction of genealogies and periodizations and calls primarily for a prophetic and speculative approach. Its fresco of the political constitution of the present renders ambiguity the virtue of being "theoretical." The gains of such confident superiority are that declarations can be made, then qualified with vague gestures and allusive generosity. It is not as though its shimmering depiction of a deeply contradictory world political reality is, as far as it goes, uninviting or without potential. Resistance should be versatile and should exploit the opportunities provided even by the power one opposes. So one can appreciate Hardt and Negri's emphasis, at one point, that Empire is not a metaphor but a concept—a living form that structures. By the same token, this move comes with its own obligations: a concept must have an object.

Empire collapses in the passage from concept to object. To take one example, the book counterintuitively argues that capitalism is driven by a logic of "renouncing pleasure" (223)—a view that many of capitalism's enthusiasts might find puzzling, since Madison Avenue has for some time sold not only commodities but a system of pleasure alluringly projected against the black-and-white backdrop of the grim Soviet bloc or the tawdry societies of Third World scarcity. Along these lines, it has been widely argued, for instance, that the United States is rapidly becoming little more than an "entertainment economy." But the authors are driven to the anachronistic Weberian notion of Protestant restraint by an identitarian logic that they never question or even foresee as a problem. Conversely, the leisure that follows from the refusal of work becomes a realm of potential pleasure and expresses itself in the following way: autonomy is that process in which labor does not produce value in manufacture but rather "valorizes itself" (294). Economics, then, is tantamount to a "revaluation of values" and *Empire*'s revolution is the worker at leisure who is himself valuable for being able to redefine value. The tautology is again imposed.

If, however, the blows to the meaningful agency of the worker as subject, and to his/her critical placement in production, are consequential, they are less so than the book's concealing of the intellectual as agent,[44] for an important aspect of new Italian thought is its well-prepared refusal to reckon with the destructive potential of the theorist's own prognoses that might, at least in principle, be the result of exaggerating the importance of mass intellectuality and the general intellect. An economy of the type Hardt and Negri describe would seem to demand an investigation of the intellectual at work—itself a prototype of immaterial labor, and perhaps its most obvious commodity. But even while dwelling on the self, the new Italians are strangely silent about the mode of the self when it comes to their theory's immediate beneficiaries. Empire, say Hardt and Negri, is "autopoietic." Aside from this word's evolutionist tinges, the view denies the agency of intellectuals in making theory. What Hardt and Negri diagnose as the dissipation of labor (or rather its erasure by way of a generalization into all spheres) is rather an echo of their own estrangement from labor.

Since the system for Hardt and Negri "constructs social fabrics that evacuate or render ineffective any contradiction . . . in an insignificant play of self-generating and self-regulating equilibria" (34), it is logical for them to conclude that the only true agency must occur within subjectivity, which is located in social fabrics but not of them. The end of labor can then be announced as though it were a vast expansion of types of labor. The reader hears about atomized constituencies, the ensemble of social forces, the atmospheric penetration of power into all spheres, but nothing of the effects of law and obligation on organization or the capacity to learn. As a result, the authors' advocacy for a post-organizational line of flight toward the general intellect appears merely as intellectual flight. In other words, the "new sovereignty" they speak of is indistinguishable from an evacuation of personnel in the sense that, robbed of the hope of making or changing anything by exertion or plan, intellectuals effect the very negative outcomes described as the original premise of their turn. The conditions to which they point when declaring the need for a theoretical rupture with the telos and conceptual modalities of the past, are the conditions they helped create by a mesmerizing diagnosis laid out in advance. At the end, the economic theory of new Italian thought is not an economics at all. At best, it is a poetics aimed at revising the meaning of the circuitry of production into the management of the self: an antediluvian *oikos*. "Self-valorization" thus implies an attempt to change the game of politics and economics in a redrawing of the field of battle. One wins, but only by redefining what victory means.

The move from the futural to the present (from the "as if" to the "is") expresses itself in a form of resistance conceived not as action but as a mode of being. In the hands of the new Italians, "being against" must always be oblique, indirect—the result not of confrontation but "defection" (212). This meeting of the Deleuzian figure of defection with Tronti's recalculation of a Marxist emphasis on the revolutionary working class can only revert—has no space but to revert—to a fixation on the great "Me" of bourgeois everyday life: "the primary site of struggle seems to emerge on the terrain of the production and regulation of subjectivity" (321). But this somewhat tame Foucauldian sentiment requires more high-octane fuel under present circumstances, and so is merged with an intricate and charged recapture of the interwar philosophy of Heidegger, who arrives in their case not directly, but filtered through the work of Hannah Arendt: "Today's corporeal mutations" (dressing in drag is one of the examples) "constitute an anthropological exodus" (215)—a flight from an unseemly preapproved being toward existentialist "being-a-whole."[45]

Reminded again of such philosophical sources, one cannot avoid returning to the putative significations of a book called *Empire* seen from a global vantage point. Ignoring development economics while commenting on Third World development, the book proclaims that "modernization has come to an end" and that "industrial production is no longer expanding its dominance over other economic forms and social phenomena" (285). This is simply nonsense. Even if it were not the case that the touted decline of basic manufacturing is usually a matter of its being exported to more-forgiving Third World zones of exploitation with relaxed environmental and labor laws, the descriptive alternatives are not between the post-industrial and the industrial. A passing glance at the global economy would easily reveal that the major alternatives are still situated between those old poles of industry and agriculture. Only an unreflectively modernist imperative would dictate that the researcher fail to grasp that in most of the world, agriculture still dominates—often in uncapitalized, traditional forms—and it is the rural citizens of Tunisia, India, or Peru rather than city denizens of Cincinnati or Cairo who represent the predominant subjectivity of labor.[46]

AGAMBEN AND THE NEW ITALIANS

My earlier use of the term "new Italian thought" alludes not only to the authors found in *Radical Thought in Italy*, but to those, like Giorgio Agamben, who have acquired an independent following, as well as to writers less self-consciously identified with the Left who draw on similar intellectual inspirations—for example, Gianni Vattimo, Roberto Esposito, and Franco Rella.[47] With the exception perhaps of Agamben, the writers owe the excitement surrounding their appearance to the radical Italian political context of autonomist movements of the 1970s.[48] Also crucial to their prominence is Negri's prolific output over forty years, his role as contributor to *Quaderni Ross* and *Potere Operaio* (two of the principal organs of *autonomia*), and his former status as a political refugee in the context of the long memory of the Italian Right, which has lately settled scores with the 1970s by jailing a number of Italian prisoners of conscience.

Ranging from etymological queries into fascist legal theory to literary-critical musings on the ethics of modernity, this work acquires the tone of a movement. Whether one is reading the philological aestheticism of Agamben, the Heideggerian homages of Vattimo or Adelino Zanini, or other pieces of writing with entirely different spiritual coordinates (for example, Carlo Varcellone's Gramscian exposés on the Italian Mafia), the characteristic themes of new Italian thought are inherently alike. Apart from the impressive character of individual performances (especially in the work of Virno), new Italian thought in its neo-communist variations represents a theoretical disposition in which the past and future blend into a numbing continuum, circling around a set of signature terms such as "weak thought" and "authentic existence."

New Italian thought, then, can be seen at least in part as a revival of the millenarian consensus of the nineteenth century that dominated the labor movement both before and after Marx. Its watchwords, then as now, are the "withering away of the state," "the abolition of property," the "classless society," and (following the title of a book by Marx's nephew, Paul Lafargue) "the right to be lazy." The self-identifying formulations of the Italians are reminiscent of each in turn: "the critique of the State form," "the constituent republic" and, as we have seen, "the refusal of work." The new Italians seem to wish in many ways to jump back to a time that escapes the need to debate what took place in interwar Marxism—the period of the Third International—which, although obsessing them, is approached only indirectly via the theoretical responses to communism in the post–World War II period. In terms of their own historical formulations, for many of these thinkers the politics of the governmental arena seemed to offer only *embourgeoisement*, the lining of pockets or a conciliation masked by the venerable fighting rhetoric of Palmiro Togliatti and other CPI forefathers. The feudal outrages of the rural South had proved surprisingly resilient and all the older encrustations of Italian-style Junkerism were being papered over by the slick advertising of modernization, motor scooters, fashionable leather jackets, and the tacky journalism of the Berlusconi media empire. Out of France and the United States rumbled an antiwar movement with Eastern and Southern longings whose inevitable corollary was a fixation on alterity as a liberating cultural dissonance. Their desire was thus to one-up radicalization itself by taking resistance to its ethical core in life beyond the mere structures of government—and here one reenters the existential redoubt of Nietzsche and his progeny.

By way of continuing to place new Italian thinking in its trajectory, one might make two other, apparently contradictory observations about its political parentage. The positive utopia of Italian radical thought is one of its most provocative and welcome features—a millenarian language as well as program that not only captures the postmodern chiliasms of Deleuze and Guattari but echoes as well the energies of historical anarchism. Although the new Italians deny that they are, technically speaking, anarchists, their critique of the state form is impossible to characterize otherwise.[49] Negri, in *The Politics of Subversion*, is entirely wed to its millenarian fervor; likewise Virno finds himself at home in anarchism's purifying and apocalyptic registers. Their philosophical project is, if nothing else, *eine fröhliche Wissenschaft* (a happy science), which may account for their insistence on not being reflected in anarchism's mirror, since such a gay science always allows its advocates a space for anti-advocacy. And theirs is undoubtedly a politics, as Agamben puts it, of "nameless terrains" and "zones of indistinction."[50] Unlike much of the politics inspired by the traditions of '68ist youth rebellions lying at the base of postwar French thought, this constellation of sympathies may well be the residual antipathy toward anarchists of a tendency formed under the umbrella (and to the left) of the PCI. At any rate, the learned barbs directed against anarchism still linger. Ingrained in their minds, as Yann Moulier points out, was not necessarily in this earlier period the erasure of all states but the delegitimation of the democratic state of Italy in the decades following the postwar Pact of Liberation. This, along with the traumas induced by the intense Italian state repression of the late 1970s and the economic restructuring symbolized by the defeats in 1980 at the Fiat auto plant in Turin, are their key formative experiences and led to the more extreme, and less interesting, blanket anarchism of the 1990s under the pressures of French poststructuralism.[51]

At first glance it may appear that Agamben is forced into this community as a form of special pleading based on the fact that he happens to be Italian, or that he happens to be an Italian who taught in France, like Negri did. But I am suggesting something more structural and pervasive than this, having to do with intellectual influence as direct borrowing as well as collective mutual citation (a process that shares certain features with what I call "flow" in chapter 7).[52] To ignore the institutional process of theory as it travels across disciplinary registers would be to fail to gauge the utility of national-cultural associations in the making of philosophical trends, as well as the preserve of the theoretical register itself, which would here be protected against its forcible inclusion into a more broadly public and interventionary discourse like that of Negri. Admittedly, the parallels I am drawing would be shallow were I merely stipulating that Negri and Agamben belong together because both are fascinated with Arendtian biopolitics or that both seemed at various moments to recast, in admiring form, the arguments of Carl Schmitt. After all, any number of other thinkers follow these trends today.

But even if it were not the case that Agamben's name is repeated in interviews with Negri, or that Agamben's coinages find their way into Negri's books, or that both Negri and Agamben idiosyncratically express their admiration for Hans Kelsen, it is also the pattern of their arguments and the echoing of common terminologies that betray a programmatic affinity, even if reached from different quarters. Both emphasize totalitarian states and the paradigm of the concentration camp as belonging together (even though concentration camps were never limited to totalitarian states). Both, in what is ultimately only a mocking echo of the Gramsci of *L'Ordine nuovo*, place their political faith in the spontaneous council, identifying the two great twentieth-century enemies of councils as the Leninist parties and the Nazis.[53] Both (following Schmitt) base their overall concept of politics on the ideas that the exception is the rule and that the simple fact of being alive ("bare life") is not only *in* politics but coincident with the political realm. Exclusion and inclusion, inside and outside (in Agamben's words) "enter into a zone of irreducible indistinction."[54]

Both, according to the rules observed above, also go to great lengths to deny they are anarchist (Agamben speaks of the weakness of anarchist and Marxist views of the state, for example, perfectly paralleling arguments wielded by Negri as well), and yet both do so by reproducing exactly the arguments of both anarchism and the Second International that the "dictatorship of the proletariat as the transitional phase leading to the stateless society is the reef on which the revolutions of our century have been shipwrecked."[55] Both want to return politics to its ontological bases, which means to constitute a state of openness—that is, as they put it, of "potentiality and actuality" (44). This revealing trace—this joint huddling around the all-important word "*potenza*"— is still another sign that we are dealing with a new Italian discursive reality that is shared rather than the mere chimera of perception.

"French theory" is now a phrase as unlikely to raise eyebrows as other banalized terms like "the Renaissance" or the "scientific community." By now, although arguably reductive, these terms strike most readers as necessary conventions. To find a common basis for such a loose assemblage of thinkers in the paterfamilias of Descartes would be misguided, since the term "French theory," if taken literally, would have to include thinkers normally outside its rubric: Henri Lefebvre, Loïc Wacquant, Réné Balibar, Paul Nizan, Michelle Mattelart, Pierre Bourdieu, and Régis Debray, among others. But the term is less diverse when one accedes to the manageable set of operative concepts that have taken hold as the result of the prominence of mostly French postwar thinkers who all knew one another, were produced by the same elite educational system whose regimented feel and incestuous unity are depicted well by, among others, Bourdieu's *In Other Words* and *Homo Academicus*. And there is no question that the trajectory of Negri's thought substantially changed during his French sojourn when he was a fugitive from the Italian state.

But one is not inclined to approach Negri as one approaches Ernesto Laclau or Agamben, regardless of the affinities in their thinking. The former's weakness has less to do with the liberal sanctities of the latter. If anything, Negri is guilty merely of a sacrificial overstatement uttered with bravery and sincerity. His invigorating analyses are also tantalizingly close to the regenerations they promise, but they are a form of ultra-leftism, rife with exaggerations that make them finally useless: "The world is a prison," "jail equals factory," and so on.[56]

As part of the same complex, Agamben nevertheless arrives at similar positions via different means. In essence, his political writing derives from the proposition that socialism and capitalism in modernity have a nefarious common project: to produce nations based on an "undivided people." This is a biopolitical project, he argues, effected by various strategies of exclusion, which have taken at times the extreme forms of strategic rape (to efface what is distinctive in an other) and extermination (to efface the other altogether).[57] Hence, the distinction in classical Rome and Greece between the private and the public person—the person who lives, breathes, and eats (on the one hand) and the person who communes, participates, and collectively acts (on the other)—has in modernity been erased. The primordial expression of exclusion can, for him, be found in the *homo sacer*, the one who can be killed but not sacrificed—a concept he derives from Roman law. With such a beginning, one has every reason to expect that his argument is based on the foundations of Western civic traditions and so refers to a perennial norm that haunts the very basis of the European polis. It is, after all, on these grounds that he proclaims "the original political relation is the ban" as though to suggest that there has been all along a fundamental illusion in Western thought about the nature of politics. All the more confusing, then, to learn that his study at the same time posits a radical break or rupture in history brought about by the Nazi genocide—a view that suggests not a norm but its violation.

What must be understood about the Heideggerian turn is that such self-contradiction is itself strategic. The uncertainty here evoked with respect to exclusion seen as permanent strategy and as a fatal new twentieth-century departure, sets up a number of dramatic claims and prescriptions. Our not knowing precisely which of two contrary forces is at work significantly enhances the argument's appeal, which permits the stitching together of a number of potentially, but not necessarily, related observations into a total fabric.

For instance, Agamben seems both surprised and disappointed that the ideals of jurists, statesmen, and reformers over the centuries were never realized—that all efforts to forge a polity based on negotiation, discussion, and the law failed to reach the standard of complete democracy. And from this he draws the conclusion that politics is de jure impossible. On the one hand, he declares, "A stable statute for the human in itself is inconceivable in the law of the Nation-State"—in other words, whereas the annals of policy deal extravagantly with *citizens*, and whereas the rights thereof are meticulously based on obligations that define who is, and is not, a citizen, the law of nations does not define human essence. Therefore, he appears to believe, it is utterly without value. From this claim regarding the eternal nature of nation-states he shifts again to his other mode of fragile temporality: "What is new in our time is that growing sections of humankind are no longer representable inside the Nation-State."[58] The shift, although incapable of being salvaged, is at least more intelligible when we grasp that the stakes for him are not to assess the law more soberly but to craft an ethical maxim: *all* political movements create conditions of unfreedom. They must be rejected not in the name of an alternative strategy but in the name of a new person—one based on "reciprocal extraterritoriality (or better yet, aterritoriality)," a permanent status of exodus or refuge. Thus, with great fanfare Agamben observes that "the status of European would then mean the going-in-exodus of the citizen (a condition that obviously could also be one of immobility)."[59] Although this gesture, as we have been seeing from other cases examined in this book, makes Agamben another interchangeable part in a highly repetitive theoretical status quo, it would be wrong to foreground this aspect of the problem. His crude conception of political purity is most troubling, paradoxically enough, at the ethical level, for his position does not simply echo that of his presumed antagonists, but derives from common sources. The extraterritoriality he endorses is precisely what is sought by, among others, the American military in pursuit of a safe haven for the "interrogation" of terrorists. I am not saying, obviously, that he would have any sympathy at all for the U.S. military, only that he unerringly applauds in a philosophical register the very principles embraced by power, that this congruence (although obscure) is not coincidental and that neither he nor his advocates ever feel compelled to address it.

If one thought that immobility here referred to a concession made in the name of a greater good, one would be mistaken. It is, by contrast, the preferred state of the anti-State in being. Just as sovereignty defined as the obnoxious and frightening total power of the state over personhood gives way in this program to sovereignty as self-possession and self-definition, so too is immobility conceived as a solution to the dead-end politics of civic life. The point for Agamben of summoning the distinction between "bare life" (*zoē*)—mere, or animal, existence—and political or social life (*bios*), which frames his narrative in *Homo Sacer*, is once again to turn negatives into positives by an act of sheer hermeneutic controversion. What Aristotle had raised as a defense of the political is here transformed into the collapse of the personal. The primitive human in Aristotle re-arises in Agamben as all that is left of the human, and all that is worth retaining. This uncertainty enhances the discussion—for "bare life" can then be seen both as the radically impoverished and horrific condition of a concentration camp prisoner and, simultaneously, as the absolute condition of the modern person as such, where nobility annexes itself to battered subjects seeking to hold on to a shred of themselves against the invasive normativity of the established order.

The primary conceptual difficulties with the biopolitical turn, unaddressed by its adherents (including Agamben) have to do with its oppressive Euronormative focus and its positing of a radical, Nazi-era break that makes the personal nothing but the political. The ultra-leftism of the position does not make it more left, but paradoxically more conservative; in the leaping to prophetic finalities all of the sensuous detail of European history is condensed and foreshortened into a predictable ritual act (the European holocaust). If the claims of biopolitics cannot be denied outright given technological developments in satellite surveillance and cloning, the resurrection of the eugenics movement, and similar invasions of the body by the state, it must be placed in a revisionary perspective all the same. One has good reason to question why in the general arc of Agamben's *Homo Sacer* there is no discussion of U.S. army experiments on soldiers, American medical experiments on African Americans, the use of chemical warfare in the trenches of World War I, tobacco addiction by company design, the brain damage produced in minority communities as a result of strategic malnutrition and neglect, phrenology, and the racial hierarchies established by the Napoleonic Code. In surveillance, is there a *qualitative* difference between the technology of the photograph for determining identity based on facial features and the fingerprint or the genetic code? Biopolitics, it appears, has existed for a very long time, if not forever. If that is so, then why must we draw conclusions that we have entered a new world?

The entire trajectory of the argument is, like everything else in Agamben's derivative work, taken whole from other writers. Arendt in *The Human Condi-*

tion (1958) already makes much of the *bios*/*zoē* distinction, although to different ends: she is interested in the way that *bios*, or the "specifically human" life (according to Aristotle) whose appearance and disappearance constitute worldly events, is "itself a kind of praxis." World events can in this way be told as a story, a biography, or a narrative. In the Cold War theorist of liberal democracy par excellence, then, we already have a proleptic formulation of life as narrative—the very idea, in other words, that contemporary theory has considered central to its particular spin on the problem of representation: that is, the concept that all knowledge and experience, because mediated by language, is subject to the wiles and snares of language or, rather, to its productive play. Not unlike the programmatic way in which abstract expressionism was ushered in to displace the figurative traditions of American social realism in painting, the poststructuralist style has, from the start, been linked to a clear and coherent political vision. For Arendt, praxis is that component of subjectivity associated with the public person—the person of the polis—although the meaning of praxis (literally "action") is expressed in Arendt's reading only by way of activities that are not aimed at a goal and that leave behind no work. Her (much reproduced) accomplishment was to make Heidegger an immediate "left" political utility; she transformed praxis into a possibility of human being, where activity is "exhausted in action" as its own meaning. In this bizarre jabberwocky world, the telos of the critic is expressed in a nonnegotiable absence of telos, and it is this self-canceling and circular motion of thought that accounts for the writing's alleged profundity. One withdraws precisely what one alleges while asserting all the while what one does not believe. This is the decisive feature of today's left-right amalgam.

ASSEMBLAGE

It is not enough to admire *Empire*'s verbal intensity and verve or to remark on the mnemonic effects of its cheeky coinages and sweeping rhythms. If the book's success is tightly bound to its rhetorical performance, there are nevertheless methodological issues embedded in the project that transcend what is normally called "style." *Empire*'s modes of telling are at least as important as its tale because of the way they symptomatically repeat gestures that have become almost automatic in contemporary cultural theory. What first strikes one about the project is its deeply incommensurable enlistment of theoretical precursors in the name of interdisciplinarity (xvi and passim). In the face of such anti-instrumentalist heavy hitters as Louis Althusser, Rousseau, Céline, and Derrida (all of whom insist on the mediations of thought), the reader may be caught up short by the book's frank utilitarianism. This utilitarianism reveals itself methodologically as "assemblage."

"Assemblage," a term taken from *A Thousand Plateaus*, refers to a methodological eclecticism that Deleuze and Guattari counterpose to science. In *Empire*, however, it is a rhetorical gesture more clearly tied to a declaration of fealties than to a counterscientific marshaling of evidence. It expresses itself as a gathering of substantively incompatible positions. In *Empire*'s assemblage, the juxtaposition of figures whose political views are mutually hostile to one another (Spinoza and Machiavelli, for instance, or Schmitt and Gramsci) is presented as the supersession of earlier divisions in pursuit of a more supple and inclusive combination. A less exacting process of distinctions can in this way pass itself off as a more inventive, less sectarian vision. Ventriloquizing the traditions of Marxist theory, Hardt and Negri reappropriate them in a more contemporary and, they would argue, more relevant way; but as with all commodities under the triumph of exchange value, the principle that matters most to them is equivalence. This style of argumentation, in fact, was already familiar to Theodor Adorno, who in 1957 condemned it as the "neutralization of culture":

> The neutralization of culture . . . indicates a more or less general reflection on the fact that intellectual formations have lost their bindingness, because they have detached themselves from any possible relationship to social praxis and become . . . objects of purely mental apprehension. . . . They become cultural commodities exhibited in a secular pantheon in which contradictory entities—works that would like to strike each other dead—are given space side-by-side in a false pacification: Kant and Nietzsche, Bismarck and Marx, Clemens Brentano and Büchner. This waxworks of great men then finally confesses its desolation in the uncounted and unconsidered images in every museum, in the editions of classics in covetously locked bookcases.[60]

The counterpart to assemblage in a formal sense is that ensemble of social forces in which Hardt and Negri place their political faith—those disparate, atomized constituencies that correspond to the interests of no class or fraction ("new constellations," in their terms). The parallel between the level of form and content is achieved by drawing on Spinoza—the great counter-Hegel of their neo-Marxism. Spinoza provides the authors with their putatively materialist, counterdialectical mantra: "immanence." The problem with employing

Spinoza for this purpose, however, is that his immanence, like their own, is oddly transcendent. In Spinoza himself there is a fundamental ambiguity about whether identifying God with the present materiality of nature outwits theology, transforming it cleverly into a materialism before its time, or only reduces the material to the mere permeating presence of God.[61] As Howard Kainz neatly puts it while paraphrasing Hegel: "There is too much God, so that man and the world are reduced to nothing."[62] Much in the manner of Spinoza's *Ethics*, one proceeds in *Empire* by way of a geometrical ordering, a system of axioms as though compensating with figural rigidity for a situation in which intuitive knowledge stands in for evidence, and freedom is a largely intellectual achievement.

My intention here is not to take on Spinoza's philosophy but to draw attention to Hardt and Negri's metaphorical Spinoza, whose deployment occurs in an assemblage of unreconciled oppositions. In this gesture as well there is a long and now forgotten history. Lucien Goldmann, for example, once paused to discuss an observation by Althusser, who had claimed, apparently, that the major philosophical question of our time is the choice between Feuerbach and Spinoza. "If I have understood correctly," writes Goldmann, "according to [Althusser], Feuerbach asserts the existence of immanent meaning. If you seek this meaning you are an idealist, or you are Spinozian if you no longer seek meaning but only the mode of production."[63] But Goldmann does not forget to add:

> We are . . . not dealing with a historical Spinoza in this instance, or with the concrete reality of his thought. We are dealing only with the second mode of knowledge and a completely mechanistic Spinoza. Basically, the alternative we are faced with is Pavlov or Hegel. Dialectical thought, at the scientific level where Marxism has situated it, rejects this alternative. It seeks simultaneously the meaning, the significant structure of the object being studied, as well as its production, its genesis, i.e., the functional need which has engendered it within a broader structure in which it fulfills a function.[64]

Empire posits a monism—the theology of the body-in-things (Spinozan immanence)—while heralding the rhizomatic decentering of the multitude, as if both structures could coexist. It prophesies the withering away of the state while insisting upon our refusal of the state or, rather, its abolition by decree. In the book, Empire's permanent "state of emergency" sits side-by-side Empire's "constituent republic" based on an unwritten constitutional structure.[65] The book's "new constellations" appear little more, finally, than philosophical organs ripped out of their original systems and rendered meaningless except as a declaration of the authors' habits of reading. To be accused simply of eclecticism would, of course, not bother Hardt and Negri per se, for they have responded dismissively in the past to this charge, as if implying that their accusers were simply scandalized by the heresy of their amalgam and had failed to see the novelty of their *combinatoire*.[66]

Notwithstanding the authors' special pleading, the problem with assemblage is, at base, epistemological. How does one borrow ideas without assuming their contextual resonances as first formulated in a system, regardless of whether such a system is summoned for contemporary use? Because Hardt and Negri ignore this logical difficulty, they have little choice but to revert to a functional relationship to the concepts they adduce. As such, their "new constellations" are rendered vulgarly pragmatic—itself a paradox, because functionalism of this type has long been associated in Continental circles with an Anglo-American anti-theoreticism. Even as their anti-orthodoxy in regard to Marxism dissipates into an evolutionary view of revolution as inevitable and inexorable (as if taken straight out of Karl Kautsky), so their Deleuzian flight from a transcendent and tainted dialectics turns out to be indistinguishable from American functionalism—moreover, an idealist utilitarianism at that, justified in the name of a "toolbox" (*Empire*, xvi).

If a discrete idea can be wrenched from its whole so that now it becomes the new autonomous whole (for example, if skepticism toward sovereignty can be taken from Schmitt without embracing his contempt for constitutional guarantees), then one has to entertain the possibility that the resulting mélange might, at least in principle, be incoherent.[67] Even if one wanted to defend an argument-by-amalgam for its power to create novel constellations, one would have to recognize the distinct risk of devising a false assemblage. But Hardt and Negri appear not to have considered this possibility. Far from being an emergent or radical Deleuzian methodological politics, eclecticism is the reverse coin of hegemonic cultural theory. By this light, assemblage appears to be the principal use value allowing the critic rapidly to shift thinkers, positions, and terminologies in order to play to a segmented or globally commodified audience of bohemians-in-training. On the terms of this logic, the diagnosis of niche marketing is niche marketing.

This can-do relationship to the archive made fashionable—because all ages, figures, and traditions are available for immediate use—gives *Empire*'s writing an aura of the eternal present even as it comfortably fits the American reader's pragmatist political unconscious. But this present poses as the future and is informed, as I have suggested, by an unacknowledged (and often misunderstood) past. My earlier depiction of *Empire* as a recapture, therefore, revisits the argument about assemblage as a mode of argumentation. For *Empire's* nomadology is indeed what Deleuze and Guattari call it: "the opposite of history" (*A Thousand Plateaus*, 23). Still, given the reverential nod of the book toward an old-left organizational past (Rosa Luxemburg in particular is deployed to this effect), Hardt and Negri want to historicize all the same, and much of *Empire* is written in a frankly historicist mode. What they lack, however, is any sense of what Raymond Williams called the "residual." *Empire's* paradoxical return is a rushing toward one past, while being unable to face another. Or, to put it differently, there is no feel in this writing for the temporal collisions of the present in which techno-culture sits side by side with the marketing of retro; new factory labor is supplemented by the reemergence of nineteenth-century workhouses and home-based cottage industries; walled suburban enclaves are policed by private militias like feudal estates; and a modern police force (nominally subject to public scrutiny) is replaced by hired guards working for a nouveau riche appropriately called the "gentry." The rhetorical form of the book, then, perfectly encapsulates its vision of history: a return and a repetition unable to see the past that tenaciously grips the present. Throughout their economic analysis, nothing of this residual character is hinted at, although it profoundly stamps the economic reality they seek to explain. Fredric Jameson shrewdly compares Deleuze to Henri Bergson, but he is really much closer to Durkheim, as we can see by turning to Perry Anderson's assessment of Durkheim:

> Durkheim's account of the development from mechanical to organic solidarity (primitive to industrial societies produced the concept of anomie—the unceasing reproduction of subjective rulelessness by a society that is defined by its ensemble of objective rules). In every case, a notion of contradiction is at the very core of the work. But it is always a "degraded" contradiction, that is *cyclical* in its movements and thereby immobile and eternal.[68]

Unable to articulate the residual as a problem, the new Italians betray its presence at every turn. The book's past is unmistakably marked by national-cultural (that is, Italian) associations. These arise, perhaps, in *Empire's* curiously scholastic modes of argumentation. In Hardt and Negri, there is a Latinate language of levels, boxes, and sets as though we had returned in an act of philological homage to an Aquinian anatomical philosophy. The neo-Aristotelian rigidity of the figures employed in *Empire* at first appear to be borrowed from positivist sociology until we see the authors draw on classical theoreticians like

Polybius, or embrace the Renaissance categories of Machiavelli, whose antique organization of points, subpoints, and definitions is fully in play as an obvious act of emulation. Such Aristotelian categories are less superficial than they are infrastructural. We are told in *Empire*, for example, that the apparatus of imperial command "consists of three distinct moments: one inclusive, another differential and the third managerial." Built neatly in a series of threes, this orrery gradually takes shape as a divinely preordained model of the cosmos. In the new sovereignty of *Empire*, which is asserted to consist of gradations of "tyranny, monarchy, and democracy" (316), each figure corresponds, analogically, to the "three global and absolute means" of "imperial control": "the bomb, money, and ether" (343).[69] This magical repetition of neat units of three underscores both the artificiality of the authors' theses as well as their playacting. They are, in their own minds, no less than the Machiavellis or Spinozas of the moment.

Philosophically, the new Italians' consolidation of a selective past is an intellectual failure they are powerless to avoid; but it is, at the same time, a deliberate strategy: it is this convenient combination we have to grasp, in fact, if we are to understand the book's interstitial logic. One final aspect of their methodological timelessness—their eternal present—makes itself felt at this juncture. For, if in political terms they heroize aspects of the Hegelian Left and draw their historical energies from it, they see dialectical thinking itself as mystificatory. Caught in the traditions floundering in Hegel's wake, outmaneuvered by his system, and left with little more than the Nietzschean option of aestheticizing thought in the micro rebellions of the will to truth, the new Italians are forced to go back to those who preceded Hegel (while, of course, silently drawing on Hegel at every step). To find a way out of Hegel's thinking they do not so much defeat him on the terrain of theory as transport themselves to a past that did not know him. Spinoza, or rather "Spinoza," the "first communist before Marx" of their creation, plays this role of anachronistic authority as *the* philosopher of modernity.

At the end of the day, though, one cannot really evaluate the book on the basis of refutations or plaudits of individual arguments and assumptions alone. It is not just this or that observation that should be placed in question but the book's entire apparatus of seeing and presenting. An adequate response to the book, in other words, demands a counternarrative because what is at issue is not simply a book but the '68ist amalgam it represents. To compose such a narrative would require more serious ground-clearing than I am at liberty to elaborate here, but it might be useful to mark the lineaments of such an effort. First, such a ground-clearing would necessitate having to understand the relationship of the anti-dialectical Nietzschean tradition to political anarchism as such.[70] It is time for intellectual history systematically to take up the demonization of the always criminal "state" in cultural theory—a state that is usually posed as an ontological category rather than a locally varied, or contradictory structure—leading to immense confusion between left and right variants of anti-capitalist positions.[71]

Equally important would be the need to explain the pattern of reverential borrowings from Marxism that involve, simultaneously, its rejection and diminishment. With respect to the new Italians, why does one need or even want a label like "communist" (as in Negri and Guattari's *Communists Like Us*) when to enlist it means inverting its traditional meanings so that, against all the weight of acquired sense and usage, it now suggests hostility to the state, to party organization, and to strategic military and class orientations? What, in short, is the need among those hostile to Marxism to assume a Marxist mantle while throwing flames at Marxist mannequins? Could it be that the term "communist" lends power by virtue of its status as an object of fear and loathing in middle-class reason, and one that cannot be outdone by anything more radical? In so many ways communism remains the ultimate margin, the far reaches of social unacceptability. Communism operates like an impassable psychological fissure and thereby provides a metaphorical frisson that, so long as it remains metaphorical, entails no risks.

Also at issue is the question of whether the theoretical legacies of '68 were really an adventure or exploration of new possibilities, or only a conservative redoubt where thinkers huddled with eyes fixed on the past.[72] One of the most striking aspects of Deleuze and Guattari's powerful evocations is the extent to which their strange and wonderful prose is studded with archaisms—allusions to medieval metallurgy, the *fratres* of primeval tribes, the autonomous craftsmen dotted along the pristine hills, the Spinozist God hovering over the world's molecules like a benign shepherd, the glorious nomadism of the Crusades. Is this antiquarianism merely a coincident element in the toolbox, or does it signify a special relationship to the past itself? In times as dark as these, such lines of flight are, perhaps, increasingly attractive, but they appear less comforting in a pact with thinkers such as Arendt, whose ideas are inseparable from Cold War America, or Schmitt, whose legal theories consciously emboldened Nazism. One is reminded of Slavoj Žižek's cogent comments on the Arendt revival: "This elevation of Arendt is perhaps the clearest sign of the theoretical defeat of the Left—of how the Left has accepted the basic co-ordinates of liberal democracy ('democracy' versus 'totalitarianism,' etc.), and is now trying to redefine its (op)position within this space."[73] It might be said that, as a matter of intellectual convergence, a Deleuzian leftism is less a neo-Marxist revamping than an old-fashioned anti-communism. The genius of capitalism, one might well conjecture, is that it can create such allies in this costume. Anti-capitalist in impulse but theoretically inoculated against the war of maneuver in all its forms, the new Italians project themselves into a futurology that largely reinvents and reinvigorates capitalism's dominant clichés.

Empire's return mounts a conception of history as a shop window filled with texts of glossy revolutionary allure. It is vital to understand Hardt and Negri's gesture toward revolutionary workers, because it marks the pathology of the paralytic moment.[74] Their writing takes the form of a conceit that has very little to do with workers, but rather the excited "quotation" of workers' recorded activities in pursuit of a transportable inner spirit wrung from this history of others' making. Dissident youth, sick and tired of the world, latch on to the discourse of the workers' movement with the sincere desire of effecting finally, and forever, what the workers' movement itself failed to achieve: the end of commodity fetishism and the alienation of labor. But *Empire* has an auteurist or culinary devotion to the events of these histories, and as such they are no longer histories but prophecies of a coming millenarian return. Each time any of the new Italians speak of workers they see an image of themselves, although that image is necessarily blurred into constructs that transcend Mexican day laborers, fast-food deliverymen, secretaries, maids, and auto mechanics. That kind of specificity tarnishes the aura of the "multitude"—a term redolent of the New Testament, embraced by the authors for evading the guilty telos of the "working class."

But the term "multitude" betrays a reverse teleology, as it were, an etiology that is religious in form: their designated "multitudo fidelium" (*Empire*, 429).[75] Negri's political and intellectual formation in 1950s Catholic radicalism in Italy may be worth some mention in this context, although it has received almost no commentary. Most reviewers have had very little to say about Negri's early inspirations in Catholic radicalism—not entirely unrelated to the universal harmony of his later vision. As an activist in L'Intesa, the organization of university Catholics in the 1950s, Negri had been "assiduous on points of doctrine" and "a fervent organizer of 'manifestations in honor of St. Anthony' and a dedicated student of St. Thomas."[76] If it is unfair to reduce Negri's choices to symptoms of his Catholic training, it is no less problematic to pretend they have no bearing on *Empire*'s methodology or on its philosophical grounding in a "materialist" theology. It should prompt interest, certainly, that a book which sees fit to dub the brilliant human rights advocate and internationalist theorist Richard Falk an "idealist" and "reformist" (417) found solace in a veiled theology.[77]

Historians of the labor movement recognize all too well the paradoxes of anarchism. The all or nothing of noncompliance resolves itself into the normality of power, because the all is always too much. This position (it used to be called ultraism) is doomed to collapse, against its will, into conservatism. The new Italians' implicit guardianship of Gramsci nevertheless prevents them from understanding that for him such ultraism reactively staked out positions so extreme that they were inoperative and, finally, arrested. Confronting the prominent south Italian philosopher Benedetto Croce, Gramsci had, among other things, dedicated himself to reclaiming ownership for the communist movement of the "ethical-political state." He rejected Croce's accusation that communism had splintered its ethical ship on the reef of the means/ends dilemma. This is an important moment in the anti-capitalist past to which Hardt and Negri allude, and yet to recover it historically—as distinct from recapturing it in a Deleuzian sense—is to see how *Empire* naively reverts to the position of Gramsci's antagonists from the 1930s. For it turns out that *Empire*'s effort to bring politics more in line with ethics resembles nothing so much as the political hermaphroditism of the German youth movements, whose "revolutionary" rhetoric Gramsci excoriated in the 1920s. Their polemics against authority were, in his opinion, right wing. We might benefit from recalling the deep irony with which he characterized their attitude of self-styled dissidence:

> Personal analysis sets itself against the principle of authority, which is attacked in all its forms: religious dogma, monarchic power, official teaching, military state, marital ties, paternal authority and above all the law that protects these frail institutions and is nothing other than coercion, restriction, the arbitrary deformation of public life and of human nature. Man is unhappy and wicked as long as he is chained by law, custom and received ideas. . . . The creative power of destruction has become an article of faith.[78]

Gramsci concluded that one simply had to accept responsibility for power. A callow optimism, like an automatic hostility to the state, was an unsophisticated, not to mention immature position. In a period of absolute authoritarianism like Gramsci's (and ours), democracy is indeed something to wish for, but is far too small a thing for the new Italians. They posit, therefore, "absolute democracy"—a rhizomatic democracy—as though the greater demand would, by definition, be the more radical one.

The slogan of *Empire*, then, might be: everything for newness provided newness is polite enough to appear in familiar forms. Given that the entire project is cast in futurological boldface, readers may miss its older structures of understanding. Although Hardt and Negri conclude that imperialism no longer exists, why wouldn't it be more likely that the new, inventive capitalism of today had simply devised a new kind of imperialism? An empire run by an information-based economy would logically realize its control through the coercive export of a national idea, blanketing alterity like a nuclear windstorm, and marking its effectiveness precisely by not being associated with the country it served, only taken on as an "us" culture? Thus, the nationless Empire of new Italian thought—"the idea of a single power that overdetermines them all, structures them in a unitary way, and treats them under one common notion of right that is decidedly postcolonial and postimperialist" (*Empire*, 9)—might only be this particular empire's national feint.[79] And that is the case.

Back in the early 1960s, Tronti's principal thesis had been that "the American workers are the hidden face of the international working class" and that "today's U.S. is the theoretical problem for the future of us all."[80] The new Italians seem now to have literally adopted his ardent faith that the United States would eventually show Europe the "never-yet-seen techniques of political use of the capitalist economic machine by the working class." The ultimate problem is that Hardt and Negri, against all expectations, fail to see the ambiguity in these words, equating Tronti's working class with the multitude of a theoretical Americana.[81] The new sovereignty is indeed, as Hardt and Negri say, that very "indeterminacy, movement, creativity, ambiguity" (39) of globalization. But perhaps they forget that, just for this reason, the dreamlike desire of fluid social boundaries effectively blurs the crude imperialism of American realpolitik. The enemy of revolutionaries in the neoliberal age is not the state—which in spite of Hardt and Negri's diagnosis, is still an extraordinarily resilient form of command—but the sovereign, freely experimenting, hybrid subjects of corporate utopia against whom the state (or one version of it, at any rate) continues to be the last refuge. The Left fights in that space, or it refuses to fight. *Empire*'s popularity, then, presents us with a dilemma. Before his death, Pierre Bourdieu observed that neoliberalism had stormed onto the ideological scene by proclaiming a revolution that was in fact a restoration.[82] The dilemma is that *Empire* does as well.

CHAPTER 7

COSMO-THEORY

The Americans . . . really are nomads. They change professions
like shoes, build houses to last 20 years and don't stay that long, so
that home isn't any specific locality. Not for nothing has the *great
disorder* spread so luxuriantly here.
—BERTOLT BRECHT, 1941

WHAT COSMOPOLITANISM POPULARLY EVOKES—among other things,
the thirst for another knowledge, unprejudiced striving, world travel, supple
open-mindedness, broad international norms of civic equality, a politics of
treaty and understanding rather than conquest—all of that can hardly be discounted, especially today. As various urban "suss" laws are upheld by the higher
courts, and as an entire people abroad is bombarded by U.S. planes for the collective sin of belonging to a race of "serial ethnic cleansers," one is tempted to
stick to the basic decency of cosmopolitanism (à la Martha Nussbaum) rather
than try to be too subtle.[1]

On the other hand, cosmopolitanism has prompted some of these very
symptoms. It is a fundamentally ambivalent phenomenon. An ethical argument for cosmopolitanism or for its nominal opposite (patriotism) cannot be
based on a formal adherence to a list of positive qualities. One's judgment of
cosmopolitanism's value or desirability, in other words, is affected by whose
cosmopolitanism or patriotism one is talking about—whose definitions of
prejudice, knowledge, or open-mindedness one is referring to. Cosmopolitanism is *local* while denying its local character. This denial is an intrinsic feature of cosmopolitanism and inherent to its appeal.

Our confusion over these preliminary observations derives from a fact
about cosmopolitanism that seems, at first, to be quite extraneous to it. In general, the term has been disorienting within cultural theory because of the the-

orist's unwillingness to analyze the marketplace in a sustained or careful way. My apparently unjustified leap into new territory might be defended by recalling the opening question of the chapter titled "The Fair, the Pig, and Authorship" from Peter Stallybrass and Allon White's widely read book, *The Politics and Poetics of Transgression.* There they ask, "How does one 'think' a marketplace?" Their provisional answer, which I take to be the *type* of point I make below, is that "the commonplace is what is most radically unthinkable":

> At once a bounded enclosure and site of open commerce, it is both the imagined centre of an urban community and its structural interconnection with the network of goods. . . . A marketplace is the epitome of local identity (often indeed it is what defined a place as more significant than surrounding communities) and the unsettling of that identity by the trade and traffic of goods from elsewhere. . . . In the marketplace pure and simple categories of thought find themselves perplexed and one-sided.[2]

Their image of opening up the center's one-sided logic to the clashing values of the outer boroughs is reminiscent of the hybridity so widely extolled in theories of cosmopolitanism. But they take us into more troubling territory with their image of a local reality translated into global terms by way of market flow—a reality, as the authors describe it, that transforms hybridity itself into a coercive lesson imposed on outlying populations. Pursuing this logic, which is uniquely accessible in a cultural analysis that attempts to "think a marketplace," Stallybrass and White find themselves questioning Mikhail Bakhtin's famous observations on the carnivalesque. They observe that "the fair, far from being the privileged site of popular symbolic opposition to hierarchies, was in fact a kind of educative spectacle, a relay for the diffusion of the cosmopolitan values of the 'centre' (particularly the capital and the new urban centres of production) throughout the provinces and the lower orders."[3]

If they treat the concept only in passing and superficially, nevertheless the authors are right about cosmopolitanism's functioning as a relay for the center's values, sublimating differences on grounds of understanding by way of a motive to export ideological products made to the measure of the world of saleable things. But I would add a point that they leave only implicit—namely, that cosmopolitanism makes sense only in the context of a specific national-cultural mood. As Stallybrass and White imply, centers tend to be where the concept has historically found its greatest acclaim. But what they do not quite express is the process by which one—benevolently, of course—expands his or her sensitivities toward the world while exporting a self-confident locality for consumption *as* the world. The problem exposed here consists of the ways in which an ideo-economic substructure is elaborately developed for the export of "idea-products" in a necessarily self-concealing act, where what is promoted has value only insofar as it proclaims that it promotes its opposite. This is a subject for theory that has too rarely been taken up, since it points toward the threatening topic of the economic function of intellectuals.

Cosmopolitanism's colloquial connotations are so overwhelmingly positive and liberal that one rarely remarks on the multipurpose ambiguity of those values it relays. Our understanding of Stallybrass and White's meaning of the term "value," for example, is humanist and ethical while dissimulating value as it is understood in the marketplace. If economic value generally rules the flow of commodities, rates of exchange, and the price of goods, nevertheless the ethical or aesthetic sense of this slippery term in cultural anthropology or literary criticism draws on an economic foundation. The passage from Stallybrass and White, although undeveloped, is extraordinarily helpful for permitting us to fold these two senses into one another. On the one hand, an attempt to imagine the relations between emergent financial interests and scholarly models is widely lacking in scholarship itself; on the other, research in the humanities finesses (without, of course, ignoring) the interconnections among languages, symbols, and objects in a social context defined by corporate incentives and a landscape of increasing monopoly over information and the means of information. The institutional role or function of the theorists themselves comes in for the least attention of all.

To tackle this complex of issues is far too daunting for a single essay, although a brief overview of a single decisive concept may be useful for illustrating a kind of inquiry that is seldom taken up in cultural studies: one that links intellectual producers to their own products in a localized matrix of intellectual work. I would like to focus on only one aspect of this matrix—the one that concerns the *flow* of the intellectual commodity known as cosmopolitanism.[4] These ideological products tend to be radically divided into disciplinary spheres of influence, or into academic versus extra-academic dichotomies that belie their actual movements. Thus, when I cite the term "intellectual" or "intellectual communities" below, I am referring not only to university professors but also to media analysts, corporate advisors, and managerial specialists, all operating within a vast division of labor that is, of course, not overseen by any command center but that nevertheless parcels out duties in a pattern that none of its actors can diagram or even fully appreciate.

At times below I focus especially on cultural theorists—that is, university intellectuals in the humanities—but only where specifically noted, for in the locality known as the United States, the role of the cultural theorist in the division of labor has been important in developing the concept of cosmopolitanism, whose ethical aura is largely an export from the humanities into other, more technical or policy-oriented formations, including branches of the social sciences and (outside the university) of government and business. In this map of interlocking arguments surrounding cosmopolitanism, my more speculative diagnoses demand a certain methodological risk. Given the constraints of space, I cannot treat all of my subjects adequately, and do not pretend to. I do, however, assume that there is something to be gained in a general approach so long as the readings themselves are not distorting. Certain facts are visible only by tracing movement across several disciplines and intellectual territories of a reasonably structured whole. I want to begin by suggesting a framework for the discussion of intellectual flow in the U.S. market and then move on to cosmopolitanism's preliminary definitions and the methodological approaches possible when studying it. I will conclude with a thesis on the nation as a "manageable community."

INTELLECTUAL FLOW AND THE MARKET

There are at least four different intellectual sectors in which the invocation of the global is taking place—a concept closely related to that of cosmopolitanism. For our purposes, globalization bears on cosmopolitanism as structure to idea. It is that purportedly new material reality to which the new ethos—cosmopolitanism—responds. The latter is, then, an ethical stance that its proponents argue grows inexorably out of exciting and revolutionary new material conditions: the mode of proper social conduct appropriate to a heretofore unseen age. In order to make sense of the force of cosmopolitanism as an ideal, one has to look at these sectors' various modes of expression, their variant proximities to power, and the lines of contact that exist or do not exist among these communities of intellectual belonging. I am not talking about "influence" here, since the process of borrowing and exchange is either unconscious or deliberately repressed.

Behind disagreements over cosmopolitanism's desirability, then, lie poorly analyzed mechanisms of flow. Intellectual communities borrow from one another without acknowledgment, pattern themselves on terms and leads taken from others that are then transformed in uncontrollable ways once they arrive in another sector for self-styled reuse. The way that cultural studies professors, 1970s dependency theorists, state department academics, pop-political commentators, and UN delegates working for NGOs all invoke the global is quite asymmetrical and quite powerfully productive of a conceptual meshing that conceals the important flows among them. The consequences of these flows are profound for those of us who think of ourselves as being involved in a theoretical enterprise that is cultural—that deals with images, arts, everyday practices, and forms of entertainment. The sharing of key motifs, key sociological assumptions, and key rhetorical tags among different levels of the intelligentsia takes places in a largely unacknowledged process of mutual echoing and shadowing.

The significance of such a diagnosis lies in its facilitating an understanding of the shape of the intellectual market, and the role of humanities intellectuals in broader networks employed by the state and business to provide a set of complementary products. Intellectuals, in other words, reach similar conclusions about the death of the nation separately but not independently. Whether business is listening is no longer controversial, as the following more or less routine quotation from management literature suggests:

> Cosmopolitanism is no longer the monopoly of the intellectual and leisure classes; it is becoming the established property and defining characteristic of all sectors everywhere in the world. Gradually and irresistibly, it breaks down the walls of economic insularity, nationalism, and chauvinism. What we see today as escalating commercial nationalism is simply the last violent death rattle of an obsolete institution.[5]

The famous gulf between the media and academic intellectuals captured so well in France by Régis Debray more than a decade ago loses much of its rigidity in postmodernism, where the university is slowly transformed into an arena where the company pays directly for intellectual services rendered and where the radical wing of theory finds new language in which to celebrate corporatism, although without explicitly wanting to or thinking that it does.[6]

What is more, the relatively powerless cultural critic longs for the audiences enjoyed by higher levels of the state and media. The policy analysts, for their part, are eager to acquire fresh thinking and an informed intellectual severity that is found in theoretical humanities circles more commonly than in their own bureaucratic enclaves. Although the academic intellectual is, in effect, the object of an out-contracting system, the cultural critic fails to theorize (or even speak openly about) this particular "crossing of borders" between the theorist and the seminar teacher, the literary critic and the feature journalist, the feature journalist and the policy analyst or think-tank strategist, or artist, or politician. Each of these sectors performs distinct, if overlapping, functions in the reproduction of the state and market and can be divided internally on the basis of its proximity to power, and the type and size of the constituencies it serves. The translation of terms and the covering of tracks is important to the ideas' use value.

In this array, humanities intellectuals have an economic function where intellectual flow might be seen as an elaborate system of playing the economic and the cultural off against one another, so that at times the prejudices of local differences can be given the solidity of economic determinations and at others the spiritual vitality of culture can humanize the bottom line. This, of course, all unfolds without deliberate plan, in the amnesiac complexities of system. The ranks of the intellectuals are not altogether fluid, but they are malleable enough for individual actors to be in doubt as to their proper place. Clearly, one can perform a function without necessarily knowing what it is, for instance. The high ethical claims of an unencumbered "value" are sustainable only in an elaborate system of distancing and dissimulation where the exercise of policy is kept separate from theory per se. Humanist ethics commands a higher price if its use value is deliberately blurred.

The demur of cultural criticism in addressing these divisions, however, has also in part to do with a bad faith that many will consider tasteless to mention. It is not out of the question, for instance, that the cultural theorist actually *wants* to be confused with his or her other—that cultural theory wants to appear part of a public sphere that it is really only gesturing toward even as it denies that this sphere is a corporate sphere. There are also local political considerations that prevent the cultural critics in an atmosphere of obligatory progressivism (almost everyone in the humanities, it appears, is, in his or her own mind at least, on the Left) from drawing lines of contact between themselves and more official representatives of public order.

What is perhaps strangest in this scenario is the assumption by the cultural theorist that his or her own national-cultural limitations are readily apparent or easily distinguishable. In spite of the sophistications of theory, which has trained us all to interrogate common sense, the critic often acts as though Americanism could not insinuate itself into cosmopolitanism without quickly being noticed. The alarms of normativity would automatically start ringing: as though the enormity of slavery or of the now somewhat ludicrous racism of Thomas Carlyle or Teddy Roosevelt was as absurd in its own time as it looks to us now, back across the decades. The contemporary version in business circles is much more humanitarian:

Whether we call the global perspective gaining a global view, a global mindset, global brains, or some other term, we are stepping into a perspective fundamentally different from the three previously described. This calls for a manager with a capability to maintain equal "mental" distance from all regions of the world. However this should not be construed as a person without any cultural anchor. Rather, the executive with the global perspective maintains that point of view with respect to his or her business or profession. A personal cultural anchor is still required for personal balance. . . . Executives with that global mind display an innate curiosity with the developments of the world.[7]

The critic is so accustomed to seeing him/herself in the process of mental, physical, or spiritual travel (self-projecting into difference) that it seems hardly possible that he or she could give comfort to a myth of nationhood, even an American one as grotesque as that of Ben Wattenberg or Fernando Valladao, who see the United States as a "universal nation," an immigrant refuge, and a polyglot, panchromatic, unity-in-diversity whose international appeal has nothing to do with its control of resources, only its moral and aesthetic superiority.[8] In cultural studies, the discourse of cosmopolitanism is never so crude as to make that argument, although it often ends up in the same place.

Implicit in my argument thus far is that culturalism performs an appreciable although elusive economic function that is especially noticeable in the debate surrounding cosmopolitanism. Economic questions, however, are really not studied in any sense meaningful to cultural life or to historical reflection in economics departments. At the same time, given its counterintuitive concepts and mathematical armature, economics tends to resist interest outside economics departments. The economy, therefore—the subject that mostly fills the chambers of government, that occupies one-quarter of every daily newspaper, and about a quarter of all news programming—is an absent signifier in cultural studies unless, of course, it has been semanticized and dissipated into a libidinal or affective sense. It is a vast unexplored territory, and clearly a missing element of the complex cultural puzzle of modernity. The great earlier cultural theories of the economy have exerted surprisingly little influence, even when their work is avidly studied in other respects.[9]

Debates in the humanities academy, its vocabularies, gestures, ideas, moods are being taken on wholesale in the worlds of business and government (Jacques Derrida, Noam Chomsky, Nelson Mandela, Michel Foucault are the subjects of corporate seminars). There is, in a prima facie sense, a continuity between the discourse of globalization in government planning and the discourse of cosmopolitanism in the humanities; or between the use of the term "cosmopolitan" in corporate advertising and global culture in a comparative

212 THE ANARCHIST SUBLIME

literature seminar. If to "globalism" and "cosmopolitanism" we add the related terms "worldliness" and "internationalism," we now have an array of words with distinct etymologies and histories of usage that lend weight to one another and mutually bolster each other's claims to reality even when (as very often now) they are programs masquerading as descriptions. The well-publicized retreats of billionaire financier George Soros at his Westchester home with Ivy League academics and thoughtful middlebrow writers like David Rieff were, after all, conducted in the name of immigrant rights and education (among other topics) in the face of threats "to the open society." It was this "open society" Soros had spent more than $1 billion enforcing in Eastern Europe after 1989 (he admits to having "messianic fantasies," although he hates Newt Gingrich, and considers himself a "failed philosopher" who studied under Karl Popper). Cosmopolitanism is, among other things, a miasmic mood in which Soros's forced injection of "capitalist freedom" in the former Soviet bloc looks appealing because the sole imputed alternative is the Christian Coalition. One sort of clarity offered by these retreats is to see how closely their motives shadow those of the cultural and academic Left. That Left, for its part, expresses its goals at times with an uncommon bluntness as the extension of Western freedom, creativity, and pleasure on a global scale.

Considering the economic function of the humanities intellectual, it is very easy to misunderstand the venomous hostility toward academic theory among the journalist watchdogs and government intellectuals. When one refines out of the venom all that is merely anti-intellectual insecurity or the patriotic recoil against the impugning of a kind of "gee, it works" functionalism, one sees that their efforts are not to make the humanities scholars close up shop or slip away into oblivion (at least those who have not bought stock in Whittle enterprises or the new correspondence-school schemes of the University of Phoenix's "e-university"). Like all managers, they want instead to tame the independent intellectuals—to submit them to the same market logic that closes off their own options for thought and creativity—to make a universal virtue out of what harangues them. Looked at sociologically or economically, they are not trying to put the cultural studies or neomodernist textualists out of business; they are trying to *keep their price down*. The humanities intellectuals themselves, then, severely misunderstand their role, constantly mistaking for a challenge to power what is actually a consecration of the pluralist mythology and aestheticist retreat for which they were hired. They raise the stakes of revolt only by bravely (and tragically) intensifying their efforts to produce, for less and less money and market recognition, precisely what power wants them to produce.

LOCATING COSMOPOLITANISM

Cosmopolitanism, in short, works by way of a self-denial that is intrinsic to its economic utility. Only such a paradox could explain the reluctance within cultural theory to explore our own resources in order to materialize a concept that in truth is too much with us.

The buzz surrounding cosmopolitanism had been anticipated and critiqued by a few scholars already in the 1980s.[10] But the proliferation of writing on the theme is a direct result of the fall of communism, and the groundwork of the concept was provided by cultural approaches to globalization that appeared in social science/humanities crossover journals of the early 1990s—especially *Theory, Culture, and Society* and *Public Culture*. But it is striking that attempts to trace the concept of cosmopolitanism historically are not found in either of these journals. With respect to cosmopolitanism, at least, good textual analyses of the major figures in the fields addressed by the journals—which conjoin the cultural and the sociological—are strangely absent. In perhaps the most famous of these kinds of sources, Georg Simmel in "The Metropolis and Mental Life" (1903), offered his later readers a relevant point of departure. He observed the city/country antagonisms at work in the origins of capitalist modernity now replayed in a globalization that is often wrongly cast as recent and novel. There he emphasizes the economic and colonial form of cosmopolitanism as an ethos:

> It is rather in transcending [the] visible expanse that any given city becomes the seat of cosmopolitanism. The horizon of the city expands in a manner comparable to the way in which wealth develops; a certain amount of property increases in a quasi-automatical way in ever more rapid progression. As soon as a certain limit has been passed, the economic, personal and intellectual relations of the citizenry, the sphere of intellectual predominance of the city over its hinterland, grow as in geometrical progression.[11]

In Simmel's considered opinion, cosmopolitanism conformed to a kind of law of colonial expansion whereby urban centers (metropolitan regions) justified their encroaching power over geopolitically dispersed, and therefore vulnerable, territories. The process, in his view, assumed the coloring of an implacable, beneficent logic. It is difficult not to see parallels between his prescience and the way in which cosmopolitanism is invoked today in a spirit of outreach and amelioration that is disarming, not least because the word captures the image intellectuals have of themselves by hinting at the proper way in fact to be an intellectual—namely, projecting outside the self in an effort to understand alien values while unconsciously translating them into terms of local usage that belie their local origins. When invoked, the term has the added merit of appearing to its users to be an antidote to discrimination, which it pretends to replace with a consummate reason.

Antonio Gramsci—to take another obvious predecessor, and one who enjoys a central position in cultural theory today—explored cosmopolitanism in great detail, and with a critical eye. Nonetheless, his conclusions on this matter play no role whatsoever in current debates over cosmopolitanism, a situation that implies how narrow our framing of the discussion has been. He distinguished the concept from internationalism while considering it an idealist detour associated with specific national formations. In one of his examples, he argues that it found expression in the abstract quest for the "universal language" of Esperanto in the early decades of the century.

As I am presenting it here, Gramsci's approach to cosmopolitanism may seem provocative, but it is very well documented. His views were neither fleeting nor ambiguous. In the late 1980s, in an essay that traced his use of the concept over his complete works, I argued that Gramsci held an attitude toward cosmopolitanism that, given contemporary understandings, was surprisingly hostile.[12] His attitude, moreover, was consonant with that of the left intellectuals of his generation.[13] This line of argument has since been convincingly taken up by Aijaz Ahmad in the context of discussing an emergent Hindu nationalism in India.[14] At any rate, despite many current readings of Gramsci (which hardly prepare one for this conclusion), the *Prison Notebooks* tirelessly record his views on the lifelessness and conservatism of Italian intellectuals. He traces their shortcomings to domestic traditions that derived, ultimately, from the role intellectuals played in Renaissance Italy, the center (in his words) of "imperial and medieval cosmopolitanism." While understanding the more familiar barriers to national harmony that come from racial and ethnic differences, Gramsci also explored the rather different process of intellectual stasis and indirection that came from a history of relative *centrality*:

> It is necessary to go back to the times of the Roman Empire when Italy, through the territory of Rome, became the melting pot of the cultured classes from throughout the Empire. Its ruling personnel became ever more imperial and ever less Latin: they became cosmopolitan. . . . From the 1500s on . . . Italian Catholicism was experienced as a surrogate for

the spirit of nationalism and statehood, and not only that, but as a worldwide hegemonic function, that is, an imperialistic spirit.[15]

The resonance of these comments for diasporic intellectuals now working in the United States is remarkable—and remarkably untheorized. One cannot lightly draw analogies, obviously, between Gramsci's Italy and the contemporary United States. But surely there is room to be astounded that someone so apparently central to contemporary writing in the humanities found cosmopolitanism so double-edged and that his demur is completely ignored in current literature.[16] He reminds us that left intellectuals of his generation thought internationalism and cosmopolitanism incompatible,[17] since internationalism acknowledges that differences of culture and polity cannot be juridically erased before the conditions exist for doing so equitably, and because internationalism insists on the principle of *national* sovereignty. There is no other way under a global nation-state system for respect to be expressed. This sort of point puzzles critics today, and the very existence of so fundamental a confusion implies that an important range of inquiries has been lost. That range might be located in the variety of complicated questions suggested by the term "market," insofar as the term is viewed as a diagnostic category for understanding the material functions and interests of intellectuals working at the crossroads of policy, social studies, and cultural studies.

One could easily add to these kinds of sources, although this is not the place to do so, for want of space. Given the background I have so far elicited, my position may be seen as hostile to cosmopolitanism, but I do not want to be misunderstood. Even though the debate surrounding the term tends to pit cosmopolitanism against patriotism, I hope it is clear that I am not arguing on behalf of an American nativism. In the current resurgence of Christian fundamentalism and jingoism in the United States (as well as in the religious revivals in other parts of the world), it takes a hard heart not to be on the side of opposing prejudice or supporting open-mindedness and alterity—all evoked, *in general*, by the term. In that sense, one should be cosmopolitan when it comes to education, tastes in art, and political solidarities if considered (paradoxically) within national frameworks. The problem being sketched out here does not conform to those senses of the term, but rather lies in the intellectual formation that Gramsci called "imperial cosmopolitanism," which is perfectly captured by the quotations from the management literature above.

We might now begin to get more specific. How has cosmopolitanism actually been studied? It has more than a single lineage. The concept has been approached, for example, in a broadly premodern sense, playing off its etymological origins in Greek cosmology (*cosmos* + *polis*) as it evolved into the Catholic universalism of Dante prior to the project of modern nationalism (the approach, for example, of Stephen Toulmin, Julia Kristeva, and Martha Nussbaum, among others).[18] It can be understood in a different, although not incompatible, way as well by focusing on the post-Kantian era of European exploration and nation building. This approach leads to a different set of questions, for it witnesses a period in which world government strategies begin to overlap with the ethical position of world culture as implied by the original Greek usage and its later adaptation by the European Church. Indeed, the raiding of the cultural concept by the governmental was one of Kant's preoccupations, as can be seen by the warnings found in his "Idea of a Universal History from a Cosmopolitan Standpoint," published in 1784. This particular approach—both a period one and one interested in the political undertones of a cultural concept—can be found in Jürgen Habermas, Bonnie Honig, Walter Mignolo, and myself.[19] And cosmopolitanism, finally, can be understood as referring to the national specificity of the United States in which a New World pluralism adapted from nineteenth-century Latin American liberation movements joins a fledgling U.S. imperial project. Here is born, in the creation of an "elect," an American exceptionalism that understands the United States as what is desired globally by all. This approach needs to be elaborated, although hints of this argument can be found elsewhere.[20] The need, above all, would be to clarify how a national-political myth of multicultural inclusion ("pluralism") dovetails, under specific conditions, with a purportedly supranational ethos of global cooperation (cosmopolitanism). I consider the ethical core of the two concepts to be identical.

To speak of cosmopolitanism's locality is to suggest its exportability (or importability). This last approach suggests that intellectual export be seen as a model for understanding how the concept of cosmopolitanism functions in U.S. intellectual circles. For certainly it is paradoxical that "pluralism" was an idea first borrowed from the Creole nationalisms of Latin America and then monopolized and exported as an American (i.e., U.S.) "new way." The concept of pluralism, which is so strongly identified with the American self-image, was originally imported into the United States from Latin America. Thus, in the national specificity of the United States, the meaning of cosmopolitanism is marked by an earlier fundamental shift in its usage after the Enlightenment, occurring for reasons both historical and regional. A New World pluralism theorized by early Caribbean travelers like Jean-Baptiste Du Tertre and Père Labat, and forged into a political ethic by Domingo Faustino Sarmiento, José Martí, and others against the background of the nineteenth-century liberation movements (and arising again in the twentieth century in *la raza cósmica* of José Vasconcelos and *lo real maravilloso* of Alejo Carpentier) was taken on—honorably at first—by North American pragmatist philosophers. In the hands of William James and John Dewey it was given a distinguished career before being officially institutionalized while gradually purified of its foreign origins—in that sense quite out of step with the inclusive intentions of the pragmatists who promoted the concept to stave off hysterical anti-immigration sentiments at the turn of the century.

Today's cosmopolitanism, then, has appeared before, appeared here, and in very similar terms. It is remarkable how little of the current research goes back to look at such moments. Where does one hear, for example, of the "Cosmopolitan Clubs" of 1912, which were accustomed to making appeals to "ideals of world brotherhood" while holding multicultural dance halls on American campuses ("Would you let your daughter dance with a Chinese or Hindu?" one pamphlet provocatively asks). Their events are reported in great detail in the *Documents of the American Association for International Conciliation*, whose contributors included William Howard Taft in a little essay titled "The Dawn of World Peace" (1911) and Norman Angell's more academic (and contemporary-sounding) essay "The Mirage of the Map: An Interrogation" (1911).[21] Leaving the early century, one might skip ahead to the immediate post–World War II era to find other precursors. A similar set of organizations arose in the left Hollywood of the late 1940s, where personalities like Clifton Fadiman and Oscar Hammerstein III held fund-raisers for the influential pamphlet series *World Government News*, performing skits to show the "myth of national sovereignty" and doing so on behalf of a strong United Nations. Both of these examples have counterparts today; the movement never really dies. Walter Cronkite's World Federalist Association, active in 1999 on behalf of good things like "sustainable development" and mutual understanding, also advocates (with an ominous ring of stewardship) a "strong international court of justice."

Again, this fundamentally Kantian illusion was particularly strong at the turn of the last century, as witnessed by the words of the famed British Radical G. Lowes Dickinson in 1908:

> I see the time approaching when the nations of the world, laying aside
> their political animosities, will be knitted together in the peaceful rivalry
> of trade; when those barriers of nationality which belong to the infancy
> of the race will melt and dissolve in the sunshine of science and art; when
> the roar of the cannon will yield to the softer murmur of the loom, and
> the apron of the artisan, the blouse of the peasant will be more hon-

ourable than the scarlet of the soldier; when the cosmopolitan armies of trade will replace the militia of death; when that which God has joined together will no longer be sundered by the ignorance, the folly, the wickedness of man; when the labour and the invention of one will become the heritage of all; and the peoples of the earth meet no longer on the field of battle, but by their chosen delegates, as in the vision of our greatest poet, in the "Parliament of Man, the Federation of the World."[22]

And the cultural invention of pluralism in the Americas that flourished in the same era specifically provided both the imperatives and the imagery to allow intellectuals a space within which to dwell when espousing an imperial cosmopolitanism from within a general progressivism. From peripheral Portugal, still in possession of the oldest of European colonial empires but now a disregarded and marginal member of the Western comity of nations, came another version of cosmopolitanism—a dream of modernity to compensate for its actual backwardness. The poet Fernando Pessoa, setting out a manifesto for the journal *Orpheu* in 1915, wrote:

What does *Orpheu* want? To create a cosmopolitan art in time and space. Ours is a time in which countries, more materially than ever, and for the first time intellectually, all exist within each other; in which Asia, America, Africa and Oceania are Europe and exist within Europe. Any European dock is sufficient . . . to have the entire earth summarised. And if I call this *European* rather than American, for example, it is because Europe rather than America is the *source and origin* of this type of civilization which serves as *norm* and *orientation* to the entire world. For this reason real modern art has to be totally denationalized; it has to accumulate within it all parts of the world. Only in this manner can you be typically modern.[23]

The locality of cosmopolitanism—here Portugal in decay—prepares us for the paradox that a political utopia like Pessoa's is constructed as aesthetic taste. The spilling over of the cultural into the political is endemic to cosmopolitanism's functionality and, in mildly different forms, reappears in the era of American hybridity's penchant for the aesthetic of the "fragment" and the conviction that rhizomatic images are, paradoxically, a "home" position, democratically familiar.

In this atmosphere, it is commonplace for even progressive journalists to assume that "common-sense international law" should "transcend outdated sovereign rights."[24] One generally does not even feel the need to defend this proposition today. We repeatedly are made to imagine that ordinary people have the same access to education, funding, and travel that intellectuals and businessmen do, and that they can exploit the same global networks of communication in a variety of foreign languages. Such mistaken assumptions are the product of the cosmopolitanism of cultural politicians who actually do live transnationally, and whose humanist/ethical outlook enlivens and, in some ways, softens their policy suggestions in the public sphere. Among the issues forgotten here are those key advantages that nations provide the global subalterns they wish to free from the tyranny of the national state—advantages that are particularly condemned by the humanists who are hostile to the myths of national belonging. And yet, any progressive vision today depends on such myths. For, outside cosmopolis, they represent the only basis for organizing opposition to the corporate carnivalesque (to echo Stallybrass and White again).

The colloquial connotations of cosmopolitanism are so irrepressibly positive that we continually see the critic "discovering" what is already the commonplace of corporate interests and official American language. National sovereignty is said to have been transcended, the nation-state relegated to an obsolete form, and the present political situation is seen as one in which newly deracinated populations, nongovernmental organizations and Web users are outwitting a new world order in the name of a bold new transnational sphere.[25]

It is primarily the cultural discourse of cosmopolitanism—a friendly discourse in the sense that it does not appear to be about politics—that prevents intellectuals from contesting this fallacious account of materialities, blinded as they are by the euphoria of a goodwill that is conveniently good business for them and theirs. For what we are really seeing is not a popular transnationalism but the substantively altered competition among nation-states—the movement from smaller polities to megastates (with China being the last remaining credible adversary to the United States). If the world were globalized in the way it is discussed in much of cultural theory, we would not be seeing such hard negotiations among the member states of the European Union nor the defections from it; we would not have the trade showdowns that periodically arise between the United States and China, the United States and Mexico, or between Venezuela and Brazil; and we would not have the national disparities existing in wage levels, ecological legislation, or the rights of judicial redress—disparities that arose historically as a result of the different ethnic compositions of the workforce as well as distinct national-political traditions. Corporations depend on these disparities, and they are enforced only by the policing operations of national governments. Equally, however, such disparities can be smuggled in through the back door even as their effectiveness is ushered out the front.

To put this more bluntly: nations continue to exist because the major players have a vested interest in their continuing. Working people need nations in order to have someone to complain to; corporations need nations in order to ensure a lack of fair competition and the absence of an equality of law, so that a dynamic flux can be maintained within a setting of monopoly. What ensures the continuity of an albeit altered nation-state system is the desirability of choices for capital mobility, so that capital can move when it finds too many regulations in one locale and more amenable legislation elsewhere. This sort of flux allows bidding and outbidding among the clients of monopoly and stands in as an impostor for the "free market" by simulating it. It is not that there is no novelty, especially demographic, in this system, or that there is no reality to what cosmopolitanism calls new world subjects, new diasporic communities, unrooted and resourceful.[26] But if one means by globalization the creation of new world subjects who are not bound by the laws and territorial limitations of locality or, indeed, are necessarily happy in their uprootedness, one is indulging in a fiction and is either missing the point or obscuring it.

The complaint with cosmopolitan discourse is not only that it falls prey to cultural fascination with new diasporic communities at the expense of questioning the market or that the culture of diasporic subjects is usually given a positive inflection in cultural theory without remarking on its coercive nature—that people often do not want to be diasporic. It is also that the discourse of cosmopolitanism is exceedingly narrow in what fascinates it, failing to link the market with imagination, and then failing to link that nexus itself to the non-Western world, which any cosmopolitanism should properly foreground. In cosmo-theory, the non-Western is, of course, always center stage. The new cosmopolitan subject, as the discourse has it, is no longer the elitist dream of poets and philosophers but a real populist fact. For the first time cosmopolitans are plebeian, nonwhite, working class, and globally varied. Why, then, does cosmo-theory so uncritically promote modernity, or see the highly prized hybrid self-consciousness of formerly subjugated peoples as a glorious arrival—a coming to modernity?

This is odd since modernity is the product of New World discovery and the management/technological breakthroughs prompted by Spanish gold, and dynamic interstate rivalries. It is striking to realize that many of the key analysts of modernity (Max Weber, Emile Durkheim—or more recently, Alain Touraine, Anthony Giddens, and Stuart Hall) have given relatively scant space to the Conquest, to colonialism, or to the imperialism that followed both. What Simmel (and after him, Guy Debord) called the "psychogeography" of modernity—the effects on mental life of the money economy expressed in the move from material goods to information, the plurality of heterogeneous claims to knowledge, the difficulty of grasping the social totality, extreme autonomization resulting from the radical division of labor, reification, the replacement of use by exchange, the rise of complex bureaucracies mediating all contacts on a colossal scale, time/space *distanciation*, and so forth—all of these familiar terms point to the colonial encounter and are fully understandable only in terms of it.[27] And yet, from conservative globalists like William Bennett and Robert Leiken to liberal sociologists like David Held, one repeatedly finds claims of proof for the "declining grip of the West over the rest of the world," as though a process of centralization and a process of decentering were indistinguishable (the same confusion of an age in which the lonely anarchist Internet hacker and the corporate takeover artist are products of the same process).[28]

Here, too, cosmo-theory arrives to dress contradiction in the garments of victory. When Giddens explores "reflexivity" (a term that also dominates the globalization writing of dissident financier George Soros), he correctly argues that reflexivity is greater as modernity develops.[29] However, he doesn't question the logic of reflexivity in this purported "declining grip of the West." Drawing on the circular impasses of theory where anarchist nomadism and aestheticism are at home with corporate monopoly and radical consumerism, his position helps finalize the West's grip, even to the point of eliminating it as a problem of critique. The telos of the imperial project is reached when the Third World subject is able to deconstruct the epistemic violence of colonialism only by way of Continental theory. What cosmopolitanism unconsciously strives for is a stasis in which the unique expression of the non-Western is Western reflexively and automatically[30]—the local self exported *as* the world. Only in this spirit could one float the truly ridiculous notion that the West was "losing its grip" on the Third World.

The imperial cosmopolitanism lying behind well-intentioned, good-spirited writing is not, for all that, a simple matter of complicity. Such a charge would fall flat, since complicity is, as it were, second nature to those trained in theory. The discursive regime asks us all to avoid complicity with Enlightenment power by staying vigilant against repressive claims of universality. Such decentering has logically moved the theorist to a form of biopolitics and specifically to a politics of the body. It was the *body*, in fact, that was cast methodically, and with explicit intention, by prewar theorists like Georges Bataille as a substitute for both party politics and dialectical negation.[31] The only way to escape complicity as such was to oppose all opposition, disagreement, or overcoming.[32] The ultimate riposte to power, in other words, was to make oneself powerless—to let power have its way, provided one was innocent of using it (a negation of the Nietzschean positions that inspired the original project). Flee-ing universals indirectly meant giving the universalizing Western state a free hand, continuing to speak under its protections and privileges as though one were absolved from its actions by inaction.

Apart from their internal contradictions, these escapes are a ruse, for they conceal the furious parallels among various intellectual sectors that are visible only in institutional settings. In fact, this invocation of complicity in theory is one of several ways in which theory's concepts outwit protest. The cultural the-orist misrecognizes him- or herself in the crazy mirror of government policy, as recent U.S. scandals show, all of them vivid examples of intellectual flow: Deleuzo-Foucauldian attacks on governmentality reverberate against a chorus of Republican calls to get the "government off our backs"; the ecstatic attention to the "subject" coincides with reduced access to citizenship in Europe and North America; and, above all, the obsolescence of sovereignty achieves its rad-ical eloquence at about the moment NATO discovers rogue ethnics in the Balkans insisting on a horrific, recidivist principle like that of the nation-state. The positions on either side of these paradoxical binarisms are not equivalent since formalisms never are. They are, however, related, and they strengthen one another in the public sphere—not as a result of conspiracy, and in the name of different gods, but above all, naively, as though intellectuals did not work for anyone or had no home.

The discourse of cosmopolitanism develops within fields of academic spe-cialization against the background of broader, and more popular, discourses. The relationship of theory to official policymaking or to the media is almost never systematically worked out. If cultural theory has usually been good about questioning its own methods—providing self-criticism as an integral part of its argument—cosmo-theory has been squeamish about analyzing the place of the researchers themselves in frameworks of interest. What is the economic func-tion of the culturalist intellectual? Where do we place the anthropologists, so-ciologists, literary critics, and cultural studies professors in the vectors of the U.S. economy? What relationship do we have to the state?

Cosmo-Theory

Above all, my choice of the term "cosmo-theory" is to suggest an unacknowl-edged consensus—one that constitutes a constellation of related premises and values. However unacceptable it might be merely to group together critics of different trainings, styles, and concrete beliefs in pursuit of a collective point, it is equally unacceptable to avoid synthesizing a visible trend in public discourse, or to avoid an attempt at characterizing it as such. Proposing to offer such a characterization clarifies issues that would not be clarified otherwise, and it goes some way toward offering an expressive and alienated truth. At any rate, that would be my defense for using a term that many will at first consider unjustifiably narrow or conflating but that is marking a collection of tendencies that are familiar. I indicate in my footnotes some of the work in which the following features can be found so as not to leave matters anonymous or to create the impression that I imagined or invented them.

What I am calling cosmo-theory begins usually by citing a very long tradition of writing and thinking on extra-national impurities, where the point is made that human populations exist in no discrete cultural, ethnic, or political realm. This unassailable observation, however, tends to be accompanied by more-questionable corollaries. Striking in its general contours are the following: First, the discourse tends to combine an overdeveloped sensitivity to significant cases of mixed forms of cultural life—usually related in vivid, anecdotal form—with a relatively weak understanding of processes of power, labor management, territorial control, or governance, as though its usefulness to arguments about government depended on its being shielded from actual power. A strong descriptive armature tends to be coupled with a weak sociological imperative. It is a discourse of "processes," "movements," unfoldings, rather than designs, projects, or campaigns. Life is described as what happens to people rather than what the holders of specific positions make or delimit.[33] It is not as though there were no role for agency in such theories, which, on the contrary, rely on excited exaggerations of activity, creativity, and plebeian initiative. But agency is almost never seen in moments of civic participation. It is primarily about subject formation. Agency, in fact, tends to be seen as a gradual process of coming to accept a fait accompli and learning to mobilize it. Modernity is "at large"—a phrase that, interestingly, implies pervasiveness as well as culpability (making the very good point, however unintentional, that modernity was like a perpetrator who had not yet been caught).

Second, cosmo-theory depends on exaggerating the degree to which people in the outlying districts of what one critic calls the "global ecumene" have actually broken with the past.[34] In cosmo-theory, modernity is generally considered to be ubiquitous—its penetration complete and largely welcome. Here one is struck by the relative absence of any substantive proof for this claim that metropolitan style, pace, or value has universally spread—a position that is almost always overstated. Even now, the villages of rural India or Latin America—with or without television—are hardly *in* modernity in any sense meaningful to cosmopolitans. Quite apart from what the cosmo-theorists are arguing, the world is largely outside modernity, although being in and out, in this sense, is naturally always a matter of degree. The point, however, is that a projection into a desired future is often mistaken in these analyses for a documentable present.

Cosmo-theory also tends to decouple individual subjects from groups of perceived material interest in which a special emphasis is placed on the imagination.[35] The media are in this way treated as a resource for the construction of imagined selves, which tend not to be discussed in terms of the polities they inhabit.[36] Whereas several theorists have given us reason to lament modernity and have rightly reminded us of its melancholy march, there is a tendency in discussions of cosmopolitanism to portray it, willy-nilly, as a benefit to which the world subject aspires.[37] In fact, part of the procedural difficulty, even obtuseness, of the ethic of cosmo-theory is that it weakens the critical impulses of non-Western thinking by assimilating them into an alien logic. The options enjoyed by individuals in local settings, for instance, are not seen in terms of their uneven forms of development. It is not so much that the individual is emphasized to the exclusion of groups, for there is space in this thinking for group sentiments, but these groups are rarely political constituencies. In an effort to leave behind oversimplified notions of media coercion or cultural imperialism, it is as if no media coercion existed at all.[38]

Stylistically, a rhetoric of ambiguity and opposition to teleological thinking prevail. This latter telos is stated as such. They are the twin poles of an aesthetic preference borrowed from the Spinozist (and later Nietzschean) genealogies of poststructuralism, primarily in Deleuze.[39] Obviously there are myriad, often contradictory, intellectual sources mingling in the serious scholarly writing of even the few globalization theorists I highlight in this chapter. "Flow" implies a largely atmospheric pressure that under conditions whose basic features have been variably present throughout the century, produces discursive hegemonies to which, in this case, we give the names "Bataille" or "Deleuze." What they developed with clarity, others found instinctively and still others took wholesale from their books.

The implications of all this, at any rate, are that cosmopolitanism effectively undermines ideals of citizenship. As the Enlightenment individual gives way to the subject, agency is passed off as creativity while ceasing to stand for production or intervention. The calculated ambiguity of the term "subject" is one of its principal attractions, meaning at once the author of an action, the subaltern of a king, and an element of speech (the nominal operative of a disembodied verb). Since theory considers individuality a term that connotes a suspiciously pre-given and stable coherence, subjectivity offers a way of talking about individuals abstracted from the speaking, thinking person (just as genealogy offers a way to talk about history abstracted from historical proof). It is a way of preserving modernity's focus on individuals without positing individuality in its confident, modernist sense. From the modernist standpoint, the individual is agential: it is author, creator, seer, often of a private world. From the postmodern, the individual's role in a rationalized society, although juridically free, is also incompatible with true agency. Thus only the subject is truly an agent, for it is so much an actor that it makes itself arbitrarily, and remakes itself constantly in the face of prescribed social roles and pseudo-universal values.[40]

If the move from individual to subject involves an abstraction and an intentional floating of meanings—one is tempted to call it an ethereality—it is accompanied by a necessary counterpart and counterweight at the conceptual level. And this, as we said above, is "the body." From modernity to postmodernity, there has been a transformation of the thinking, active will into the body. The individual of old has now been bifurcated, so that what used to be identifiable within a single entity now requires two. In this thinking, the body and the subject together make the individual, although the discourse deals with the latter like a volatile chemical mixture, treating neither together, at the risk of social explosion. If postmodernity separates the whole into autonomous fields when it comes to the person, then by extension the *citizen* (or the person in his or her juridical, national, or political form) is the result of tying together what had before been separate. The foreign/domestic dichotomy is replaced in theory by the hybrid subject, instinctively returning to the American self-image of pluralism as though part of a great money-laundering operation in which Continental theory played the role of a shady bank. Although attacked, citizenship is never actually endangered under postmodernism. It is simply turned into a fungible category based on a very unfungible national/political reality that denies its own existence: the American. This "American" is fully, although deceptively, capable of being performed by diasporic intellectuals, and in the cosmoplitan moment, this is frequently the case.

In a number of ways, then, our debates fail to examine histories central to the term's formation. These debates, moreover, have often been dependent on an eminently literary or philological practice that has often been associated with *genealogy*. This very popular term, derived from Nietzsche, is a crucial anchoring device for the poststructuralist common sense that informs the current discussion of globalization in a variety of disciplines, not just in the humanities. It would be saying too much to say it was intrinsic to the field, but it does inform many of the uses of cosmo-theory as it flows back into the humanities from policy circles, government, and the social sciences—a theory now repoliticized with case studies of actual states, peoples, and periods. This cartography of American intellectuals demands a few words on the relationship of cartography to genealogy itself. Both are a translation of time into space; both change the unfolding of history into a fixed synchronic schema. What, then, is genealogy?

Nietzsche presents it as a counterhistorical technique that does not posit the utility of a thing as its origin. Genealogies critically engage with the changing interpretations of the meaning of concepts and institutions in order to show their current expression in a long history of unrelated and contradictory articulations. A genealogy, as Nietzsche invents it, cannot be exhaustive, since phenomena can only partially be known by their relationships. Because inaccessible, origins themselves give way to the family lineage, which is a fluctuating sameness that may traverse time but without voluntary practice or guiding intelligence, a legacy-in-blood, recorded inexorably in language (the etymology) as a word's "parentage."

Foucault similarly saw in the genealogy an adamantly counterhistorical knowledge, a way of practicing history without being historical. His arguments (derived from Nietzsche) were necessarily based on a past, on the authority of the actual, but for rhetorical reasons he emphasized contingencies rather than stabilities, complexities rather than continuities, perspectives rather than false objectivities. I am precisely *not* involved in a genealogy in these senses. I do not think history can be avoided by changing history's name or by indulging in the subterfuge of both using and disavowing a past—both relying on its proof value and destabilizing the very concept of proof. My point is rather to reinstate a contentious binarism latent in intellectual practice—a practice that may not want to dwell on its own agency or interests but that never relinquishes it either.

I want to capture the sense of fluidity among constituencies in a setting of interested knowledge where the economic is translated into the ethical for reuse in a variety of economic spheres mediated by culture. Since this is all happening in a global confrontation of civilizations, one's response to the genealogical method—whose metaphorical associations are rather embarrassingly related to blood, family, and immutable hierarchy—should be different. Theory's job is not (as many argue) to emphasize the contingency of origins, but rather to stress the priority of origins over understanding. Another way to re-pose the problem of origins by the light of such a priority is to ask: what is it about *American* value that prevents cultural critics from looking closely at their economic function in promoting globalization?

If theory has insistently taught us to reject origins and be suspicious of foundations—which in geopolitical terms is usually seen as being culpably related to mythical projects of nation forming—it is because the recourse to ur-communities and earlier peoples is usually intended to authenticate attempts to consolidate governments in the present. We might recall that Foucault translated Nietzsche's original concept of the genealogy in the context of being a member of a repressed sexual minority and a devout anti-Hegelian. Genealogy was his preferred methodological mode because it was anti-developmental, anti-organic, anti-historical in Hegel's sense of seeing individuals as part of social universals, and of societies as developing through active intelligence and effort toward a goal or end. However, recognizing that if one remains in the sumptuously static world of the synchronic, one lacks interest as well as authority, Foucault the genealogist had to find a way of appealing to history without accepting its corollaries. The germ of the original concept in Nietzsche remains at the core of this fundamentally duplicitous operation of practicing history while not practicing it. Nietzsche's intention, unlike Foucault's, was to claim rights for aristocratic privilege and *Rangordnung* (hierarchical ranking)—a deeply recidivist and explicitly racialist concept in Nietzsche's original text (although this reading is conventionally denied). The genealogy, because it was about family, recalled not agency and change but the genetic inevitabilities of paternity; at the same time, it apotheosized etymology as if to say that history is fundamentally about words ruling people, the willful creation of a truth embedded in a linguistic trace. So my point, finally, is to say that if the method of genealogy conceals the very source-specific patriotism and racialist filiations that it pretends to get past, cosmo-theory attempts, through its own genealogical pretensions at worldliness, to override the veiled Americanism to which it aspires. Cosmopolitanism is the way in which a kind of American patriotism is today being expressed.

Nevertheless, thematically cosmo-theory is generally aware of the danger of imperial apologetics. The critic states his or her opposition to "reckless American expansion" and is vocal about the dangers of an uncritical multiculturalism.[41] The emphasis is therefore on the American *government*, where all of its suspicion lies, expressing its deeper philosophical commitment to a wariness toward states in themselves. Caution toward the American state is, however, accompanied by a defense of internationalism as a form of American influence seen as the components of American cultural life that have become international. International arrangements are therefore divided between "state-saturated" societies and "anti-statist" ones, with China usually standing in for the former while market/media capitalism is aligned with the latter. The United States in these articles is quite remarkably considered a weak-state society.[42] Indeed, this is the distinction that fuels both the emphasis on culture (that which exists outside the state as well as outside the intermediary realm of civil society) and the view that a capitalist popular culture is not only recuperable but expressive of a deep liberatory drive. The corporate boardroom, as one critic ludicrously puts it, is a "public space" and mass cultural phenomena like, say, rap demonstrate the continual creativity of capitalism as a culture.[43]

Along with arguing for the naturally cosmopolitan character of intellectuals as a group, the cosmo-critic argues that there is a natural alliance between the American cultural Left and Third World constituencies on whose behalf the former speaks in domestic contexts, and whose presence (imaginary or actual) is marshaled for salutary means at home. Outside the United States, the cultural is said to be already political, and the cultural Left learns from, while solidarizing with, those constituencies, arriving finally at the important understanding that the cultural is also political *at home*.[44] Corollaries of this self-serving idea are the following: that the cultural Left is inherently internationalist and that it obtains its political results via a process of indirection. Neither one of these contentions is true, but they fuel a substantial portion of culturalist analysis.

STATELESSNESS: THAT IS, THE AMERICAN STATE

Cosmopolitanism implies a theory of nations, although it is only in the context of the market that such a theory can be seen clearly and judged. Flows of influence on the nation among different constituencies of intellectuals bring us back to the problem of characterizing a diverse collection of beliefs within recognizable trends. Again, these constituency-wide tendencies have the character of a separation of powers or of segmented intellectual duties within a broader, national project.

In the field of academic cultural studies, for example, the nation is typically considered obsolete *at the same time* that it is said to be founded upon (1) a dangerous, murky, racialist essentialism, (2) a statist conception of coercion, and (3) patronizing welfarism. This is a position that I have argued elsewhere was self-contradictory, if unashamed (in Julia Kristeva and Anthony King, for example).[45] In the different arena of popular political commentary and among official government academics, the nation is considered (1) still resilient, and forms the political landscape of the foreseeable future, but (2) is a dangerous, murky, racialist essentialism that it would be best to transcend with the universalist values of the West in the form of Pax Americana, seen as some new form of "international cooperation" or "international law" (Huntington, Kissinger, Archibugi).[46] The view might be further ventriloquized in this way: (3) let us have less nation and more *state*, but a modified state, not one that micromanages corporations or regulates business enterprises at the expense of growth. Let it be one not limited by national boundaries, one that functions by the rule of law rather than by the brutal power politics of invasion or imperialism (the argument, mutatis mutandis, once used by Walter Lippmann).

The illogical array of views of the state is therefore, twofold, and a merging of positions between the first and second set of groups is always possible under conditions of intellectual flow, as happens often among the pop futurologist and the writers of commercial travelogues (Pico Iyer, Robert Kaplan, Thomas Friedman). Their mixture of fear-mongering cameos of tribal bloodletting entertains its audience while driving home moral lessons about the barbarism of national allegiances. In this ubiquitous genre—which saturates academic writing and feature journalism equally—the author expresses bemused sympathy for the fly-ridden faces of starving children while writing with metropolitan detachment, arriving at conclusions posed as confessions: these traumas are curable only with help from the outside (that is, us).[47]

For their part (and to consider still another intellectual sector), corporate strategists and Western politicians tend to argue that states should recognize their interests in stimulating growth by freeing the market from the state's controls (Robert Reich, William Baumol, Robert Rubin, Jeffrey Sachs).[48] Here the argument urges us to have a stronger state when it comes to dismantling habeas corpus, or instituting stronger prison sentences and border patrols, as well as adding a new wing of government that functions as part of the state but is not called the state, and proclaims its independence from it, and that is on that basis absent of democratic controls (the fourth estate). Above all, the state under globalization *ensures that the mobility of capital outpaces the mobility of labor*. Globalization means heightened border controls.[49]

What one is forced to conclude is that nation-states are not only, in the overused terminology du jour, imagined communities. They are rather manageable communities. The state as coercive negotiator presides over a community that it must, by definition, be capable of managing. But that is not all. What it is capable of managing becomes inexorably what must be ruled. What the state *can* manage, it eventually *does* manage. It does this by virtue of a law that is militarily enforced, as well as by the ideology of nation, although cultural theory has been inordinately focused only on the latter in recent decades, dwelling on the national print media or images of racial belonging or patriarchal privileges whose combinatory effects at the affective level of signs and tastes and discursive networks have provided the basis for the mass hysteria of national myth and its coercive corollaries. But these important dimensions of nation-making have been overstated. They tend to lapse into an idealistic euphoria that underestimates the practical force of management.

If one does, by contrast, explore the managerial dimension, nations begin to appear more a matter of default than of manipulative mythology. Until recently, there was no way around them historically because no coercive or hegemonic apparatus was capable of managing the entire earth (in spite of imperial attempts to do so by Egyptians, Macedonians, Turks, Mongols, Mughals, Romans, Britons, Germans, and more recently, North Americans). Administratively speaking, nations are discrete units for the organization of profit making, resource extraction, and the perpetuation of unequal social relations; they are also, within the framework of a world system of nations in which enormous disparities in national power exist, structures that permit local or indigenous peoples to draw a boundary between what is theirs and what is not theirs, between what is open to the outside and not open. In this latter, very seldom talked-about, sense, the nation protects the weak and is their refuge. For like cosmopolitanism, nations are local. They are manageable in two directions, since they allow the state to manage the subalterns, and the subalterns to petition the state within the context of a rhetoric of the popular—a notion of cultural family and shared identity.

It is not clear, then, how much importance should be given to the common distinction between state and nation, since the difference is itself superseded in actual practice. The transition from the tributary state to the modern nation-state in the Romantic period might be seen as the result of a management crisis created by foreign conquest and the wealth that it generated.[50] This was the endpoint and fruition of a three-centuries-long era of primitive accumulation based on slave labor, an immense extraction of foreign booty, the creation of entirely new global markets (rather than the penetration of existing markets), and the *encomienda* system.[51] The passage from what historians traditionally call colonialism to imperialism proper in the high nineteenth century called forth the nation in the form of a management crisis. Fences had to be set up at home in order to clarify jurisdiction over the spoils abroad. The massive cultural confrontations of global settlement and business organization dictated a reactive fear of difference, not primarily out of psychological mechanisms of "forming the self" in the irrational arena of xenophobic being but rather on the grounds of not being the beings branded by skin or by tongue as the owned, the occupied, the laborers. In part, the nation was the result of a desire, again for reasons of jurisdiction, to codify the differences between home and territory, receiver and giver, owner and owned.

The debate over the fate of the nation today takes place as a debate over nations *as such*. With some exceptions, no fundamental distinction is entertained between those created by imperial expansion and those created, some three centuries afterward, by the peoples resisting that expansion. To argue today that the nation is dead is, then, doubly vexed: on the one hand, for ignoring the prognoses of the makers of policy who know quite well this isn't so; and on the other, for borrowing uncritically from the perspective of the makers of policy who would like to replace many states (seen as pathetically belated, fictional, and unviable) with one or two: a truly world state whose character and systems of value they had a crucial role in determining. In this latter case, they would not (of course) be explicitly built *in the name of* any existing nation, only serving its interests in a mediated way. Here we return to the cosmopolitan fantasy that has existed in the medieval church and, in its modern form, in Kant's *Perpetual Peace: A Philosophical Essay* (1795). However, now it is conducted under the rubric of a Realpolitik composed of rapid deployment forces, carrier jets, cruise missiles, and satellite surveillance. A national idea based on America as a universal nation—hegemonized through popular culture, fashion, and the Internet—can be imagined for the first time. The global management problem, many now argue, has been solved, and thus Kant's ideal is possible for the first time. The real debate—although it is never put in these terms—is this: is the globe now manageable? If so, then it is on its way to becoming a single nation, which is the situation that most cultural theory refers to—fatally and cosmopolitically—as "transnationalism."

Pondering the reality of the political economy of the nation known (still) as the United States, one sees the ambiguity that a term like "globalization" creates. For even as it implies the integration of networks of trade, information, and finance in a single global marketplace, it points to a primary beneficiary. Apart from having a vastly superior military and apart from being the runaway leader in computer and information technologies, the United States *thinks* globally, and it does so as a matter of time-tested national mythos as well as more recent ideological mobilization. That is, its population is famously, and by tradition, multicultural as well as being constantly renewed by new waves of innovative influx from foreign lands; its labor force has been purged of most union interference to job relocations; and at the level of small business as well as at the level of the corporation, the Internet style of market interaction is accepted as inevitable and now fully under way as a matter of mass-cultural popularity. The industries in which it excels are precisely the ones designed for the postindustrial charge of the global economy: entertainment, software, the service industries, consulting, media. As Thomas Friedman rightly although ob-

noxiously puts it, "globalization is us." And this (we might call it, "crypto") nationalism is in play in any buoyant assessment of the coming global culture.
This, of course, is not to say that the concept is not also a matter reckoned with
in Brussels, or in the economic planning rooms of China and Singapore; or that
U.S. capitalism has no competitors powerful enough to modify or rechannel (if
not veto) its decisions.

What one confronts, then, is a series of misunderstandings. In high modernity, one spoke of the universal values of humanism, the dignity of labor, freedom of speech and assembly, and other universals that culminated, honorably,
in 1945 with the UN's Universal Declaration of Human Rights (and it is these
universals that have been mercilessly attacked by postmodern theory). But paradoxically, the universal becomes fully possible only in postmodernity, although it is a universal of a different type—the universality of the media and
its coextensive reach, as well as the inability to escape its penetration by virtue
of its very ephemerality.[52]

We have to be very cautious, then, of positing anything like a diasporic public sphere, the hopeful vision of nonwhite, non-Western exiles in metropolitan
enclaves making good while making do. Many of the strategies of immigrant
communities or of domestic subterraneans (the ghosts of the census) or of political refugees—all busily crossing borders, of course—are precisely not about
stateless subjects taking the view that their very being alone constitutes a kind
of resistance to those who resent the beings they are. They are instead about establishing the right to lead in cultural matters, the right to export a collective
identity in such a way that borders are not effaced but enhanced, protectively
and by civic plan. Were intellectuals not so reluctant to explore their economic
roles, they might be championing the efforts—in southern Mexico, Venezuela,
Brazil, Palestine, Portugal, and elsewhere—of establishing sovereignty, this as
opposed to constructing intricate theoretical edifices designed to explode the
very ability to imagine it. Such a project does not clash with articulations of
new forms of transnational organizing, global cultural links, or cross-border
theorizing. The two responsibly imply one another.

CHAPTER 8

THE SOUTHERN INTELLECTUAL

THE IDEAS ATTRIBUTED THESE DAYS TO Antonio Gramsci's lonely, even renegade, genius were already commonplace in Italian and interwar communism. Far from being the received wisdom on Gramsci, this fact is intertwined with a second and equally discounted one: that the primary departures of his work derive from his thinking about European colonialism, race, and myths of empire, which are themes that weave their way through the *Prison Notebooks.*

There were two primary reasons for Gramsci to have seen the importance of colonialism for his broader concerns. His youthful work in social linguistics at the University of Turin had introduced him to the problems of hegemony (a common term in linguistic circles) and its attendant focus on minority languages.[1] In addition, his obsession with the theme of the "country and the city" was a natural focus for him and his contemporaries given party debates over the self-determination of Russia's ethnic and regional minorities in the context of land reform. In other words, many of the conflicts in studies of colonialism and the European empires—including the tone and ire of antagonistic positions within it—first emerged between 1919 and 1945. A reasonable conclusion would be that the popularity of Gramsci in postcolonial theory is a muted consequence of this fact. Or to put this another way, Gramsci embodies his era's anti-colonial energies, and because these are regularly downplayed, he has come to represent a uniqueness of vision that was, in fact, not unique.

In this chapter, I am interested in offering a kind of map of Gramsci's influence during the turn. The genre I am employing here, which has to do with the reception of the great Italian thinker, is fairly common. Some have looked at Gramsci and English criticism, for example; others, at post-1968 Continental Europe, pre-1960s Italy, and specific disciplines like history.[2] There is a Crocean Gramsci, a Gentilean idealist Gramsci, a Togliattian Gramsci as party man, and even a fascist Gramsci.[3] But if V. G. Kiernan in 1977 had already begun to look at Gramsci's views of the "other continents," no one has really considered how profoundly those views affected, often negatively, the new study of colonialism and postcolonialism after the 1970s during the rise of theory and the new Christian Right.[4]

The very first thing to notice is a striking paradox. Almost every postcolonial text in the last two decades has deferred to Gramsci's authority, but few went back to immerse themselves in his writing with the view of mastering it or learning from it in a novel way. All of his political journalism and many of the *Prison Notebooks'* unanthologized passages remain largely unknown to the critics who cite him. Gramsci's own theses, styles of thinking, or points of departure are in these circles still received at second hand.[5] It is difficult to find work in postcolonial studies that does *not* cite Gramsci, but there is usually little claim to provide an exposition of his work as such. The objective is usually more pro forma: a narrative act of allegiance within a frame provided by four of his signature terms: "hegemony," the "subaltern," "passive revolution," and "common sense."

The second thing to notice is that these signature terms, as they are interpreted, run into problems when measured against his life and times. Given that Gramsci held a ministerial post in the Italian parliament, it is doubtful that hegemony could mean, as most postcolonial critics believe, a one-sidedly ideological element of rule in a specifically non-governmental power. The "subaltern," for its part, is invoked to turn readers' attentions towards race, ethnicity and gender despite Gramsci's tendency to focus on what he called "corporatist" organization (which is to say, sectoralist belief cultures based on flexible class identities). "Passive revolution" is used to suggest an incomplete social transformation resulting from colonial occupation, which is not wrong but very partial, since Gramsci was positively invested in Fordist modernity, and wrote of passive revolution in the context of the mutual military invasions of the European powers in the nineteenth century. These powers often occupied their neighbors in order to push through the social and economic changes the home country itself failed to achieve. "Common sense," finally, intimates for the postcolonial theorist the innate, undervalued genius of the subaltern: that which lies outside and above the theoretical pretensions of Western reason. This view ignores Gramsci's efforts to break the stranglehold of the Church and bureau-cracy over the peasantry, his loathing for Italian clerical reaction, and his dis-paraging comments on the bookishness (*libresco*) of the theoretical avant-garde (their "critical criticism," in his ironic words).

On balance, there is a remarkable, and almost perfectly symmetrical, dis-junction between the diagnosis Gramsci provides of intellectuals from rural, pre-capitalist, or colonized regions and the widespread attraction to his work in postcolonial studies. Although it is never expressed in this fashion, Gramsci, it turns out, addresses a situation very similar to that experienced today by postcolonial intellectuals writing in diasporic settings of the imperial and for-merly imperial capitals. These "Southern intellectuals" (in his vocabulary) had historically formed the basis of an imperial intellectual caste from the time of the Roman Empire that in many ways resembles the postcolonial condition, al-though far less flatteringly than we are accustomed to suppose.

In a theoretical climate like our own, where empirical verifiability is often conflated with "empiricism" and condemned in turn as positivism, it is difficult to build a case—as I propose to do here—for better and worse readings of Gramsci. Wouldn't that just be once again to fetishize the archive? It might make more sense, though, to recognize that apart from the serious critical chal-lenge to correct interpretations, callow invocations of "post-empiricism" are often little more than an alibi for satisfying oneself with thumbing a close-at-hand copy of *Selections from the Prison Notebooks* in order to avoid having to do a more taxing kind of research—including the reading of the texts of Gram-sci that do not appear in that well-known anthology, or that do appear there but are more accurately translated elsewhere (let alone the original Italian ver-sions). To point this out is not to pretend that discourses do not devise realities, or that interpretations are not acts of creation. But saying so does not allow one to escape the external tribunals for verbal statements, which are finally rather fragile in relation to the world of things. Janet Abu-Lughod, among others, has invoked this kind of distinction while arguing for a standard of evidence based, at the very least, on "triangulation."[6] Gramsci himself managed to keep theo-ries of language and practical historical work in a productive tension, and it is good to remember that theories also have histories that uncomfortably reveal the interests at stake in one rather than another epistemological faith, as I at-tempt to show below.[7]

A crucial aspect of that history in Gramsci's case, at any rate, is the trans-formation of the Italian thinker into a self-alien object. One might argue that it is through Gramsci that interwar Marxist traditions are strangely dominant today, but only in disguised and diffused forms. They enter our discussions alongside reactively anti-Marxist traditions as though the two were a merging of complementary positions. The interwar period's antagonisms are concealed or skimmed over, and these couplings are for most critics no longer even troubling. Walter Benjamin, Theodor Adorno, Ernst Bloch, Mikhail Bakhtin, Louis Aragon, on the Left; Martin Heidegger, Filippo Tommaso Marinetti, Oswald Spengler, Ernst Jünger, Carl Schmitt, on the Right, but all mined selectively, instrumentally, and idiosyncratically. The contemporary critic's project is always some variant of a sweeping claim to break from historicism, escape totalizing thought, and question man. Under these signs, Benjamin as well as Heidegger emerges as a critic of historicism without any regard for the chasms separating their positions or politics. The highly experimental anti-fascist Bloch and the Orientalist, populist prophet Spengler are both said to find chiliastic solace in the religious impulse. Gramsci's thought is in this way posed as being logically entwined with Heidegger and Georges Sorel, as though Gramsci could comfortably occupy the camp of German aesthetic nihilism with its fear of civilizational decline and its ponderous explanations of world history in terms of racial classifications.[8] If one protests that this jumbling of attributions and intentions suffers from sloppiness or bias, one is condemned as being too rigid.

The now-routine linkages between the right and left wings of the interwar intelligentsia are not entirely fatuous, however. Both groupings found common ground in metaphors of the peasantry, and much more needs to be said about these peculiar obsessions about why both fixated on the fact, as well as the image, of the non-Western world. Here is where I believe Gramsci comes alive and has most to offer today, not least because he clearly diagnosed the blending of hostile traditions that I have just tried to cast in doubt. The following passage is entirely typical of the *Prison Notebooks*. The degree to which it sounds alien to the Gramsci fashioned by postcolonial studies is both immediately obvious and arresting. He goes so far here as to argue that philosophy in the 1920s and 1930s looked up to Marxism, and while seeking to turn it against itself, simply plagiarized it:

> Historical materialism has no need for extraneous support: it is itself so robust that the old world turns to it to supply its own arsenal with some more effective weapons. This means that while historical materialism is not subjected to hegemonies, it has itself started to exercise a hegemony over the old intellectual world. This happens in reciprocal ways, naturally, but that is precisely what needs to be thwarted. The old world, while rendering homage to historical materialism, seeks to reduce it to a body of

subordinate, secondary criteria that can be incorporated into its idealist or materialist general theory.[9]

These injunctions—their very possibility—open up a number of needed demands for revision, for they confound the assumptions of the cultural Left of the last three decades.

If four signal terms from Gramsci's canon resonate through the postcolonial writing that extols him, two of his concepts—"transformism" and "Southernism"—have nothing like the same currency. In my reading, I would like to foreground both and suggest they have a position of centrality to his theory of intellectuals that has not been recognized. Seen this way, they proleptically allude both to the field of postcolonial studies and to the very process by which he has been assimilated into it. The first term refers to political syncretism as political decline—the joining of formerly hostile constituencies in which the Left in effect becomes the Right (a proposition, obviously, with a good deal of relevance to what I have been calling the "turn"). The second is more complicated; it refers to a political quietism purveyed by intellectuals whose authority is enhanced by claims to foreignness—to transnational credentials that validate their consultative capacities in the imperial centers where they constitute an intellectual diaspora.

GRAMSCI'S POSTCOLONIAL RECEPTION (1942–1992)

Gramsci enters postcolonial studies already riven down the middle, although the split is not evident before the 1970s. We have to remind ourselves that our ability to see Gramsci as an intellectual presiding over a corpus of written work is the result of a complicated historical undertaking. In his lifetime, no one understood him to be an *author*—someone who created ideas requiring exegetical effort. Seeing him in this way required the work of now largely forgotten people from the 1940s.[10] Already dead by 1937, with Mussolini still firmly in power, Gramsci the writer and thinker was the posthumous product of allies from the communist movement who arranged his notes, thematically ordered them, reconstructed his booklists, and saved the manuscripts from destruction by spiriting them away to the Soviet Union, where they were first carefully edited.

Gramsci's major superstructural themes (as well as his economic ones) were, of course, Gramsci's own, but the way in which his entire corpus was organized around them emerged from editorial decisions made by intellectuals from the Communist Party of Italy (PCI). So although it may come as a surprise to some, we have to reckon with the historical fact that the emphases on culture, on civil society, and on the role of intellectuals were constructed and highlighted by Gramsci's communist redactors. It was *their* perspective, not that of a later generation of skeptical readers intent on reading him "against the grain" of his communist affiliations. The now familiar categories under which Gramsci's project is organized already appeared in the first published version of the *Prison Notebooks*, the Einaudi edition (1947–1951). As hermeneutic specialists and curators, his first editors brought together the person and his work, and these early exegetes summoned testimonies of cohorts, friends, and likethinkers who experienced the actual contexts of composition that had attended Gramsci's writing.

The paradox of Gramsci's reception in the postcolonial field is not hard to locate, but once stated, throws an entire lineage into disarray. It is this: the revival of Gramsci by intellectuals invested in the new turn represented by Eurocommunism in the mid-1970s, and then later, the first formation of the tenets of what would later be called post-Marxism (which largely relied on this Eurocommunist Gramsci for its points of departure)—staked their claims of Gramsci's radical difference from classical Marxism in one sense above all. The primary thing for them—and it occupies all their rhetoric—is that he had developed theoretical modes of understanding that were applicable to the modern, media-saturated capitalist state. The debates in India, however,—which perhaps culminated in the writing of Partha Chatterjee, Ranajit Guha, and others in the 1980s—staked their claims on Gramsci's departure from interwar Marxism in quite another way. The primary thing for them was that he developed theoretical modes of understanding applicable to the developing world, to feudal incrustations and religious backwardness, to weak and wavering bourgeoisies seeking ways to construct hegemony. He was, above all, the analyst useful to the *colonial* situation. It is not simply that this contradiction is never mentioned but that it reveals the plasticity of interpretation when forming an intellectual object-for-use. In the black communities of Britain, Stuart Hall intuitively understood this bipolar appeal of Gramsci and attempted to unify the two positions by speaking of the racial identities of diasporic subjects within a class-bound, still semi-monarchical modern Britain. However, it is not only the structural asymmetry of the positions I am pointing to, which are obvious when juxtaposed in this way; it is rather that the debates in India that Chatterjee alludes to in 1986 drew their energies from the Eurocommunist revival. They have no incidental relationship to one another, but represent a direct line of convergence. Their Gramsci is the Gramsci of the turn.

This trajectory is the result of an abrupt shift in the common sense surrounding the nature of Gramsci's achievement. The rereading of Gramsci, we should recall, took place in the course of debates in an evolving, and dying, Italian Communist Party (PCI) in the late 1960s and 1970s. Seeking respectability within a parliamentary framework, and needing to remold the image of its chief intellectual icon, the Party demanded a new Gramsci. He was produced ultimately not by the PCI but by one of its newfound allies: the Socialist parliamentary official Norberto Bobbio, a professor who had already overseen dissertations on the Italian leader in the 1950s. His "Gramsci and the Conception of Civil Society" (1967) crafted a reading that helped forge a Eurocommunist version of the man, which was being developed at the same time by Leonardo Paggi and others.[11]

Almost everything about Gramsci in the better-known (and later) work of Chantal Mouffe and Ernesto Laclau's *Hegemony and Socialist Strategy* (1986) is anticipated by Bobbio (see chapter 5). His is the text for all later post-Marxist readings, even if its learned disquisitions on Hegel and civil society in the opening pages are quite unlike subsequent work in both method and tone. Constructing his case out of plausible partialities, Bobbio famously asserted that Gramsci represented a radical refinement of Marxism, that his work privileged the superstructure over the economy, held the war of position (that is, a reform-oriented or situational politics) to be the only viable strategy in the West, built a conceptual wall between state and civil society, located all effective political work within civil society's realm of cultural, nonparty activity, and warned of the penetration of the state into nonstate spheres. Although somewhat commonplace today, his bold declarations that "Gramsci's reversal [of power] happens within the superstructure itself" and that he gave "primacy . . . to the ideological factor over the institutional factor" were surprising to readers of the time.[12] Bobbio's reading was appealing not only because of his political and academic stature but also because his essay studiously and tendentiously returned Gramsci to a past before Marx—to Hegel himself in the "pure" form in which Croce had conceived him—in order to argue that Gramsci, turning Hegel on his head, believed "the state is not an end in itself" (142). Bobbio's substantive claims proved to be highly exportable, and they carried with them the imprimatur of having developed within Gramsci's native Italy, where detailed research on him had always surpassed that elsewhere, as well as within the now reoriented circles of the PCI.

In the wake of Bobbio's essay, which itself had been prompted by an important conference in Cagliari in 1967 held to reconsider Gramsci's legacy, Continental European intellectuals of the New Left developed what might be called a "'68ist Gramsci," picking up where Bobbio left off but adding new emphases of their own. They completed and popularized the post-Marxist reading that had been manufactured for conjunctural ends, fixing it for posterity with Chantal Mouffe's influential anthology *Gramsci and Marxist Theory* (1979), which included Bobbio's essay and contained an introduction that stressed its decisive importance. The '68ist reading stipulated that Gramsci's primary usefulness, as yet unexplored, lay in the foundation of a new *theory*—that is, not a set of ideas with theoretical implications, but a body of thought that, *as* thought, had the effect of finding in theory a Marxism that could now properly be distilled as Gramscian. A set of patented gestures toward cultural populism in the somewhat claustrophobic hegemonies of stable and prosperous Western societies became the essence of Gramscism as theory.[13]

The most important interlocutor for the '68ist theorists was, as this emphasis on theoretical praxis might suggest, Louis Althusser. As Mouffe put it in her anthology, "if the '60s had been the era of Althusserianism, the '70s was the era of Gramscism," leaving no doubt about her intention of yoking the two thinkers together in a pantheon defined by rupture.[14] Several of the collection's contributors argue that Gramsci represented a bridge to the New Left with his work on the "articulating practices" of discourse—an emphasis that allied his project for them with that of Foucault as well as Althusser. The struggle, they felt, had shifted from revolution to radical democracy (a phrase associated with Mouffe but first popularized by Bobbio). Gramsci, for them, had anticipated not only in his views but in his methodology a poststructuralist ethics of dispersion, instability, and displacement. This New Left Gramsci sought a continuity with an old Left that could be recuperated, but only on altered terms.

However, this was not the only line of Gramsci scholarship descending from his original Italian commentators—a scholarship, it should be said, that attempted in important ways to document the predictive capacities of interwar Marxism as a body of thought not requiring the correctives putatively effected upon it by post-Marxism. If the macro-political developments of Eurocommunism set the stage for a general reconsideration of that iconic past, and if countercultural intellectuals influenced by Althusser went on to create a post-Marxist Gramsci, they did so only with competition.[15] Critics in both England and the United States emerged who were able to elicit from the historical record a portrait in keeping with the tenor and foci of Gramsci's original strategies. Having taken the trouble to work through the first generation of Italian scholarship, these critics were writing as the first Eurocommunist renderings appeared but were altogether different in their emphases, and indifferent to what they saw as a facile and forced reinterpretation. The dichotomy between the two approaches represented in some ways an Anglo-American/ Continental split. Not an established group, they saw themselves elaborating a non-sectarian left intellectual culture per se, unfettered by the conjunctural needs of either a party or a preexistent philosophical movement (as had occurred in Italy and France).

Perry Anderson's "The Antinomies of Antonio Gramsci" (1976–1977) is among the most significant pieces of writing from this constellation.[16] The length of a small monograph, the essay was a crushing riposte to the post-Marxist Gramsci then emerging on the Continent. It remains the most careful explanation of Gramsci's oeuvre in essay form available in English. Along with Anderson, scholars like Joseph Femia, Michael Löwy, Gwyn Williams, Alistair Davidson, John Cammett, and others provided the first political biographies of Gramsci in English, the first sustained studies outside Italy of the prison writings, and the first systematic treatment of Gramsci's organizing in Turin.[17] Grouped here, of course, would also be Geoffrey Nowell Smith and Quintin Hoare—the most important redactors of Gramsci in the English-speaking world. In addition to coediting *Selections from the Prison Notebooks* (1971)— whose notes, glossaries, and emendations have defined the limits of understanding of Gramsci for three decades—Hoare edited the two volumes of Gramsci's *Selections from Political Writings*, which are still not widely read, even though they disrupt and reorient Gramsci's meanings in vital ways.[18]

On the one hand an Althusserian, on the other a left-philological, tradition presented themselves as options following the 1970s, when, for the first time, Gramsci's work extended beyond the communist movement into circles that found him acceptable in part because of the Eurocommunist gloss. I am using the term "philology"—Gramsci's formal discipline at the University of Turin— here to speak of a tradition of left scholarship that is both textual and historical. Such an approach fit nicely with the Gramsci described by Palmiro Togliatti, who knew him personally and who found in him a "taste for exact information," and a "disdain . . . even moral repugnance, for improvisation and superficiality" marked by laborious historical and archival research.[19] For Gramsci, philology meant "to go back to the source and arrive at a plausible explanation."[20]

The postcolonial appropriation of Gramsci has thus been a mixture, even if it was not seen as such. In India, a historiography that extolled research on the lives and practices of history's subalterns preceded Gramsci's broader internationalization and owed its existence to the wide dissemination of E. P. Thompson's *Making of the English Working Class*, which had been reverently received in India, culminating in a conference in Thompson's honor in the late 1970s. Rajnarayan Chandavarkar has recently pointed out that subaltern studies' early cues were borrowed wholesale from Thompson—with respect to the representation of a pre-industrial working class not found in official histories, and sensuous depiction of the agency of society's lower social strata.[21] One of Thompson's colleagues in the British historians group, Kiernan, was also noteworthy in creating a postcolonial Gramsci, but here as an absence rather than an influential force. Kiernan had apprenticed in India and been active as a scholar there for years. It was he who published the first essay specifically addressed to Gramsci's writing on colonial themes: "Antonio Gramsci and the Other Continents" in *New Edinburgh Review* (1977).[22]

Sumit Sarkar (1973), Asok Sen (1976), Bipan Chandra (1986), Partha Chatterjee (1986), and Sudipta Kaviraj (1992) all relied on Gramsci for key argumentative moves and general theoretical orientation. But with the exception of Sarkar, the author of a seminal history of modern India, Gramsci has usually been brought in not for the purpose of enriching a discussion of subalternity already begun but to effect a departure from the subalternism pioneered by left historicism. Despite Thompson's leads, the emphasis in subaltern historiography shifted in the 1980s from the agency of social actors to an essential subalternity based on "the assertion of an irreducibility and autonomy of experience"—a shift that drove Sarkar, one of subaltern studies' founding members, to becoming one of its harshest critics.[23] In response to Bobbio's omnipresent, innately tyrannical "state," subaltern studies rushed to what Ranajit Guha portrayed as the "resistant presence" of the marginalized, whose very being was an affront to state authority. In Rosalind O'Hanlon's critique of subaltern studies, resistant presence is skeptically described as an altogether too unified and autonomous "insurgent consciousness of mind" consisting of a "violation of signs" through "speech . . . bodily gestures and social space, clothing, means of transport."[24] O'Hanlon partly praises this move as an "antidote to instrumentalist notion[s]" of action, and it must be said that despite the extremes to which such dubious resistance was pushed in the work Guha inspired, his own adjudications of the many forms of resistance—which extend from food riots to caste conflict—are eloquently posed, militating against scholars who see Indian resistance as a footnote to British history.[25]

In Latin America, a similar trajectory of reception was being traced during the same years of the turn and even somewhat earlier.[26] Intellectuals there debated Gramsci's work from the time of the first appearance of *Letters from Prison* in Argentina in the late 1950s (well before the Bobbio remodeling). By 1963, a formal group of Gramscians had even assembled themselves under the title "Past and Present" (a title of one of Gramsci's volumes from *Prison Notebooks*), dedicated to reading and expanding his texts while applying them creatively to an unfolding Latin American reality.[27] José Aricó recounts how Gramsci's ideas—important throughout the active Left—exploded "with the force of a volcano" in the mid-1970s into broader, nonactivist circles in contact with European theory.[28] One of these early Gramscians from the 1950s, Juan Carlos Portantiero, portrayed the evolution from the philological to the '68ist Gramsci in some detail in his introduction to *Los usos de Gramsci* (1977). An activist and scholar familiar with the Italian critical literature, a bemused Portantiero described Gramsci's utilitarian insertion into the new theoretical milieus created by the arrival of a certain French theory. Illogically, though inexorably, these ideas spread through the communities of the Left, not so much correcting the earlier readings of Gramsci as expunging them. A great wall was erected, closing off the thought of a generation as though it had never existed. Powerless to oppose the gathering force of the new critical mainstream, Portantiero could only protest that concepts like "hegemony," "historic bloc," and other ostensibly Gramscian departures were in fact not his alone but the property of "the world communist movement."[29]

Both the South Asian and Latin American examples paint a similar picture. The earlier work of Thompson, Kiernan, Sarkar, Portantiero, and others was shunted to the side. A decisive break from their already well-developed critical apparatus was enacted in ways both precipitous and startling. By the 1980s, when postcolonial studies was coming into its own within American and British universities, the newly enlisted Gramsci appeared, and he was resolutely derived from the Eurocommunist turn. Inexplicably, the varied philological scholarship that hitherto had been so important played absolutely no role in this postcolonial Gramsci. What we confront here in a practical sense is not whether cultural theory in its current guises is epistemologically preferable or morally or politically salient, but whether it has damaged a generation's ability to think and react. The attitude of poststructuralism toward knowledge was more clearly defined by the erasure of an earlier hermeneutic tradition than by any interpretation of knowledge in the poststructuralist text. This peremptory shift in the understanding of Gramsci was possible because the peripheries of empire and the peripheries of metropolitan being were merged at the outset as a single problematic in the minds of its academic practitioners. Local knowledge, the gradual or dispersed quality of revolution, and the multiplicity of actors falling under the rubric of the subaltern all seemed naturally to flow from the concerns of theory and (by extension) from the Bobbio/Mouffe Gramsci.

Although the actual history of the '70s split is not generally known, it is perhaps unintentionally invoked whenever one hears the common appeal that we read Gramsci "against the grain." This ubiquitous, if informal, injunction is everywhere today, and it has the advantage of implying an inventive reapplication of stale material as well as the integrity to resist a chorus of formulae. An inadequate textual knowledge or a lack of philological accuracy can, in this way, be dealt with under the aegis of a brave and inventive calling. But resistance to orthodoxy is no clear-cut matter and requires a closer inspection if one is to appreciate its often surprising results, as Gayatri Spivak argued when she upbraided Foucault and Deleuze for turning Maoism into the "eccentric phenomenon of French intellectual Maoism," referring to the latter as "a harmless rhetorical banality."[30] Spivak accused them of creating an alibi for the sovereign Subject of history, and of having no answer for (indeed, not even noticing) the insufficiency of "micrological texture[s] of power" for explaining the "macrological" problems of "global capitalism."[31] Neil Lazarus puts his finger on a similar problem when he quotes Adorno on the importance of "hating tradition properly."[32] Our response to the demand to read Gramsci against the grain must be that we first need to know the grain. A reversal of meaning is always possible, of course, but it can too easily slip into being a substitution of another formula in which one *always* finds Gramsci to mean exactly the opposite of what he says.

None of this is to suggest that some of the theory attacked by Spivak and Lazarus does not continue to liberate readers, giving them the freedom to pursue a style of historiography attentive to the wiles of self-censorship, the illusions of authorship, and the preordained thinking of philosophical pragmatism or mechanistic social science. Gramsci's caution about neglecting national-cultural contexts also comes into play here, not only in the dissonances between 1970s Maoism as found in France and in the United States, but in so-called post-structuralism, which was and is politically incomparable in the two countries, as well as others. In Germany, the mere mention of Foucault or Heidegger is likely to risk ridicule from the conservative center of academia, thereby closing off new lines of inquiry. It is important, then, that my criticisms not be misunderstood. The Anglo-American intellectual configuration in which a coercive and disingenuous reading of Gramsci took hold traveled along the formidable imperial circuits that the English-speaking countries enjoyed throughout the turn. It did this, however, by way of a French translation whose specific violence towards meaning is not generally known and still widely uncontested.

THE ALTHUSSERIAN PRISM

As an overall political project, post-Marxism is not limited to one type of reading or a single author's work. And yet, the degree to which Gramsci has played a decisive role in establishing a new relation to the past is striking. Prominent debates over post-Marxism in the late 1980s in *New Left Review*, we may recall, took the form of an exchange over Laclau and Mouffe's *Hegemony and Socialist Strategy*, a book that effectively spliced Althusserian and Foucauldian modes of argumentation onto a Eurocommunist political program, thereby taking Althusser himself into political terrain he had not foreseen, and arguably did not endorse.[33] In addition to evoking Gramsci with the word "hegemony," the book built its entire analysis of radical democratic politics on what it called the "Gramscian watershed." More than others, this was the book that served simultaneously to place Gramsci at the center of American and British cultural theory and to make post-Marxism the default position within postcolonial theory. Journals like *New Formations*, *Social Text*, and *Marxism Today* enthusiastically embraced its findings while converting them into general laws. Schools of thought arose—the British "New Times" critics, for example—that codified its claims as forms of received wisdom. Its tenets coincided with the "reforms" of communism in the 1970s, but went significantly beyond them into an anti-statist rather than a merely reformist politics—a position already present, if inchoate, in Bobbio. Mouffe, for example, at the close of that decade expressed a collective fear at the "ever-increasing intervention of the state in all areas of society."[34]

On this ambiguous basis—for if the state has expanded so thoroughly it might also be said to have dissipated into meaninglessness—*Hegemony and Socialist Strategy* shifted the focus from laborers to identitarian constituencies; from struggles over wages and land to a new "proliferation of struggles" involving subaltern subjectivity; from "economism" to "articulation"—in other words, from explanations based on material interests to those based on immaterial desires and self-understandings—a pattern of argument with which we are now all deadeningly familiar.[35] Laclau's Althusserian credentials had their own distinctive past. His earlier book *Politics and Ideology* was already beginning to prevail in the cultural studies wing of Latin American Gramscism, supplanting the traditions, described by Aricó, which had been lived by a foundational generation of scholar-militants.[36] Laclau's career in Latin America, moreover, lent authority to his discussions of "combined development" and the peripheral mentality underlying hegemony's contingent nature, and so further underlined the implicit Gramsci/non-Western link—even in work, like Laclau's and Mouffe's, that was profoundly European in focus.[37]

Althusser not only gave post-Marxism its methodology; he had the paradoxical effect of appearing to open out philosophy's sterile quibbles to an exciting constellation of repressed radical thinkers from an era of actual mass movements. Seminar students already predisposed to the vocations of theory were, in their own minds, moved by Althusser in a more insurgent direction. It was a fundamentally contradictory process. The generation most influenced by Althusser had been cut off from the left traditions of the interwar period by the hiatus of the Cold War. This dual movement clouded debate. In the view of left philology, Althusserianism was a naive restatement of older positions, cloaked in strident language but animated by middle-class sentimentality; in that of newly politicized graduate students, it was a revolutionary deepening that made their own customary arena of books and classrooms a vital and revolutionary space.

Gramsci provided a bridge between the two mutually canceling theoretical and political postures. Indeed, it was Althusser who cast himself as entering the scene to complete and systematize what Gramsci had begun: "To my knowledge, Gramsci is the only one who went any distance in the road I am taking."[38] That "road" had three branches that others would later follow: the repudiation of historicism and Hegelian dialectical thought, the promotion of philosophy itself as a form of political intervention, and the adoption of a structural language that intimated the materiality and relative autonomy of the superstructural realm.[39] Althusser coins many of the arguments that later become routine in this constellation. It is he, for example, who first sets up Lukács as the bad interwar Marxist and intellectual foil for the good Gramsci. If, Althusser argued, Marxism was a "new philosophy, a 'philosophy of praxis,'" Lukács could offer the project no assistance because he was "tainted by a guilty Hegelianism."[40] Other guilty Hegelians—Rosa Luxemburg, Karl Korsch, Anton Pannekoek, Lev Davidovich Bronstein, Arturo Labriola—either went unread or were not given the privilege of attaining the status of theory. When Althusser uses the striking phrase "Marx, Engels and Gramsci," then, he signals his intention of making interwar Marxism invisible. All that passed between the texts of Marx and postwar Marxism is thrust outside of the discussion.[41] As the Third International's shadow, Gramsci had to become, for Althusser, its controversion as well.

Although Althusser never actually worked through Gramsci's texts (and in his autobiography he tells us that this was also true of Marx, although his defenders read this revelation also "against the grain"), this constraint had little effect on his effulgent reception. In *Reading Capital*, Althusser announced he would not pay attention to Gramsci's actual words until he had determined whether they were *organically* related to his philosophy and his "delicate work of genius."[42] He put this in a related way somewhat later, to "make visible a latent logic," what Althusser problematically called a "symptomatic reading."[43]

By these maneuvers, the myths Althusser initiated were passed on like misspellings in medieval transcriptions. He, for example, was under the impression that Gramsci coined the term "hegemony"; others have since repeated the claim—but the term goes back to the nineteenth-century Russian labor movement and was first popularized by Plekhanov.[44] Like his followers, Althusser was unfamiliar with the Italian intellectual traditions that informed Gramsci's writing, unaware of what Gramsci read while in prison, the details of his organizational ties, or his extensive writings about colonies, race, and the relationship of both to fascism. That this model of argument has been taken up throughout postcolonial criticism is uncontroversial; that it did so under the name of Althusser is equally demonstrable. Stuart Hall, Ajit Chaudhury, John Beverley, and others all concede that their Gramsci came *through* Althusser, which is to say not only that they are pointed in a direction independently followed, but that they come to recognize Gramsci's importance by way of Althusser's symptomatic comments on Gramsci.[45] All of them see Gramsci's relation to Althusser in the latter's emphasis on complexifying the model of coercive apparatuses, his focus on representation and ideology, his nondenominational expansion of the field of allies, and his sublimation of theory.

The contours of Althusserian logic, which so excited his contemporaries, have today become so standard that they amount to a kind of reflex. Spatial mappings step in to displace immanent critique. Against causation, one poses juxtaposition; against interrelationships and determinations, a theory of levels and overdetermination. The Althusserian concept of *structure*, for instance, which is etymologically redolent of the architectonic thrust of "theoretical science" (in his terms), overtly relies on spatial thinking, a language of levels, spheres, terrains: what Thompson famously dubbed the Althusserian "orrery" (Thompson, 100). The convenient methodology of symptomatic reading rendered him helpless to account for Gramsci's obvious and emphatic anthropological humanism. He was left with having not only to deny the historicist bent in Gramsci, but to ignore a distinguished heritage of interpreters from Croce to Guido Morpurgo Tagliabue to Galvano Della Volpe, who all reinforced precisely this aspect of Gramsci's thought even as they reviled it.[46] Their revulsion perhaps makes the accuracy of their observations all the more plausible. Gramsci's manner of giving relaxed attention to specific and actual cases, at any rate, has for some been an occasion to rebuke interwar Marxism for its purported abstractions (since Gramsci is said to depart from that Marxism), but for the Althusserians, interestingly, the conjunctural imagination is exactly what Gramsci is said happily to have avoided, since, in the face of all the evidence in the tainted archive, this was the Gramsci they needed.[47]

Whether Gramsci is labeled historicist or structuralist, all his readers are evidently constrained to summon him for one reason and one alone: to repudiate dialectical reason. The political unconscious of the new Gramscianism after the late 1970s is more or less unanimous, and finds its way even into the more nuanced writing of Edward Said: "Gramsci is not interested in mediating, transmuting, overcoming and all those other Hegelian processes by which antinomies are somehow resolved, but he's really interested in actually working them out as discrepant realities physically, on the ground."[48] The assumption here is interesting, since to most left Hegelians the contradiction simply would not exist, as Said himself observed in his early writing on Joseph Needham and Raymond Williams (see chapter 3). Gramsci repeatedly argued that dialectics always sought its material ends "on the ground" and, from Ludwig Feuerbach onward—which is to say in the lineages seized upon and developed by Marx—defined itself against other modes of philosophical thought precisely by focusing on the sensuously human, active consciousness formed in contact with a plenitudinous world. Gramsci would have heartily agreed with Feuerbach's comment that dialectics negotiates the "anti-scholastic, sanguine principle of French sensualism" on the one hand, and the "scholastic stodginess of German metaphysics" on the other.[49]

Inasmuch as Feuerbach critiqued Hegel, his critique was avowedly Hegelian. As Feuerbach puts it: "Whatever becomes real becomes so only as something determined. The incarnation of the species with all its plenitude into *one* individuality, would be an absolute miracle, a violent suspension of all the laws and principles of reality; it would, indeed, be the *end of the world*."[50] This tradition of conceiving thought as that which material involvements condition and create is by its nature *conjunctural* and *contingent*. It is precisely the Hegelian strain that poststructuralism misunderstands or traduces, but above all appropriates, that faintly repeats the very emphasis on plurality and difference codified in the first great critics of Hegel: the Young Hegelians, but without any of their accompanying commitments to political positioning and skepticism toward academic formulae. This is Gramsci's Hegelian tradition.

In the end, it is impossible to deny that Gramsci's intellectual project was built around immanent contradictions. To portray him as hostile to dialectical reason, if serious at all, would have to be a willful act of interpretive sabotage. For his work is riddled with the same determinate negations found throughout the Young Hegelians. One need not read far in his texts to appreciate the revelation he found in arguing that only a militarized party could be an ethical standard-bearer; that at the heart of Italy's cosmopolitan role in papal Europe lay a deeply parochial nationalism; that intellectuals, to keep abreast of modernity, were themselves the agents of intellectual self-cancellation in their new form as functionaries of industry and state and commercial propaganda. If

these examples are mediated enough to keep the matter ambiguous, biographical details nail the point down firmly. Gramsci was not at all reluctant to advocate a high school pedagogy based on Hegel and dialectics—a plan he elaborated at a number of points in the *Prison Notebooks*.[51] But to point out
something so fragile as the facts perhaps misses the larger point about the sociology of knowledge. In the semanticized milieu of Gramsci's reception, it
seems not to matter whether one promotes theoretical science or abjures it (Althusser vs. Said), or whether one is for or against historicism (Chatterjee vs.
Della Volpe). All that matters is reliably invoking Gramsci as having been
against a manner of thought universally known and more lately condemned:
dialectics.

The post-1970s mood for all of this unanimity-in-difference is embodied
best, perhaps, by Stuart Hall, whose essays advanced Gramsci's reputation
among younger scholars from the 1980s on. Not a postcolonial critic per se,
Hall is one of the most original analysts of race and social democracy in the
post-colony of black Britain, and the author of one of the most widely cited
short statements on the ideological constants of the field as such: "When Was
'the Postcolonial'?"[52] Hall expressed in Althusserian language an accurately
Gramscian attitude when he asserted that Gramsci stood for "difference and
specificity." Always referring to actual British immigrants or recent government
policies, Hall moreover applied Gramsci to his own specific historical moment,
rightly insisting that Gramsci refuses "any idea of a pre-given unified ideological subject" and that "the ideological field is always, for Gramsci, articulated to
different social and political positions, [but] its shape and structure do *not* precisely mirror, match or 'echo' the class structure of society."[53] Hall repeats and
enriches Mouffe's somewhat overstated thesis that, for Gramsci, capitalism did
not develop as a process of proletarianization: "The transition to socialism
[was] . . . not strictly class-based."[54] The concept of the subaltern was a way
for both Hall and Mouffe to shift the emphasis from labor to race—a shift repeatedly enacted in postcolonial studies in the spirit of exclusion rather than
inclusion.

Almost never contained in these otherwise welcome renditions of Gramsci's broad and balanced mind is—again—a philological care for context and
detail. These sentiments are rather ethical in the narrow sense—pure statements of position, for, after all, the subaltern was in large part Gramsci's euphemism for the proletariat, which he used to evade the prison censors as well
as to articulate the multiple faces and differential forms of wage laborers in a
global, Fordist system. The term was a reclamation on his part as well as a rebuke to reactive theorists like Max Weber who sought new categories such as

"status" to accompany and crowd out the analytic of class. It was one of those shared codes arranged with his movement correspondents, taken from the now-forgotten worlds of Italian current events and in direct conversation with the grand early-century debates within the new discipline of sociology. My reminder of this legacy does not directly contradict Hall, who is quite right about one part of his attribution. The code word does, in fact, nicely evoke Gramsci's sense of expanding the limits of social actors and according a new layering to the definition of the occupants of society's lower depths.

On other issues, however, Hall's unfamiliarity with Gramsci's texts leads to uncharacteristic blunders—the product, one suspects, of the Bobbio/Mouffe accents governing his interpretations. He claims at one point, for instance, that Gramsci had little to say about the non-European world or about the relationship of imperial nationals to the capitalist center: "Actually . . . Gramsci does not write about racism and does not specifically address those problems."[55] To think that he did, argues Hall, would be to "commit the error of literalism." But then what can one make of this fairly typical aside in one of Gramsci's letters from 1930 (whose counter-Eurocentric sensibilities sound strikingly modern)?:

> This eminent Massis, who is dreadfully afraid that Tagore's and Gandhi's Asiatic ideology might destroy French Catholic rationalism, does not realize that Paris has already become a semicolony of Senegalese intellectualism. . . . One might, just for a laugh, maintain that, if Germany is the extreme outcrop of ideological Asianism, France is the beginning of darkest Africa and the jazz band is the first molecule of a new Euro-African civilization![56]

Far from a passing interest, race preoccupied Gramsci. The problem of race (and colonialism) is literally everywhere in the Prison Notebooks and deeply inflects the political writing and early journalism. Italy, he reported, suspectly favored Garibaldi in accounts of the Risorgimento because he, rather than Mazzini, was a "blond hero."[57] Gramsci's analytical interest in problems of ethnicity and color can also be seen in his discussions of Maurice Muret's The Twilight of the White Races (1929), which was only one of several popular treatises forecasting the decline of Europe in the face of the colonial uprisings that accompanied the Russian revolution (Muret specifically accentuated the anti-colonial dynamic unleashed by the revolution).[58] Indeed, race very often makes its appearance in the guise of the psychology of colonialism, which had been of interest to Gramsci even as a twenty-year-old in Turin. In one passionate outburst, for example, he wrote:

A student has assassinated the English governor of the Indies; or the Italians have been defeated at Dogali; or the *boxers* have wiped out the European missionaries—and then horror-stricken old Europe inveighs against the barbarians, against the uncivilized hordes, and a new crusade against these unfortunate peoples is announced . . . whole races of noble and intelligent people have been destroyed or are in the process of dying out. The liquor and opium that their civilizing masters distributed to them in such abundance have done their damaging work.[59]

In general, we may say that Gramsci's importance for Hall, like his importance for Althusser, is that his project is taken on as a duplicate of the critic's itself. His recuperation is seen (à la Althusser) as his completion. If Althusser saw himself traveling down the road of theoretical praxis, Hall sees Gramsci playing an identical role to his own, albeit in another era—namely, as strategic interpreter of a new right bloc that has vanquished the Left, and from which we must now learn.[60] To understand Margaret Thatcher's authoritarian populism and to admire its ability to rally mass sentiments at a libidinal level is, as Hall points out, a Gramscian imperative.

This is an important insight on Hall's part. It is true that Gramsci tended to learn by absorbing the lessons of the popular conservative forces of his day. He was constantly reading such varied antagonists as Giovanni Gentile, Frederick Taylor, Croce, Sorel, and Luigi Pirandello. He regularly consulted *Critica fascista* throughout his stay in prison and, in matters large and small, modeled his arguments as answers to those in the ascendant of modern thought, whatever their persuasion. Hall understands this motivation and uses it to great advantage. But the critical break between him and Gramsci occurs over the matter of overcoming: what Gramsci saw as the supersession of his adversaries by a fuller explication of a more comprehensive, more subtly differentiated, worldview still found (for him) in Marxism as a self-correcting, epochal orientation as distinct from a source prematurely cast aside.

Against that spirit, it is worth dwelling for a moment on the tone of Hall's "Gramsci and Us," which exemplifies that of the Bobbio/Mouffe axis and gives a sense of its historical mission. In the name of opening up new lines of inquiry, Hall's essay asks us repeatedly to reject various left positions out of hand. "The old Fabian thing," Hall bitingly states at one point, is "exhausted," "dead," "over." So too is social democracy's "little smidgeon of Keynesianism. . . . Nobody believes in it any more. . . . They know in their bones that life is not like that any more."[61] Never pausing to define this "they" (or for that matter, this "nobody"), Hall simmers with complaints from older wars. His admonitions to discard the past take on the air of a necessary displacement. He searches for adjectives to describe Gramsci's rare sophistication, referring to it as "complexifying," "supple," "subtle," "fluctuating," "multiaccentual," "flexible." In the same place looms a series of counter-adjectives ("pre-given," "simple," "abstract," "sketchy," "unvaried") ascribed to unnamed people.[62] The culprits appear only under vague monikers: "explanations . . . more traditional to marxist theorizing," "traditional emphases," "some versions of marxism," "the old mechanical economism," and so on, as though playing to an audience that didn't need to know who these culprits were or what and when they had written.[63]

As a mark of the movement, Hall's relentless charges of orthodoxy invite exercises in moral judgment rather than strategic assessments. Neglecting detail, Hall adopts a prerogative that tends to fixate on the person of Gramsci while making him separable from his own text—a model widely followed in the Bobbio/Mouffe lineage.[64] It is in this incarnation that Gramsci becomes something like the patron saint of postcolonial theory. As a person in the world, Gramsci is particularly suited to the task of flailing Marxism from within because of his inability to respond to his interpreters, his long sequestration, his death before World War II, and his embodiment, as it were, of his theory's purported shift from class to other forms of marginalized identity by virtue of his being from the impoverished south of Italy. In a theoretical climate marked by the recoil from citizenship and law, the communist Gramsci, as person, is ideally configured in that he never wielded power and so cannot be accused of abusing it. Gramsci, one could say, is attractive to them *because he lost.*

In spite of this trend to glorify his persona, his New Left commentators might very well have been appalled by Gramsci had they met him in the 1920s. He would likely have seemed to them humorless, uselessly passionate, reclusive, and inflexible (he was, after all, considered by several acquaintances to have an "imperious personality").[65] All of this is to say that the Bobbio/Mouffe axis that has overwhelmed Gramscian usage in the name of a radical democracy from below is inattentive, finally, to the practical philosophical mood and style of the man who claimed, again from prison, that "a revolution is a genuine revolution and not just empty, swollen rhetorical demagoguery, only when it is embodied in some type of State, only when it becomes an organized system of power. Society can only exist in the form of a State, which is the source and the end of all rights and duties."[66]

These are words that bring us to the related problem of orthodoxy, which in many ways descends from, or is a part of, the Althusserian prism. Clearly the reason Gramsci alone among Third International Marxists could play the role of bridge to the New Left, or be an acceptable entryway into interwar Marxism for postcolonial theorists has to do with exceptional personal qualities found in Gramsci himself. One does not want to dispute the central claim of the Bobbio/Mouffe axis about Gramsci's being unique, and uniquely attractive for new conditions. Just as they say (and just as writers such as Walter Mignolo, R. Radhakrishnan, Hall, and Chatterjee correctly repeat), the fluidity and resilience of mind toward concrete situations and real people, the avoidance of "mechanically repeating scientific and theoretical formulae" (as Gramsci puts it) existed in Gramsci's writing to a spectacular degree—arguably more than in the work of many others within the Marxist tradition, or any other tradition for that matter.[67]

No question, Gramsci as an individual was a remarkable combination of talents. That he was able to write the documents that attest to his movement's broadmindedness was partly the result of the accident of his being in prison (and therefore of having the time to record them), but it also had to do with his exceptional quality of mind and his desire to write, as his voluminous (and for the most part sparkling) pre-prison journalism shows. To be a man of intellectual bent, one who toils over minor distinctions or who drives himself to learn many languages or master the graceful intensities of literature and philosophy and history all at once, and yet to be, at the same time, a person repelled by pomposity or elitism, driven to a simplicity of expression, and dedicated to jettisoning a philological career in order to improve the lot in life for the poor and disenfranchised, sacrificing his life to organize—clearly that combination did not arise very often in the Third International, nor in any other grouping or institution.

So it would be vain to protest too much when hearing today's Gramscians declare that his work is not typical of his Marxist contemporaries (or followers) and that it represents a break from their thinking. However, we cannot forget that Gramsci neither thought of himself, nor did his contemporaries think of him, as being exceptional in his attitudes or formulations (which, after all, he had the opportunity of publishing in great quantities before 1926). These formulations were concrete, they avoided dogmatic certainties, they emphasized disparate social strata within class blocs, and so on. We ascribe the name "Gramsci" to these attitudes and formulations because this gifted writer and thinker found himself in the unusual situation of being able to depict, with some detail and careful afterthought, the views that those in his movement had come to learn were necessary, more honest, and more likely to yield success. The fact is that he thought along the lines of many of his contemporaries who never wrote their findings down.

He disparaged bohemia, had little time for anarchist youth whose revolts against authority might, with just a little effort, be seen as counterparts for many of the constituencies heralded in contemporary cultural theory.[68] Gramsci spoke harshly of the "band of gypsies" and "political nomad[s]" in Italy, whom he disparaged as "not dangerous things."[69] The Gramscian "self"—as important as it has become for the ethical warrant of his findings—is mythologized beyond recognition. The fragmentary nature of his utterances, often posed as deep interpretive problems, is actually an invitation to those who wish to read "against the grain." This fortuitous circumstance is passed off as a barrier heroically overcome. Hall writes that "Gramsci was never a 'marxist' in either a doctrinal, orthodox or 'religious' sense."[70] This is very true, but it might equally be said of all those Marxists we still consider valuable enough to read today—the ones, incidentally, who form the core of postwar literary and cultural theory in a variety of disciplines (Lukács, Bertolt Brecht, V. N. Vološinov, Rosa Luxemburg, Henri Lefebvre, Christa Wolf, Adorno, Benjamin, Bloch, Williams). The job still waiting to be done, it would appear, requires more than merely calling one's opponents dogmatic.

In this context, it may be instructive to pay attention to the way Gramsci himself weighed in on the charge of dogma.[71] His quarrel with Croce, after all (the nature of which is spelled out plainly in a series of letters—through Tatiana Schucht—to Piero Sraffa in April and May of 1932) attempted to repudiate exactly the complaints against Marxism later launched by writers like Hall and others in the Bobbio/Mouffe tradition. Croce gave voice to their accusations much earlier and worded them in almost exactly the same terms. It is worth considering Gramsci's response at some length:

> Of what does the innovation brought about by Croce consist? . . . We can concretely say that Croce, in his historico-political activity, makes the stress fall exclusively on the moment in politics that is called the moment of "hegemony," of consensus, of cultural direction, to distinguish it from the moment of force, of coercion, of legislative, governmental, or police intervention. In truth one cannot understand why Croce believes that this postulation of the theory of history should be capable of definitively liquidating all forms of the philosophy of praxis. The fact is that precisely during the same period in which Croce was shaping this self-styled cudgel of his, the philosophy of praxis, in its greatest modern theorists, was being elaborated in the same direction and the moment of "hegemony" or cultural direction was precisely being reevaluated in opposition to the mechanistic and fatalistic concepts of economism. It has indeed been possible to maintain that the essential trait of the most modern philosophy of praxis resides precisely in the historico-political concept of

"hegemony." It therefore seems to be that Croce is not "up-to-date" on the research and bibliography of his favorite studies or has lost the capacity to be critically oriented.[72]

Two features of this passage leap out. First, that the concept of hegemony (as that which involves the cultural as well as the coercive, or statist, dimension) characterized the general stage of Marxist theory in Gramsci's time. It was not, in other words, Gramsci's insight as he saw the matter. Second, that economism—the key charge of Althusserians against an older Marxism—was already a pejorative within the Third International, where it meant a restriction of one's political objectives to struggles over wages or, contrarily, a mechanistic view of revolution, positing that resistance was automatic or inevitable as a result of increasing immiseration.[73] Clearly, neither Gramsci nor his movement thought of him as heterodox. He published his largely uncontroversial views in voluminous quantities of journalistic writing and intra-party circulars before 1926. His ideas became "Gramscian" when he found himself in prison and so was able to depict with afterthought the views of an entire movement to which he belonged. He delved more fully and shrewdly into the issues that concerned his circle, but they too believed as he did.[74]

It is easier to celebrate the singular, auratic author than the collective character of a movement. This would be one explanation for characterizing Gramsci's authority as autonomous when there is so much counter-evidence. The distinction, at any rate, between Gramsci and the numerous and nameless party functionaries in Germany, Italy, or the Soviet Union who spoke uninterestingly of class struggle and the revolutionary party is not a distinction between Marxism and its beyond, but one between a nuanced commentator and dutiful popularizers or managerial types (analogous, say, to the distinction between John Rawls and a Democratic Party convention speaker). Since communism was a mass movement, its popularization inevitably led to formulaic slogans. How Gramsci would have regarded the political shifts of the post–World War II period will always remain unknown, but we do know that in his time dismissals of Marxism by progressive intellectuals and the media were carried on in exactly the same terms as today. More important, we know how he responded:

That many so-called theoreticians of historical materialism might have fallen into a philosophical position similar to medieval theologism and might have made of "economic structure" a sort of "unknown god" can perhaps be proven; but what would it mean? It would be as though one were trying to judge the religion of the Pope and the Jesuits and were to talk about the superstitions of the peasants of Bergamo. Croce's position on historical materialism seems to me similar to the position of Renaissance man on the Lutheran Reform: "Where Luther enters, civilization disappears," said Erasmus, and yet the historians and Croce himself today recognize that Luther and the Reformation stand at the beginning of all modern philosophy and civilization.[75]

Gramsci suggests here that Third International Marxism was epochal; it stood to its future as the Reformation did to its own. He even found at times unexpected benefits in what were, admittedly, oversimplifications: the "initial poverty of historical materialism—unavoidable in a theory disseminated among the masses—will enable it to expand."[76] The whole point of his famous early newspaper article in *Avanti!*, "The Revolution Against *Capital*" (1917), was to show that in the time of Marx, "Marxists" were "contaminated by positivist and naturalist encrustations" but later generations of Marxists had exploded those older inanities.

Subalternity

In its emphasis on *absolute* and universal contingency, the Althusserian tradition ended up in a paradox. Privileging scientific "practice," it evolved by inches and in mixed theoretical company into a discourse of ineffable subalternity. These conflictual origins lie embedded in the theoretical problem of subalternity today, which expresses itself in an intractable division: are we to understand the subaltern as an active historical agent or as an ethically decisive being-in-the-world? Which of these two faces of subalternity inspire its use today, as well as our tireless return to the concept? The first version evokes a world of alliances and blocs, of leadership acting in the name of specific interests, and a collective subject that erupts into a transformative force. The second version intimates a form of life whose philosophical perspectives are shielded from an imposed and always arrogant rationalism—a life privileged only insofar as it *remains* subaltern. Rather than marking a condition to be overcome, the latter portrays subalternity as a sacred refuge, a dark secret space of revelation.

Although representing a classic fissure in postcolonial studies between opposition as action and opposition as a demand for recognition, both views draw on the resources available from Gramsci's concept of common sense, which is the theoretical term in his repertoire that seems most clearly to capture his vision of the subaltern. In the milieu in which postcolonial studies developed, the gesture of avowing marginality soon became dominant. Far from being limited to the theory circles first enlisted by Bobbio/Mouffe, it arose in more traditional historiographic work. It is evident, for instance, in Partha Chatterjee's seemingly routine injunction "not to inject into popular life a 'scientific' form of thought springing from somewhere else, but to develop and make critical an activity that already exists in popular life."[77] This gesture is paradigmatic, although many postcolonial critics have been even less guarded, seeing a structural blockage between the stable facts of history and the occult freedom of the lower depths. In postcoloniality, the experience of existing outside and permanently estranged from public participation or intervention in politics is cast as noble. In an essay that contrasts Gramsci and Foucault, R. Radhakrishnan has nicely characterized this latter view: by opposing argumentation based on historical proof, theory sees itself opening up a space where "subjugated knowledges can announce and pursue their insurrection."[78]

Theory leans on the postcolonial, is even parasitical of it, in the sense that an occult subalternity is conceived as theory's deepest and most irreducible value. The abject image of Third World marginality forms the projected moral center of metropolitan thought itself in its poststructuralist phase. One typically finds, then, two mutually exclusive but complementary interpretations. Either, like Chatterjee, one suppresses the textual evidence to insist that Gramsci gave subalternity an existential value or one argues (more accurately) that Gramsci sought to explode subalternity, and then goes on to condemn him for doing so. An instance of the latter, which is perhaps more common, can be found in a recent postcolonial anthology where the critic José Rabasa applauds Gramsci's embrace of plebeian wisdom but bristles at his efforts to push common sense beyond its reactive function. Gramsci is "blind to the folkloric," condescending to it because he considered it merely an educable, potential thought rather than the mysterious and final thought of a pure powerlessness. In a gesture common to postcolonial studies, Rabasa goes so far as to deny that the "form of life of the subaltern can be contained within the objectification of the intellectual," who must therefore stop trying to instruct the dispossessed and instead modestly submit to their vigilant dispossession. Otherwise one falls into the trap of "vanguardism."[79] The celebration of subalternity as such requires that no programmatic effort at "upliftment" be permitted because the latter always smacks of intellectual and political arrogance.

Although Althusserians have largely dictated the view of Gramsci within postcolonial studies, the part of his oeuvre that has been addressed has to do with culture, ideology, and the state. Moreover, the stress on theory as science intimated a leadership role for intellectuals that hardly accorded with an anti-vanguardism. The discourse of subalternity, by contrast, derives from a some-what different Heideggerian inspiration. In recent decades, these traditions have been popularized by some of the earlier proponents of the Althusserian Gramsci as seen, for example in Mouffe's recent anthology on Heidegger's po-litical friend and ally Carl Schmitt.[80]

This Heideggerian turn is evident not only in complementary fields like globalization theory but in the philosophical margins of postcolonial studies itself, a point articulated in Ian Hacking's *Historical Ontology*, Kaja Silverman's *World Spectators*, and Jacques Derrida and Gianni Vattimo's *Religion*, to take only three recent examples.[81] Heideggerian enthusiasms in postcolonial criti-cism per se can also be widely found.[82] If Foucault determined the themes and modes of postcolonial studies more than any other thinker (with the exception of Marx), he also conceded that his "entire philosophical development was de-termined by [his] reading of Heidegger."[83] So it is perhaps not surprising that Heidegger is so prominent as an influence behind the scene, even when not fil-tered through the Derridean screen where we would most expect to find him. Heidegger has provided an important repertoire for expressing the political in-stincts of the maturing field of postcolonialism.

The Heideggerian retreat into ontology, enacted to counter the renewed vigor in materialist philosophies of history and epistemology in the interwar decades, permitted an idealization of the objective self. Along with the Freu-dian (and later Lacanian) "other," this irreducible, grounded self became a compensatory homage to the Third World, a muffled acknowledgment of the encroachments of the anti-colonial movements then forcing their way into Eu-ropean consciousness via the Russian revolution, against which Heidegger was reacting, even as he ransacked Lukács's *History and Class Consciousness* in order to adapt the concept of reification for his own purposes. Today this highly structured discourse of authenticity, counter-Enlightenment, and sensuous "peasant" consciousness "thrown into" the world floods postcolonial writing. Ideas are absorbed through French intermediaries even in those cases where the borrowers are unaware of their ultimate points of departure.

In late subaltern studies, the borrowings from Heidegger are, however, ex-plicit. Guha, for example, has declared his intention to abandon historicism in favor of Heideggerian aesthetic being; Dipesh Chakrabarty announces that Hei-degger is his "icon" and seeks to displace history with the concept of memory.[84] In a phrase derived from Nietzsche's critique of historicism, Chakrabarty con-siders subaltern memory paradoxically sacrosanct, since those who summon it create a necessary past by finding the "memory they need"—an oddly instru-mental view for a professional historian.[85] Writers as diverse as Enrique Dussel,

Michael Taussig, and Gauri Viswanathan have lately argued, with a good deal of justification, for the liberatory potential of subaltern belief systems taken to be innately religious. Here Gramsci is often considered the honorary forebear of such criticisms by virtue of his sympathetic analyses throughout the *Prison Notebooks* of a resistance carried out in the otherwise constricting terms of a stagnant rural Catholicism.[86] Despite the decidedly *anti-*religious religiosity of the German existentialist, many of the valorizations of religion in postcolonial theory complement Heideggerian positions in this new streamlined form; like him, they teach that it is the subaltern who teaches intellectuals about life in that astounding way in which Heidegger portrays himself as a village shopkeeper whose wisdom is crafted, unpretentious, and earthy—much like the protagonist of Knut Hamsun's novel *Growth of the Soil*. Dedicated to thought as though it were a hard, round object modeled out of the clay of language, Heidegger represents himself as a seer, but not properly speaking an "intellectual," since such a title would carry with it offensive cosmopolitan connotations.

Heidegger's place in postcolonial studies has, above all, to do with his metamorphosing a putative thingliness into an aesthetic revelation of being. Inasmuch as historians, anthropologists, and sociologists in postcolonial studies have taken their leads from literary criticism, Heidegger's sensuous world, which opens out before an intuitive truth where art is perceived as an "uncon-cealing," has proven deeply attractive. So unlike, say, Hall, the Foucauldian Gramsci of Gyanendra Pandey and the Derridean Gramsci of Homi Bhabha veer toward a political poetics that demands a different rhetorical register than Althusser's, although without abandoning his ethical postulates, which are taken to be absolute and which are therefore indefatigably present in one or another metaphorical package.[87]

Hence, although Heidegger is the emblem, in Chakrabarty's words, of the "plural ways of being human . . . contained in the very different orientations to the world—the 'worlding' of the earth in Heidegger's language," Chakrabarty employs many of the same charged adjectives earlier present in Hall without changing their theoretical function.[88] In the new rhetorical mode, an older pattern persists: Chakrabarty is drawn to "the plurality that inheres in the 'now,' the lack of totality, the constant fragmentariness, that constitutes one's present."[89] Heidegger is by no means a pronounced source in all postcolonial theory, and yet his turning away from knowledge to being is a philosophical gesture that has proven irresistible, in part because it elevates the overly pragmatic discourse of identity politics to a more dramatic plane without changing its substance. But such a turning is also influential because, in Heidegger's actual work, it is accompanied by a Delphic simplicity of expression repetitively performed, grounded in a homely vision of cottages, copses, forest paths, and airy mountain landscapes.

Grafted onto the teleology of a struggle against Eurocentrism (again, alien to Heidegger himself), Heideggerianism yields a hybrid product. The hybrid, expressed as resistant presence in Guha's and others' work, is a term that lies at the heart of subalternity and is understood to be the essential resistance of the voiceless. The goal of critique is here seen to preserve ontological resistance, to nurture its existence as a jumbled, useless, noble, suffering, revelatory excess.[90] None of the macro consequences of subaltern agency are ever worked out, only the clarity of negation. One understands what one must be *against*. What one is *for* is contained only in the heraldic bodies of people not seen, voices not heard.

The influence of Heideggerian thought, as if in some bizarre homage to the antipodal positions of the interwar era, is so widespread that it encompasses work without any direct interest in it or apparent awareness of it. Chatterjee's expert analysis of hegemony, in *Nationalist Thought and the Colonial World*, is at the same time a sustained study of the Indian independence movements as a "passive revolution" (Gramsci's term for a new political order imposed without a fundamental reordering of social relations, usually by way of foreign invasion). The analysis is wonderfully attentive to Gramsci's sense of contradiction as Chatterjee lays out the argument that the Indian national movement created a culturally based "non-Western being"—an essentialized Indianness—thereby driving a wedge between two traditional objectives of the nationalist project: technological modernization and the equation of the national with the non-Western.[91] This positively inflected allusion to the soil-rooted absoluteness of national being may or may not have been borrowed from Heidegger's modern application of German Romanticism, but it is nonetheless neatly congruent with such borrowings, openly enacted by Chatterjee's colleagues in the subaltern studies collective. As such, the passive revolution of capital, Chatterjee argues, was no "blocked dialectic," as Gramsci had thought. Rather, "the strategic relations of forces between capital, precapitalist dominant groups, and the popular masses can be seen as a series of contingent, conjunctural moments," working in concert toward a beneficial end.[92]

The problem with deifying subalternity as a mode of being is that it renders truly critical thinking difficult. Chatterjee's analysis of passive revolution, for instance, cannot account for simple backwardness. The ability, or willingness, to identify and name the "backward" is rendered unthinkable on purely ethical grounds. This is very far from Gramsci's way of thinking, for he had frequently described how the native intelligentsia, without naming it, strategically enlisted backwardness as a new epistemology of otherness to be preserved against met-ropolitan encroachments. It is ironic that, in drawing on Gramsci, subaltern studies has no feel for that dimension of passive revolution having to do with decay. That is to say, there is no sense of Gramsci's elaborate analysis of that pattern of stagnation, corruption, and paternalist infantilization obtaining in feudal or semifeudal pockets of the peripheral world familiar to anyone from the Indian, and not just Italian, countryside. The typically Gramscian evoca-tions of the sated, decadent lords, living in crumbling houses of former grandeur, parasitically collecting taxes, cannot be found in the latter-day ren-ditions of his theses on subalternity. One might ask where in postcolonial stud-ies we find an adequate discussion of the strongmen, the henchmen of small business and capitalized agriculture, who terrorize the farmers in the name of ancient privilege? Where are the Padre Brescianis—that is, the lowbrow literary popularizers of the superstitions of Catholic dogma (a major concern of Gramsci's prison writing)? Certainly in this genre of Gramsci's thought, there is little recourse to religion as a positively coded value, whatever may be the merits of its transvaluation for his adherents.

In contexts that might have seemed relevant to the subaltern studies enter-prise, these lines of inquiry would have placed Hindu mythology, and indeed peasant resistance itself, in an embarrassing location vis-à-vis the contempo-rary political realities of Indian Hindutva ("Hindu-ness"). They would have necessitated removing the portrayal of the indigenous Indian agency of the subaltern from a context imagined as a silent fight against imperial domination to a much more graded and contradictory series of struggles in which the sub-altern is the oppressor (as, for example, in the anti-Muslim reprisals in Gujarat in the early 2000s).[93] In his famous footnote at the end of "On Some Aspects of the Historiography of Colonial India," Guha is careful to express the fluidity of the dichotomy between elite and subaltern, but he does so in only one direc-tion. Local elites, he observes, may take on the air of subalterns in national con-texts (as small landholders, for example); and those in the civil service may be subalterns in the context of the English cricket clubs. What is elided are those moments in which racialized or ethnicized subjects (either at home or in dias-pora) can themselves dominate and constrain political alternatives by a logic of displaced abjection. As I hope to enlarge upon in the next section, this insight was central to Gramsci's theorization of the modern intellectual as the inheri-tor of what he called "Southernism."

The emphasis on the ethical as distinct from the political is a polarization in post-Marxist theory that remains in Gramsci, by contrast, a productive ten-sion. My point here, in other words, is not to vilify the ethical as a squeamish, liberal, or unworthy objective. All of Gramsci's pre-prison writings in various ways dedicate themselves to answering questions related to that goal. Does socialism mean the end of all private property? Does it mean the complete absence of all differentiation among individuals under a given political structure: that is, a strict, juridically enforced, blind equality? What, in fact, is the place of the *individual*? These writings all imply that there existed a certain prefabricated notion of what socialism is supposed to be (one widely circulated by the Catholic Church, by popular accounts in the press, and by the "learned" writings of certain popularizing intellectuals in widely selling books) that Gramsci was eager to correct or amend. What is the dialectic between discipline and freedom? What kind of person do we want to be—or is it even a question of being rather than making such a person? But the "making" of people sounds so authoritarian. How do we resolve the tensions that exist between the militarization of the soul required to vie for power (rather than just talking about power, or the endless taking of positions) and the openings for self-determination that are possible only after taking it? If our position is that culture is conditioned in advance by material conditions, then precisely how are they connected? Why should we not be looking for changes in culture first (and perhaps forever) rather than bothering with the state? What is the relationship of ethics to politics?

One has to recall—as the Althusserian and Heideggerian traditions of postcolonialism never do—that in his writing on civil society and the state, Gramsci gave provisional answers to these questions (posed when he was still a young man) after he had gone to prison. He saw the state as having three interrelated dimensions. First, it was tantamount to government, so that whether it was a regulating state, monarchical, constitutional, parliamentary, or fascist, one aspect of its operations was comparable to that of a "nightwatchman" (as he put it)—coercive, police-like, reactive. Second, the state was the institutional embodiment of the party that effectively ran it, just as the party was the state *in nuce*. Hence, any political organization had the responsibility of working out a way of living, a way of learning, of teaching, of following orders and accepting them that forecast the ethos of the regime it was trying to build. Finally, the state could be seen as equivalent to civil society (Hegel's "ethical-political state"). It was educative, private, public, leaderly (*dirigente*). It referred both to the collective cultural gathering places and to practices that have no explicit political function. The state plays a role in the political or cultural life that lies outside the state.[94]

These are the kinds of considerations more vitally related to Chatterjee's analysis of passive revolution, I would argue, than his elision of social function in favor of racialized being—a move that is structurally related, moreover, to the denial of debt to the less prized traditions of the interwar period, as I have argued above. This gesture is not at all limited to one thinker; it is general.[95] Chatterjee's important and accomplished historical work with its embrace of a strategic myth of Indianness, neglects important issues of divided interest among Indians in the colonial context and makes it more difficult to find potential allies among the already othered political subjectivities of the Left.[96]

Like others in his Marxist milieu (for example, M. N. Roy, José Carlos Mariátegui, Ernst Bloch), Gramsci spoke about disjunct temporalities and comparative cultural value in a sense very close to many postcolonial studies' latter-day representations, although very much from within the purview of Marxism rather than as a corrective to it. More significantly, in the 1920s and 1930s it was common on both the Left and the Right to see the Russian revolution as a revolt against the necessity (in Gramsci's words) of a "Western-type civilization."[97] Gramsci's question "Why should [Russians] wait for the history of England to be repeated in Russia?" seems to presage current concerns, leaving nothing out, but it is not recognized as doing so, and the entire drift of contemporary theory denies that it does.[98]

If the subaltern is eagerly taken on as a welcome expansion of the categories of oppression, then the irony underlying Gramsci's reception is the license it has given to an exaggerated focus on the struggle over hegemony's moral center, whose corollary is the supposed autonomy of the subaltern realm. The persistent arrogance of imperial rule produces a contradictory backlash against the critic with the temerity to describe it. Along the lines of shooting the messenger, the charge of crudity is easily deployed when one asks that the brutally coercive aspects of imperial power be considered along with its more subtle ideological forms. In this climate, it has become impertinent to wonder whether an occult subalternity that appears resurgent in the literature really evades the vanguardist gestures of uplift against which it seems so resolutely posed. One might well see it as imputing a belief system that effectively demands passivity.[99]

Gramsci counterposes to such moralizing the concept of politics as sacrifice. Politics may sully and, in some cases, destroy its actors, but without it, the humiliation of the vulnerable goes uncontested. He viewed subalternity as a status to be changed rather than an already complete "resistant presence" precisely because he viewed the subaltern as a matter of shifting, temporally defined interests rather than the repository of suprahistorical, rural, or religious desires or impervious counterlogics. Having no desire to "give voice" to the essential wisdom of the subaltern, or to glorify subalternity as such, Gramsci repeatedly made clear in his writing the need for the training and discipline provided by education, national-popular literature, and other practices that would in essence eradicate subalternity.

The intense focus on the ideational essence of subalternity rather than the alterable status of actual subalterns is analogous to the one-sided reading of Gramsci's superstructural emphases within contemporary theory. These tend to discount (quite unlike Gramsci himself) the structuring role of armies, demographics, and the extortions of Christian charity. Because formerly colonized governments are typically sites of weak hegemony, the opportunities for transformation through culture seem most likely there: yet another way in which theory is parasitical on the non-Western. The world afar can be neatly counterposed to the consolidated hegemonies of advanced capitalism, with the result of glorifying the foreign in essays that seek to hold up the fragmentary silent subject as a kind of model that then symbolizes the location of the transnational researcher. As a result, little attention is paid to the internal divisions that replicate the inequalities now safely slotted under the sign of colonialism and Western reason.

The ill-formed modernity found in so many peripheral polities becomes, in this way, the sign of a false progress rather than (as in Gramsci) a limited solution to social inequalities shored up by stagnation and the paralysis of tradition. The critic counterposes to this false modernity not so much an indigenous philosophy ("subalternity") as a romantic nihilism borrowed from the anti-Enlightenment wing of European thought. Under the guise of indigenism, we have an exalting of Europe that is at once oppressive and self-deprecating: Heidegger as the liberatory voice of the Third World subject.

SOUTHERNISM

To consider the "southern intellectual" as Gramsci meant the term is a messy proposition, since it fits no flattering correspondences between victims and worthy leaders. Returning to Gramsci's analysis of the southern intellectual is likely to appear impolite and jarring today, for it seems to point an accusing finger at what we ourselves now call the postcolonial intellectual.

The problems posed by the intelligentsia of economically undeveloped rural regions are of particular interest in a supposedly globalized world.[100] And yet it remains among the most provocative aspects of Gramsci's writings, and it specifically relates to some of the themes we have been developing in this book in regard to the Heideggerian turn, which among other things devised a praxis of spectatorship—that is, a politics of inactivity. One must keep in mind that both Giovanni Gentile and Benedetto Croce as southern intellectuals, especially the former with his "actualist" philosophy formulated after a long apprenticeship in Marx, exemplified for Gramsci an idealist "improvement" of Marx to which Gramsci was deeply hostile, and which parallels very closely the politics of the post-1970s turn.

We know from one of Gramsci's earliest prison letters that his unfinished essay "Some Aspects of the Southern Question" (1926) provided a microcosm of his project in the *Prison Notebooks* as a whole.[101] The conventional view about the essay is that it launched his work on subaltern consciousness and addressed the intrinsic value of Italy's most invisible sectors, whose distance from the metropolitan centers could not be seen as a backwardness to be cured but an autonomous and respectful counter-reason (a reading putatively borne out later in Gramsci's lengthy investigations into folklore, popular literature, and, as I have been saying, "common sense").[102]

But to grapple with this reading requires our reminding ourselves what Gramsci had tried to establish in his theory of intellectuals as such.[103] In the Bobbio/Mouffe tradition, that theory was taken to be an invitation to harden the claim that a left politics resided in philosophical critique, a view structurally based on the apparently privileged position of intellectuals in information societies. This view of the intellectual's centrality is, I have been arguing, discordant with Gramsci's overall views. For one thing, he insisted that one could only "affirm in," not "realize through," philosophy, since believing in philosophy as itself a politics would be "just a religious utopia."[104] Although there is overwhelming evidence for Gramsci's antipathy to the "theoretical praxis" of his day—seen, for example, in his many attacks on Otto Bauer—historical analogies of this sort are not likely to be convincing to those in the Bobbio/Mouffe lineage.[105] A more convincing riposte for demonstrating what Gramsci thought of "theory" in its present sense can be found by returning to his accounts of its conditions of existence. Above all, one finds this in the "Southern Question" essay. Actually, the *Prison Notebooks'* more famous passages on intellectuals, later reprinted in the widely read Hoare/Nowell Smith selections, were written four years after the essay and should be properly seen as elaborations of it.[106]

The centrality of "Southernism" to his theory of intellectuals is best understood by working back from later, more celebrated passages in *Selections from the Prison Notebooks.* We may recall briefly the genesis of Gramsci's theory of intellectuals. Although he had possessed an enviable library in Rome, his prison reading consisted overwhelmingly of literary ephemera, particularly magazines, reviews, and some select books. Readers of the *Prison Notebooks* are inevitably struck by the number of entries responding to minor newspaper critics. As such, the overall movement of his ideas took shape in response to public opinion and current events, including those unfolding before his eyes (and against his will) by influential public intellectuals such as Sorel, William James, and René Fülöp-Miller.[107] He sought to learn from their appeal and to master the energy they tapped while challenging their antipathy toward socialist prospects. In a letter from prison in 1930, for example, he states: "My entire intellectual formation has been of a polemical order; even thinking 'disinterestedly' is difficult for me, that is, studying for study's sake. . . . Ordinarily, I need to set out from a dialogical or dialectical standpoint, otherwise I don't experience any intellectual stimulation. . . . I want to feel a concrete interlocutor or adversary."[108]

In fact, an overlooked facet of Gramsci's theory of intellectuals is that it represents a direct engagement with Henri de Man's *The Psychology of Socialism* (1926) which he read in Italian translation immediately after its appearance in 1929.[109] Gramsci borrowed heavily from de Man's categories and emphases, setting his own opinions in relief but also showing their convergence. A member of the Belgian labor movement and later the leader of the Belgian Labor Party, de Man wrote his book as a systematic critique of the Marxist conflation of working-class interests with socialist goals. Writing with sympathy for socialist objectives, he nevertheless sought to expose what he saw as the fatal logical flaw at the heart of Marxism, which had a fallacious "theory of motives" and repeatedly foisted the interests of intellectuals (a "new sociological class," in de Man's view) onto laborers: "the working masses are the dough, whereas the ideas of non-proletarian intellectuals are the yeast" (28). The middle section of his immensely popular book comprises two prominent chapters: "Intellectuals and the State" and "The Socialism of Intellectuals." It is striking how closely the following passage forecasts the opening gambit of Gramsci's famous prison-era essay on intellectuals, which begins with the statement that "non-intellectuals do not exist . . . even the relationship between efforts of intellectual-cerebral elaboration and muscular-nervous effort is not always the same. . . . *Homo faber* cannot be separated from *homo sapiens*."[110] And now de Man:

> I need hardly say that the term "intellectual" does not involve any higher valuation of the intelligence requisite for some particular kind of work. When we speak of an intellectual we are thinking of a kind of work which, instead of needing an expenditure of physical force, needs the practice of intellectual judgments that presuppose the acquirement of particular

kinds of knowledge in the mental domain. It does not follow that the intellectual is a better-informed or a more intelligent person than the manual worker or the peasant; he is merely one who uses his intelligence in a different way, and the knowledge he needs in his occupation is directed towards a different end, and therefore has a different character. (200)

For de Man, intellectuals mastered the cultural realm but increasingly took on the all-important functions of the state in the form not of scholars and artists but of bureaucrats, technicians, and moralists. They performed their duties independently of the interest of capitalists and workers. The guidance of the state had passed "into the hands of professional specialists" (202), and therefore parties (including the Socialist Party) exhibited the same problematic confusion between leaders and led. Although "a socialist society could easily dispense with the ragtag and bobtail of Bohemia . . . it could not continue to exist without the good will of engineers, men of science, school teachers, able civil servants, and statesmen" (228).[111] Like Gramsci, de Man emphasized the overall characteristics of the social system, which depended "far less upon the way in which political and social power are, at a given moment, distributed among different classes, than upon the motive for work, upon the juridical principle, upon the moral aim, and upon the cultural content, which determine the attitude of all classes" (220).

Despite taking his cue from these leads, Gramsci set out to contradict de Man's assertion that "Marxists will not recognize the existence of the class of intellectuals" (209). He bristled at de Man's psychologizing of social interest, his reckless dependence for his theory of change on intellectual "volition," and his routine equation of communism and fascism as the "refuge of the ultras . . . congenial to the destructive nihilism of . . . thwarted individualists" (226). Marxism, Gramsci insisted, did have an implicit theory of intellectuals that he was attempting to make explicit. So, while he recognized the new importance of intellectual work captured with passing accuracy by de Man himself, Gramsci wanted to explode the wrong-headed view that intellectuals were a separate class. Rather, they acted with different degrees of consciousness in the service of others, and the very nature of their existence militated against their having a set of unique goals or interests. To make these counterarguments, Gramsci drew on the theses already sketched out in "Some Aspects of the Southern Question."

Gramsci's theory, then, conceives the role of theorists as complementary to the *technicians* of capital. He puts the matter very clearly in a number of places, but no more so than in 1930: "in the modern world, technical education, implicitly related to industrial labor . . . forms the basis of the 'new intellectual': it is on this basis that one must work to develop the 'new intellectualism.'"[112] Accordingly, the famous division between "organic" and "traditional" intellectuals is not, as is often said, a distinction between progressive critical minds and old-style humanists, aesthetes, or "men of letters." In fact, the term "organic intellectual"—which plays such a prominent role in the opening pages of *Selections from the Prison Notebooks*—does not exist in Gramsci's original Italian until later in the essay, and then only in a subordinate, offhanded way (not as a definitive category). He is instead speaking of intellectuals *who organize*—who are aware of their place in a field of political interests. Hoare and Nowell-Smith are improvising when they first introduce the term. Gramsci's distinction, moreover, is not normative; it was possible to be a politically abhorrent organic intellectual, as indeed he shows with most of his examples, which include the "permanent persuaders" of the media, lawyers, clerks, and the factory pencil pushers of American Fordist industry.[113]

The key point, however, is this: Gramsci's "Southernism" did not merely illustrate his theory of intellectuals in a special case. It was its vital basis. If the new intellectual was "intellectual-constructor, organizer" and "superior to the abstract mathematical spirit" of an earlier stage of industry, it was a sign that "technique-as-work" was evolving toward "technique-as-science and to the 'humanistic-historical' concept, without which one remains a 'specialist' and does not become a 'leader' (specialist in politics)."[114] In other words, urban industry had developed uses for traditional humanistic intellectual activity; the propagandists and managers of capitalism could not lead if they contented themselves with statistics of efficiency. The traditional intellectual—whom Gramsci identifies as being of "the rural type"—is in this account far from outmoded. Rather, what he considers dated is "technique-as-work" divorced from its "humanistic-historical concept."

It is in the "Southern Question" essay that Gramsci describes the part played by rural intellectuals in the imperial-industrial state. This functional humanist role of philosophical organization was, in Italy's case, largely played by intellectuals from the South. Much of Gramsci's writing on intellectuals in *Prison Notebooks* is dedicated to illustrating how in other metropoles at other times, this role was similarly performed *by diasporic intellectuals from dependent regions*. This point is established with an elaborate chain of historical observations. In the Roman Empire, Gramsci notes, traditional intellectuals emerged from the "freed men of Greek or Oriental origin" following Caesar's proposal to "attract to Rome the best intellectuals from all over the Roman Empire, thus promoting centralisation on a massive scale."[115] The separation of intellectuals from the "large masses" was, in this way, not only social but "national and racial." This principle of separability persists following the collapse of the empire in the distinction between "German warriors and intellectuals of ro-manised origin," and then later in Catholicism, which from its base in Rome set out to develop intellectuals "in a number of the more important countries" for the purposes of consolidating Church rule. One counterpart to this strategy (a variant) occurred in France of the eighteenth and nineteenth centuries, where a fetishized culture was conceived as a "function of . . . outward radiation and of imperialistic and hegemonic expansion in an organic fashion." In the United States, Gramsci finds yet another adaptation of the diasporic role. There the "necessity of an equilibrium [was] determined . . . by the need to fuse together in a single national crucible with a unitary culture the different forms of cul-ture imported by immigrants of differing national origins."[116] Specifically, he speaks of the value of Negro intellectuals for the influence they could exert on the African masses: "American expansionism [will] use American Negroes as its agents in the conquest of the African market and the extension of American civilization."[117]

Again, it is the "Southern Question" essay that helps us determine whether these later elaborations of "Southernism" actually state what they imply— namely, the historical familiarity of the situation in which foreign intellectuals are recruited to perform empire's traditional tasks. At one end, the essay traces the imagery of the southern peasantry disdained by the worker-soldiers in the northern factory towns. But if this aspect of the essay is most remembered, the latter half, which addresses the southern intellectual, presages the process Gramsci dubs "Southernism." The latter part is more important not only be-cause the essay was left unfinished but because it dovetails with Gramsci's later theoretical contribution on the new kind of intellectual created by Fordism— "the technical organizer, the specialist in applied science."[118] Southernism was, as it were, an answer to this image and reality of an oppressive modernity, throwing up a type of intellectual who prevailed because of the required char-acteristics of "order and intellectual discipline" (328).

When Gramsci first speaks in the essay of "the southern intellectual" he is not talking about philosophers or academics but administrative functionaries, the upper clergy, and local potentates. Such functional figures played a key role in holding on to an older model of the intellectual (which he would later call the "traditional intellectual"), although they were not themselves exemplars of it. The southern intellectual had its own characteristics: "democratic when it faces the peasantry, reactionary when it faces the landowners and government" (328).

As a group, the southern intellectuals developed from the "rural bourgeoisie," says Gramsci, and were characterized by a "refined hypocrisy" and "an extremely refined art of deceiving" (329). They mediated between the great landholders and the peasantry, forming "a monstrous agrarian bloc . . . overseeing the *status quo*." But there was, he continued, another intellectual bloc above the agrarian one, which served to prevent too many cracks from forming in it. Those from this type of southern intellectual were the "most active reactionaries of the entire peninsula": Giustino Fortunato and Benedetto Croce (333).[119] Precisely because of their ambivalent position above (in terms of status and privilege) and below (in terms of a regional peripheral status and the stigma of backwardness), they prompted "all the cultural initiatives by middle-ranking intellectuals that have taken place this century in Central and Northern Italy" (333). The grotesque disproportion of the system that created them allowed them to be both spokespersons for an entire region and, at the same time, utterly cut off from and hovering over the anonymous social beings whose existence provided them with a resonant importance because of the constituents they only purportedly represented.

The radical nature of their separation accounted for their privileges, which could be translated into impressive individual accomplishments not easily found in the Protestant, utilitarian confines of the bourgeois self-made man: "There have always existed and still exist great accumulations of culture and intelligence in single individuals or small groups of great intellectuals, while there is no organization of culture at a lower level" (333). Dialectically, the poverty of "home" in the region of Italy's Third World South made the expansiveness of the southern intellectuals' interests compelling and inevitable; with little to fascinate it in the permanent stasis of tradition, the endless obeisance, the tired reenactments of hierarchy and corruption, the southern intellectual turned outward, focusing his brilliance on big ideas with an almost limitless amount of leisure time and the luxury of resources. To suggest that this is dialectical is to remark that for Gramsci, there is no paradox in this Janus-faced disposition. Thrust forth by a system governing territories unencumbered by modernity, the southern intellectual was decidedly not a modern urban technician. He was rather a rural ideocrat who monopolized the large, synthetic concepts that alone hardened and naturalized bourgeois norms, making them spiritual, and as such, exportable as Italy's contribution to the globe. Tied to "European and hence world culture," they steered restless youth "along a middle way of classical serenity of thought and action" (334). Croce, in Gramsci's opinion, detached "the radical intellectuals of the South from the peasant masses and made them participate in national and European culture" (334). Lest we take these judgments to be limited to his pre-prison thought, it was in 1931 in *Prison Notebooks* that Gramsci expanded these ideas with one of many related observations of immediate relevance to postcolonial studies: "In relation to the people-nation," he wrote, "the indigenous intellectual element is more foreign than the foreigners."[120]

The political ambivalence of theory is echoed in every aspect of this Crocean project, and it should make us interrogate, as Gramsci did, the function of intellectuals in an ostensible era of transnationalism. What uncomfortable, even self-defeating, role do postcolonial intellectuals play in this process? As we have seen in the case of Gramsci's reception, postcolonial critics stake their claims on anti-Eurocentric principles even as they exemplify key features of Euro-American global culture, particularly when articulating its sine qua non: indifference toward the social and civic (although not occult or personal) movements for emancipation of the continuing colonial periphery. Sarkar has rightly pointed out the parallels between the attacks on Enlightenment rationalism that were the prelude to fascism in Gramsci's Italy and those found on the left wing of today's cultural theory.[121]

It would be reckless to posit a direct correlation between postcolonial intellectuals from, say, India and Latin America, and Gramsci's southern intellectuals. The two formations are, after all, distinct in some respects, and there is moreover a difference between a settled, aristocratic, and Olympian expectation (as in the Crocean model) and the troubled, academic role played by diasporic intellectuals in the anti-intellectual environment of the United States. Indeed, the Americanism that Croce feared, and that Gramsci wrote about as a coming future, now defines the present. Even more, postcolonial intellectuals are often the products of a radical formation, committed (if contradictorily) to challenging a uniquely European value and to a fundamental reordering of knowledge that derives more from countercultural than elitist sources, as was the case with their southern Italian predecessors.[122]

But, if Southernism is the Gramscian concept most relevant to postcolonial studies, the similarly neglected concept of "transformism" is the most relevant to the cultural theory upon which that field is based.[123] Derived from historical writing on the Risorgimento, transformism was creatively reapplied by Gramsci to refer to progressive circles in his own time. It described for him a process in which "Left and Right parties tended to merge in terms of program" and "new formations arose to assert the autonomy of the subaltern groups, but within the old framework."[124] Transformism described the inexorable logic of progressive groups' imperceptibly and unselfconsciously adopting conservative positions.

It is widely conceded that ours is a period when culture has become an economic category. But how are we to understand this claim? I am suggesting that cultural theory in recent decades personifies this statement as much as it analyzes it, endorsing an imperial and pragmatic self-image of America as multicultural refuge and site of opportunity. The expressive word reigns supreme in the realm of the self-making subject—a view expressed in theory not pragmatically but in the exalted Crocean terms of a struggle over language and the ethical soul now cast as a series of micro-battles with the colonial episteme. Gramsci forces us, somewhat rudely, into recognizing a different possibility: that diasporic intellectuals from the periphery (as well as domestic intellectuals who project themselves into a perceived diasporic sensibility) act as technicians of the soul, steering youth "along a middle way of classical serenity in thought and action," while speaking on behalf of a "world culture" presided over by imperial benefactors. If that possibility sounds outrageous, it also testifies to the distance separating Gramsci from the temporizing of the present. Postcolonial studies needs to appreciate how many of its questions were theorized by Gramsci's generation, from which we are all still borrowing.

The history of Gramsci's reception is not a minor or localized concern of cultural theory. Eurocommunism's effect on the supposedly unrelated strategies of renewal labeled post-Marxism weighs heavily on postcolonial studies as well as mainstream discourses in anthropology, political science, and international relations. It is this history, I have tried to argue, that needs to be understood in order to be overcome.

NOTES

INTRODUCTION: CULTURES OF BELIEF

1. Patricia White, *Uninvited: Classical Hollywood Cinema and Lesbian Representability*, Theories of Representation and Difference (Bloomington: Indiana University Press, 1999).

2. University of Minnesota Press catalogue, spring 2003.

3. Another way of defining "theory" is the monopolization of *theory*—the latter referring to thinking about thought; about the methodologies of intellectual inquiry as such; about the patterns of consciousness, outside individual cases, that enable thinking itself. So by using "theory" I am also referring to the resistance of its practitioners to conceding this act of appropriation, and to clarifying this confusion between part and whole. As I use it in this chapter, theory would include (but not be limited to) Lacanian psychoanalysis, deconstruction, and the discursive reading, but not, for example, the critical theory of the Frankfurt School, theories of space and place, reflexive sociology, institutional media theory, or studies of imperialism. Theory was often defined by its practitioners in the 1980s as the science of representation conceived as rhetoricity and literariness. But it was posed as applying to all human activity, not merely literary objects, and from this claim were derived its claims to political saliency, which have so fatally stamped themselves on a generation of humanists.

4. Note Lefebvre's disparaging remarks about structuralism in *Critique of Everyday Life*, vol. 2 (London and New York: Verso, 2002), 176: "*Structuralism* proceeds by privileging structure absolutely, and by absorbing within it the other terms we are considering, along with the relations they designate. Without admitting to do so, it

substantifies it, presenting it as an essence and as something intelligible, thus acting as a belated marriage broker between Aristotelian ontology and a Platonism which dares not speak its name. Stability becomes both active and formal, the prototype and model for the real."

5. Sebastiano Timpanaro, *On Materialism* (London: New Left Books, 1975), 171, 188.

6. See, for example, Sergei Bocharov's essay in Caryl Emerson, ed., *Critical Essays on Mikhail Bakhtin* (New York: G. K. Hall, 1999); and Gary Saul Morson's essay in Gary Saul Morson and Caryl Emerson, eds., *Rethinking Bakhtin: Extensions and Challenges* (Evanston: Northwestern University Press, 1989).

7. Mikhail Bakhtin, *The Dialogic Imagination* (Austin: University of Texas Press, 1981), 291–92.

8. See, among others, Michael Payne, ed., *Life After Theory* (New York: Continuum, 2003).

9. Timpanaro, *On Materialism*, 171.

10. This five-year stretch has primarily an American significance. Clearly this kind of shift could be located much earlier—for instance, in France in the first attempts in the 1950s by Lévi-Strauss and Louis Althusser to displace the legacy of Sartre. Although decisive for the institutionalization of the ideas in the United States, the years I have marked as the turn are not meant to be exclusive, nor neatly confined to that span of years alone.

11. Kristin Ross, *May '68 and Its Afterlives* (Chicago: University of Chicago Press, 2002); Angelo Quattrochi and Tom Nairn, *The Beginning of the End: France, May 1968* (London and New York: Verso, 1998); Bernardo Bertolucci, director, and Gilbert Adair, scriptwriter, *The Dreamers* (Twentieth Century Fox, 2004).

12. Edward Said, "Secular Criticism," in *The World, the Text, and the Critic* (Cambridge, Mass.: Harvard University Press, 1983), 23.

13. Pierre Bourdieu, *Outline of a Theory of Practice* (Cambridge: Cambridge University Press, 1977), 164.

14. I discuss Vico's role in Said's work in "Edward Said and Comparative Literature," *Journal of Palestine Studies* 33, no. 3 (Spring 2004): 23–38, and in "The Critic and the Public: Edward Said and World Literature," in Hakem Rustom and Adel Iskander, eds., *Edward Said: Emancipation and Representation* (Berkeley: University of California Press, 2005).

15. Edward W. Said, introduction to the Fiftieth Anniversary Edition, *Mimesis: The Representation of Reality in Western Literature,* by Erich Auerbach, trans. Willard R. Trask (Princeton: Princeton University Press, 2003), xii. Auerbach's work "arose from the themes and methods of German intellectual history and philology; it would be conceivable in no other tradition than in that of German romanticism and Hegel."

16. Among them, Fredric Jameson, "Symptoms of Theory or Symptoms for Theory?" *Critical Inquiry* 30, no. 2 (Winter 2004): 403–8. Surprisingly, Jameson takes a position similar to that of Paul de Man: "I believe that theory begins to supplant philosophy (and other disciplines as well) at the moment it is realized that thought is linguistic or material and the concepts cannot exist independently of their linguistic expression" (403). Timpanaro has effectively ridiculed the view that the neces-

sary link between thought and linguistic expression leads to anything like a theory of *discourse* (indeed, this link is central already in the work of Kant). On the exaggerations and belatedness of the "linguistic turn" in general, see above all Raymond Williams, "Language," in *Marxism and Literature* (New York and Oxford: Oxford University Press, 1977), 21–44.

17. Timpanaro, *On Materialism*, 171. This style was characterized by Timpanaro as "the flaunting of an anti-empirical, ultra-theoretical and rigorously mathematizing epistemology, on the one hand, and decadentist and *existentialistic* poses—'literary' (in the worst sense of the word) flirtations—on the other."

18. For a case in point, see Gianni Vattimo, *Belief* (Stanford, Calif.: Stanford University Press, 1999), which links the history of Christian revelation with that of a nihilist strain in Nietzsche and Heidegger.

19. Alexander Hamilton, James Madison, and John Jay, *The Federalist Papers*, Encyclopedia Britannica Great Books of the Western World, vol. 43 (Chicago: University of Chicago Press, 1952), 23.

20. Theory's relationship to historical socialism is, I am saying, generally appropriative. See the journal *The Responsive Community* (Summer 2002), where Stanley Fish summons the fearful portrait of a U.S. senator peering down an oaken table to ask a frightened English professor, "Are you now or have you ever been a postmodernist?"

21. Louis Hartz, *The Liberal Tradition in America* (New York: Harcourt, Brace, and World, 1955), 297, 295.

22. I am not suggesting that Butler is unfamiliar with the Hegelian Marxist tradition, for she apprenticed in it; nor is my point that Butler has not continued to write, often approvingly, of aspects of Hegelian philosophy as she does, for example, in *Subjects of Desire: Hegelian Reflections in Twentieth-Century France* (New York: Columbia University Press, 1987). I am referring here only to the disavowed essentialism that reigns among those invested in her writing in actual intellectual settings (see also note 24 in Chapter 5).

23. Julia Kristeva, *Crisis of the ~~European~~ Subject* (New York: Other Press, 2000) (the adjective "European" can be erased while remaining visible because for Kristeva *all* subjects are European to the extent that reason and individuality are Europe's original export to the world.), and Julia Kristeva, *Revolt, She Said* (New York: Semiotext(e), 2002). For more on this point, see Dušan Bjelić, "The Balkans: Europe's Cesspool," *Cultural Critique* 62 (Fall 2005). Unlike Huntington, Kristeva is willing to attack the market: the logic of business "begins by protecting and stimulating but ends up with the closed system of supply and demand" (*Crisis of the ~~European~~ Subject*, 143); in the West "the unemployed [are] forbidden to work and earn a living" (*Revolt, She Said*, 32). Her critique, as she later makes clear, follows Heidegger in locating the problem not in anything so pedestrian as productive or social relations as in "productivism" and "technical reason" (*Crisis of the ~~European~~ Subject*, 122).

24. Kristeva, *Revolt, She Said*, 65.

25. Ibid., 36.

26. Ibid., 81.

27. Ibid., 34.

28. Lucien Goldmann, *Lukács and Heidegger: Towards a New Philosophy* (London: Routledge and Kegan Paul, 1977).

29. Corey Robin, "The Ex-Cons: Right-Wing Thinkers Go Left!" *Lingua Franca*, February 2001, 26.

30. Giorgio Agamben, *Homo Sacer: Sovereign Power and Bare Life* (Stanford, Calif.: Stanford University Press, 1998), 181.

31. Ibid., 6.

32. Slavoj Žižek is one critic who has brilliantly challenged the religion of the middle way—for example, in *Did Somebody Say Totalitarianism? Five Interventions in the (Mis)use of a Notion* (New York and London: Verso, 2001)—but also in a manner designed to make his own culture of belief ambiguous.

33. Kristeva, *Crisis of the ~~European~~ Subject*, 114.

34. Lyotard, "The Wall, the Gulf, the System," in *Postmodern Fables*, trans. Georges Van Den Abbeele (Minneapolis: University of Minnesota Press, 1997), 67–82.

35. G. W. F. Hegel, *Hegel's Philosophy of Right*, trans. T. M. Knox (Oxford: Oxford University Press, 1952), 165.

36. Herbert Marcuse, *Reason and Revolution: Hegel and the Rise of Social Theory* (1941; Amherst, N.Y.: Humanity Books, 1999), 211.

37. Hegel, *The Philosophy of History* (New York: Colonial Press, 1899), 7.

38. Marcuse, *Reason and Revolution*, 211.

39. Edmund L. Andrews, "FCC Is Said to Seek an End to Preference on Sex and Race," *New York Times*, June 22, 1995.

40. R. Terry Ellmore, *Broadcasting Law and Regulation* (Blue Ridge Summit, Pa.: Tab Books, 1982), 209; Celia W. Dugger, "Woman's Pleas for Asylum Put Tribal Ritual on Trial," *New York Times*, April 15, 1996.

41. William B. Ray, *FCC: The Ups and Downs of Radio-TV Regulation* (New York: Ames, 1990).

42. See Robert Quinn, "Defending 'Dangerous' Minds," *Items and Issues* 5, nos. 1–2 (Spring/Summer, 2004): 2.

43. "Privashing" refers to published books that, because of political offensiveness or the threat of lawsuits, are neither advertised nor distributed.

44. For another example, see Thomas Wagner, "Blair Urges Apology in 'Nazi' Flap," *Philadelphia Inquirer*, February 17, 2005. Ken Livingston, the mayor of London, was upbraided by his nemesis, Prime Minister Tony Blair, for remarks that Blair called "anti-semitic." Livingston was being interviewed by the *Evening Standard*, a British tabloid. Averse to its brand of journalism, Livingston asked the reporter, ironically, if he had been "a German war criminal. . . . You are just like a concentration camp guard. You are just doing it because you are paid, aren't you?" The critique of the reporter's cynicism—his complicity with the paper's political agenda for the sake of advancement—was evidently missed. Blair's charge stemmed from the fact that the reporter was Jewish, something Livingston apparently did not know at the time of the interview. Unmentioned in the subsequent reporting was that Livingston's identity has always been politically defined (the article referred to him as "Red Ken," a disparaging moniker frequently used by British conservatives). He was deemed guilty of mocking another's religious and ethic identity—a charge that effectively

displaced Livingston's real critique, which was directed toward the corporate media. In such ways is identity mobilized to forestall criticism and obscure the fact that the critic was himself the victim of discrimination.

45. "There is also a sort of game that I play. . . . I often quote concepts, texts and phrases from Marx, but without feeling obliged to add the authenticating label of a footnote with a laudatory phrase to accompany the quotation. . . . But I quote Marx without saying so, without quotation marks, and because people are incapable of recognizing Marx's texts I am thought to be someone who doesn't quote Marx" (Michel Foucault, *Power/Knowledge*, ed. Colin Gordon [New York: Pantheon, 1972], 52).

46. Beatriz Sarlo, interview by Cecily Marcus, July 17, 2002, Buenos Aires. This quotation is taken from Marcus's dissertation, "Culture Under Ground: Argentina's Last Dictatorship, 1976–1983" (University of Minnesota, December 2004).

47. Santiago Kovadloff, "La siembra del miedo," in *Argentina—Un oscuro país: Ensayos para un tiempo de quebranto* (Buenos Aires: Torres Agüero Editor, 1983), 17. Cited in Marcus, "Culture Under Ground."

48. Perry Anderson, "Stand-off in Taiwan," *London Review of Books* 26, no. 11 (June 3, 2004): 13.

49. For a compilation of such instances, see Joel Kovel, *Red Hunting in the Promised Land* (New York: Basic Books, 1994). Evidence outside the United States is as easy to find. In a typical example, the journalist and memoirist John Ross recalled "one of the ugliest lynchings in Mexico's modern political history [that] took place in Canoa, Puebla during the 1968 student strike down in Mexico City, when the local priest accused four young mountain climbers of being Communists—they were burnt at the stake in the church courtyard, a page right out of the Holy Inquisition. Local priests have often incited mobs to lynch outsiders—dozens of radical schoolteachers were murdered by lynch mobs in rural alphabetization campaigns during the presidency of Lazaro Cardenas in the 1930s. Cardenas was perceived by the Catholic Church to be an 'atheist Bolshevik'" (John Ross, *Blindman's Buff* 56, January 29–February 4, 2005).

50. Editorial, *Nation*, September 6–13, 1999.

1. The Barbaric Left

1. Martin Heidegger, "The Way to Language," in *Basic Writings*, ed. David Farrel Krell (San Francisco: HarperCollins, 1993), 397–426; Paul de Man, "The Rhetoric of Blindness," in *Blindness and Insight: Essays in the Rhetoric of Contemporary Criticism* (Minneapolis: University of Minnesota Press, 1983), 102–41; Walter Benjamin, "The Task of the Translator," in *Illuminations*, ed. Hannah Arendt (New York: Schocken, 1968), 83–110.

2. Samuel P. Huntington, *The Clash of Civilizations and the Remaking of World Order* (New York: Simon and Schuster, 1996).

3. The merits of the all but universally held view that classical Greece provides the foundation for European individualism, freedom, and rationality have rarely been

questioned. The role of Persian art and military prowess, the prevalence of Isis and Osiris cults, as well as the frankly authoritarian and piratical values of Homer's *Iliad* are all reasons to express some skepticism about the neatness of the official story. But other intriguing leads can be found as well—for example, this passage from W. K. C. Guthrie, *The Greek Philosophers: From Thales to Aristotle* (London: Routledge, 1950), 22: "While in the Eastern part of the Greek world the Ionians were absorbed in the first attempts at a scientific explanation of the Universe, in the West the Pythagoreans were setting up the ideal of philosophy as a way of life, and the philosophic brotherhood as a kind of religious order."

4. Charles Taylor, *Sources of the Self: The Making of Modern Identity* (Cambridge, Mass.: Harvard University Press, 1989), 27, makes a similar point. The answer to the question "Who am I?" cannot be one's name or genealogy. "To know who I am is a species of knowing where I stand. My identity is defined by the commitments and identifications which provide the frame or horizon within which I can try to determine from case to case what is good, or valuable, or what ought to be done, or what I endorse or oppose."

5. Jean-Francois Lyotard, *The Differend: Phrases in Dispute* (Minneapolis: University of Minnesota Press, 1988), 48–49, 140.

6. Tomás Borge, "*El Arte como herejía,*" in *Hacia una política cultural* (Managua: Ministerio de cultura, 1982), 61–68.

7. Ernst Bloch, *Heritage of Our Times,* trans. Neville and Stephen Plaice (Berkeley: University of California Press, 1991), 97–137.

8. Johannes Fabian, *Time and the Other: How Anthropology Makes Its Object* (New York: Columbia University Press, 1983).

9. The sort of bohemia, in short, found in Leonel Rugama rather than Baudelaire, the Rugama that Ernesto Cardenal described as "ex-theological student, Marxist" hanging out in the "Cafeteria La India" who believed that "revolution is the communion with the species." See Steven F. White, *Modern Nicaraguan Poetry* (Cranbury, N.J.: Associated University Press, 1993), 186.

10. Borge, "*El Arte como herejía,*" 62 (my translation).

11. "Eurocapitalism" is an ironic reference to the premature market reform era of the 1970s known as "Eurocommunism," which saw the first glimmerings of what later produced, in theory, Ernesto Laclau, Chantal Mouffe, and Slavoj Žižek. The internal reforms of the European Communist Parties in the late 1970s were associated with the names Santiago Carillo, Enrico Berlinguer, and Georges Marchais, the respective heads of the Communist Parties of Spain, Italy, and France. Launched by Carillo's *Eurocommunism and the State* (1977), it professed an acceptance of pluralist democracy, an end to internationalist aspirations for communist rule, and a qualified acceptance of the market along social democratic lines. See Vernon V. Aspaturian, Jiri Valenta, and David P. Burke, eds., *Eurocommunism Between East and West* (Bloomington: Indiana University Press, 1980).

12. Daniela Dahn, *Westwärts und nicht vergessen* (Berlin: Rowohlt, 1996), 7, 33, 148.

13. Wolf Wagner, *Kulturschock Deutschlands* (Bonn: Rotbuch Verlag, 1996), 36.

14. Michael Weck, as quoted in John Borneman, "Time-Space Compression and the Continental Divide in German Subjectivity," *New Formations* 21, 112.

15. Hans-Joachim Maaz, *Behind the Wall: The Inner Life of Communist Germany*, trans. Margot Bettauer Dembo (New York: Norton, 1995), 83.

16. Julia Kristeva, *Crisis of the ~~European~~ Subject* (New York: Other Press, 2000). What appears to broaden her interrogation beyond the merely ethnocentric is actually a statement of redundancy, and that which is asserted is at the same time coyly withdrawn.

17. Ibid., 177.

18. Ibid., 134. By the same token, it is true that the West too comes in for criticism. It is rocked by a "failing Oedipal subjectivity" in which people can no longer express their feelings, sensations, or desires, making use instead of "collective schemas" borrowed from the media, which tend to "robotize" them (128). Addiction, vandalism, and cynicism are often the result.

19. Ibid., 140, 150.

20. Ibid., 166–67.

21. Ibid., 168–69.

22. Ibid., 171–72.

23. Christa Wolf, *Parting from Phantoms: Selected Writings, 1990–1994* (Chicago: University of Chicago Press, 1997), 297.

24. Jürgen Habermas, "What Does 'Working Off the Past' Mean Today?" in *A Berlin Republic: Writings on Germany* (Lincoln: University of Nebraska Press, 1997), 37–38.

25. Jürgen Habermas, *The Inclusion of the Other: Studies in Political Theory*, ed. Ciaran Cronin and Pablo De Greiff (Cambridge, Mass.: MIT Press, 1999).

26. I am thinking of Samia Mehrez, "Translation and the Postcolonial Experience," in Lawrence Venuti, ed., *Rethinking Translation: Discourse, Subjectivity, Ideology*, 120–38 (New York: Routledge, 1992); Abdelkebir Khatibi, "La Loi du partage," in M. Bencheikh and C. Develotte, eds., *L'Interculturel: Reflexion pluridisciplinaire*, 11–14 (Paris: L'Harmattan, 1995); Abdelkebir Khatibi, *Love in Two Languages*, trans. Richard Howard (Minneapolis: University of Minnesota Press, 1990); and Carol Maier, "Towards a Theoretical Practice for Cross-Cultural Translation," in Anuradha Dingwaney and Carol Maier, eds., *Between Languages and Cultures: Translation and Cross-Cultural Texts*, 3–15, 21–38 (Pittsburgh, Pa.: Pittsburgh University Press, 1995).

27. Wolf, *Parting from Phantoms*, 122: "In general, we in the East knew more about the West and about living conditions there than our Western colleagues knew and know about us and the conditions of our lives, simply because we were more interested."

28. Edouard Glissant, *Caribbean Discourse* (Charlottesville: University of Virginia Press, 1995). On the matter of cultural translation, see Harald Kittel: the search for adequate linguistic equivalents "is ahistorical because as a rule the postulate of *equivalent* (or *adequate*) translation fails to take into account the cognitive aims and conditions prevailing in different places and cultural epochs" ("The 'Gottingen Approach' to Translation Studies," in Kurt Mueller-Vollmer and Michael Irmscher, eds., *Translating Literature/Translating Cultures: New Vistas and Approaches in Literary Studies*, 5–6 [Stanford, Calif.: Stanford University Press, 1998]).

29. Rey Chow, *Primitive Passions: Visuality, Sexuality, Ethnography, and Contemporary Chinese Cinema* (New York: Columbia University Press, 1995), 182–202.

30. Glissant, *Caribbean Discourse*, 125. Acts of intentional linguistic distancing are wonderfully parodied in the outrageous episode of *Monty Python* where a publisher stands accused at the Old Bailey of putting out a Hungarian-English phrase book filled with spurious translations designed to confuse foreign tourists by rendering questions like "Can you direct me to the railway station?" as "Please fondle my buttocks" (Stephen Budiansky, "Lost in Translation," *Atlantic Monthly*, December 1998, 81). Intentional mistranslation in Cold War contexts is not uncommon. See Julio Cortázar's *Nicaraguan Sketches* (New York: Norton, 1989), 86, where his declarations on behalf of socialism—"the best and most legitimate portrait of life"—are excised from the English version. What Cortázar actually wrote is found in the Spanish original, *Nicaragua, tan violentemente dulce* (Buenos Aires: Muchnik, 1984), 11, 16.

31. Although postcolonial critiques of deconstruction are not common, they do exist. See Mustapha Marrouchi, "Decolonizing the Terrain of Western Theoretical Productions," *College Literature* 24 (June 1997): 1–34, and Ian Adam, "Oracy and Literacy: A Postcolonial Dilemma," *Journal of Commonwealth Literature* 31, no. 1 (1996): 97–109.

32. This view is similar to that of Mehrez in "Translation and the Postcolonial Experience." To Mehrez, various postcolonial texts "have succeeded in forging a new language that defies the very notion of a 'foreign' text that can be readily translatable into another language. . . . Postcolonial anglophone and francophone literature very often defies our notions of an 'original' work and its translation" (121–22). However, she goes on to develop a thesis that in my opinion evades the problem. She imagines that these texts operate "in between" cultures, equally at odds with their national bases and the coercive "imperialist" readings that greet them. She is after what she calls a "global" reading. Given the political ghosts haunting actual, nationally specific, acts of reception, such a view is frankly utopian.

33. Mikhail Bakhtin, *The Dialogic Imagination: Four Essays*, ed. Michael Holquist, trans. Caryl Emerson and Michael Holquist (Austin: University of Texas Press, 1981), 360–61.

34. See Gary Saul Morson and Caryl Emerson, eds., *Rethinking Bakhtin: Extensions and Challenges* (Evanston, Ill.: Northwestern University Press, 1989). Also, Caryl Emerson, *The First Hundred Years of Mikhail Bakhtin* (Princeton, N.J.: Princeton University Press, 1997); and Peter Hitchcock, ed., "Bakhtin/'Bakhtin': Studies in the Archive and Beyond," Special issue of *South Atlantic Quarterly* (Summer 1998).

35. George Steiner, *After Babel* (London and New York: Oxford University Press, 1975).

36. Raymond Williams, "The Welsh Industrial Novel," in *Problems in Materialism and Culture* (London and New York: Verso, 1980), 213–29.

37. I. A. Richards, *Basic English and Its Uses* (New York: Norton, 1943); C. K. Ogden, *The System of Basic English* (New York: Harcourt, Brace, 1934); George Orwell, *Orwell: The War Broadcasts*, ed. W. J. West (London: BBC, 1985), 284–89.

38. Andreas Huyssen, *Twilight Memories: Marking Time in a Culture* (New York and London: Routledge, 1995), 41.

39. Thus, ritually, Sembene Ousmane, Ngugi wa Thiongo, or Claribel Alegría would be invoked with a repetitiveness that eventually robbed them of their power to be seen

in terms of the East/West conflict—albeit translated readily into English. Of course, the problem is not so much that of a set of writers who represent, in toto and neatly, a specific politics as it is with those aspects of many frequently cited writers who went unmentioned: the activist Nadine Gordimer of *The Burger's Daughter* rather than the racial alien of *July's People*; the César Vallejo of the novel *El Tungsteno*, as distinct from the Vallejo of *Poemas Humanos*. The matter of the East/West ideological is literally untranslatable in Western book markets. It lingers as a politico-exotic, but cannot be uttered with denotative clarity. It is the unutterable.

40. It was not only supposedly socialist writing from the former colonies that suffered—being thought unmetaphorical, brutely autobiographical, or naively historical (and one says this in spite of the open door given selected texts of this variety, always in a controlled atmosphere of synecdochic representation). Literary reception of translated works has also shown a lack of enthusiasm for modernist or experimental writing by those considered not political enough, those who do not fit the injunction that the Third World writer embody politics in a readily consumable form. See Clarice Lispector, *The Stream of Life*, trans. Elizabeth Lowe and Earl Fitz (Minneapolis: University of Minnesota Press, 1989); Dambudzo Marechera, *The House of Hunger: A Novella and Short Stories* (New York: Pantheon, 1978).

41. Jacques Rancière, *On the Shores of Politics*, trans. Liz Heron (New York: Verso, 1995), 42.

42. Consider, for example, Langston Hughes in Latin America, his youthful living experiences with his father in Mexico, his later translations of Cuban poetry, his friendship with Nicolás Guillén (one of the leaders of Cuban *negrismo* between the wars and a devoted communist after 1959), alongside his efforts to translate black rhythms (*The Book of Swing*) and communism (*Jesse B. Simple*) to popular audiences. How did these types of translation come together? How were they related?

43. Walter Benjamin, *Illuminations*, ed. Hannah Arendt, trans. Harry Zohn (New York: Schocken, 1968), 84.

2. Nativism

1. Salman Rushdie, "One Thousand Days in a Balloon," *New York Times*, December 12, 1991. My emphasis.

2. Their claims were, however, largely untrue. The detailed readings of *The Satanic Verses* by ardent Muslims were numerous. See, for example, M. M. Ahsan and A. R. Kidwai, eds., *Sacrilege Versus Civility: Muslim Perspectives on the "Satanic Verses" Affair* (Leicester, U.K.: Islamic Foundation, 1991); Shabbir Akhtar, *Be Careful with Muhammad: The Salman Rushdie Affair* (London: Bellew, 1989); Munawar Ahmad Anees, *The Kiss of Judas: Affairs of a Brown Sahib* (Kuala Lumpur, Malaysia: Quill, 1989); Mohammad T. Mehdi, *Islam and Intolerance: A Reply to Salman Rushdie* (New York: New World Press, 1989); and Mutaharunnisa Omer, *The Holy Prophet and the Satanic Slander* (Madras, India: Women's Islamic Social and Educational Service Trust, 1989).

3. Fred Halliday, *The Making of the Second Cold War* (London: Verso, 1983).

4. George Orwell's seminal essay of 1945, "Notes on Nationalism," is one of those places. See my discussion in *At Home in the World: Cosmopolitanism Now* (Cambridge, Mass.: Harvard University Press, 1997), 141–44. Among its many contemporary counterparts is Samuel Huntington's *The Clash of Civilizations and the Remaking of World Order* (New York: Touchstone, 1997).
5. Rushdie's defense of the novel has always formed one of his principal political interventions, and it overlaps explicitly with his critique of the neoliberal state and his defense of immigrant rights. It has also dovetailed with his awareness of the Cold War context of his own writing, evident above all in his romance with Eastern and Middle European novelists and intellectuals, whom he has frequently reviewed (Günter Grass, Andrei Sakharov, Siegfried Lenz).
6. Tariq Ali, "Abdelrahman Munif's *Cities of Salt*," *Marxism Today* (1991).
7. This is not to say that Rushdie did not often complain of the ignorance of Western reviewers toward his Subcontinental literary inspirations. If in "Is Nothing Sacred?" Rushdie recalled that the "surrealism and modernism and Marx" of his upbringing complemented rather nicely the change and flux inherent in Hinduism, with its multiple gods, it was another way of saying that the critics' free use of the label "postmodern" for his fiction was the result of their poverty of references. His metafictional games had their sources less in French theory than in the "Mimic me Truth" narrative of the 1940s British Indian novelist G. V. Desani, the spiraling digressions of the Storyteller of Baroda, or indeed, Bollywood itself.
8. In a kind of reflex repetition of the floating of this view of Rushdie the postmodernist by Kum Kum Sangari's "The Politics of the Possible" (in Abdul JanMohamed and David Lloyd, eds., *The Nature and Context of Minority Discourse*, 216–45 [New York: Oxford University Press, 1989]), one finds Gyan Prakash arguing that Rushdie shares postmodernism's hostility to "grand totalizing theories," disclosing in *Midnight's Children* the "fable-like character of real history" ("Writing Post-Orientalist Histories of the Third World: Perspectives on Indian Historiography," *Cultural Critique* 32, no. 2 [April 1990]: 383–408).
9. Salman Rushdie with Geraldine Brooks, "Salman Rushdie: My Lunch with a Condemned Man," *New Republic* 207, no. 5 (July 27, 1992): 22–25.
10. Phone interview with the author, July 1995.
11. Cynthia Ozick, "Rushdie in the Louvre," *New Yorker*, December 13, 1993, 69–79.
12. Agha Shahid Ali, "A Secular Muslim's Response—*The Satanic Verses* by Salman Rushdie," *Yale Journal of Criticism* 4, no. 1 (Fall 1990): 296.
13. Ali Mazrui, *Michigan Quarterly Review* 28, no. 3 (Summer 1989): 347–71.
14. Fred Halliday, "The Fundamental Lesson of the *Fatwa*," *New Statesman and Society*, February 12, 1993, 17. Aamir Mufti, "*The Satanic Verses* and the Cultural Politics of 'Islam,'" *Social Text* 31/32 (1992): 277–82.
15. Halliday was not alone. Several other essays condemned Rushdie's fair-weather friends with a similar virulence. See, for example, Geoffrey Wheatcroft, "The Friends of Salman Rushdie," *Atlantic Monthly*, March 1994, 22–43.
16. See, for example, Nawal El-Saadawi, *Woman at Point Zero*, trans. Sherif Hetata (London: Zed, 1983); Hanan al-Shaykh, *Women of Sand and Myrrh*, trans. Catherine Cobham (London: Quartet, 1989); Etel Adnan, *Sitt Marie Rose: A Novel*, trans.

Georgina Kleege (Sausalito, Calif.: Post-Apollo, 1982); Andrée Chedid, *The Return to Beirut* (1985; reprint, London: Serpents' Tail, 1989; Assia Djebar, *Women of Algiers in Their Apartment* (1980; reprint, Charlottesville and London: University Press of Virginia, 1992); Naguib Mahfouz, *Palace Walk*, trans. William M. Hutchins and Olive E. Kenny (1956; reprint, New York and London: Doubleday, 1989); Tayeb Salih, *Season of Migration to the North*, trans. Denys Johnson-Davis (London: Heinemann, 1969); Tahar Ben Jelloun, *L'enfant de sable* (Paris: Éditions de Seuil, 1985).

17. Srinivas Aravamudan, "'Being God's Postman Is No Fun, Yaar': Salman Rushdie's *The Satanic Verses*," *Diacritics* 19, no. 2 (1989): 7.

18. Feroza Jussawalla, "Post-Joycean/Sub-Joycean: The Reverses of Mr. Rushdie's Tricks in *The Satanic Verses*," in Viney Kirpal, ed., *New Indian Novel in English: A Study of the 1980s* (New Delhi: Allied, 1990).

19. Salman Rushdie, *Imaginary Homelands: Essays and Criticism, 1981–1991* (London: Granta, 1991), 161.

20. Ibid., 159. The essay was written in 1983.

21. See my reading of the novel in "Salman Rushdie," in George Stade, ed., *British Writers*, 4:433–58 (New York: Scribner's, 1997).

22. Salman Rushdie, "Can Hollywood See the Tiger?" *New York Times*, March 9, 2001. A similar, and welcome, critical edge can be found in his novel *Fury*, where, arriving in New York, the protagonist, Malik Solanka, wonders: "Might this new Rome actually be more provincial than its provinces; might these new Romans have forgotten what and how to value, or had they never known? Were all empires so undeserving, or was this one particularly crass? . . . Who demolished the City on the Hill and put in its place a row of electric chairs, those dealers in death's democracy, where everyone, the innocent, the mentally deficient, the guilty, could come to die side by side? Who paved Paradise and put up a parking lot? Who settled for George W. Bush's boredom and Al Bore's gush?" ([New York: Random House, 2001], 87).

23. Feroza Jussawalla, "Rushdie's *Dastan-e-Dilruba: The Satanic Verses* as Rushdie's Love Letter to Islam," *Diacritics* 26, no. 1 (Spring 1996): 50–73. She is at her most ahistorical when she quotes, without proviso, Rushdie's "Why I Have Embraced Islam" to substantiate her peculiar argument that Rushdie is alienated from Hindu India. His essay was conjunctural, defensive, and later embarrassing to him. He repudiated it.

24. Ibid., 50. Her blunt claim that *The Satanic Verses* is not a novel—indeed, that Rushdie does not write "novels"—is a spectacular case of the excesses of nativist reading. Evidence to the contrary does not deter her. See, for example, Rushdie's "In Defense of the Novel, Yet Again," *New Yorker*, June 24, 1996, 48–54; "A Dangerous Art Form," *Third World Book Review* 1 (1984): 3–5; or, "Fact, Faith, and Fiction," *Far Eastern Economic Review* 143, no. 9 (March 2, 1989).

25. The point is made in surprisingly similar terms by Sara Suleri in "Whither Rushdie?" *Transition* 51 (1991): 199, and by Dipesh Chakrabarty, *Provincializing Europe* (Princeton, N.J.: Princeton University Press, 2001), 28.

26. Aamir R. Mufti, "Reading the Rushdie Affair: 'Islam,' Cultural Politics, Form," in Richard Burt, ed., *The Administration of Aesthetics: Censorship, Political Criticism, and the Public Sphere*, 307–39 (Minneapolis: University of Minnesota Press, 1994).

27. See Rushdie's critique of this sort of resistance in his review of the Black Audio Film Collective's documentary, *Handsworth Songs*, in *Imaginary Homelands*, 115–17.

28. Rushdie, *Imaginary Homelands*, 384.

29. Suleri, "Whither Rushdie?" 198–221.

30. Salman Rushdie, "Fighting the Forces of Invisibility," *Washington Post*, October 2, 2001.

31. Hindus in India were incensed by the novel's parody of Bal Thackeray, the leader of an ultra-right Hindu revivalist party, Shiv Sena. Maharashtra State considered banning the novel, but the attempt was repelled by India's Supreme Court in February 1996.

32. See Salman Rushdie, "The Most Dangerous Place in the World," *New York Times*, May 30, 2002, and "Kashmir, the Imperiled Paradise," *New York Times*, June 3, 1999.

3. HUMANISM, PHILOLOGY, AND IMPERIALISM

1. It is probably the only thing that Aijaz Ahmad and his critics, right and left, agree on: Said the Foucauldian.

2. See, for example, E. San Juan's arguments in "The Limits of Postcolonial Criticism: The Discourse of Edward Said," *Against the Current* 77 (November/December 1998): 28–32.

3. Edward Said, "East Isn't East: The Impending End of the Age of Orientalism," *Times Literary Supplement*, February 3, 1995, 3–4.

4. It may be that not all of his readers willingly grant that these books constitute a trilogy. As Said himself puts it, "All of these essays were written as I was working on three books dealing with the history of relations between East and West: *Orientalism* (1978), *The Question of Palestine* (1979) and *Covering Islam* (1981), books whose historical and social setting is political and cultural in the most urgent way" (*The World, the Text, and the Critic* [Cambridge, Mass.: Harvard University Press, 1983], 27). Further citations for this book, in text and in notes, appear as *WTC*.

5. The way Said employed Julien Benda's famous phrase "*Les trahison des clercs*" in this American context has been misunderstood, in my opinion, by Aijaz Ahmad, who may have scored points in his remarks on Said's approach to Marx's writing on India but who falsely concludes that Said was urging—as Benda did—that literary intellectuals reject political involvements. The exact opposite is true. See, for example, "Third World Intellectuals and Metropolitan Culture," *Raritan* (Winter 1990): 3, 9, 27–50; and *WTC*, 14–15.

6. For his mixed views on nationalism, see Jennifer Wicke and Michael Sprinker, "Interview with Edward Said," in Michael Sprinker, ed., *Edward Said: A Critical Reader*, 231–32 (Oxford, U.K., and Cambridge, Mass.: Blackwell, 1992).

7. Edward Said, *Beginnings: Intention and Method* (Baltimore and London: Johns Hopkins University Press, 1975), 368–70.

8. It is easy enough to demonstrate that Said's emphasis on philology does not constitute an analysis of the sort promoted with justification by some Marxist critics of postcolonial studies, who quite rightly point out that a theory of imperialism and culture that ignores theorizing capitalism (its definition, its historical changeability,

its future) is severely limited. It is quite another matter, however, to dehistoricize the issue by collapsing the early 1980s into the late 1990s in order to assert that Said's literary focus was in the latter context evasive or abstract. By contrast, he was militating against the conceptual and epistemological conservatism of poststructuralism at a time when few understood its implications.

9. Surely a paradoxical outcome for a lineage that traces so much of its inspiration from Heidegger. The usually unmentioned contradiction entailed by the outcome is precisely the point I am making here—or rather, am suggesting that Said tentatively made.

10. For an interesting link, see Foucault's essay "La Situation de Cuvier dans l'histoire de la biologie" (May 1969), *Thales: Revue d'histoire des sciences et de leurs applications* 23, no. 1 (January–March 1970): 63–92. For Said's phrase, see *Orientalism* (New York: Vintage, 1978), 132–35. All other citations for this book appear in the body of the text.

11. Paul A. Bové, *Intellectuals in Power: A Genealogy of Critical Humanism* (New York: Columbia University Press, 1986), 1–38.

12. Paul A. Bové, *In the Wake of Theory* (Hanover, N.H.: Wesleyan University Press, 1992), x.

13. Bové, *Intellectuals in Power*, 218.

14. I do not, however, think critics like San Juan, Eagleton, or Amin are wrong in pointing out what Said misses in the socialist theorists he borrows from. He is particularly weak on Marx, for example. The problems, though, do not lie in Said's supposed theoretical idealism or in his being unclear about his political goals. The most valid claim to be made against Said from the Left, it seems to me, is that he was opposed to organizational commitments, an issue that needs to be taken up in a different context.

15. For a sense of his milieu, see his retrospective comments about his close personal acquaintance and confidant Eqbal Ahmad in an essay for *Le Monde diplomatique* in March 2003: "I enlisted a friend, the late scholar and political activist, Eqbal Ahmad, who had expert knowledge of U.S. society (and was perhaps the world's finest theorist and historian of anti-colonial national liberation movements), to talk to Arafat and bring other experts to develop a more nuanced model for the Palestinians during preliminary contacts with the U.S. government in the late 1980s."

16. See, for example, "The Politics of Knowledge," *Raritan* 2, no. 1 (Summer 1991).

17. On the other hand, that latter book is not the radical break in Said's thinking that some have claimed. On the contrary, it is the place where Said makes good on his observation in *Orientalism* that "there is still a general essay to be written on imperialism and culture" (24). There are no doubt many methodological changes in emphasis between the two books, including the much freer way Said has of invoking materialist categories—"territory" as *land*, colonization as physical occupation—but another decisive difference is *Culture and Imperialism*'s positioning of non-European intellectuals for the first time at center stage.

18. Said at one point draws a comparison directly between Foucault and Schwab, for example. Although both represent something positive in the general theoretical climate (as explained above), he does distinguish between them. Foucault is "rather

ambiguous," whereas Schwab is "uncompromising" and "unstinting." Schwab "gives flesh to such of Foucault's statements as are unquestionably true" (*WTC*, 259).

19. See Rosalind O'Hanlon and David Washbrook, "After Orientalism: Culture, Criticism, and Politics in the Third World," *Comparative Studies in Society and History* 34, no. 1 (January 1992): 141–68. The authors correctly argue that *Orientalism* was "fused and extended into a distinctive amalgam of cultural critique, Foucauldian approaches to power, engaged 'politics of difference,' and postmodernist emphases on the decentered and the heterogeneous." They go on to say, also correctly, that these assumptions are "mistaken" (142).

20. For the French texts, I am giving the dates of English publication on the grounds that postcolonial studies is primarily the work of U.S. and British intellectuals, most of whom do not read French as a matter of course.

21. See Stephen Greenblatt, "Towards a Poetics of Culture," in H. Aram Veeser, ed., *The New Historicism*, 1–14 (New York: Routledge, 1989). The ostensible positioning of New Historicism between Marxism and poststructuralism is here credited to Foucault's "extended visits" to the Berkeley campus "during the last five or six years of his life" (1).

22. Examples include Timothy Mitchell, *Colonizing Egypt* (Cambridge: Cambridge University Press, 1988); Christopher Miller, *Blank Darkness: Africanist Discourse in French* (Chicago: University of Chicago Press, 1985); Robert Young, *White Mythologies: Writing History and the West* (London and New York: Routledge, 1990); and of course, the extensive work of the Subaltern Studies collective, whose first readily available volume in a series was Ranajit Guha and Gayatri Chakravorty Spivak, eds., *Selected Subaltern Studies* (New York and Oxford: Oxford University Press, 1988).

23. See James Clifford, "On *Orientalism*," in *The Predicament of Culture* (Cambridge, Mass.: Harvard University Press, 1988), 255–76; Dennis Porter, "*Orientalism* and Its Problems," in Patrick Williams and Laura Chrisman, eds., *Colonial Discourse and Post-Colonial Theory: A Reader*, 150–61 (New York: Columbia University Press, 1994). The exception to this chorus is, again, Bové's insightful *Intellectuals in Power*, which alludes to Said's cautioning against "the wholesale importation of Foucault into the academy" and to his warning against "the quietistic temptations of Foucault's textual practice" (219).

24. Jonathan I. Israel, *Radical Enlightenment: Philosophy and the Making of Modernity 1650–1750* (Oxford: Oxford University Press, 2001), 666.

25. Edward Said, "Interview," *Diacritics* 6, no. 3 (Fall 1976): 32.

26. The Foucault he creates in these pages is one who stands for "history" and for a critique of broad "cultural formations" and "networks" of state power as distinct from what Said considered the "stunning silence" toward materialist histories on the critical "Left" (*WTC*, 169)—in other words, a Foucault that many Foucualdians today would not recognize.

27. See Said, *Culture and Imperialism*, 26: "Foucault also turned his attention away from the oppositional forces in modern society which he had studied for their undeterred resistance to exclusion and confinements—delinquents, poets, outcasts, and the like—and decided that since power was everywhere it was probably better to concentrate on the local micro-physics of power that surround the individual.

The self was therefore to be studied, cultivated, and if necessary, refashioned and constituted."

28. See, for example, his late interview with W. T. J. Mitchell, in Paul A. Bové, ed., *Edward Said and the Work of the Critic: Speaking Truth to Power* (Durham and London: Duke University Press, 2000), where he charges the French thinker with using epistemology as a "theatrical instrument" (42) and with "dramatiz[ing] himself" (43).

29. *Beginnings: Intention and Method* (Baltimore and London: Johns Hopkins University Press, 1975), 316. All other references to this book will occur in the body of the text.

30. Taken whole, Said's grouping of Chomsky, Kolko, and Foucault—much like the Jameson of the *Political Unconscious*—may be seen as an attempt to outwit theory by promoting radical social thinkers while appropriating problematic "structuralists"—by highlighting, in other words, and even by blowing out of proportion, those aspects of their work that are recuperable.

31. See particularly Dennis Porter, here: "Whereas the second set of propositions implies the existence of a place of truth, of the possibility of emergence from hegemonic discourse into a beyond of true knowledge, the first set denies the idea of any knowledge pure of political positioning. The contradiction is never fully resolved in Said's book" (*"Orientalism* and Its Problems," 151).

32. Richard Hofstadter, *Social Darwinism in American Thought* (Boston: Beacon, 1992), 128–29.

33. "A history of the different modes by which, in our culture, human beings are made subjects" (Michel Foucault, *Remarks on Marx: Conversations with Duccio Trombadori*, trans. R. James Goldstein and James Cascaito [New York: Semiotext(e), 1991], 9).

34. Criticism is "a method or system acquired . . . by social and political conviction, economic and historical circumstances, voluntary effort and willed deliberation" rather than "birth, nationality, profession" (*WTC*, 25).

35. R. K. Dhawan, *Comparative Literature* (New Delhi: Bahri Publications, 1987).

36. Fritz Strich, *Goethe and World Literature* (London: Routledge and Kegan Paul, 1949).

37. Edward W. Said, introduction to the Fiftieth Anniversary Edition, *Mimesis: The Representation on Reality in Western Literature*, by Erich Auerbach, trans. Willard R. Trask (Princeton, N.J.: Princeton University Press, 2003), xv.

38. Said, "Secular Criticism," 21.

39. Wicke and Sprinker, "Interview with Edward Said," 230.

40. Said, introduction to the Fiftieth Anniversary Edition, x, xix, xxxi, xx. There is an "absence in America of such universal novelistic figures as Solzhenitzyn, or the Egyptian Naguib Mahfouz, or Gabriel García Márquez—writers for whom mimesis with a profoundly moral social engagement is still potent" (Said, "Contemporary Fiction and Criticism," *Tri-Quarterly* 33 [Spring 1975]: 255).

41. Edward Said, "Roads Taken and Not Taken in Contemporary Criticism," in *WTC*, 151; and "Interview," *Diacritics*, 41.

42. "Secular Criticism," 2. See also "Interview," *Diacritics*, 38: "To some extent we are technicians doing a very specialized job; to a certain degree also we are keepers of,

kept by, and tutors to the middle and upper classes, although a great deal of what we are interested in as students of literature is necessarily subversive of middle class values."

43. Edward Said, "A Sociology of Mind," *Partisan Review* 33, no. 3 (Summer 1966): 444.

44. "Interview," *Diacritics*, 39.

45. Edward Said, "Traveling Theory," WTC, 238.

46. Edward W. Said, "Between Chance and Determinism," *Times Literary Supplement*, February 6, 1976, 67.

47. Edward Said, in Wicke and Sprinker, "Interview with Edward Said," 260. He continues, specifically addressing the expressions of Marxism within the Palestinian movement: "Take the Popular Front, which declares itself a Marxist movement. . . . They could be described in other ways, but those of a classical Marxist party they are not. Its analyses are not Marxist. They are essentially insurrectionary and Blanquist, dispiriting to the organization of the PFLP and also 'the masses,' whom they seem to address. They have no popular base, never did" (260).

48. Georg Lukács, "Reification and the Consciousness of the Proletariat," in *History and Class Consciousness* (Cambridge, Mass.: MIT Press, 1971), 128. The emphasis is Lukács's.

49. Ibid., 145.

50. Edward W. Said, introduction to the Fiftieth Anniversary Edition, xii.

51. The point here is how much of his work has been dedicated to problems of intellectual *presentation*. See Timothy Brennan, "Places of Mind, Occupied Lands: Edward Said and Philology," in Michael Sprinker, ed., *Edward Said: A Critical Reader*, 92 (Oxford, U.K., and Cambridge, Mass.: Blackwell, 1992).

52. Michel Foucault, "*Sept propos sur la septieme ange*," Preface to Jean-Pierre Brisset, *La Grammaire logique* (1883; Paris: Tchou, 1970). A work very much at odds with Said's antipathy to the "curious veering toward the religious" in American literary criticism (*WTC*, 292).

4. GLOBALIZATION'S UNLIKELY CHAMPIONS

1. Bartolomé de Las Casas, *Breuissima relacion de la destruycion de las Indias* [The Destruction of the Indians] (Sevilla: s.n. 1552); Sir Walter Raleigh, *The discoverie of the large, rich and bevvtiful empire of Guiana, with a relation of the great and golden citie of Manoa (which the Spanyards call El Dorado) and the prouinces of Emeria, Arromaia, Amapaia, and other countries, with their riuers, adioyning* (London: Robert Robinson, 1596); Michel de Montaigne, "On Cannibals," in *Les Essais de Michel seignevr de Montaigne* (Paris: Abel L'Angelier, 1595).

2. Francoise de Graffigny, *Letters from a Peruvian Woman* (1752; New York: Modern Language Association, 1993); Voltaire, *Candide: Ou l'optimisme* (1759; Paris: Maisonneuve et Larose, 2001); Abbé Raynal (Guillaume-Thomas-François), *Histoire philosophique et politique des établissements et du commerce des Européens dans les deux Indes* (1770; Oxford: Voltaire Foundation at the Taylor Institution, 1991); Adam Smith, *An inquiry into the nature and causes of the wealth of nations* (Dublin: Printed for Whitestone, 1776); Jeremy Bentham, *Colonies, commerce, and constitutional law:*

Rid yourselves of Ultramaria and other writings on Spain and Spanish America, ed. Philip Schofield (Oxford: Clarendon and New York: Oxford University Press, 1995).

3. Karl Marx and Friedrich Engels, *The Communist Manifesto* (1848; New York: Monthly Review Press, ca. 1998); Karl Marx, *Capital: A Critical Analysis of Capitalist Production*, vol. 3, ed. Frederick Engels, trans. Samuel Moore and Edward Aveling (London: Sonnenschein, Lowery, 1897); Herman Melville, *Moby-Dick* (1851; New York: Norton, 2002); J. A. Hobson, *Imperialism: A Study* (London: Allen and Unwin, 1902).

4. R. B. Cunningham Graham, *The Imperial Kailyard: Being a Biting Satire on English Colonisation* (London: Twentieth Century Press, 1896); William Morris, *News from nowhere: or, An epoch of rest, being some chapters from a utopian romance* (New York: Longmans, Green, 1901); Karl Kautsky, "Ultra-imperialism," *New Left Review* 59 (1914; January/February 1970); Vladimir Lenin, *Imperialism: The Highest Stage of Capitalism* (1917; London: New Left Books, 1975).

5. Fernand Braudel, "Economies in Space: The World Economies" and "By Way of a Conclusion: Past and Present" in *The Perspective of the World*, vol. 3 of *Civilization and Capitalism, 15th–18th Century* (New York: Harper and Row, 1984). William McNeill, *The Rise of the West: A History of the Human Community* (Chicago and London: University of Chicago Press, 1963); Marshall Hodgson, *The Venture of Islam: Conscience and History in a World Civilization* (Chicago: University of Chicago Press, 1974).

6. V. G. Kiernan, *The Lords of Human Kind: European Attitudes to the Outside World in the Imperial Age* (London: Weidenfeld and Nicolson, 1969); Leften Stavros Stavrianos, *Global Rift: The Third World Comes of Age* (New York: Morrow, 1981); Eric R. Wolf, *Europe and the People Without History* (Berkeley: University of California Press, 1982).

7. André Gunder Frank, *Capitalism and Underdevelopment in Latin America* (New York: Monthly Review Press, 1967); Walter Rodney, *How Europe Underdeveloped Africa* (London: Bogle L'Ouverture Publications and Dar es Salaam: Tanzania Publishing House, 1972); Theotonio dos Santos, *Imperialismo y dependencia* (Mexico City: Ediciones Era, 1978).

8. Oliver Cromwell Cox, *The Foundations of Capitalism* (New York: Philosophical Library, 1959); Immanuel Wallerstein, *The Modern World-System: Capitalist Agriculture and the Origins of the European World Economy in the Sixteenth Century* (New York: Academic Press, 1974); Samir Amin, *Unequal Development: An Essay on the Social Formations of Peripheral Capitalism* (New York: Monthly Review, 1976).

9. Jawaharlal Nehru, *The Discovery of India* (New York: John Day Company, 1946); Mao Zedong, *On Contradiction* (New York: International Publishers, 1953); Ernesto Che Guevara, *Guerrilla Warfare*, trans. J. P. Morray (from Spanish), prefatory note by I. F. Stone (1961; New York: Vintage, 1969); Frantz Fanon, *The Wretched of the Earth*, trans. Constance Farrington, preface by Jean-Paul Sartre (New York: Grove Press, 1963); Patrice Lumumba, *Lumumba Speaks: The Speeches and Writings of Patrice Lumumba*, ed. Jean van Lierde, trans. Helen R. Lane, introduction by Jean-Paul Sartre (Boston: Little, Brown, 1972); Ho Chi Minh, *Selected Works* (Hanoi: Tricontinental, 1960). For a closer look at the interwar sources of postcolonial studies,

see Benita Parry, "Liberation Theory: Variations of Themes of Marxism and Modernity," 125–49, and Timothy Brennan, "Postcolonial Studies Between the European Wars: An Intellectual History," 185–203, both in Crystal Bartolovich and Neil Lazarus, eds., *Marxism, Modernity, and Postcolonial Studies* (Cambridge: Cambridge University Press, 2002).

10. David Harvey, *The Condition of Postmodernity: An Enquiry Into the Origins of Cultural Change* (Oxford, U.K., and Cambridge, Mass.: Blackwell, 1998).

11. Pierre Bourdieu, "Uniting Better to Dominate," *Items and Issues* 2 (Winter 2001): 3–4; John Bellamy Foster, "The Rediscovery of Imperialism," *Monthly Review* 54, no. 6 (November 2002): 1–16; Thomas Friedman, *The Lexus and the Olive Tree* (New York: Farrar, Strauss, and Giroux, 1999).

12. Anthony Kwame Appiah, "Is the Post- in Postmodernism the Post- in Postcolonial?" *Critical Inquiry* 17 (Winter 1991): 336–51; Aijaz Ahmad, *In Theory: Classes, Nations, Literatures* (London and New York: Verso, 1992); Arif Dirlik, *The Postcolonial Aura: Third World Criticism in the Age of Global Capitalism* (Boulder, Col.: Westview, 1997); Graham Huggan, *The Postcolonial Exotic: Marketing the Margins* (London: Routledge, 2001).

13. By "interestedness" I mean positions that are a matter of social convenience rather than the acknowledgment of inconvenient facts: for example, the bookish philosopher Derrida's prioritizing of writing over speaking in a culture of televisual secondary orality, or New Criticism's unyielding principle of the self-enclosed, nonreferential artwork during the political freeze of the 1950s. But this is not to say that one cannot transcend sectoral, class, or cultural interestedness. The logic of raising "interest" as a category to the surface for discussion is precisely to bring this conclusion about.

14. Zygmunt Bauman, *Globalization: The Human Consequences* (New York: Columbia University Press, 1998); Mike Featherstone, *Global Culture: Nationalism, Globalization, and Modernity* (London: Sage, 1990); Anthony Giddens, "The Contours of High Modernity," in *Modernity and Self-Identity: Self and Society in the Late Modern Age* (Stanford, Calif.: Stanford University Press, 1991), 10–34; Giorgio Agamben, *The Coming Community* (Minneapolis and London: University of Minnesota Press, 1993).

15. Giddens, "The Contours of High Modernity."

16. Immanuel Kant, *Perpetual Peace: A Philosophical Essay on History*, 1795, trans. and ed. Lewis White Beck (New York: Bobbs-Merrill, 1963), 85–135; Stephen Edelston Toulmin, *Cosmopolis: The Hidden Agenda of Modernity* (New York: Free Press, 1990); Julia Kristeva, *Nations Without Nationalism* (New York: Columbia University Press, 1993).

17. Richard Falk and Andrew Strauss, "On the Creation of a Global People's Assembly: Legitimacy and Power of Popular Sovereignty," *Stanford Journal of International Law* 36, no. 2 (2000): 191–219; Richard Falk and Andrew Strauss, "Toward a Global Parliament," *Foreign Affairs* (January/February 2001): 212–20.

18. Leslie Sklair, *Sociology of the Global System* (Brighton: Harvester Wheatsheaf, 1991).

19. Jagdish Bhagwati, "Why Globalization Is Good," *Items and Issues* 2, nos. 3–4 (Winter 2001): 7–8; Félix Guattari and Toni Negri, *Communists Like Us* (New York: Semiotext(e), 1985).

20. George Soros, *The Crisis of Global Capitalism: Open Society Endangered* (New York: Public Affairs, 1998).

21. Fernando Valladao, *The Twenty-first Century Will Be American* (London: Verso, 1995); Bauman, *Globalization*.

22. Friedman, *The Lexus and the Olive Tree*; Paul R. Krugman, *The Age of Diminished Expectations: U.S. Economic Policy in the 1990s* (Cambridge, Mass.: MIT Press, 1997).

23. Lewis H. Lapham, *The Agony of Mammon: The Imperial World Economy Explains Itself to the Membership in Davos, Switzerland* (London and New York: Verso, 1998); J. M. Blaut, *The Colonizer's Model of the World: Geographical Diffusionism and Eurocentric History* (New York and London: Guilford, 1993); Samir Amin, *Transforming the Revolution: Social Movements and the World-System* (New York: Monthly Review, 1990); Pierre Bourdieu, "Neo-liberalism, the Utopia (Becoming a Reality) of Unlimited Exploitation," in *Acts of Resistance: Against the Tyranny of the Market*, trans. Richard Nice (New York: New Press, 1998), 94–105.

24. Henry Kissinger, *Diplomacy* (New York: Simon and Schuster, 1994).

25. Immanuel Wallerstein, *The Politics of the World Economy: The States, the Movements, and the Civilizations* (Cambridge and New York: Cambridge University Press, 1984); Janet Abu-Lughod, "On the Remaking of History: How to Reinvent the Past," in Barbara Kruger and Phil Mariani, eds., *Remaking History*, 111–29 (Seattle: Bay Press, 1989).

26. Tony McGrew, "A Global Society?" in Stuart Hall, David Held, and Tony McGrew, eds., *Modernity and Its Futures* (Cambridge, U.K.: Polity Press and Blackwell, 1992).

27. Neil Lazarus, *Nationalism and Cultural Practice in the Postcolonial World* (Cambridge and New York: Cambridge University Press, 1999); Neil Lazarus, "The Fetish of the 'West' in Postcolonial Theory," in Crystal Bartolovich and Neil Lazarus, eds., *Marxism, Modernity, and Postcolonial Studies*, 43–64 (Cambridge: Cambridge University Press, 2002); Neil Lazarus, "Doubting the New World Order: Marxism and Postmodernist Social Theory," *differences* 3, no. 3 (1991): 94–138; Fernando Coronil, *The Magical State: Nature, Money, and Modernity in Venezuela* (Chicago: University of Chicago Press, 1997); Edward Said, *Culture and Imperialism* (New York: Knopf, 1993).

28. Arif Dirlik, "Place-Based Imagination: Globalism and the Politics of Place," in Roxann Prazniak and Arif Dirlik, eds., *Places and Politics in an Age of Globalization*, 15–51 (Lanham, Md., and Oxford: Rowman and Littlefield, 2001); Saskia Sassen, *Globalization and Its Discontents* (New York: New Press, 1998).

29. Ulf Hannerz, "Cosmopolitans and Locals in World Culture," in Mike Featherstone, ed., *Global Culture: Nationalism, Globalization, and Modernity* (London: Sage, 1990), 237–51; Martha C. Nussbaum, with respondents, *For Love of Country? Debating the Limits of Patriotism*, ed. Joshus Cohen (Boston: Beacon Press, 1996); Timothy Brennan, *At Home in the World: Cosmopolitanism Now* (Cambridge, Mass.: Harvard University Press, 1997).

30. Bourdieu, "Neo-liberalism, the Utopia (Becoming a Reality) of Unlimited Exploitation," 95.

31. Hodgson, *The Venture of Islam*; Cromwell Cox, *The Foundations of Capitalism*.

32. David Landes, *The Wealth and Poverty of Nations: Why Some Are So Rich and Some So Poor* (New York: Norton, 1998); McNeill, *The Rise of the West*.

33. Santos, *Imperialismo y dependencia*; Frank, *Capitalism and Underdevelopment in Latin America*; Rodney, *How Europe Underdeveloped Africa*.

34. Justin Rosenberg, *The Follies of Globalisation Theory* (London: Verso, 2000). A more detailed description of this process can be found in Ahmad, *In Theory*; Lazarus, *Nationalism and Cultural Practice in the Postcolonial World*; and Epifanio San Juan, *Beyond Postcolonial Theory* (New York: St. Martin's, 1998).

35. Blaut, *The Colonizer's Model of the World*; Gale Stokes, "Why the West?" *Lingua Franca*, November 2001, 30–39.

36. Ronald H. Chilcote, ed., *Imperialism: Theoretical Directions* (Amherst, N.Y.: Humanity Books, 2000); William K. Tabb, "Capitalism and Globalization," in ibid., 315–21; Anthony Brewer, *Marxist Theories of Imperialism* (London: Routledge and Kegan Paul, 1980)

37. Nikolai Bukharin, *Imperialism and World Economy* (1917; New York: Monthly Review, 1973); Bukharin and Rosa Luxemburg, *Imperialism and the Accumulation of Capital: An Anti-Critique* (1921; New York: Monthly Review Press, 1972).

38. Karl Polanyi, *The Great Transformation* (New York and Toronto: Farrar and Rinehart, 1944).

39. Benedict Anderson, *Imagined Communities: Reflections on the Origins and Spread of Nationalism* (London and New York: Verso, 1983); Eric Hobsbawm, *The Age of Empire: 1875–1914* (London: Cardinal, 1987); Eric Hobsbawm and Terence Ranger, *The Invention of Tradition* (Cambridge and New York: Cambridge University Press, 1983).

40. Bourdieu, "Neo-liberalism, the Utopia (Becoming a Reality) of Unlimited Exploitation"; Samir Amin, *Capitalism in the Age of Globalization: The Management of Contemporary Society* (London and Atlantic Highlands, N.J.: Zed Books, 1997).

5. THE ORGANIZATIONAL IMAGINARY

1. Kenneth Gergen (1991) as quoted in Ronald E. Hopson and Donald R. Smith, "Changing Fortunes: An Analysis of Christian Right Ascendance Within American Political Discourse," *Journal for the Scientific Study of Religion* 38, no. 1 (March 1999): 1, 58.

2. Thus prompting the charge of contradiction—I suppose like Walter Kauffman's strangely counter-Nietzschean claim that because Nietzsche excoriated the Germans he was not a German nationalist!

3. Martin Lechner (1989) as quoted in Hopson and Smith, "Changing Fortunes," 37.

4. Hopson and Smith, "Changing Fortunes," 58.

5. Angelo Quattrocchi and Tom Nairn, *The Beginning of the End: France, May 1968* (London and New York: Verso, 1998).

6. Karl Marx, "Theses on Feuerbach," *The Marx-Engels Reader*, ed. Robert C. Tucker (New York: Norton, 1978), 145.

7. Jacques Derrida, *Writing and Difference* (Chicago and London: University of Chicago Press, 1978).

8. The refashioning of a politics of engagement and its transformation into "transgression" finds its paradigmatic expression in Georges Bataille, "The Sorcerer's Apprentice," in Denis Hollier, ed., *The College of Sociology, 1937–1939*, 12–23 (Minneapolis: University of Minnesota Press, 1988).

9. "All political and economic arrangements are not worth it, that precisely the most gifted spirits should be permitted, or even obliged, to manage them: such a waste of spirit is really worse than an extremity. . . . At such a price, one pays far too dearly for the 'general security'" (Friedrich Nietzsche, excerpts from *The Dawn*, in *The Portable Nietzsche* [New York and London: Penguin, 1982], 82).

10. *New York Times*, December 20, 1998, 35.

11. Even a superb journalist like Alexander Cockburn falls prey to a view that discounts conspiracy theory out of hand. He believes that because John F. Kennedy's policies were impeccably consonant with those of the Cold War establishment, therefore the CIA, rogue military personnel, and the Mafia could never think him a dangerous communist. I disagree with this reading on the grounds that it fails to contend with the sheer lunacy of right-wing exegesis in the United States. Cockburn's intelligent exposé of the paranoid style in American politics—particularly effective when he lampoons "pwogwessive" conspiracy theories—blinds him to the persistent fact of conspiracy as an everyday political mode.

12. Ruth Shalit, "The Man Who Knew Too Much," *Lingua Franca*, February 1998, 32–40; Margaret Talbot, "A Most Dangerous Method," *Lingua Franca*, February 1994, 24–40.

13. Talbot, "A Most Dangerous Method," 38.

14. Jack Hitt, "Permission Granted Upon Request," *Lingua Franca*, November/December 1993, 6.

15. Lisa DePaulo, "The Sixteenth Minute," *Mirabella*, July–August 1998, 76.

16. William Martin, "The Christian Right and American Foreign Policy," *Foreign Policy* 114 (Spring 1999): 1, 66.

17. Despite losing purchase temporarily after failing to force Clinton out of office, the NCR was victorious in selling George W. Bush as the pro-choice, Spanish-speaking politician of "compassion" during the presidential race of 2000. In the 1998 elections, 22 of its 28 favored candidates were defeated; after 2000, it arose as again the major force. The important point here is that both Gary Bauer and Pat Buchanan defended their opportunistic approach (this unseemly meddling with principles) in order to gain force "vote after vote after vote." In other words, religious myth always proved secondary to political strategy.

18. Hopson and Smith, "Changing Fortunes," 8–9.

19. A prominent exception can be found in Félix Guattari and Toni Negri's *Communists Like Us* (New York: Semiotext(e), 1990), a culturalist text that explicitly addresses organizational questions (see especially 146–47). It does so, however, in a sense reminiscent of Catalonian anarchism, with much talk of the "illusory choice between capitalism and socialism" (71).

20. See, for instance, Neil Larsen, *Modernism and Hegemony: A Materialist Critique of Aesthetic Agencies* (Minneapolis: University of Minnesota Press, 1990), xxix–xxxi,

102–3; Norman Geras, "Seven Types of Obloquy: Travesties of Marxism," *Graduate Faculty Philosophy Journal* (1991): 81–115.

21. Judith Butler, "Merely Cultural," *Social Text* 52/53, nos. 3/4 (Fall/Winter 1997): 265–77.

22. Judith Butler, "A 'Bad Writer' Bites Back," *New York Times*, March 20, 1999.

23. Theodor Adorno, *Prisms* (1955; Cambridge, Mass.: MIT Press, 1995), 24.

24. Kristin Ross, "Establishing Consensus: May '68 in France as Seen from the 1980s," *Critical Inquiry* 28, no. 3 (Spring 2002): 654.

25. It could be objected that Butler herself established a scholarly past in regard to Hegel, about whom she has written with authority. This is true, and I would not deny the importance of her work in this or other regards. But her place in the drift of theory's anti-Hegelian posture is a corollary of her deployment of Hegel. In *The Psychic Life of Power: Theories of Subjection* (Stanford: Stanford University Press, 1997), she attempts the unenviable task of demonstrating that Hegel's *Phenomenology* looked forward to Foucault by adopting a "dystopic" outlook on the subject in the "Lordship and Bondage" section. Foucault's chastisement of the regulatory mechanisms governing the production of subjects is, according to her, prefigured in "Hegel's account of the bondsman's liberation into various forms of ethical self-beratement." This counter-reading of the theorist of the active subject in civic life, par excellence—which, among other things, ignores the frank hostility of these later writers toward Hegel—does not stop there. It goes on to show that Hegel's text "forecloses" the "Nietzschean and Freudian account of conscience" as well—a position, I would argue, that is possible only because Butler conflates Hegel's critique of religious transcendence with a rejection of "ethical imperatives." This allows her to link Hegel with the Nietzsche of *On the Genealogy of Morals*.

26. Eric Lott, "Boomer Liberalism," *Transition* 78 (Spring 1999): 24–45.

27. Butler, "Merely Cultural," 265.

28. That an older radicalism itself in Lott's mind "crumbled when women, blacks and queers made their own movements" (35) is a startling illustration of the confusion that results when one fails to consider cultures of belief. Here, the doxa of the self-expressive subject formed the limit text of middle-class aspirations so that now first-wave feminism, community anti-racism, and the legacies of Stonewall themselves were repudiated for their essentialism or for their merely civic forms of engagement.

6. THE EMPIRE'S NEW CLOTHES

1. Antonio Gramsci, "The Futurists," N1, item 124, *The Prison Notebooks*, vol. 1, ed. Joseph A. Buttigieg (New York: Columbia University Press, 1992), 211.

2. While it is certainly clear enough why the book became prominent, it is also important to insist that its success is perplexing. There are any number of more consequential and better-written books on globalization, new labor, anarchist responses to the contemporary state, identity politics, and, for that matter, the writing of Deleuze and Guattari. *Empire*, in other words, is not formidable and wrong, as

some have described it. As an ambitious recharting, it simply doesn't measure up to the early Baudrillard, say, or lately, Žižek.

3. Michael Hardt and Antonio Negri, *Empire* (Cambridge, Mass. and London: Harvard University Press, 2000), 66.

4. In addition to the coverage in the *New York Times* and on the Charlie Rose show—neither of which has shown much interest in long books of theory that quote Polybius and Rosa Luxemburg—see the coverage, for example, in Michael Elliott, "The Wrong Side of the Barricades," *Time*, July 23, 2001, 39. Elliott interestingly avers that Hardt and Negri are really on to something, provided they lose the Marx, who only gets in the way.

5. See Hardt and Negri, *Empire*, 62, on Deleuze and Guattari's "apparatus of capture."

6. For example, *Theory, Culture, and Society* 7, nos. 2–3 (June 1990), Special Issue on "Global Culture," ed. Mike Featherstone; Anthony King, ed., *Culture, Globalization, and the World System: Contemporary Conditions for the Representation of Identity* (London: Macmillan, 1991); David Yergin and Joseph Stanislaw, *The Commanding Heights: The Battle Between Government and the Marketplace That Is Remaking the Modern World* (London: Macmillan, 1998); David Held, *Democracy and the Global Order: From the Modern State to Cosmopolitan Governance* (London: Macmillan, 1995).

7. Anthony Giddens, *Modernity and Self-Identity: Self and Society in the Late Modern Age* (Stanford: Stanford University Press, 1991), 9.

8. This is a standard view in conservative international relations circles, but also (and more surprisingly) in left social studies. Benjamin Lee, for example, inexplicably considers the United States (as opposed to China) a "weak-state" society. See "Critical Internationalism," *Public Culture* 7, no. 3 (Spring 1995): 581. But does he not, then, concur with Deleuze and Guattari's formulation on the *Urstaat* in *Anti-Oedipus*? "It is beneath the blows of private property, then of commodity production, that the State witnesses its decline" (Gilles Deleuze and Félix Guattari, *Anti-Oedipus: Capitalism and Schizophrenia* [1972; Minneapolis: University of Minnesota Press, 1983], 218). Capitalism is here cast as a savior: it saves us from the excesses of (in Deleuze and Guattari's words) the fearful "Asiatic state."

9. For a fuller discussion of council communism and related interwar tendencies, see Paul Mattick, *Anti-Bolshevik Communism* (London: Merlin Press, 1978). Note especially 83–85.

10. It is especially Agamben who articulates the ontological loathing for government that characterizes all new Italian thought: a virtual "polisophobia." In Agamben's retelling of the work of Carl Schmitt—and *Homo Sacer* is largely Schmitt's *Crisis of Parliamentary Democracy* written in a different style—he attacks the "democratico-revolutionary tradition" by showing its inability to escape the exception that governs all law. Thus Schmitt's original critique of Weimar liberalism is enlisted as evidence of the original sin of governments of all types (Agamben, *Homo Sacer: Sovereign Power and Bare Life*, trans. Daniel Heller-Roazen [Stanford, Calif.: Stanford University Press, 1998], 40).

11. Paolo Virno and Michael Hardt, eds., *Radical Thought in Italy: A Potential Politics* (Minneapolis: University of Minnesota Press, 1996).

12. Hardt, "Introduction: Laboratory Italy," in Virno and Hardt, *Radical Thought in Italy*, 1.

13. For political background, see Mark Gilbert, "Italy's Third Fall," *Journal of Modern Italian Studies* 2, no. 2 (1997): 221–31; Alexander Stille, "Italy: The Convulsions of Normalcy," *New York Review of Books*, June 6, 1996, 42–46; Rudi Ghedini, "After the Fall of Bologna: The Decline of Italy's Red City," *Le Monde Diplomatique*, September 2000. The contemporary Italian situation is well presented in Vittorio Bufacchi and Simon Burgess, *Italy Since 1989* (London: Macmillan, 1998).

14. Antonio Gramsci, *Selections from the Prison Notebooks* (New York: International Publishers, 1971), 125.

15. Ibid., 126.

16. Malcolm Bull, "You Can't Build a New Society with a Stanley Knife," *London Review of Books* 23, no. 19 (October 4, 2001): 3.

17. Although invariably marked by circumspection, not all of the public response has been adulatory. Gopal Balakrishnan ("Virgilian Visions," *New Left Review* 5 [September/October 2000]: 143–49) faults *Empire* for its "series of dubious assumptions"; John Kraniauskas ("Empire, or Multitude: Transnational Negri," *Radical Philosophy* 103 [September/October 2000]: 35) is skeptical of the book's "neo-positivist ontology of becoming" (35).

18. At times dismissive of *Empire*'s argument, Bull too is circumspect. He swings from condescension to overpraise as though worried that a blunter contestation would consign him under the current hegemony to the ranks of the out-of-touch. When one reflects on what books are excluded by Bull's judgment—Alexander Cockburn's *Corruptions of Empire*, Thomas Frank's *One Market Under God*, Ellen Meiksins Wood's *The Pristine Culture of Capitalism*, John Ross's *Shadows of Tender Fury*, Fredric Jameson's *The Cultural Turn*, and Giovanni Arrighi's *The Long Twentieth Century*—the statement seems not only unmeasured, but absurd.

19. "New Times" is associated with circles around the (now defunct) British journal *Marxism Today* in the late 1980s and early 1990s. They argued that systemic transformations in capitalism had forced the Left to place a new emphasis on consumerism, abandon the emphasis on industrial labor, and jettison the goals of the welfare state. See Stuart Hall and Martin Jacques, eds., *New Times: The Changing Face of Politics in the 1990s* (London and New York: Verso, 1990).

20. There are in practice too many distractions in the course of reading a book like *Empire* to be deterred by its preparatory ideas—ones that are often groundless but that have acquired the status of truth by repetition. These ideas may nag at the reader's attention, but since there is already so much else that needs a response, the reader fails to contest them, fearing that the debate has already moved on to another place. To question the predicates, at any rate, is seen as lagging behind the game, for the participants have already agreed to agree about ideas whose truth value is based above all on the number of times they are repeated.

21. Neil Smith, *Uneven Development: Nature, Capital, and the Production of Space* (New York and London: Blackwell, 1984).

22. It is beyond the scope of this essay to provide a critique of post-Fordist conceits, but readers may want to consult the following concise accounts of the problems found

in them: Neil Lazarus's "Doubting the New World Order: Marxism and Postmodernist Social Theory," *differences* 3, no. 3 (1991): 94–138; Alex Callinicos, *Against Postmodernism: A Marxist Critique* (Oxford: Polity Press, 1990); and Daniel T. McGee, "Post-Marxism: The Opiate of the Intellectuals," *Modern Language Quarterly* 58, no. 2 (June 1997): 201–25.

23. According to Varcellone, the phrase animated the entire movement throughout the 1970s and functions now in the present as a structure of feeling (Virno and Hardt, *Radical Thought in Italy*, 2); for "the will to be against," see Hardt and Negri, *Empire*, 274. As a political concept, the "refusal of work" is far from unexpected, however. As Edouard Glissant points out in *Caribbean Discourse* (Charlottesville: University Press of Virginia, 1989), the refusal of work was long the strategy of Rastafarianism.

24. Mario Tronti, *Operai e capitale* (Torino: Einaudi, 1977).

25. Mario Tronti, "The Strategy of Refusal," *Semiotexte* 3, no. 3 (1980): 30.

26. There are also suggestive parallels between new Italian thought and those new ambivalent left/right tendencies of post-unification Europe described by Douglas R. Holmes in *Integral Europe: Fast-Capitalism, Multiculturalism, Neofascism* (Princeton and Oxford: Princeton University Press, 2000), 44, 46, 56. Holmes's ethnography (he did his fieldwork in, among other places, Northern Italy) investigates a new political hybrid in a reconfigured Europe that works within the counter-Enlightenment traditions of German Romanticism, opposes the ideals of modernity, and looks to build a collectivity that champions a holistic "integralism." Both sharing and rejecting key parts of this amalgam, new Italian thought teeters at its edges. Although the integralists reject the supranational aims of the European Union, their concept of collectivity is strikingly similar, taken from the social modernism of Jean Monnet in France of the 1940s in pursuit of the "formation of broad and unlikely alliances" as well as the "delineation of unusual possibilities." Holmes goes on to discuss the links between integralism and an earlier neo-Thomist tradition of social Catholicism out of which Negri grew (see below).

27. Timo Ahonen and Markus Termonen, interview with Norbert Trenkle in *Krisis*, originally made for the Finnish magazine *Megafoni* (http://megafoni.kulma.net).

28. Who pays for this "citizens' income" is, of course, an unanswered question. Trenkle concedes that the proposal makes sense only in the advanced countries and that the debt might very well fall on "the rest of the world's humanity" (ibid.).

29. See Virno, "The Ambivalence of Disenchantment," in Virno and Hardt, *Radical Thought in Italy*, 20, 26, 28.

30. Robert Reich, *The Work of Nations* (New York: Knopf, 1991); Anthony Giddens, "The Contours of High Modernity," in *Modernity and Self-Identity*, 10–34.

31. Virno and Hardt, *Radical Thought in Italy*, 132.

32. See Negri, *Marx Beyond Marx* (Brooklyn: Autonomedia/Pluto, 1991), especially 1–21, and Virno and Hardt, *Radical Thought in Italy*, 13–36. Anyone familiar with the Left over the last three decades knows how repetitive this return to the *Grundrisse* is. Already in 1978, E. P. Thompson was reminding readers that the *Grundrisse* was, after all, a series of notes, that it remained unfinished, and that it was, in the mind of its author, superseded by the more accomplished work of a later period. To pur-

sue the directive of revisiting the *Grundrisse* now demands some special justification, which readers of the new Italians never receive.

33. The passage is found in the Martin Nicolaus translation (London: Penguin, 1973), 705.

34. Antonio Negri, "Twenty Theses on Marx: Interpretation of the Class Situation Today," in Saree Makdisi, Cesare Casarino, and Rebecca E. Karl, eds., *Marxism Beyond Marxism*, 165, 172, 175 (New York and London: Routledge, 1996).

35. In "A-Way with Their Wor(l)d: Rural Labourers Through the Postmodern Prism," *Economic and Political Weekly* 28, no. 23 (1993): 1162–68, Tom Brass traces the conservative heritage of the popular culture *as* resistance thesis. His analysis can be applied to Hardt and Negri's revolution of the already is: "An almost identical concept of non-confrontation with the state, a form of indirect political action known as the 'theory of small deeds,' was actually pioneered by Russian populists during the late 19th century [Utechin 1964]. More importantly, much of the theory which prefigures the 'resistance' framework is already present in an earlier text by James Scott [1968: 94 ff., 119 ff.] where he endorses both the 'limited good' argument of George Foster [1965] and the 'culture of poverty' thesis advanced by Oscar Lewis [1962]" (1163).

36. The uses of Heidegger in new Italian texts is seen clearly in Massimo de Carolis, who defines "autonomy"—his goal—in terms of "an authentic and complete existence," which requires being "exposed to the world" so that one might "dismantle at the outset the myth of a pure subject" (Virno and Hardt, *Radical Thought in Italy*, 43). It takes us closer to new Italian method when we appreciate this articulation of the existential in terms of the economic. As he puts it, the "world is now for us," since "exoticism" has been liquidated and there is no such thing any longer as "a full and concrete alterity," a phrase that—like much of Heidegger's influence—vastly strengthens the discourses of Eurocentrism. For an excellent analysis of the disingenuous attractions to Heidegger on the Italian left, see Renate Holub, "Italian Heidegger Affairs," in Nancy A. Harrowitz, ed., *Tainted Greatness: Antisemitism and Cultural Heroes*, 173–89 (Philadelphia: Temple University Press, 1994). A concise account of the specific convergence in recent Italian thought of Heideggerian categories with a new strain of devoutly Catholic forms of philosophical meditation can be found in Romano Luperini, "Tendencies of Criticism in Contemporary Italy," *Rethinking Marxism* 5, no. 1 (Spring 1992): 32–43.

37. Which is to suggest that Heidegger is not an unproblematic source for them (as he is, for example, for Derrida, Franco Rella, or Agamben). He is a tragic philosopher in their opinion. Also, Hardt and Negri attack postmodernism at one point as "the poisonous culture of the 1980s" and the benefactors of a de facto corporate cheerleading (Virno and Hardt, *Radical Thought in Italy*, 7; Hardt and Negri, *Empire*, 137–39).

38. "The globalization of markets, far from being simply the horrible fruit of capitalist entrepreneurship, was actually the result of the desires and demands of Taylorist, Fordist, and disciplined labor power across the world" (Hardt and Negri, *Empire*, 266).

39. Richard Falk and Andrew Strauss, "On the Creation of a Global People's Assembly: Legitimacy and Power of Popular Sovereignty," *Stanford Journal of International Law* 36, no. 2 (2000): 191–219; and Richard Falk and Andrew Strauss, "Toward a Global Parliament," *Foreign Affairs*, January/February 2001, 212–20.

40. Whatever critique one might offer of the political legacies of the Russian revolution, anti-Bolshevik Marxism typically ends by "discovering" the beauty of the United States, which is then weirdly taken to have realized socialism's original aims in spite of its annihilation of actual socialists. C. L. R. James, to take only one example, seriously argued in the 1950s that American popular culture accurately registered working-class interests, and witnessed a flawless correspondence between the popular will and a government forced to do its bidding: the people had come to power!

41. For *Empire*'s concept of the constituent republic and its analysis of the state, see, for example, *Labor of Dionysus: A Critique of the State-Form* (Minneapolis: University of Minnesota Press, 1994). For its slogan of the "mass worker," its view of work as an "environment" or "ecology," and its emphasis on the subjectivity of labor, see *The Politics of Subversion*. For its theories of *Grundrisse* and the nature of "value," see *Marx Beyond Marx*.

42. Saskia Sassen, *Globalization and Its Discontents* (New York: New Press, 1998), xxix; and *The Global City: New York, London, Tokyo* (Princeton, N.J.: Princeton University Press, 1991), 3–34. *Empire* takes its discussion of "non-places" from Marc Augé.

43. Hardt and Negri's July 2001 op-ed piece in the *New York Times* offered a startling illustration of ambivalence in cultural theory, in this case self-serving. Written to explain what the anti-globalization protesters at the Genoa summit *really* wanted, the article concluded—in spite of the protesters' emphatic declarations to the contrary—that the Genovese rebels were not against globalization. In what must have come as great relief to the editors of the *Times*, the authors further argued that the insurgents did not see the United States as the major antagonist in the new global order (which also contradicts the protesters' reported statements). The prominence of the forum in the *Times* undoubtedly moves readers to associate Hardt and Negri's work with the rebelling forces, as though proof of their prophetic and radical aims. Actually, the analysis indicates their practice of shoehorning movements into the theses of *Empire*. Michael Hardt and Antonio Negri, "What the Protesters in Genoa Want," *New York Times*, July 20, 2001.

44. Political organization itself, in their words, should be seen as a kind of "Exodus." Because new Italian thinkers have found success primarily abroad in the American theoretical establishment (that is, in a kind of exodus), the theorist's person is analogized in the nomadism of labor, which is cast as a restless "refusal and search for liberation"—rather than the typically coercive migration of workers to harvests or factory towns fleeing landlords or a callous police force (Hardt and Negri, *Empire*, 234–35, 212–13).

45. Interesting, if troubling, are the historical traces found in the word "anthropological." Seeing the traditional political parties in shambles in the Italy of the 1970s, Pier Paolo Passolini decried the new radicalism as a consumerist hedonism modeled on the American type. He called it an "anthropological mutation." What revolted Pas-

solini inspires Negri, who here appears to quote Passolini against himself. See Richard Drake, *The Revolutionary Mystique and Terrorism in Contemporary Italy* (Bloomington: Indiana University Press, 1989), 154.

46. The authors do, however, concede that agriculture is economically dominant in India or Nigeria, but they consider this insignificant since it is "subordinated to industry" (*Empire*, 282). The comment appears to be a toss-off and is, moreover, a superficial formulation. But it is revealing. Why would the dominant sector of an economy be rendered irrelevant to the subjectivity of labor simply because another sector had "subordinated" it? That condition would only make it more relevant.

47. See, for example, Gianni Vattimo, *The End of Modernity* (Baltimore: Johns Hopkins University Press, 1991), which lays out the concept of "weak thought" taken up by Alfredo Zanini in the Virno and Hardt anthology; and Franco Rella, *The Myth of the Other* (Washington, D.C.: Maisonneuve Press, 1994). Roberto Esposito's *Bíos: Biopolitica e filosofia* (Torino: Biblioteca Einaudi, 2004) is one of the most sustained presentations of the general claims of the biopolitical turn, and it shares Agamben's points of departure—namely, that philosophy has utterly changed since Nazism, which launched a Thanatopolitics (a politics based on death), now a central feature of a "post-human" age in which a proper "sovereignty" shifts to control of one's body. Hardt and Negri spell out their differences with Agamben in *Empire* (366, 421).

48. As Rossana Rossanda tells the story (in "Two Hundred Questions for Anyone Who Wants to Be Communist in the 1990s," in Virno and Hardt, *Radical Thought in Italy*, 61–77), autonomia evolved from a fertile series of practical political encounters that took place in Italy during the 1970s. For writers and activists like Paolo Virno, Paolo Pozzi, and Luciano Ferrari Bravo, this was no May '68, as in France, but a decade-long skirmish that left indelible marks on the fragile Italian state. Alternative newspapers, student-worker linkages, and activist study circles operated in an atmosphere of endemic governmental crisis and corruption, and within an established communist popular culture, formulating what they called the "frontist line." The enthusiasms of that remarkable period are still evident in all of their writing (and especially marked in the resilient Negri), although it is now cast in a polylingual, cross-disciplinary mélange inflected by Franco-German theory and post-Fordist economics. In often very personalized narratives, Rossanda, Lucio Castellano, and others testify to a historical trajectory that brought student radicals, disgruntled unionists, and the cultural underground from an industrially based left consensus to a fractured grouping of defiant youth and now aging professors struggling to hold on to an ethic of opposition at a time when the substance of rebellion had for them already become ambiguous.

49. "The question is not should the state be destroyed in order to establish a democratic society but when is the right time to do so" (Michael Hardt, in Thomas Dumm, interview with Michael Hardt, "Sovereignty, Multitudes, Absolute Democracy," *Theory and Event*, http://muse.jhu.edu/journals/theory_&_event/v004/4.3hardt .html).

50. Agamben, *Homo Sacer*, 187.

51. Yann Moulier, introduction to Antonio Negri, *The Politics of Subversion* (Cambridge, Mass.: Polity Press, 1989), 8.

52. By the word "flow," I mean not simply influence but the air of inevitability that surrounds certain concepts traveling through the intellectual market, where the borrowing of ideas is concealed in order to replay a theatrical act of discovery of what is already hegemonic, so that the predominant can continue to enjoy the status of the emergent.
53. Virno and Hardt, *Radical Thought in Italy*, 42.
54. Ibid., 9.
55. Ibid., 12.
56. Negri, *Marx Beyond Marx*, xvi.
57. Agamben, *Homo Sacer*, 179
58. Giorgio Agamben, "Beyond Human Rights," in Virno and Hardt, *Radical Thought in Italy*, 162.
59. Ibid., 163.
60. Theodor Adorno, *Beethoven: The Philosophy of Music* (Stanford, Calif.: Stanford University Press, 1998), 141.
61. Warren Montag has shown that Spinoza tends to tell us three stories at once: "the story of God, the story of Nature and the story of God-as-Nature, or, the story of transcendence, the story of immanence and the story of transcendence as immanence" (Warren Montag, *Bodies, Masses, Power: Spinoza and His Contemporaries* [London and New York: Verso, 1999], 4, as quoted in Kraniauskas, "Empire, or Multitude: Transnational Negri," 36).
62. Howard P. Kainz, *An Introduction to Hegel: The Stages of Modern Philosophy* (Athens: Ohio University Press, 1996), 21.
63. Lucien Goldmann, "The Social Structure and the Collective Consciousness of Structures," in William Q. Beolhower, ed., *Essays on Method in the Sociology of Literature*, 87–88 (St. Louis: Telos, 1980).
64. Ibid., 88.
65. Similarly, although the authors claim to despise dialectical thinking (Hardt and Negri, *Empire*, 161), they are forced repeatedly to assume its logic (without, of course, commenting on the fact): Empire, they argue, "has now been fully realized" by way of the "deterritorializing power of the multitude" that "calls for and makes necessary [Empire's] destruction" (24–25, 61). What is this if not routine Hegelian negation?
66. For example, in Thomas Dumm's interview with Michael Hardt, "Sovereignty, Multitudes, Absolute Democracy," 6.
67. As Jürgen Habermas was pointing out long before the Schmitt revival took shape in the English-speaking world, Schmitt plays a curious role in current cultural theory. His approach to the political is about freeing political actors from ethical constraints in the practice of sovereign power. He plays a compensatory role here, saying what the authors are unwilling to enact—that is, striking the note that is absent from their discourse. His conservative credentials bring his views more in accord with the conservatism that attends the neoliberal age to which the new Italians form an adversarial adjunct. And yet, since Schmitt was radical in his earlier period, he has been cleansed by the decades into a new acceptability—a conformism that is not a conformism. See Habermas, "The Horrors of Autonomy: Carl Schmitt in Eng-

302   6. THE EMPIRE'S NEW CLOTHES

lish," in *The New Conservatism: Cultural Criticism and the Historians' Debate* (Cambridge, Mass.: MIT Press, 1989), 128–39.

68. See Perry Anderson, "Components of the National Culture," *New Left Review* 50, no. 9 (July/August 1968): 3–58.

69. In this sense, at least, the book shares with Agamben an untroubled embrace of European Romanticism's view of the classical *fons et origo*. To this degree, Agamben not only refers to many of the same philosophical sources but also provides the basis for them. As a result, whatever his differences, he shares with Hardt and Negri an amazing confidence in the transhistorical validity of classical etymologies (see *Empire*'s discussion of "*posse*" and "*esse*," for example)—a confidence that appears not so much redolent of Nietzschean genealogy as simply quaint. Agamben's positions on states, power, and the body derive from the lexicons of Mediterranean antiquity as though modernity were merely an anagoge of the Greek and Latin linguistic mind.

70. As Holmes points out in *Integral Europe*, the Sorelians "emphasized the potential of a cultural assemblage to serve as the basis of collectivity. . . . They sought to formulate a politics that could . . . engage directly the human substance of an integral lifeworld." Nicola Badaloni has also shown how Sorel is key for understanding the interwar period, from which many of the new Italian ideas are drawn, including its ambiguous political location. A theory that abandoned "the theme of the necessity of socialism and its replacement by a combinatory of various possibilities, connect with the co-penetration of the juridical and the economic. He presented this result (in a way which does not differ from that at which, fifty years later, the structuralist school of French Marxism was to arrive) as the authentic thought of Marx." Results are achieved "in spite of man's intellectual consciousness." See Chantal Mouffe, *Gramsci and Marxist Theory* (London and Boston: Routledge and Kegan Paul, 1979), 82.

71. And nowhere more emphatically than in *Anti-Oedipus*, where Deleuze and Guattari write: "*There has never been but a single State*, the State-as-dog that 'speaks with flaming roars'" (the latter part of their statement is a quote from Nietzsche) (192). In response to that singular evil, on the very next page, they posit "the dream of a spiritual empire, wherever temporal empires fall into decadence" (193). And this dream gives us *Empire*.

72. See, for example, Thomas Frank and Matt Wieland, eds., *Commodify Your Dissent* (New York: Norton, 1997).

73. Slavoj Žižek, *Did Somebody Say Totalitarianism?* (London and New York: Verso, 2001), 3.

74. One illustration of this element in Negri's work can be found in *Labor of Dionysus*, 28–29.

75. Throughout the *Prison Notebooks*, Gramsci describes the scholastic national-cultural training of Italian high intellectuals and the Catholic excrescences on modern thought that had remained resilient in the face of modernization. It is ironic that the new Italian amalgam—in particular Negri, whose status as a prisoner gives him a superficial resemblance to Gramsci in the minds of younger theorists—would gain from association with Gramsci's prior fame. One could say—above all

in their Sorelian echoes—that they were the cult he sought to expose. See the entries on Sorel in Antonio Gramsci, *Prison Notebooks*, vol. 2, 58, 98, 112, 123, 139–41, 168–72, 193–94, 235.

76. Drake, *The Revolutionary Mystique and Terrorism in Contemporary Italy*, 52.

77. In this respect, and in recognition of the interwar political lineages on which *Empire* quietly draws, one might recall the words of Henry de Man: "Young people do not so much want a new economic theory or a new way of explaining history, as a new outlook on life, and indeed a new religion. Since Marxism does not offer them this, they turn away from it" (*The Psychology of Socialism*, trans. Eden and Cedar Paul [London: George Allen and Unwin, 1926], 22).

78. Antonio Gramsci, *Prison Notebooks*, vol. 2, Q3, item 3 (1930), 8–9.

79. But they do acknowledge the U.S. efforts to do so: "The contemporary idea of Empire is born through the global expansion of the internal U.S. constitutional project" (182), a process they unexpectedly welcome in spite of the rather less than revolutionary tenor of a "constitutional project" and in spite of the U.S. military agency for such expansion.

80. Tronti, "Workers and Capital," *Telos* 14 (Winter 1972): 40, 62.

81. Ibid., 62.

82. Pierre Bourdieu, "The 'Globalization' Myth and the Welfare State," in *Acts of Resistance* (New York: New Press, 1998), 35.

7. Cosmo-Theory

1. Martha C. Nussbaum, with respondents, *For Love of Country? Debating the Limits of Patriotism* (Boston: Beacon, 1996). For all its merits, this famous exchange constructed a false dichotomy: either cosmopolitanism or American patriotism. Mainstream critiques of cosmopolitanism from the Left became in this way impossible.

2. Peter Stallybrass and Allon White, *The Politics and Poetics of Transgression* (Ithaca, N.Y.: Cornell University Press, 1986), 27.

3. Ibid., 38.

4. The term may recall Arjun Appadurai's important concept of "global flow," although I am attempting to distinguish my usage from his by focusing on strongly bordered domestic intellectual zones. See his *Modernity at Large: Cultural Dimensions of Globalization* (Minneapolis: University of Minnesota Press, 1996), 27–48. In an unpublished essay, Eva Hudecova points out that in the countries of actually existing socialism, cosmopolitanism was the way Eastern European individuals were initiated into capitalism with the promise of the paraphernalia of a culture of leisure. Cosmopolitanism "functioned as a trigger for that constantly deferred desire for consumption that citizens of the Eastern bloc had no way to satisfy. Thus Slavenka Drakulic's example of every run-down coffee house across Eastern Europe being named 'Cafe Europa,' aspiring to evoke a Viennese flavor, and thus effortless world travel."

5. Robert D. Buzzell, John A. Quelch, Christopher A. Bartlett, eds., *Global Marketing Management: Cases and Readings* (Reading, Mass.: Addison-Wesley, 1995), 26.

6. Régis Debray, *Teachers, Writers, Celebrities: The Intellectuals of Modern France*, trans. David Macey (London: Verso, 1981).

7. H. David Hennessey and Jean-Pierre Jeannet, *Global Account Management: Creating Value* (Chichester: John Wiley and Sons, 2003), 232. For a longer treatment of how transnational corporations are still nation-identified, still culturally bound by the national preconceptions of their managerial stratum, see Timothy Brennan, *At Home in the World: Cosmpolitanism Now* (Cambridge, Mass.: Harvard University Press, 1997), 155–62.

8. Ben Wattenberg, *The First Universal Nation* (New York, Free Press, 1991); Fernando Valladao, *The Twenty-first Century Will Be American* (London and New York: Verso, 1996).

9. Georg Simmel, *The Philosophy of Money* (Boston and London: Routledge and Kegan Paul, 1978); Georges Bataille, *The Accursed Share: An Essay on General Economy*, vol. 1 (New York: Zone Books, 1991); Jean Baudrillard, *For a Critique of the Political Economy of the Sign* (St. Louis: Telos Press, 1981); Guy Debord, *Society of the Spectacle* (1967; New York: Zone Books, 1995); and Fredric Jameson, *The Cultural Turn* (London and New York: Verso, 1998).

10. Timothy Brennan, "Cosmopolitans and Celebrities," *Race and Class* 31, no. 1 (July–September 1989): 1–20; Ulf Hannerz, "Cosmopolitans and Locals in World Culture," Mike Featherstone, ed. *Global Culture: Nationalism, Globalization, and Modernity* (London; Newbury Park, CA: Sage, 1990), 237-51.

11. David Frisby and Mike Featherstone, eds., *Simmel on Culture* (London: Sage, 1997), 181–82.

12. Timothy Brennan, "Literary Criticism and the 'Southern Question,'" *Cultural Critique* 11 (Winter 1988–1989): 87–114.

13. See, for example, M. N. Roy, the Bengali delegate to the Third International: "The dissolution of the Communist International is not a vindication of antinationalism. As a matter of fact, Communist internationalism is not an antithesis of nationalism. The CI, from its very beginning, stood for national freedom of all peoples" (M. N. Roy, *The Communist International* [Bombay: Popular Printing Press, 1943]).

14. See Aijaz Ahmad, "Fascism and National Culture: Reading Gramsci in the Days of the Hindutva," *Social Scientist* 21 (March–April 1993): 3–4. Without taking up the issue of "cosmopolitanism" in Gramsci directly, several other studies lend support to the thesis. See Joseph Buttigieg, introduction to Antonio Gramsci, *Prison Notebooks*, vol. 1 (New York, 1992); and V. S. Kiernan, *Imperialism and Its Contradictions* (New York: Routledge, 1995).

15. Antonio Gramsci, *Quaderni del carcere*, ed. Valentino Gerratana (Turin: Einaudi, 1975), vol. 1, 371, Q 3, item 88. The volume contains several passages on the "cosmopolitan function of Italian intellectuals."

16. "The 'national' relation is a result of a unique 'original' combination (in a certain sense) that must be understood and conceived in its originality and uniqueness if one wants to control and direct it. No doubt that development strives towards internationalism, but the point of departure is 'national,' and it is from this point of departure that one must start out" (*Quaderni del carcere*, vol. 3, 1729, Q 14, item 68, my translation). See also vol. 1, 284–85, Q 3, item 2.

17. Michael Löwy, "Marx and Engels Cosmopolites," in *Fatherland or Mother Earth? Essays on the National Question* (London: Verso, 1998), 5–29. Löwy does note, however, that there is ambiguity in the Marxist tradition on the matter of cosmopolitanism.
18. Stephen Toulmin, *Cosmopolis: The Hidden Agenda of Modernity* (New York: Free Press, 1990); Julia Kristeva, *Strangers to Ourselves* (New York: Columbia University Press, 1991).
19. Jürgen Habermas, "Kant's Idea of Perpetual Peace: At Two Hundred Years' Historical Remove," *The Inclusion of the Other: Studies in Political Theory* (Cambridge, Mass.: MIT Press, 1998), 165–202; Walter Mignolo, "Globalization, Civilization Processes, and the Relocation of Languages and Cultures," in Fredric Jameson and Masao Miyoshi, eds., *The Cultures of Globalization*, 32–53 (Durham and London: Duke University Press, 1998); Bonnie Honig, "Ruth, The Model Emigré: Mourning and the Symbolic Politics of Immigration," *Political Theory* 25, no. 1 (February 1997): 112–36.
20. Enrique Dussel, *The Underside of Modernity* (New York: Prometheus Books, 1996); Roberto Fernandez Retamar, *Caliban and Other Essays* (Minneapolis: University of Minnesota Press, 1989); Arif Dirlik, *The Postcolonial Aura* (Boulder: Westview, 1997).
21. *Documents of the American Association for International Conciliation*, a series of privately published pamphlets. The piece by Louis P. Lochner on the "cosmopolitan club movement" observes that "during the last decade the complexion of the American student body has undergone a remarkable change. From being national and local institutions our large universities have become international temples of learning. . . . With the coming of the foreigner there has developed one of the most interesting movements known in college life—the banding together of students from all countries in international or cosmopolitan clubs, aptly termed 'miniature Hague Conferences' by Baron d'Estournelles de Constant." In his contribution the year before, Taft remarked that "the United States has a mission, besides developing the principles of the brotherhood of man into a living, palpable force, it seems to me that it is to blaze the way to universal arbitration among the nations." He later defends the exclusion of immigrants on the principle that international law allows that "every country may admit only those whom it chooses."
22. G. Lowes Dickinson, *A Modern Symposium*, 26–27 (1908), quoted in Bernard Porter, *Critics of Empire: British Radical Attitudes to Colonialism in Africa, 1895–1914* (London: Macmillan, 1968), 331.
23. Quoted in René Jara, "A Design for Modernity in the Margins," in Anthony L. Geist and José B. Monleón, eds., *Modernism and Its Margins: Reinscribing Cultural Modernity from Spain and Latin America* (New York and London: Garland, 1999), 282–83.
24. Kai Bird, "Another Course in Kosovo," *Nation*, June 14, 1999, 5. A similar view appears in Slavoj Žižek, "Against the Double Blackmail," *Nation*, May 24, 1999, 22. Žižek counsels readers to abjure nations, urging that we back "*transnational* political movements and institutions" rather than national ones while drawing on unanalyzed popular associations of the national form with dictatorship and the (always criminal) "state."

25. For a welcome challenge to this chorus, see Peter Marcuse's "The Language of Globalization," *Monthly Review* 3, no. 52 (July–August 2000): 23–27.

26. One has to acknowledge some excellent work in this field—for example, that of Manuel Castells.

27. Guy Debord, *Theory of the Dérive, and Other Situationist Writings on the City*, ed. Libero Andreotti and Xavier Costa (Barcelona: Museu d'Art Contemporani de Barcelona, 1996), 18.

28. Samuel Huntington, *The Clash of Civilizations and the Remaking of World Order* (New York: Touchstone, 1997); Anthony Giddens, *The Consequences of Modernity* (Stanford, Calif.: Stanford University Press, 1990).

29. George Soros, *The Crisis of Global Capitalism* (New York: Public Affairs, 1998), 3–83.

30. In spite of her courageous and liberatory exchange with Richard Rorty, Martha Nussbaum's points of departure are more exclusively European than necessary at this late date. Alongside his Greek philosophical originals, Rabindranath Tagore is tokenized in her essay .

31. A comprehensive critique of the "body" as an analytic category in social philosophy has yet to be written. The focus is developed in the affective emphases of Spinoza's *Ethics* (so central to Deleuze) and in Nietzschean megalomania, where his stress on the salutary pain and discomfort of his own body becomes the project of philosophical "seeing." For some leads on the trend, see Pierre Bourdieu, "Belief and the Body," *The Logic of Practice* (Stanford, Calif.: Stanford University Press, 1990), 66–79; Emily Martin, "The End of the Body," *American Ethnologist* 19, no. 1 (1992): 121–40; Nancy Fraser, "Foucault's Body Language," *Unruly Practices* (Minneapolis: University of Minnesota Press, 1989), 55–66; Mike Featherstone, Mike Hepworth, Bryan S. Turners, eds., *The Body: Social Processes and Cultural Theory* (London; Newbury Park, CA: Sage, 1991); and Terry Eagleton, *The Illusions of Postmodernism* (Oxford: Blackwell Publishers, 1996), 69–92.

32. Georges Bataille, "The Sorcerer's Apprentice," in Denis Hollier, ed., and Betsy Wing, trans., *The College of Sociology*, 14 (Minneapolis: The University of Minnesota Press, 1988).

33. Roland Robertson, *Globalization: Social Theory and Global Culture* (London: Sage, 1992).

34. Ulf Hannerz, *Transnational Connections: Culture, People, Places* (New York and London: Routledge, 1996).

35. Stuart Hall, "Cultural Identity and Diaspora," in Jonathan Rutherford, ed., *Identity, Community, Culture, Difference* (London: Lawrence and Wishart, 1990), 224.

36. Arjun Appadurai, *Modernity at Large: Cultural Dimensions of Globalization* (Minneapolis: University of Minnesota Press, 1996), 35. Nevertheless, explicit attention to civic and political forms of cosmopolitanism frequently arise in international relations scholarship without abandoning the cultural tropes honed in ethnography and literary criticism. Note the work, for example, of W. Kymlicka, *Multicultural Citizenship* (Oxford: Clarendon, 1995).

37. For an example of this welcome questioning of modernity, see Dipesh Chakrabarty, "The Difference-Deferral of a Colonial Modernity: Public Debates on Domesticity in British India," in David Arnold and David Hardiman, eds., *Subaltern Studies VIII:*

Essays in Honor of Ranajit Guha, 50–88 (Bombay, Calcutta, Madras: Oxford University Press, 1995); and Partha Chatterjee, *The Nation and Its Fragments: Colonial and Postcolonial History* (Princeton, N.J.: Princeton University Press, 1993).

38. Nestor García Canclini, *Hybrid Cultures: Strategies for Entering and Leaving Modernity* (Minneapolis: University of Minnesota Press, 1995), 212.

39. The relationship between Deleuzian theory and cosmo-theory can be seen, for example, in Antonio Negri and Michael Hardt's *Empire* (Cambridge, Mass.: Harvard University Press, 2000).

40. James Clifford, "Traveling Cultures," in Lawrence Grossberg, Cary Nelson, and Paula Treichler, eds., *Cultural Studies* (New York and London: Routledge, 1992), 107.

41. Bruce Robbins, "Some Versions of U.S. Internationalism," *Social Text* 45 (Winter 1995): 97–123.

42. Benjamin Lee, "Critical Internationalism," *Public Culture* 7, no. 3 (Spring 1995): 581.

43. Bruce Robbins, "Sad Stories in the International Public Sphere: Richard Rorty on Culture and Human Rights," *Public Culture* 9, no. 2 (Winter 1997), 209–32.

44. Pheng Cheah, "Given Culture: Rethinking Cosmopolitical Freedom in Transnationalism," in Pheng Cheah and Bruce Robbins, eds., *Cosmopolitics: Thinking and Feeling Beyond the Nation*, 290–328 (Minneapolis: University of Minnesota Press, 1998).

45. Julia Kristeva, *Strangers to Ourselves*, trans. Leon S. Roudiez (New York: Columbia University Press, 1991); Anthony King, *Urbanism, Colonialism, and the World Economy: Culture and Spatial Foundations of the World Urban System* (New York: Routledge, 1990). As I argued above, this emphasis has its roots in the continually replayed cosmopolitanism of earlier eras. A by no means rare view on the "end of the nation state" can be found, for example, in Hannah Arendt's *Imperialism* (San Diego and New York: Harcourt Brace Jovanovich, 1951), particularly in the final chapter, "Decline of the Nation-State; End of the Right of Man," which conforms depressingly to the mood of the postwar period. Not surprisingly, Arendt's book has been rediscovered lately and is frequently cited.

46. Huntington, *The Clash of Civilizations and the Remaking of World Order*; Henry Kissinger, *Diplomacy* (New York: Simon and Schuster, 1994), 23–24.

47. Pico Iyer, *Tropical Classical: Essays from Several Directions* (New York: Alfred A. Knopf, 1997); Robert D. Kaplan, *The Ends of the Earth: A Journey at the Dawn of the Twenty-first Century* (New York: Random House, 1996); Thomas L. Friedman, *The Lexus and the Olive Tree* (New York: Farrar, Strauss, and Giroux, 1999).

48. Robert Reich, *The Work of Nations: Preparing Ourselves for 21st-Century Capitalism* (New York: Alfred A. Knopf, 1991); William J. Baumol, *Privatization, Competitive Entry, and Rational Rules for Residual Regulation* (Hobart: Department of Economics, University of Tasmania, 1997); Jeffrey Sachs and Katharina Pistor, eds., *The Rule of Law and Economic Reform in Russia* (Boulder: Westview, 1997).

49. Although the single currency and open passport of the European Union would seem to contradict this statement, both have been accompanied by much stricter regulations governing the entry into Europe of peoples from Africa, Asia, and the Caribbean. A strengthening of border patrols and surveillance between the United States and Mexico by the Immigration and Naturalization Service has similarly accompanied the NAFTA accords.

50. Samir Amin, *Delinking: Toward a Polycentric World* (London: Zed Books, 1990).

51. This view is tentatively put forward by K. M. Pannikar in *Asia and Western Dominance* (London: Allen and Unwin, 1953), although not in this context. Enrique Dussel works along similar lines in his essay "Beyond Eurocentrism: The World-System and the Limits of Modernity," in Jameson and Miyoshi, *The Cultures of Globalization*, 15.

52. Guy Debord, *Comments on the Society of the Spectacle* (New York and London: Verso, 1990).

8. THE SOUTHERN INTELLECTUAL

1. The key figure in this line of argument has been Franco Lo Piparo, *Lingua intellettuali egemonia in Gramsci* (Bari: Laterza, 1979), work that forms the basis of a study by Peter Ives, *Gramsci's Politics of Language: Engaging the Bakhtin Circle and the Frankfurt School* (Toronto: University of Toronto Press, 2004). For an excellent account of the effect of Gramsci's linguistic studies on his general theories as they relate to Sardinia and Gramsci's "southern" origins, see Stefano Selenu, "Alcuni aspetti della questione della lingua sarda attraverso la diade storia-grammatica: Un'impostazione di tipo Gramsciano" (Ph.D. diss., University of Bologna, 2003).

2. Chantal Mouffe and Anne Showstack Sassoon, "Gramsci in France and Italy: A Review of the Literature," *Economy and Society* 6, no. 1 (February 1977): 31–68; A. B. Davidson, "The Varying Seasons of Gramscian Studies," *Political Studies* 20, no. 4: 448–61; Elsa Fubini, *Gramsci e la cultura contemporanea* (Rome: Riuniti-Istituto Gramsci, 1970); Geoff Eley, "Reading Gramsci in English: Observations on the Reception of Antonio Gramsci in the English-Speaking World, 1957–82," *European History Quarterly* 14 (1984): 441–78.

3. Richard Bellamy, "Gramsci, Croce, and the Italian Political Tradition," *History of Political Thought* 11, no. 2 (Summer 1990): 313–17; Palmiro Togliatti, "Il leninismo nel pensiero e nel azione di A. Gramsci," *Studi gramsciani, Atti del convegno tenuto a Roma nei giorni 11–13 gennaio 1958* (Rome: Riuniti, 1969), 16–19; Umberto Calosso, "Gramsci e l'ordine Nuovo," *Quaderni di Giustizia e Liberta* 2 (August 1933): 71–79; Davidson, "The Varying Seasons of Gramscian Studies." For a good overview of Gramsci's U.S. reception in contrast to his Italian, see Joseph Buttigieg, "La circolazione delle categorie gramsciane negli Stati Uniti" in Maria Luisa Righi, ed., *Gramsci nel mondo*, 137–48 (Rome: Fondazione Istituto Gramsci, 1995).

4. V. G. Kiernan, "Antonio Gramsci and the Other Continents," in *Imperialism and Its Contradictions*, ed. Harvey J. Kaye (New York: Routledge, 1995), 171–90.

5. An interesting exception is R. Radhakrishnan, "Toward an Effective Intellectual: Foucault or Gramsci?" *Diasporic Mediations: Between Home and Location* (Minneapolis: University of Minnesota Press, 1996), 32. His is one of the most independently minded essays on Gramsci in postcolonial studies.

6. Janet Abu-Lughod, "On the Remaking of History: How to Reinvent the Past," in Barbara Kruger and Phil Mariani, eds., *Remaking History*, 110–11 (Seattle: Bay Press, 1989).

7. Raymond Williams found a way to characterize what was new, and not new, in the "turn to language," diagnosing the ideological strain that transformed a very familiar set of observations on language (which had existed for many centuries) into a tendentious campaign under the aegis of structuralism in the late 1960s and 1970s. See *Marxism and Literature* (Oxford and New York: Oxford University Press, 1977), 21–44.

8. John Beverley, *Subalternity and Representation: Arguments in Cultural Theory* (Durham and London: Duke University Press, 1999), 32; Karin Bauer, *Adorno's Nietzschean Narratives* (Buffalo: SUNY Press, 1999), 190–91.

9. Antonio Gramsci, *Prison Notebooks*, vol. 2, ed. and trans. Joseph A. Buttigieg (New York: Columbia University Press, 1996), 156; N[otebook] 4, item 14.

10. Nor was this early exegesis limited to Italy. It was the small activist circles of the international communist movement that disseminated Gramsci's work prior to the 1960s. This tradition, it should be said, is still very much alive. See Emanuele Saccarelli's well-researched account of the critique of Stalinism in Gramsci's work, "The Mummy, the Professor, and the Cannibal: The Contemporary Uses and Marxist Reclamation of Antonio Gramsci," unpublished essay, San Diego State University, 2004.

11. Norberto Bobbio, "Gramsci and the Conception of Civil Society," in Richard Bellamy, ed., *Which Socialism? Marxism, Socialism, and Democracy*, trans. Roger Griffin, 139–61 (Minneapolis: University of Minnesota Press, 1987); Leonardo Paggi, "Gramsci's General Theory of Marxism," in Chantal Mouffe, ed., *Gramsci and Marxist Theory*, 113–67 (London and Boston: Routledge and Kegan Paul, 1979).

12. Bobbio, "Gramscii and the Conception of Civil Society," 151, 154.

13. The Russia of Gramsci's youthful inspirations, after all, did not apply, since it was a semi-developed, peripheral region of the European world—a resonant point for postcolonial theory in that it alluded to the unforeseen, and certainly unanalyzed, affinity of the Russian revolution with the anticolonial movements.

14. Mouffe, *Gramsci and Marxist Theory*, 1.

15. A paradoxical outcome, since Althusser was neither Eurocommunist nor post-Marxist. One might see him, by contrast, as committed to the integrity of a party Marxism filled with classical reverence for the textual corpus of Marx. His brief was merely to demonstrate Marxism's relevance to a structuralist theory that was then ascendant—that Marxism could be, and had to be, attractive to those who practiced philosophy and for whom thought was an avocation.

16. Perry Anderson, "The Antinomies of Antonio Gramsci," *New Left Review* 100 (1977): 5–80.

17. Joseph Femia, "Hegemony and Consciousness in the Thought of Antonio Gramsci," *Political Studies* 23, no. 1 (1975): 29–48.

18. The view of Gramsci that is based on a reading of his complete works in Italian and the recovery of his local contexts and intellectual sources is pursued today by such incisive redactors as Joseph Buttigieg, Frank Rosengarten, Richard Bellamy, Emanuele Saccarelli, and David Forgacs. Later studies of Gramsci's political theory and cultural and literary relations with interwar philosophy carried on this meticulous attention to history and the archive. See Anne Showstack Sassoon, *Gramsci's Poli-*

tics (Minneapolis: University of Minnesota Press, 1980); and Renate Holub, *Antonio Gramsci: Beyond Marxism and Postmodernism* (London and New York: Routledge, 1992).

19. Davidson, "The Varying Seasons of Gramscian Studies," 451.

20. Ibid.; and Antonio Gramsci, *Letters from Prison*, vol. 2, ed. Frank Rosengarten, trans. Raymond Rosenthal (New York: Columbia University Press, 1994), 275.

21. Rajnarayan Chandarvarkar, "'The Making of the Working Class': E. P. Thompson and Indian History," in Vinayak Chaturvedi, ed., *Mapping Subaltern Studies and the Post-colonial*, 50–71 (New York and London: Verso, 2000).

22. V. G. Kiernan, "Antonio Gramsci and the Other Continents," in Harvey Kaye, ed., *Imperialism and Its Contradictions*, 171–90 (New York and London: Routledge, 1995).

23. With Sarkar, Tom Brass, Gayatri Chakravorty Spivak, and David Washbrook, O'Hanlon has provided a crushing riposte to subaltern studies. See Rosalind O'Hanlon, "Recovering the Subject: Subaltern Studies and Histories of Resistance in Colonial South Asia," *Modern Asian Studies* 22, no. 1 (1988): 189–224; and Rosalind O'Hanlon and David Washbrook, "After Orientalism: Culture, Criticism, and Politics in the Third World," *Comparative Studies in Society and History* 32, no. 1 (January 1992): 141–67.

24. O'Hanlon, "Recovering the Subject," 203, 205.

25. Ranajit Guha, *Dominance Without Hegemony* (Cambridge, Mass.: Harvard University Press, 1997), 89–95.

26. Although there is not the space here for a comprehensive comparison of Gramsci's reception in other parts of the formerly colonized world, useful additions to the other sources I cite here can be found in Michele Brondino and Tahar Labib, eds., *Gramsci dans le monde arabe* (Tunis: Les Editions de la Mediterranee, 1994); and Raul Burgos, "The Gramscian Intervention in the Theoretical and Political Production of the Latin American Left," *Latin American Perspectives* 122 (January 2002): 9–35.

27. The entire history of Gramsci's career in Latin America is narrated in José Aricó, *La cola del diablo: Itinerario de Gramsci en América Latina* (Caracas: Editorial Nueva Sociedad, 1988). See especially 11.

28. Ibid., 12.

29. Juan Carlos Portantiero, *Los usos de Gramsci: Escritos políticos, 1917–1933* (Mexico City: Ediciones pasado y presente, 1977), 55.

30. Gayatri Chakravorty Spivak, "Can the Subaltern Speak?" in Cary Nelson and Lawrence Grossberg, eds., *Marxism and the Interpretation of Culture* (Urbana and Chicago: University of Illinois Press, 1988), 272.

31. Ibid., 279.

32. Neil Lazarus, *Nationalism and Cultural Practice in the Post-colonial World* (Cambridge: Cambridge University Press, 1999), 1–15.

33. Ernesto Laclau and Chantal Mouffe, *Hegemony and Socialist Strategy: Towards a Radical Democratic Politics* (New York and London: Verso, 1985).

34. Mouffe, *Gramsci and Marxist Theory*, 4–5.

35. The theory of the "new social movements" was already alive in the interwar period, as Gramsci's skeptical comments show: "The question of the importance of women in Roman history is similar to the question of the subaltern classes, but up to a cer-

tain point: 'masculinity' can be compared to class domination only in a certain sense; it therefore has greater importance for the history of customs than for political and social history. Another extremely important observation must be made about the inherent dangers of the method of historical analogy as a criterion of interpretation" (*Prison Notebooks*, vol. 2, 195; N 3, item 18).

36. José Rabasa, "Of Zapatismo: Reflections on the Folkloric and the Impossible in a Subaltern Insurrection," in Lisa Lowe and David Lloyd, eds., *The Politics of Culture in the Shadow of Capital*, 405 (Durham: Duke University Press, 1997).

37. Laclau and Mouffe, *Hegemony and Socialist Strategy*, 48.

38. Louis Althusser, *Lenin and Philosophy and Other Essays* (New York: Monthly Review, 1971), 142.

39. For Marx, Lenin and Gramsci . . . philosophy is fundamentally *political*" (ibid., 12). If the eleventh thesis on Feuerbach ("philosophers have only interpreted the world, the point, however, is to change it") had generally been taken as a declaration of philosophy's limits, Althusser in "Lenin and Philosophy"—with virtuosic cheekiness—considered it a call for a new philosophy that would transform the world.

40. Louis Althusser, *For Marx* (New York and London: New Left Books, 1969), 114.

41. This is why it is puzzling that Thompson's great polemic against Althusser has come down to us as a battle against "Stalinoid mystagogues." Perhaps it seemed so in 1978, but it is easier in retrospect to see that Althusser's attack on humanist Marxism grew out of that New Left conservatism diagnosed by Jürgen Habermas in his debates with Michel Foucault. It was very far from Stalinism—a point Perry Anderson alludes to in *Arguments Within English Marxism*. On this point, see Richard Wolin, "Antihumanism in the Discourse of French Postwar Philosophy," *Labyrinths* (Amherst: University of Massachusetts Press, 1995), 175–209.

42. Louis Althusser with Etienne Balibar, *Reading Capital* (London: New Left Books, 1970), 126, 131.

43. Ibid., 143, 131, 126 ff.

44. Stuart Hall, "Gramsci's Relevance for the Study of Race and Ethnicity," in *Stuart Hall: Critical Dialogues in Cultural Studies*, 425 (London and New York: Routledge, 1996); Rabasa, "Of Zapatismo," 405. For the history of the concept "hegemony," see Richard Bellamy's introduction to *Pre-Prison Writings*, ed. Richard Bellamy (Cambridge: Cambridge University Press, 1994), xxvii.

45. Ajit Chaudhuri, "From Hegemony to Counter-Hegemony: A Journey in a Non-Imaginary Unreal Space," *Economic and Political Weekly* 23, no. 5 (January 30, 1988): 19–22; Hall, "Gramsci's Relevance for the Study of Race and Ethnicity," 418, 420.

46. Mouffe, *Gramsci and Marxist Theory*, 7.

47. A concrete case of this logic is found in Ajit Chaudhury's essay cited above. Partha Chatterjee's response to Chaudhury's essay is a useful summary of the reservations with the Althusserian model. See "On Gramsci's 'Fundamental Mistake,' " *Economic and Political Weekly* 23, no. 5 (January 30, 1988): 24–26.

48. Edward Said, "An Interview with Edward Said," *boundary 2* 2, no. 20 (1993): 2, 13.

49. Ludwig Feuerbach, "Provisional Theses for the Reformation of Philosophy," in Lawrence S. Stepelevich, ed., *The Young Hegelians: An Anthology*, 164 (Atlantic Highlands, N.J.: Humanities Press, 1997).

50. Ludwig Feuerbach, "Towards a Critique of Hegelian Philosophy," in Stepelevich, *The Young Hegelians*, 98 (Feuerbach's emphasis).

51. And offhandedly, in the *Letters*. He worked through Hegel on the history of philosophy in the late 1920s, and Croce's book, *Hegel*. Gramsci read philosophy on the fly, often at second remove: books like *Summary of the History of Philosophy* by Guido De Ruggero or the publisher Laterza of Bari's *Piccola Biblioteco Filosofica*. Perhaps this is why at one point he laments that dialectics "has not yet been manualized" (*Letters from Prison*, vol. 1, 256, 258).

52. Stuart Hall, "When Was 'the Post-Colonial'? Thinking at the Limit," in Iain Chambers and Lidia Curti, eds., *The Post-Colonial Question: Common Skies, Divided Horizons*, 242–60 (New York: Routledge, 1996).

53. Hall, "Gramsci's Relevance for the Study of Race and Ethnicity," 412, 433–34, 439.

54. Mouffe, *Gramsci and Marxist Theory*, 9.

55. Hall, "Gramsci's Relevance for the Study of Race and Ethnicity," 416.

56. *Letters from Prison*, vol. 1, 128.

57. Antonio Gramsci, *Selections from Political Writings, 1910–1920*, ed. Quintin Hoare, trans. John Mathews (1977; Minneapolis: University of Minnesota Press, 1990), 4.

58. Maurice Muret, *Le crépuscule des nations blanches* (Paris: Payot, 1926).

59. *Selections from Political Writings, 1910–1920*, 3.

60. Stuart Hall, "Gramsci and Us," in *The Hard Road to Renewal: Thatcherism and the Crisis of the Left* (London and New York: Verso, 1988), 163 ff.

61. Ibid., 170.

62. Hall, "Gramsci's Relevance for the Study of Race and Ethnicity," 412, 433, 434, 439; Hall, "Gramsci and Us," 168, 163.

63. Hall, "Gramsci's Relevance for the Study of Race and Ethnicity," 433, 430, 428.

64. O'Hanlon, "Recovering the Subject," 215.

65. *Letters from Prison*, vol. 1, 5.

66. Gramsci, *Pre-Prison Writings*, 97.

67. Antonio Gramsci, *Selections from the Prison Notebooks*, ed. Quintin Hoare and Geoffrey Nowell Smith (New York: International Publishers, 1971), 196–98

68. "[Ford] has a corps of inspectors who check on the private lives of the workers and impose on them a certain regimen. . . . We Europeans are still too bohemian, we believe that we can do a certain kind of work and live as we please, like bohemians: naturally, machinism crushes us and I mean machinism in a general sense, as scientific organization that encompasses also intellectual work. We are too romantic in an absurd way and not wanting to be petit bourgeois we fall into the most typical form of petit bourgeoisism that is precisely bohemianism" (*Letters from Prison*, vol. 1, 356).

69. *Prison Notebooks*, vol. 2, 47; N 3, item 46.

70 Stuart Hall, *Stuart Hall: Critical Dialogues in Cultural Studies* (London and New York: Routledge, 1996), 412.

71. Hall, "Gramsci and Us," 169.

72. *Letters from Prison*, vol. 2, 169.

73. To pursue this issue, see "Some Theoretical and Practical Aspects of Economism," *Selections from the Prison Notebooks*. This may be the moment to state that Laclau

and Mouffe's *Hegemony and Socialist Strategy* routinely confuses the world of Karl Kautsky with the world of Rosa Luxemburg, Paul Mattick, and Adorno: in other words, this influential book repeats the Third International's critique of the Second International's "economism" (already a cliché in the 1920s) while condemning the legacy of the Third International as "economist." It is not clear whether this is incompetence on Laclau and Mouffe's part, or a strategic subterfuge.

74. A sense of how non-heterodox Gramsci's views were among his colleagues might be gathered from the sheer familiarity of his ideas to his Italian contemporaries. See *Letters from Prison*, vol. 2, 66: "In ten years of journalism I wrote enough lines to fill fifteen or twenty volumes of 400 pages each, but they were written for the day and, in my opinion, were supposed to die with the day. I have always refused to permit the publication of a collection of them, even a limited one."

75. Ibid., vol. 1, 365.

76. *Prison Notebooks*, vol. 2, 33; N 3, item 34.

77. Partha Chatterjee, *The Nation and Its Fragments: Colonial and Post-colonial Histories* (Princeton, N.J.: Princeton University Press, 1993), 199.

78. R. Radhakrishnan, "Toward an Effective Intellectual: Foucault or Gramsci?" 32.

79. Rabasa, "Of Zapatismo," 408, 424.

80. Chantal Mouffe, ed., *The Challenge of Carl Schmitt* (London and New York: Verso, 1999).

81. A concise account of the specific convergence in recent Italian thought of Heideggerian categories with a new strain of devoutly Catholic forms of philosophical meditation can be found in Romano Luperini, "Tendencies of Criticism in Contemporary Italy," *Rethinking Marxism* 5, no. 1 (Spring 1992): 32–43.

82. Iain Chambers, "Signs of Silence, Lines of Listening," in Chambers and Curti, *The Post-colonial Question*, 50; Demetrio Yocum, "Some Troubled Homecomings," in Chambers and Curti, *The Post-colonial Question*, 221–27; Arturo Escobar, "Imagining a Post-Development Era? *Social Text* 31/32 (Spring 1992): 20–56; Hall, "When Was 'the Postcolonial'?" 255.

83. Didion Erebon, *Michel Foucault* (Cambridge, Mass.: Harvard University Press, 1991), 30.

84. Guha's comments were delivered at a speech at Columbia University in February 2001, Chakrabarty's in a lecture at the University of Minnesota in April 2001. See also Chakrabarty, *Provincializing Europe: Post-colonial Thought and Historical Difference* (Princeton, N.J.: Princeton University Press, 2000), 18, 143–44.

85. Ibid., 143–44.

86. Enrique Dussel, *The Invention of the Americas: Eclipse of the "Other" and the Myth of Modernity* (New York: Continuum, 1995); Michael Taussig, *Shamanism, Colonialism, and the Wild Man: A Study in Terror and Healing* (Chicago: University of Chicago Press, 1986); Gauri Viswanathan, *Outside the Fold: Conversion, Modernity, Belief* (Princeton, N.J. Princeton University Press, 1998).

87. Gyanendra Pandey, "The Prose of Otherness," in David Arnold and David Hardiman, eds., *Subaltern Studies VIII* (Delhi: Oxford University Press, 1994), 188–221.

88. Chakrabarty, *Provincializing Europe*, 241.

89. Ibid., 243.

90. Again, this argument is posed in the negative, as that which one is *against*. See Denzil Saldanha, "Antonio Gramsci and the Analysis of Class Consciousness: Some Methodological Considerations," *Economic and Political Weekly* (Special Issue): 11–18. For a critique of "subaltern thought" from a Foucauldian point of view, see Veena Das, "Subaltern as Perspective," in Ranajit Guha, ed., *Subaltern Studies VI*, 310–24 (Oxford and New York: Oxford University Press, 1992).

91. Partha Chatterjee, *Nationalist Thought and the Colonial World: A Derivative Discourse* (Minneapolis: University of Minnesota Press, 1986), 75.

92. Sumit Sarkar has cast these same events (and Chatterjee's reading of them) in a very different light in "The Fascism of the Sangh Parivar," *Economic and Political Weekly* 28, no. 5 (January 20, 1993): 163–67. Extolling the "fragment" in this way, he insists, amounts in the current political climate of India to a desire for a recidivist embrace of pre-colonial princely states ruled by religious affiliation. There is an embarrassing romanticism about the indigenous ruling classes, and a forgetfulness about the abject social consequences of these appeals to retaining a "traditional" past. As Chakrabarty has himself recently observed, it is striking to notice that Indian Muslims, for example, play no role whatsoever in Chatterjee's study. See also Chaturvedi, *Mapping Subaltern Studies and the Post-colonial*, 300–23.

93. Part of this point—although not with reference to Gramsci's actual writing—has been made by David Washbrook, Tom Brass, and others. See Brass, "A-Way with Their Wor(l)d: Rural Labourers Through the Postmodern Prism," *Economic and Political Weekly* 28, no. 23 (1993): 1162–68; and O'Hanlon and Washbrook, "After Orientalism," 141–67.

94. *Selections from the Prison Notebooks*, 244, 247, 259.

95. Walter Mignolo's proposal for a "subaltern rationality," for example, with its "core . . . in race"—this as opposed to what he calls undifferentiated "Marxist thinking"; or in Prakash's defanging of historiography in the name of a postcolonial truth identity operating against the "White mythology" of Marxism (Walter Mignolo, "(Post)Occidentalism, (Post)Coloniality, and (Post)Subaltern Rationality" in Fawzia Afzal-Khan and Kelpana Seshadri-Crooks, eds., *The Pre-Occupation of Postcolonial Studies*, 86–118 (New York: Routledge, 1996); Gyan Prakash, "Post-Colonial Criticism and Indian Historiography," *Social Text* 31/32 (Spring 1992): 15–18.

96. One is struck, similarly, not only by the prominence of gods and goddesses in Chakrabarty's *Provincializing Europe* but by the role he accords modernity there. Chakrabarty portrays peripheral development in such a way that Marxism is collapsed into a historicist formula of "stagism," exporting to the "not yet" of empire a model of modernity taken from another's history. If one leaves alone the reductionism of the term "Marxism" (which like "the Enlightenment" is used almost invariably in such analyses with a leaden simplicity), Chakrabarty's concern is a valid one, although the charge is hardly unique to him, since it is a commonplace within postcolonial studies. He is understandably worried by any historiography that sees India only in terms of a developmental schema that portrays its present as a lack and a lapse. But as I have been at pains to argue, the narrative of the break from interwar Marxism, which Gramsci is inaccurately said to exemplify, has prevented critics from seeing their return to meanings and goals they ostensibly confound.

97. *Selections from Political Writings, 1919–1920*, 34.

98. Ibid., 36.

99. But see Radhakrishnan's more modulated view. He argues finally for the dissimilarity of the two thinkers. Gramsci "commits 'man' to a field of relationships" that still accord him agency, whereas Foucault is involved in the Nietzschean project of "sacrifice of the subject" to the processes of knowledge (49). Although Foucault is said to be against the arrogance of political "representation," Radhakrishnan observes that his "'outsider' politics . . . in spite of its best intentions of 'letting the masses be,' ends up in a prescriptive mode telling the masses what they should know" (55).

100. For Gramsci's discussion of his plan to publish a book on intellectuals, see his letter to Tatiana Schucht of September 7, 1931, *Letters*, vol. 2, 65–68.

101. *Letters from Prison*, vol. 1, 83; Timothy Brennan, "Literary Criticism and the 'Southern Question,'" *Cultural Critique* 11 (Winter 1988–1989): 87–114.

102. Asok Sen, "The Frontiers of the 'Prison Notebooks,'" *Economic and Political Weekly* (Special Issue) 23, no. 5 (January 30, 1988): 32; Beverley, *Subalternity and Representation*, 5. The subaltern studies historians tend to see in the Enlightenment only a disdain for superstition and "religious backwardness." As Alex Callinicos and others have shown, such an argument is ahistorical. It depends on our disregarding Enlightenment thinkers who do not fit the model—among them J. G. Herder, Constantin Francois Volney, Victor Schoelcher, and others—who explicitly extolled the internal coherence and separable value of non-European cultures. Gramsci is enlisted in this effort on the grounds that he spoke to subaltern consciousness *as it actually was* rather than to Lukács's famous "imputed consciousness" from *History and Class Consciousness*.

103. It is significant that Gramsci's estimation of his own writing, always modest, approaches confidence only in regard to his work on intellectuals, which is the only piece of his prison research that he actually planned to publish during his lifetime. As above, see the letter to Tatiana Schucht of September 7, 1931, *Letters*, vol. 2, 65–68.

104. *Prison Notebooks*, vol. 2, 195; N 4, item 45.

105. In the essay "Critical Criticism," Gramsci alludes to this famous phrase from Marx's parody of Bruno Bauer in *The Holy Family* and *The German Ideology*: "The Bauers of this world have not been cured of their liking for scrambling up concepts and facts into fantastic pseudo-philosophical concoctions" (*Pre-Prison Writings*, 43). Gramsci goes on to say that an article he is then reading makes a big deal out of the "sterilization of Marx's doctrines at the hands of the Positivist Socialists" but that this point is "hardly a great discovery."

106. *Selections from the Prison Notebooks*, 3–23.

107. René Fülöp-Miller was the author of the widely read *Geist und Gesicht des Bolschewismus* (1926), translated into English in 1929.

108. *Letters from Prison*, vol. 1, 369.

109. In a letter to Tatiana on June 3, 1929, he requested that the book be sent to him, and he did, in fact, read it in prison immediately before writing his main entry on intellectuals in the following year. In several notebooks, long passages are dedicated to de Man.

110. *Selections from the Prison Notebooks*, 9.
111. Deriving, like Gramsci, from Pareto's writing on "elites," de Man in this way antic-ipated James Burnham's famous theory of the bureaucratic class formulated in the United States in 1940, and looked forward to even more recent studies on the pro-fessional managerial class.
112. *Prison Notebooks*, vol. 2, 242; N 4, item 72.
113. This point is almost without exception confused in postcolonial studies even when it appears to be clarified. For a recent example, see Kalpana Seshadri-Crooks's de-fense of Homi Bhabha's notion of the organic intellectual as an "unstable identity," in Afzal-Khan and Seshadri-Crooks, eds., *The Pre-Occupation of Postcolonial Studies*, 15–16.
114. *Prison Notebooks*, vol. 2, 243; N 4, item 75.
115. *Selections from the Prison Notebooks*, 17.
116. Ibid., 20.
117. Ibid., 21.
118. *Pre-Prison Writings*, 328.
119. The intensity of Gramsci's abreaction to Croce's politics (as distinct from his in-tellectual and methodological brilliance) can be seen in the fact that he accuses him of outright complicity with fascism. See *Letters from Prison*, vol. 2, 181–82.
120. *Prison Notebooks*, vol. 2, 63; N 3, item 63.
121. For a sensitive reading of the pros and cons of this process, see Benita Parry, "Lib-eration Theory: Variations on Themes of Marxism and Modernity," in Crystal Bar-tolovich and Neil Lazarus, eds., *Marxism, Modernity, and Post-colonial Studies* (Cambridge: Cambridge University Press, 2001), 125–49; Lazarus, *Nationalism and Cultural Practice in the Post-colonial World*; and Anthony Appiah, "Is the Post- in Postmodernism the Post- in Post-colonial?" *Critical Inquiry* 17 (Winter 1991): 336–57.
122. One exception can be found in Sen, "The Frontiers of the 'Prison Notebooks,'" 31–36; Hall mentions the term in passing in "Gramsci's Relevance" (438) but does not discuss it.
123. *Selections from the Prison Notebooks*, 58–59.
124. Sarkar, "The Fascism of the Sangh Parivar," 163–67.

Thompson, E. P., 241–242, 311*n*41
Timpanaro, Sebastiano, 2, 10, 274–275*m*6
Togliatti, Palmiro, 189, 241
Totalitarianism. *See* State
Touraine, Alain, 220
Transformism, 237, 271
Translation: creating works of proper domestic literature, 63; cultural political in
case of Borge, 47–49; cultural political in
context of German reunification, 50–54;
as cultural in postcolonial theory, 54;
decay of impulse toward Third World, 61;
East/West ideological as untranslatable in
Western book markets, 280–281*n*39; emphasis on politics disabling appreciation,
61; of fiction, blurring national belonging, 59–60; of first accounts of travelers
to New World, 59; intentional mistransla-
tions in Cold War contexts, 280*n*30; internalized by author before writing begins, 62–63; as intriguingly impossible
task, 63; of language compared to cultural
codes, 44; loanwords in, 52, 75; operating
within networks of conditioning and expectation, 60; as problem of belief, 46; as
problem of East/West or North/South,
47; problem of intra-national language
disjunctions, 57; publishing as industry in
setting of empire with victorious dissemination, 60; racialism and ideologies af-
fecting, 46; readers drawn to manageable
foreignness, 60; of story from *afar* echoing *here*, 45; theories of, inquiries for, 59;
transparency of language to invaders, 61;
in World English, 61; *See also* Language
Transnationalism/transnationals, 96, 131, 231
Travelogues, 229
Trilling, Lionel, 113
Trinh, T. Minh-ha, 13
Tripp, Linda, 155
Tronti, Mario, 177–178, 204
"Turn," the: as belated, 275*m*6; bringing
politics of "being," x, xi; cast incorrectly
in terms of identity politics, x; credos reinforced with interpretive violence, ix;

crushing social democratic vision, xii; far
right wing permeating government, 100;
generational aspects of recognition of, 5;
humanities entering political mainstream, 5; as joining of formerly hostile
constituencies of left/right, ix, 237; lacking notions of equality, civic betterment,
or affirmative action, 15; as period from
1975–1980, ix, 274*n*10; as period of misun-
derstanding of Said, 107; subsequent suppression of particular beliefs, xii; vibrancy of pre-1970s ideas, 24; *See also*
Heideggerian turn

Ultraism, 203
Ungleichzeitigkeit (temporal incommensurability), 48
Union movement. *See* Labor union
movement
United States: America as multicultural
refuge and site of opportunity, 272;
American critics as functionaries of
state, 99; American obsession with
ethnic identity as authority, 114; anti-
statism as routine in American universities, 148; Bush Administration's authoritarian policies, 28; censorship in and
outside of, 29–30; cosmopolitanism as
expression of American patriotism,
227; cosmopolitanism as New World pluralism joining imperial project, 216; cosmopolitanism as pluralism, 216; cosmo-
theory's defense of internationalism as
form of American influence, 227; cosmo-
theory's veiled Americanism, 227;
Empire fitting mainstream perception
of America's global influence, 172; freedom of speech/conscience protections
absent from Constitution, 26; globalization as Americanization of foreignness,
129; as globalization's primary beneficiary, 231–232; globalization with underlying American ideology, 132–133;
hegemonized through popular
culture, fashion, and Internet, 231;

DATE DUE

Demco, Inc. 38-293